Best wishes

With regards
Shahid Jameel

DISRUPTIVE TECHNOLOGIES AND MUSLIM SOCIETIES

From AI and Education to Food and Fintech

DISRUPTIVE TECHNOLOGIES AND MUSLIM SOCIETIES

From AI and Education to Food and Fintech

Editors

Shahid Jameel

David C Clary

Oxford Centre for Islamic Studies, UK

World Scientific

NEW JERSEY • LONDON • SINGAPORE • BEIJING • SHANGHAI • TAIPEI • CHENNAI

Published by

World Scientific Publishing Europe Ltd.

57 Shelton Street, Covent Garden, London WC2H 9HE

Head office: 5 Toh Tuck Link, Singapore 596224

USA office: 27 Warren Street, Suite 401-402, Hackensack, NJ 07601

Library of Congress Cataloging-in-Publication Data
Names: Jamīl, Shāhid, editor.
Title: Disruptive technologies and Muslim societies : from AI and education to food and fintech / editors, Shahid Jameel, Oxford Centre for Islamic Studies, UK, David C Clary, Oxford Centre for Islamic Studies, UK.
Description: New Jersey : World Scientific, [2025] | Includes bibliographical references and index.
Identifiers: LCCN 2024035237 | ISBN 9781800616288 (hardcover) | ISBN 9781800616295 (ebook) | ISBN 9781800616301 (ebook other)
Subjects: LCSH: Finance--Islamic countries. | Islamic countries--Technological innovations.
Classification: LCC HG187.4 .D57 2025 | DDC 332.0917/67--dc23/eng/20241203
LC record available at https://lccn.loc.gov/2024035237

British Library Cataloguing-in-Publication Data
A catalogue record for this book is available from the British Library.

For any available supplementary material, please visit
https://www.worldscientific.com/worldscibooks/10.1142/Q0481#t=suppl

Desk Editors: Balasubramanian Shanmugam/Rosie Williamson/Shi Ying Koe

Typeset by Stallion Press
Email: enquiries@stallionpress.com

https://doi.org/10.1142/9781800616295_fmatter

About the Editors

Professor Shahid Jameel is Sultan Qaboos bin Said Fellow at the Oxford Centre for Islamic Studies, where he leads the project on Science, Technology and Environment in Muslim Societies (STEMS). He is also a Research Fellow at Green Templeton College, University of Oxford. He served as the Founding Director of the Trivedi School of Biosciences at Ashoka University, India (2020–2021) and the CEO of the Wellcome Trust's partnership with the Government of India (2013–2020). Professor Jameel trained as a biochemist and virologist and carried out research on human viruses at the International Centre for Genetic Engineering and Biotechnology, New Delhi, India (1988–2013). He is the recipient of the Shanti Swarup Bhatnagar Prize in Medicine, the highest mid-career science award of the Government of India. He is also an elected fellow of all three Indian science academies.

Professor Sir David C. Clary FRS is Emeritus Professor of Chemistry at the University of Oxford, UK. He was the President of Magdalen College, Oxford, from 2005 to 2020. He is an elected fellow of many academies, including the Royal Society, the Royal Society of Chemistry, the Institute of Physics, the American Physical Society, the American Association for the Advancement of Science, the American Academy of Arts and Sciences, and the International Academy of Quantum Molecular

Science. During 2009–2013, he was the first Chief Scientific Advisor to the UK Foreign and Commonwealth Office. In 2016, he was knighted in the Birthday Honours of Queen Elizabeth II for services to international science. He is a Senior Advisor to the project on Science, Technology and Environment in Muslim Societies at the Oxford Centre for Islamic Studies.

https://doi.org/10.1142/9781800616295_fmatter

Contents

https://doi.org/10.1142/9781800616295_fmatter

Introduction

Shahid Jameel* and David C. Clary†

Oxford Centre for Islamic Studies, Oxford, UK

**shahid.jameel@oxcis.ac.uk*

†david.clary@magd.ox.ac.uk

At the Oxford Centre for Islamic Studies, a new project on "Science, Technology and Environment in Muslim Societies" has been initiated. SJ is the principal investigator, and DCC is the senior advisor for the project. In the regular seminar series associated with our project, we noticed that speakers frequently chose to talk about how disruptive technologies were having a significant influence on Islamic countries or Muslim societies. These talks brought up several interesting aspects, including how cultural and ethical challenges were arising in the adoption of some new technologies, which are unique to Muslim societies. Consequently, we considered it would be timely to commission and edit this volume of invited and peer-reviewed chapters on *Disruptive Technologies and Muslim Societies*. We had contributions from countries throughout the Islamic world, including Pakistan, Malaysia, Morocco, Saudi Arabia, Turkey, and Qatar. We also had some contributions from authors based in the Western world who had a particular interest in the introduction of disruptive technologies to Muslim societies.

We found that the 17 chapters submitted to the volume could be broadly divided into five areas, but with several overlaps. These areas are artificial intelligence, science and technology, health and education, food systems, and fintech. The chapters show that disruptive technologies are inducing significant changes in Muslim societies and Islamic countries that are paralleling those in the Western world, but often with subtle differences that the authors were encouraged to discuss.

1. Artificial Intelligence

Just as the internet, the world wide web, and mobile phones have changed the world, there are now major developments in the applications of machine learning and artificial intelligence (AI) that are producing an analogous disruption in all spheres of human activity. AI can present major challenges to Muslim societies, as the training datasets used for machine learning can have significant biases. For example, the books, journals, and other publications used as the fundamental fitting information to enable AI algorithms to produce new prose largely come from the Western world and can produce biased outcomes for some important topics.

The chapter "Islam and Decentralized Artificial Intelligence Systems: Ontologies and Common Sense" by Biliana Popova and Mazhar Ali Bari discusses these challenges and advocates for the development of epistemic maps in AI which are tailored to Islamic communities, fostering more meaningful interaction among these communities. The establishment of such maps is proposed as a means to mitigate instances of epistemic violence and to facilitate the emergence of decentralized AI systems as viable alternatives.

The chapter by Muhammad Adil Iqbal and Najimdeen Bakare on "Muslim Societies and the Rise of Artificial Intelligence: Impacts, Challenges, and the Way Forward" further discusses the responses and reflections of Muslim societies toward AI. The discussion is centered on how diverse Muslim societies, particularly those beyond the Western sphere, engage with the new technologies and modernity. Drawing primarily from existing secondary sources, this qualitative exploration also delves into the epistemic dimensions of the topic.

"Leveraging Historical Responses and Islamic Perspectives for AI in 21st-Century Healthcare in Muslim Societies" is the title of the chapter by Ajwah Nadeem and colleagues. The application of AI to healthcare represents one of the most direct benefits arising from the new technology and can have an immediate impact. The chapter delves into the intricate historical, sociopolitical, and jurisprudential factors shaping the integration of AI in global healthcare, with a particular focus on Muslim societies. The roles of various stakeholders, including governments, Muslim scholars, and human–computer interaction developers, are examined in their haping of perceptions and adoption of advanced medical technologies. Case studies explore Islamic bioethics and shed light on the diverse mechanisms facilitating integration. The chapter seeks to provide a multidisciplinary viewpoint to enhance comprehension of the complexities involved with using AI.

News media can have major influences on politics and views in societies. Forms of AI have been used for many years in the news area, which has always been one of the first to use new technology due to the immediacy of the information that is required. There has, however, been an acceleration in more sophisticated AI applications recently. The chapter by Subhra Priyadarshini on "How Artificial Intelligence is Changing Newsrooms" discusses these features and examines how both Muslim and Western societies are adapting to the dynamic landscape of news dissemination and the differences which are arising.

2. Science and Technology

New science can have a huge influence when the technology arising from it is broadly applicable throughout societies. The dangers of climate change demand radical and disruptive technological solutions that are the subject of intensive research in laboratories and institutions around the world. Carbon capture technologies are of particular interest in regions with their own major oil or gas industries, and this includes several countries of the Islamic world. The chapter "Fossil Fuel Decarbonization and Plastics-Waste Conversion to Hydrogen and High-Value Carbons: Pure Science Behind Two Emerging Disruptive Technologies" by Peter Edwards and colleagues describes a major collaboration between the Oxford Petrochemical Research Centre and the King Abdulaziz City of Science and Technology in Saudi Arabia. Their joint research project involves the development of new techniques to capture and then transform carbon dioxide emissions into carbon-neutral synthetic fuels by using green hydrogen. This collaboration has also spearheaded research in utilizing plastic waste as a valuable resource by employing microwave catalysis to produce clean hydrogen and high-value materials.

An innovative technology to tackle the escalating global waste disposal challenges amid the backdrop of climate change is also the topic of the chapter by Erfan Ibrahim on "Waste to Value Technology: The Key

Enabler for Sustainability in Muslim Societies." This chapter presents a detailed technical and financial framework for commercially viable and scalable waste management solutions. The new technology aims to address the waste disposal issues prevalent in Muslim societies while concurrently fostering employment opportunities, producing valuable fuel and soil enhancement products, and generating carbon credits to aid in achieving net-zero targets.

A different area where scientific advances are producing new insights is architecture. Caravanserais have traditionally provided places for merchants and traders to access local markets and meet and interact with people from across vast regions. They can also serve as a showcase of the aesthetic and cultural essence of Islamic architecture. The chapter by Güzden Varinlioğlu and Özge Börekçi titled "Toward a Geospatial and Temporal Experience of Islamic Architecture: Caravanserais of Anatolia" investigates the evolution of these unique architectural marvels over time by employing digital tools to generate precise spatial data. Their work provides a systematic and parametric insight, integrating information gleaned from previous research on caravanserais which is cross-referenced with data collected onsite.

3. Health and Education

Occasionally, a scientific breakthrough emerges with profound potential for advances in health. Gene editing is poised to be one such discovery. This is the subject of the chapter by John Parrington, Ali Alhoshani, and Ali Hanbashi on "The Great Promise and Potential Perils of Genome Editing for the Islamic World." They emphasize that gene editing can be applied to virtually any cell type in diverse plant or animal species, spanning bacteria to humans, and also offers the ability to either completely disable gene function or subtly modify it by introducing mutations. They also explain that the tools required for gene editing are relatively straightforward to prepare and are well within the grasp of individuals possessing molecular biology expertise, reagents, and equipment. Consequently, laboratories worldwide, including those in several countries of the Islamic World, are embracing this technology to investigate bacteria, plants, or human cell cultures.

Addressing maternal mortality remains a global imperative, with weaknesses in health systems playing a significant role in deaths worldwide. The integration of digital technologies holds promise for accelerating progress and bolstering maternity services on a global scale. This is the subject of the chapter by Jane Hirst with the title "Digital Technologies for Improving Pregnancy Care." The chapter advocates the adoption of digital health innovations to bolster pregnancy and maternity services, offering a series of case studies that explore both the potential benefits and challenges associated with their widespread implementation. Although the examples provided are not directly specific to Muslim societies, they offer insights that could be relevant to addressing challenges encountered in these societies worldwide.

The COVID-19 pandemic was the most significant health crisis of recent times throughout the world. The chapter by Shahid Jameel, with the title "How the COVID-19 Pandemic Impacted Learning in Islamic Countries," examines how the pandemic influenced education and learning. A standardized global evaluation of students and education systems, conducted every three years across approximately 80 countries, was used to provide the basic information for the study. The chapter describes how prolonged school closures and digital access disparities in Islamic countries during the pandemic particularly disadvantaged girls. It also found that disadvantaged students in Islamic countries were more resilient than those in other countries. Furthermore, immigrant students were found to outperform non-immigrants in countries with large expatriate populations. Several Islamic countries spend generously on education and stand to benefit from studying the strategies employed by the best global education systems.

The influence of disruptive technologies on higher education is the subject of the chapter by Ahmad Fauzi Ismail and colleagues on "Disruptive Innovation and Muslim Societies: The Need for Reforms in Higher Education." Recent initiatives undertaken by the Malaysian government and the Universiti Teknologi Malaysia (UTM) to foster a culture of invention-based education are discussed. It is emphasized that universities should establish clear strategies and programs aimed at instilling innovation as a fundamental practice among students and academics while also fostering collaborative partnerships with industry.

4. Food Systems

Innovation in the production of food has huge potential across all countries and societies. The chapter with the title "Food System Innovations to Feed a Growing Global Muslim Population" by Sophie Attwood,

Eman Alkhalawi, and Cother Hajat describes the significant challenges within food systems confronting burgeoning global populations. The focus is on high-growth Muslim-majority countries where food security, human health, and environmental sustainability are paramount concerns. The potential for plant-based diets, which enhance access to alternative protein sources, is emphasized within the framework of Islamic religious beliefs and the unique practices inherent to Muslim communities.

The topic of food is also discussed by Saher Hasnain in the chapter "Food System Transformation: A Society-Based Approach." Research on food system transformations has predominantly been confined to abstract or localized levels, often lacking practical engagement with societies. This chapter shifts the focus toward societies as intermediaries, facilitating connections between transformations occurring at local levels and broader regional and global changes, with examples from Muslim societies. It is emphasized that this framework offers a socially and spatially inclusive approach to examining food system transformation, ultimately contributing to a resilient and food-secure future.

Legal aspects of food production and consumption can present interesting challenges. This is the subject of the chapter by Nour-Eddine Qaouar titled "On the Consumption of Blood-Based Foods in Light of Two Old, Yet New, Legal Cases." The consumption of blood-based foods in Islamic countries is considered by analyzing two legal cases – insects and sugar – studied by premodern scholars. For insects, the chapter delves into authoritative and conflicting opinions from the four major schools of Islamic law. In the case of sugar, the proposed prohibition of sugar consumption by some scholars in 19th-century Morocco due to the perceived presence of blood is also described. The influence of these older legal cases on food consumption in modern Muslim societies is discussed.

5. Fintech

Another area where disruptive technologies are producing significant changes is fintech. The chapter by Ahmet Faruk Aysan and Muhammad Fazlurrahman Syarif is on "Fusion of Blockchain and Islamic Fintech: Unlocking New Possibilities in SME Financing, Financial Well-Being, and Trade Financing." It describes how Islamic fintech is utilizing modern technology to provide Sharia-compliant products, ensuring adherence to Islamic ethical standards in transactions. The radical new opportunities associated with blockchain technology are also discussed. It is emphasized that the new financial technologies have the potential to support the significant growth and advancement of SME (small- and medium-sized enterprise) financing, financial well-being, and trade financing.

Zakat is the obligation of Muslims to donate a portion of their wealth each year to charity. The chapter by Kinan Salim, Wan Nuriqlima Wan Mohd Noor, and Shamsher Mohamad Ramadili Mohd, with the title "The Potential Applications of Artificial Intelligence in Managing Zakat Funds," investigates the transformative impact of AI on the collection and distribution of Zakat funds. An examination is carried out on the utilization of AI to streamline collection procedures, accurately identify eligible recipients, and ensure efficient fund allocation. The challenges and ethical considerations associated with integrating AI into religious and social welfare contexts are also discussed.

Erdal Harunoğullari's chapter on "An Analysis of Disruptive Technologies in Muslim Societies: Economic, Financial, and Ethical Implications" scrutinizes the Islamic ethical principles governing the use of new technology and evaluates its influence on economic inclusivity and social equity. Existing regulations, strategic insights, and present-day case studies of technology adoption in different regions are examined. The chapter explores emerging patterns and advancing technologies shaping Islamic civilizations while also outlining the associated challenges and opportunities.

The editors hope that these contributions by several domain experts will add new information on disruptive technologies as these get accepted by Muslim societies and adopted in Islamic countries. We thank World Scientific Publishing for joining us in this effort.

Part I

Artificial Intelligence

https://doi.org/10.1142/9781800616295_0001

Chapter 1

Islam and Decentralized Artificial Intelligence Systems: Ontologies and Common Sense

Biliana Popova[*,‡] and Mazhar Ali Bari[†]

[*]*Al Akhawayn University, Ifrane, Morocco*

[†]*Ghulam Bari Foundation, CognoVation, Riyadh, Kingdom of Saudi Arabia*

[‡]*b.popova@aui.ma*

Abstract

An *epistemic map* is a conceptual tool used to represent knowledge or beliefs within a particular context. This chapter argues for the creation of epistemic maps for different Islamic epistemic communities, enabling them to meaningfully interact with each other and other epistemic communities without being solely subjected to centralized artificial intelligence (AI) systems' epistemological principles and dynamics. We argue that the creation of epistemic maps will reduce the possibility for epistemic violence and, moreover, will pave the way toward the creation of *decentralized* AI systems as alternative choices. In order to create epistemic maps for specific Islamic epistemic communities, we claim that domain-specific ontologies should be combined with domain-specific common sense; this combination constitutes the concrete epistemic map.

1. Introduction

Questions of intellect, causality, potentiality, probability, determination, free will, and how these relate to different types of knowledge production, construction, governance, and embodiment have been central to Islamic philosophy for centuries. Examples include the works of Ibn Rushd, Ibn Bajja, Ibn Tufayl, Ar-Razi, Ibn ‘Arabi, and others dedicated to defining what constitutes intellect, passive and active intelligence, and common sense and whether *domain-specific common sense* exists or if it is shared across cultures, spaces, and times. Furthermore, are morality and ethics related to intelligence? Are intelligence and common sense related to the legitimization of power? Are knowledge and common sense foundational to judicial and moral reasoning? Or, are customs and identity construction more important for justice on a greater scale? What is the scale to begin with: should universals be placed above particulars? Are universals atemporal or are they time-related?

When one opens an old book, these questions emerge from every page. But, one then closes the book and proceeds to engage with social media or the latest Muslim chatbot application. There, a completely different world emerges – a world where the main questions concerning Islam are predominantly centered around ritualistic aspects, creating the perception that Islam is primarily absorbed in its ritualistic dimensions with minimal attention to other facets.

Imam Al-Ghazzali [1] would perhaps object to these remarks (in our opinion), and certainly proclaim that the sacred rituals are as important as the acts of *Ijtihad* and knowledge of the ritualistic aspects of Islam cannot be minimized compared to mental *Ijtihad* practices (p. 55) – both matter. And we, of course, agree with the Imam. Nevertheless, this state of affairs bothers us. Islam today feels marginalized not in a physical but in a metaphysical sense. It feels as though the religion is used primarily to provide specific instructions for very specific, ritual-based inquiries. As for the bigger questions, such as “What is life?”, “What is our role in it?”, and “How do we coexist with others?”, many Muslim chatbots either respond in a neoliberal or utilitarian manner or simply and over-moralizingly state, “this chatbot is meant to give information on *salat* and *zakat* and Ramadan and not to such questions.”

Many current applications, such as Muslim chatbots, Islamic finance programs, and others, have nothing *Islamic* about them, except for the use of Islamic-related terms. This is not surprising at present: artificial intelligence (AI) systems are centralized, and their underpinning ideology is formed by the initial dataset collected in specific geopolitical contexts (efforts to include other datasets are underway; yet, the predominant data are from the Northern and Western hemispheres) and with the epistemological principles of utilitarianism and neoliberalism. Most applications that claim to be Islamic are usually constructed from centralized AI datasets and semantic maps. In other words, most applications are developed based on a centralized collection of information and patterns; the data used to train and develop the AI models typically originates from a single, unified repository or source. Is that terrible? No, of course not; we are not claiming that.

Here, we claim that while centralized AI systems were the necessary beginning of AI development, we believe that the creation of decentralized AI systems, which function with different, filtered datasets – not those sourced from a single, central repository but instead gathered from diverse locations or contributors and operate on different epistemic principles – would enrich the field of AI and limit future occurrences of epistemic violence.

This chapter is based on the belief that Islam, as a religion and protector of humanist values, has much to offer in terms of knowledge. In addition, it is worth capturing this knowledge and enabling it to be used by different communities across the world. Creating decentralized AI systems, based on Islamic epistemic maps, could enrich both Islam (the ability to view religion through AI lenses) and AI development. After all, religious studies and the humanities remain the sole disciplines of knowledge sustaining the belief that there is more to humans than mere representatives of a biological species, with psychological problems, socially and economically determined behaviors, and chemical imbalances.

We claim that currently, the possibility of epistemic violence is high, and that Islam, as a knowledge framework and as a philosophy of life and governance, is being further marginalized. We claim that the creation of Islamic epistemic maps for different epistemic communities would facilitate the development of decentralized AI systems, serving as alternatives to centralized AI systems for various aspects of life.

We also argue that the concepts of "epistemic maps" should be disambiguated, conceptualized, and operationalized. In this chapter, we try to introduce a possible conceptualization of epistemic maps as a translation tool between social and humanist realities and AI.

In the chapter, we first define what epistemic violence is, how it is usually presented in literature, and which definition we use. Then, we present the existing scholarly work on domain-specific (Islamic knowledge) ontologies and the current scholarly work on AI common sense. We argue for the need to create a *domain-specific Islamic common sense*. We claim that the amalgamation of Islamic AI ontologies with Islamic domain-specific common sense would lead to the creation of Islamic AI epistemic maps. This would serve as the basis for decentralized AI systems; however, it would also facilitate meaningful dialogue, communication, and negotiation among different Islamic epistemic communities.

2. On Epistemic Violence

Much of the scholarly literature on epistemic violence focuses on the imposition of hegemonic narratives and discourses on others (*others* in all its connotations). Such critiques touch upon many scholarly fields: critiques of legal, academic, and popular discourses addressing epistemic ignorance and violence regarding issues of gender and sexuality [2–5]; critiques of different types of epistemic violence present in religious discourses and practices [6–11], and critiques of Western (hegemonic) normative discourses imposed by different international institutions and approaches to globalization [12–15]. The suggested approaches to studying and countering epistemic violence are also diverse: from proposed methodologies for identifying epistemic violence to propositions for new engagements with different epistemic communities and new ways to *resist* imposed hegemonic epistemological dominance.

Few authors question whether practices of prescribing solely negative and violent traits to Western epistemological and paradigmatic dominance are, on their own, a form of epistemic violence that reduces the imagery of the *West* to an amalgamated essentialist hyperbolic representation and the imagery of the *rest* to agentless, victimhood-based representations. Vickers [16] is an exception to this, and we believe that further research in this vein is necessary in order to avoid essentialist representations of any epistemic communities – be they hegemonic or not – and to facilitate a proactive engagement with their specific knowledge construction and production practices.

It is challenging to disambiguate *epistemic violence* as a concept, as it has many manifestations and is interpreted differently in different contexts. Nevertheless, for this particular study, we attempt to give a working definition that will serve as an axiomatic basis for further elaboration of our principal arguments. Epistemic violence in literature is often presented as the process of indoctrinating a certain population into ideologies and beliefs *foreign* to its phenomenological epistemologies or as a discriminatory mechanism through which certain beliefs and epistemological systems are marginalized in favor of others to secure or establish the domination or power of political and social agents [17–21].

To establish our understanding of epistemic violence, it is essential to introduce our broad definition of an "epistemic map." We employ this term to describe the informal and frequently implicit arrangement of sociocultural, political, and ideological assumptions and beliefs regarding knowledge management and production. In simpler terms, an epistemic map serves as an organizational framework for beliefs about who is entitled to produce knowledge, what qualifies as knowledge, who is deemed suitable to oversee it, and other related inquiries. We further discuss the term "epistemic map" in the following section.

We conceptualize epistemic violence as the act of imposing one epistemic map and its embedded and underpinning principles on an epistemic agent (an individual or a community), either by intentionally disregarding or annihilating their own epistemic maps or by not acknowledging the existence of their maps. Further, in our view, epistemic violence can be imposed either overtly by declaring the intention to impose an epistemic map on a certain agent (as typically seen in colonial and totalitarian regimes of the 20th century) or covertly by appearing to accept existing ontologies while substituting contextualized common sense principles and mechanisms to the point where an independent agent's map becomes completely obliterated. This is an approach widely applied in neoliberal politics, as described, for example, in Nielsen's work [22].

The creation of decentralized AI systems capable of supporting the development of temporally bound, contextualized epistemic maps will enable the creation of negotiation mechanisms that could lead to more balanced power dynamics and interactions among different epistemic agents. Here, we specifically argue for the creation of *Islamic* epistemic maps that capture and operationalize Islamic ontologies, as well as the fundamental, contextually-specific religious principles and beliefs (domain-specific common sense) in concrete epistemic communities within Islamic social contexts.

The exploration of Islamic epistemological paradigms and their manifestations in the contemporary Westernized world, along with the consequential impact on Muslim communities and societies, has been a focal point for numerous philosophers, including Arkoun, Jabiri, Nasr, Abu El Fadl, Sardar, and Mernissi [23–28] among many others. Though important, discussing in detail how their and other contemporary Muslim philosophers' contributions would be paramount for developing refined Islamic epistemic frameworks should be the focus of another, separate study. Our argument here is based on the often-emphasized belief that epistemic violence cannot be eradicated as long as there are significant imbalances in knowledge production and power.

We are also arguing that ensuring a more equitable dialogue among different political, social, and religious paradigms will not be achieved merely by *restraining* more powerful or dominant agents; rather, it requires enabling all epistemic agents to participate in the global AI scene and to share their universality as well as their particularity.

3. On Epistemic Maps

The term *epistemic map* has been used more frequently in economic and psychological scholarship than in social and cultural studies. In the field of education, Metelerkamp *et al.* [29] argue that systems such as Net-Map can identify informal knowledge networks and thus enable community-based actors to better understand these networks within their respective career fields. In our opinion, it is paramount that we have the means to engage with networks of informal knowledge, yet they continue to be understudied in the field of social science. Most research in this area is found in management and economics studies [30–32].

Goldfarb and Yan [33] present a study in which they evaluate an economic theory by designing different epistemic maps and measuring data in different contexts. Their approach to the design of epistemic maps consists of capturing existing empirical assumptions within a concrete context, identifying different types of variables, and evaluating manifestations of theoretical consistency. One of their aims was to estimate the relationship between coverage mismatch and excess value: *excess value* manifests where the empirical assumption is overestimated (and does not significantly affect objective reality) and *coverage mismatch* manifests where the empirical assumption is completely missing from the rationalized ontological architecture.

In the context of this chapter's focus, the following can serve as an overgeneralized example of how their model can be understood if we are engaging with a specific Islamic epistemic community: In any formal Islamic ontological architecture, the concept of "compassion" could be disambiguated, refined, and strictly conceptualized. Yet, in a specific epistemic community, the principle of compassion can be expressed in strikingly different ways, in very different situations, and by diverse actors or agents. The mismatch between the formal ontological representation of the concept and its practical manifestation would be one of the focuses of studies constructing the epistemic map of said community.

We take this study as the basis for our proposed model for epistemic maps. We propose that a contextualized epistemic map should consist of *domain-specific ontologies* as well as *domain-specific common sense.* The domain-specific ontologies extract semantic, symbolic, and rationalized relations among concepts that are significant to the local body of knowledge. They represent the architecture of formal knowledge representation. A lot of research [34–36] (discussed in Section 5) has been conducted in this direction, especially in terms of extracting ontologies from Islamic data (primarily textual data) and developing systems for formal Islamic knowledge management. We discuss these in the following section.

Nevertheless, we argue that these studies alone are not enough to develop Islamic epistemic maps. In addition to the domain-specific ontologies, an Islamic epistemic map should include dynamic mechanisms capable of outlining the *empirical assumptions* of a certain epistemic community. We call this *domain-specific common sense*.

We also argue that the disambiguation of concepts and the establishment of their semantic relations and taxonomic hierarchies is not enough. While Islam is a religion of the book, it is also a lived, lively, and organic religion – knowledge of sacred texts has never been considered enough to be a good Muslim. Personal responsibility, community engagement, and the ability to contextualize lessons and guidance from sacred texts have always been paramount in the phenomenological experience of Islam. If all the studies focus solely on extracting ontologies for Islamic knowledge management, the risk of epistemic violence is significant. Ontological structures imposed on epistemic communities without considering their informal Islamic knowledge network structures, their contextual assumptions about the world, society, social structures, and power dynamics are troubling, as they engender possibilities for epistemic violence as grave as the instances where utilitarian ontologies are imposed on specific epistemic communities (one of the great objections to neoliberalism).

For the development of different Islamic epistemic maps, it is necessary that, in addition to domain-specific ontologies, *domain-specific common sense systems* also be developed. These would be platforms where users or agents could identify themselves as participants or representatives of specific epistemic communities, thereby facilitating the organization of informal empirical social assumptions and other fundamental interactions and embedded dynamics.

If such context-specific epistemic maps can be constructed by applying theories of mind, assemblage theory, game theory, or other emerging theories as well as Islamic *kalam* and philosophy, it would then be possible to create decentralized meta-platforms and structures in which communication and meaning-making between and among different epistemic communities are based less on dynamics of domination and subordination and more on dynamics of meaningful negotiation. Meta-structural platforms will enable us to develop an *epistemic logic* for formalizing group dynamics, as suggested by Constantini *et al.* [37]. We agree with this approach, and their focus on principles of dynamics and implicit structure, but argue that religious, cultural, and social assumptions should be relied upon rather than psychological and cognitive assumptions.

In a certain sense, we are arguing for the opposite of what Nihei [14] is defending. We claim that the inclusion of diverse epistemic agents in creating universal, diverse, and just epistemic maps is a worthy endeavor, yet it would be insufficient on its own. We claim that, in addition, there is a need for the development of *contextually intelligent* epistemic maps that capture the *epistemic injustices* specific to particular epistemic communities. They would constitute epistemic injustices only if imposed on the communities or used for discriminatory purposes and power struggles. Whether these are *just* or *unjust* is a subjective question that, we argue, can only be studied if epistemic maps become a reality, allowing people to negotiate meaning among different maps and according to different circumstances. In other words, we argue that knowledge production will always remain *biased* in a certain way, and labeling those biases as unjust may constitute an ethical fallacy, thereby negating the notion of human free will. Believing that knowledge production can be entirely unbiased is not a human-centered approach to knowledge production; rather, it is quite a totalitarian one. While we agree with the usefulness of some standardized, universal (inclusive, tolerant, global) epistemic networks for regulating global interactions, we also argue that context-specific epistemic maps should be developed to better understand and engage with domain-specific, human-centered (religious and cultural), time-bound knowledge production.

It is important to note that we believe epistemic maps should be constructed based on the principles of positive theories: how people actually behave, what they actually believe and infer in different situations, what actual informal knowledge comes into play in their interactions, etc., rather than the principles of normative theories that focus on ideal scenarios and how people *should* behave. The main aim of creating epistemic maps is to understand and negotiate meaning and not to judge or impose external (to the epistemic community) moralistic principles by force or coercion.

In the following sections, we first present an overview of the progress made in the development of Islamic knowledge management and Islamic ontology extraction systems and their significance and use. Then, we present an overview of the relevant work on the development of AI common sense and how it relates to the development of domain-specific common sense. Finally, we argue that the creation of Islamic epistemic maps should combine both domain-specific ontologies and domain-specific common sense.

4. On Domain-Specific (Islamic) Ontologies

AI ontology can be broadly defined as the formal representation of the structure of knowledge in a specific domain. Ontology extraction aims at specifying the concepts in a specific domain, their attributes, and the relationships between them [38–40]. The general approaches to extracting ontologies, especially from unstructured texts within a specific field, are numerous; however, in this section, we focus only on the literature that engages with Islamic domain-specific ontologies.

Many researchers have proposed that Islamic ontologies can be extracted first from the most important Islamic texts, such as the Quran and the Hadith. Kamran *et al.* [34] propose developing an ontology-driven *knowledge graph*, extracted from the Hadith corpus, by basing it on web-based ontology representation in accordance with residual derivative fuel (RDF) standards. Such an approach would facilitate meaningful engagement with Hadith texts by students of Islam as well as other users.

Ta'a *et al.* [35] argue for the need to construct Al-Quran ontologies based on semantic approaches that include (in addition to the usual conventional knowledge management methods such as taxonomies, hierarchies, and tree structures) domain-specific architectures and categories such as the instructions *mutasyabiha* and *muhkamat* and their disambiguation. This approach includes the possibility of linking the core text to *Tafsir* and translations from different languages.

Mohamed *et al.* [41] propose the development of a Quranic semantic search tool, in which the ontology extraction is done manually based on the classifications developed by Mushaf Al-Tajweed. Beirade *et al.* [36], on the other hand, base their Quranic ontology on the classifications presented by Mu'ajam al Mufahras Li Alfath Quran Al Karim and develop it by using Protégé 2000 open source software in OWL (Web Ontology Language) format.

Most of these approaches to creating ontologies, based on the sacred texts of the Quran and the Hadith, are lexico-syntactic approaches that rely on natural language processing (NLP) of Arabic. This, in turn, raises key questions: Arabic is considered a low-NLP resource language [42,43], so there is always the need to combine transfer learning approaches and multi-task learning approaches, and more recently, to incorporate bidirectional pre-trained models such as AraBERT and AraGPT [44]. Another aspect related to the Arabic language and the Quran is, of course, that the classical Arabic used in the Quran holds a sacred status and differs significantly from Modern Standard Arabic. This has been addressed by many authors; for example, Abood *et al.* [45] argue that word sense disambiguation (WSD) approaches utilizing open-domain dictionaries such as WordNet may prove insufficient when applied to the Quranic text and could be misleading. Therefore, they argue that a domain-specific WSD approach is needed – an approach that uses restricted training data. They propose using the Yarwosky algorithm for training in the Quran domain-specific WSD.

Another approach to ontology creation, which is not entirely lexico-syntactic, involves the use of *axiomatic ontology learning* that supports formal-logic-based reasoning. This approach can be used with sources that are not only in Arabic but also in other languages. Its aim is to form both a regular (definitional form) and generalized (axiomatic form) description logic ontology [46]. In addition, numerous recent scholarly works have focused on developing Islamic knowledge ontologies for various aspects of human life, aiming to create ontology learning methods for engaging with the sacred texts (the Quran and the Hadith). These are based on a larger corpus of texts in order to produce specific outcomes.

One such example is the automated Islamic *fatwa* generation system, in which the researchers propose using latent Dirichlet analysis to model *fatwa* texts. They suggest that the dataset should be constructed through web scraping of public websites. The data then trains the topic classifier and the QA engines. The classification is evaluated through recurrent- and transformer-based approaches. Then, based on the user's questions, a topic-specific expert QA system is triggered, which then generates retrieval-based answers [44].

Another approach is to use the taxonomies of chatbots and QA systems to generate answers to jurisprudential questions, as proposed by Jamal *et al.* [47]. They argue that the chatbot system can be trained using a text classification model based on jurisprudence texts written by one Islamic scholar. They used Bayesian networks and naïve Bayes as machine learning algorithms and a string-to-word vector filter in order to classify the text data. Training chatbot systems through specific text classification models based on different datasets (from public websites to texts by specific Islamic scholars) opens up many possibilities for rethinking the overall classification of jurisprudential texts and their use in contextualized epistemic communities.

Aside from the scholarly work focused on Islamic jurisprudence, there have been quite a few researchers focusing on narrowly defined domain-specific ontology extraction. One such example is the development of TibbOnto, a semantic ontology representation of *Tibb Al-Nabawy* – prophetic medicine based on Hadith. This ontology has been developed with the aim of potentially generating treatment recommendations based on Islamic knowledge [48]. We believe that such domain-specific ontologies need not be restricted to only a dataset based on Hadith texts. It would be interesting to include a larger dataset that could consist of *Kalam, Fiqh,* and *Falsafa* texts dedicated to Islamic medical practices.

Another interesting domain-specific ontology, developed by Othman *et al.* [49] is related to providing *Do'a* and *Zikr al-Mā'thur* for counseling services in high schools. The ontology was created in Protégé, and it functions as a dynamic knowledge-based platform for a semantic web. It is aimed at facilitating the provision of authentic answers for *Do'a* and *Zikr al-Ma'thur* to questions related to stress relief, dealing with bullying, addiction, and other relevant cases for high school students.

We argue that such domain-specific ontologies would be an adequate starting point for the development of epistemic maps because the epistemic community that the *Do'a* and *Zikr al-Ma'thur* ontology engages with is clearly defined: high school students in Malaysia. Hence, this is one example we could use to argue that, in addition to domain-specific ontologies, it would also be useful to develop knowledge representations of domain-specific common sense (informal knowledge networks, pre-existing assumptions, etc.), and then, by combining both the ontology and the common-sense representations, we would obtain a concrete epistemic map specific to concrete epistemic communities. This, we claim, can be done in all spheres of life.

A significant number of scholarly efforts have been directed toward developing domain-specific ontologies related to Islamic knowledge in the sphere of Islamic economics and finance. Aboubacar *et al.* [50] designed the Islamic finance ontology, OntoFIS. They use the Protégé editor for the design of the ontology and RDF, RDFS, and OWL as knowledge representation tools. They manually identify the key concepts and then encode them in the appropriate language. In their conclusion, they propose that, in order to expand the database used for the further enrichment of the ontology, they will consider web scraping techniques in their future work. Keltoum *et al.* [51] take a different approach in designing an ontology for Islamic finance and banking called IFBO. They, too, use the Protégé tool and OWL language; however, they chose to apply the NeOn methodology for the ontology engineering process because it allows for reusability, contextualization, and continuous evolution.

Among the wide-ranging studies in Islamic finance, the work by Zouaoui *et al.* [52] has a very specific focus: they develop AraFamOnto, which is an ontology-based inheritance calculation system. The ontology is built manually by the researchers by identifying key concepts and their attributes and hierarchical relations from within Islamic inheritance law. The researchers used the Protégé editor and Apache JENA to build the semantic web, and their dataset consists of 50 real families.

OntoAndalus is an ontology designed by Almeida *et al.* [53] for pottery artifacts from Al-Andalus by using standard semantic web ontologies for archaeological studies. They chose DUL as a foundational ontology in order to enrich the conceptualization of the domain. They demonstrated how competing interpretations of one artifact can be modeled in individual artifact descriptions. OntoAndalus allows for the multifaceted analysis of artifacts by considering their functionality, composition, and competing descriptions.

There are two main concerns regarding these domain-specific ontology extraction and construction approaches. First, centralized datasets and semantic maps are used in most cases. This, on the one hand, ensures the standardization and universalization of the ontologies, while on the other hand, it raises questions regarding the filtering processes in large dataset engagement. This, we argue, is the *lesser* worry, as it has been addressed by multiple researchers who either constructed the ontology manually or considered alternative approaches to the creation of filters for large datasets and centralized semantic map engagement. Second, the greater worry is that all domain-specific ontologies are presented as universal and totalized representations of knowledge. However, there is no consideration of the different *madhabs*, different schools of thought, and, of course, specific epistemic communities.

In the end, this tendency to represent Islam as a totalized, disembodied truth diminishes the chances of *separatism* – "We all are Muslims, we all share the same knowledge" is its message. Yet, this practice greatly increases the possibilities for epistemic violence. Islam is a living and lived religion; it cares for specific individuals and their communities. This aspect – the living, vibrant aspect of Islam – is completely ignored by this totalized and disembodied truth approach to Islamic ontologies.

5. On AI Common Sense

When discussing the notion of common sense, the literature examines two related, but different, concepts. The first is described as *intuitive reasoning*, and the second is *rationalistic probabilistic reasoning* [54,55]. They are related because the human ability to read a situation is strictly related to the ability to identify causal relations in the physical and social worlds, to evaluate the significance of the situation in a broader sense, and, based on that, to undertake actions appropriate to the situation in accordance with human values and estimations about the most useful means to reach certain ends (be they narrowly or broadly specified).

Despite this relationship, we examine these two definitions separately. The first involves *intuitive reasoning* – the cognitive management of intuitive inferences humans make about the implicit structures, dynamics, and causalities that exist in the physical and social worlds [54]. Intuitive human reasoning, and its compositional nature, is contrasted with the formulations of machine learning discriminative tasks [55]. Intuitive reasoning can be linked to abductive reasoning – the ability to generate explanatory hypotheses based on partial information. Or, as suggested by Hasselberger *et al.* [56]: the ability to learn implicit causal structures from limited data. In the same spirit, Zhu *et al.* [57] describe human causal learning as a rational Bayesian process that constitutes the acquisition of abstract causal structures.

In 2005, Matuszek *et al.* [58] proposed that machine learning requires a core of knowledge that makes the incorporation of new knowledge automatic and contextualized. The Cyc knowledge base aims to build a consistent, formalized representation of the world. They explain that the Cyc system has three components: a knowledge base, an inference engine, and a natural language system. While this system seems useful for facilitating the development of AI common sense in general, we believe it is more pertinent to the development of inference reasoning related to the *physical world*, whereas our focus here is to discuss possibilities for creating domain-specific common sense relevant to the *social world* of different epistemic communities.

Hasselberg *et al.* [56] argue that one of the key characteristics of common sense is the ability to understand a situation by choosing the most effective and meaningful features while ignoring all irrelevant details. Choi [55] differs, claiming that it is not necessary for humans to discriminate among an infinite number of possibilities in order to choose the most optimal one; he claims, rather, that this is typical of computational reasoning. We argue here that the truth lies somewhere in between. While we do not believe that human intuitive reasoning is a process of cognitive discrimination among an *infinite* number of possibilities, we do believe that it is a process of discrimination among possible scenarios measured against *possible* narratives or stories that an individual holds to be true. In this sense, we agree with some of the core principles applied in the development of Aesop, as studied by Mao *et al.* [59]. Common sense, in addition to being an abductive reasoning mechanism, is also strongly related to human abilities of storytelling and compositional approaches to reality.

So, in terms of the aspect of common sense that manifests itself in the ability of humans to *read a situation*, Hasselberger *et al.* [56] argue that this ability reflects a process of adjudicating and constantly monitoring and evaluating the progress on different ongoing activities (both short and long term) and different possible ends or goals. They also argue that common sense can be defined as the holistic practical awareness, which enables humans to understand the significance of a situation both in relation to its immediate context and in relation to the wider backdrop of one's life experiences as a whole.

We argue that, while their definition is relevant overall and valid for human intuitive reasoning about the physical world (and even in this aspect, we cannot completely agree with them), our understanding aligns more closely with the definitions presented by Meo *et al.* [59] and Choi [55] – common sense is the ability to read a situation according to impromptu hypotheses formed based on partially presented data. We argue here that, furthermore, hypotheses are formed by relating them to existing abstract epistemic and ethical narratives or stories that exist in the human consciousness prior to the presentation of the specific partial data. These narratives can be analyzed on an individual level. As Hasselberger *et al.* [56] implicitly suggest, each person has their own individual stories, priorities, and ongoing activities, all of which come into consideration when interpreting a specific situation. However, these matters can also pertain to a cultural or religious community level. We are interested in the narratives or stories that each epistemic community forms in relation to social situations, as these serve as the background of all hypotheses constructed through abductive reasoning in particular social situations.

In terms of developing algorithms that capture human-like abductive reasoning, Choi [55] proposes the inference algorithm DeLoren, which uses *past observations* and *future observations* as inputs to construct practical intelligence hypotheses. They also mention existing AI systems for common-sense abductive reasoning that use language-based formalism, such as COMET and Delphi (the latter also includes language-based moral reasoning).

The hypotheses produced by abductive reasoning are usually generalizable and transferable to other situations in which the objects and actors involved may differ, but the underlying principles remain the same. Zhu *et al.* [57] propose another approach to achieve this in AI. They propose that there should be a paradigm shift from big data for small tasks to small data for big tasks, which they claim could be achieved thanks to the functionality of deep neural networks (DNNs), fueled by hardware acceleration.

So, to sum up, we argue that the first aspect of *common-sense* reasoning is the ability to understand and evaluate a situation in terms of causal relations among objects, actors, and dynamics, through both abductive reasoning and the ability to connect the particular setting to a *complete picture*, story, or narrative about its composition; the significance of some partial data and the insignificance of other partial data; and the significance of the entire setting *vis-à-vis* other settings.

The second aspect of common sense discussed in the literature is what Zhu *et al.* [57] define as a manifestation of "the rational choice theory; that is, a rational person's behaviour and decision-making are driven by maximizing their utility function" and the ability to "achieve their intentions rationally by maximizing their utility while minimizing their costs, given their beliefs about the world" (p. 330). Hassellberger *et al.* [56] define it as the sensitivity humans have toward means that are both effective and appropriate for the situation.

In terms of *task completion*, there is an overall agreement that humans' common sense is not merely about skillfully completing narrowly defined tasks. Hasselberger *et al.* [56] differentiate between *intelligent engagement in activity* – by which they clarify that merely accomplishing a task efficiently does not constitute common sense and that, rather, it is the ability to accomplish it within the framework of a deep understanding of the concrete situational context – and its relation to other, broader, life-related contexts.

Zhu *et al.* [57] on the other hand, argue that common sense in task completion is also the ability to have an "organic paradigm of generalization, adaptation, and transfer among various tasks" (p. 312). In other words, it is not enough to accomplish a given task by maximizing the utility function and understanding its significance *vis-à-vis* a broader context; rather, one must also be able to construct and sustain an organic paradigm of generalization and adaptation that will ensure the transferability of skills and knowledge. In addition to understanding causal relations that are fundamental to human common sense, they also argue that intentionality plays an important role in the process of goal-setting and hence the efficiency level of task completion. Furthermore, they argue that, because intentionality plays such an important role, the ability to understand and predict the intentions, and thus the behavior of other agents, is also an important aspect of common-sense reasoning. In our argument for *domain-specific AI common-sense* development, we can consider other agents' intentionality, desires, and mental states only within the framework of cultural and religious stories and narratives that emerge from specific epistemic communities.

One last aspect of human common sense reasoning, discussed in the literature, is the problem of human goal-setting. Unlike machines, humans rarely have pre-set concrete goals [60], and even if they do, they constantly reevaluate situations and redefine and reset goals accordingly. This is achieved through an organic bidirectional interplay between the partial data humans perceive and their needs and goals, which Zhu *et al.* [57] claim should be developed in computer vision systems.

Hasselberger *et al.* [56], on the other hand, argue that humans pursue a variety of tasks that are broadly defined and that criteria for success could never be implemented fully because of the constantly changing context within which long-term, broadly-defined activities unfold. Hence, rather than focusing on aspects and criteria for *successful completion of tasks*, common-sense reasoning development should be more focused on non-monotonic reasoning, approximate concepts, and formalized contexts [60].

In order to develop the utilitarianism or rational choice aspect of common sense, we agree that some of the most efficient methods would include virtual simulations and other virtual and augmented reality platforms and systems, including video games, as proposed by Hutson [61].

6. On the Need for Domain-Specific Common Sense

We argue that, in order to be able to design specific epistemic maps for specific epistemic communities, there is first a need to combine both Islamic knowledge ontologies and domain-specific common-sense frameworks. The aims of the latter will be to capture and map implicit knowledge associations, implicit causal relations (including their cognition), the intentionalities of specific agents in their social roles, and the compositional narratives or stories that different epistemic communities use to contextualize social situations. This would be based on which metrics of axiomatic and causal discrimination occur as processes for determining goals, the significance of the specific situation, and probable desirable imagined outcomes.

In this sense, we propose something similar to the system conceptualized by Yu *et al.* [62], where the development of large-scale *design knowledge semantic networks* will facilitate the capture of contextual and implicit knowledge. This can be used later for cross-domain structures, which can in turn serve as a foundation for weighted, directed graphs with interconnected nodes. However, cross-domain knowledge engineering can only occur if specific epistemic maps for specific epistemic communities have first been designed.

We argue that one of the methods to create such maps could entail the following process: Different Islamic formal ontological architectures are superimposed on domain-specific common-sense architectures, the latter being a product of specific epistemic communities. A domain-specific common-sense architecture is constructed separately from the formal ontological architecture and is based on narratives (language-centered or multimodal) produced by members of the epistemic community. These narratives serve as the foundation for formalizing the prevailing hypotheses about reality among the members of that epistemic community and their corresponding structures of causality, approaches to probabilistic thinking, and meaning-making approaches that establish relations between the immediate context and broader narratives.

This is followed by a process of identifying excess value (where the assumptions represented in the domain-specific common-sense architecture are overestimated by the members of the epistemic community, either *vis-à-vis* the formal ontological architecture or *vis-à-vis* reality) and a process of identifying coverage mismatch (where the assumptions represented in the domain-specific common-sense architecture are missing from the formal ontological architecture) [33].

The result of this entire process would be an epistemic map related to a specific Islamic epistemic community.

None of this would be possible, however, without first developing domain-specific common sense.

We believe that the creation of such epistemic maps would significantly influence the advancement of decentralized AI systems. Moreover, their impact would extend to the approaches and methods we employ when engaging with Islam as a religion that matters to many people around the world.

7. Conclusion

In this chapter, we have argued that the sole reliance on centralized AI systems, large datasets, and semantic maps could eventually lead to the occurrence of different kinds of epistemic violence. Specific Islamic knowledge could be lost and replaced by solely utilitarian-based, global narratives, discourses, and knowledge production. Therefore, we first discussed the meaning of epistemic violence and its conceptualizations in academic literature. Following that, we proposed our definition of epistemic violence, based on which we further developed our arguments. We then examined existing practices and approaches to Islamic knowledge domain-specific ontology construction, noting that most of the ontology extraction work focuses on a totalized representation of Islam that does not recognize different contextualized understandings of various *madhabs*, schools of thought, and community-based conceptualization traditions. We believe that computer scientists should collaborate with Islamic scholars in order to construct more robust Islamic ontologies.

Next, we discussed how *AI common sense* is conceptualized by different scholars, and we argued for the need to develop *domain-specific common sense*, which would represent the informal knowledge, implicit causal relations, compositional (and contextualizing) stories, and narratives of specific Islamic epistemic communities. The combination and integration of both Islamic ontologies (formal representations of domain-specific knowledge) and domain-specific common sense would enable the creation of Islamic epistemic maps particular to specific communities. That, in turn, would enable different epistemic communities to interact meaningfully among themselves while minimizing the potential for epistemic violence by relying on decentralized AI systems, which would serve as alternatives to the current centralized ones.

References

[1] Al-Ghazzālī AH. The incoherence of philosophers [Tahāfutal-falāsifah]. Cairo: Dāral-Ma'ārif; 1961.

[2] Cayli Messina B. Breaking the silence on femicide: How women challenge epistemic injustice and male violence. *Br J Sociol.* 2022;73(4):859–884.

[3] Lim-Bunnin LL. 'And every word a lie': Samoan gender-divergent communities, language and epistemic violence. *Women Stud Abstr.* 2020;34:76–91.

[4] Milwertz C, Bu W. Non-governmental organising for gender equality in china – joining a global emancipatory epistemic community. *Int J Hum Rights.* 2007;11(1–2):131–149. https://doi.org/10.1080/13642980601176308.

[5] Segalo P, Fine M. Under lying conditions of gender-based violence – decolonial feminism meets epistemic ignorance: Critical transnational conversations. *Soc Pers Psychol Compass.* 2020;14(10):1–10.

[6] Auga U. Decolonizing public space: A challenge of Bonhoeffer's and Spivak's concepts of resistance, 'religion' and 'gender.' *Fem Theol.* 2015;24(1):49–68.

[7] Goto CT. Experiencing oppression: Ventriloquism and epistemic violence in practical theology. *Int J Pract Theol*. 2017;21(2):175–193.
[8] Lebens S. Proselytism as epistemic violence: A Jewish approach to the ethics of religious persuasion. *Monist*. 2021;104(3):376–392.
[9] Kiyimba K. An analysis of the epistemic link between the Catholic religion and violence in Uganda's history. *J Study Relig*. 2017;30(1):26–51.
[10] Naidoo M. Undoing epistemic violence in religious leadership in African theological education. *To be published in Pract Theol.* [Preprint] 2023;1–13.
[11] Sandberg S, Colvin S. 'ISIS is not Islam': Epistemic injustice, everyday religion, and young Muslims' narrative resistance. *Brit J Criminol*. 2020;60(6):1585–1605.
[12] Chilisa B, Mertens DM. Indigenous made in Africa evaluation frameworks: Addressing epistemic violence and contributing to social transformation. *Am J Eval*. 2021;42(2):241–253.
[13] Iveković R. Epistemological fractures: The decline of western paradigms. Beyond the current epistemic hegemony? *J Postcolon Writ*. 2019;55(6):755–768.
[14] Nihei M. Epistemic injustice as a philosophical conception for considering fairness and diversity in human-centered AI principles. *Interdiscip Inf Sci*. 2022;28(1):35–43.
[15] Tittensor D, Clarke M. Epistemic violence and the rise of the pseudo-secular Islamic FBO in the age of the 'religious turn' in development. *Muslim World* (Hartford). 2022;112(1):167–187.
[16] Vickers E. Critiquing coloniality, 'epistemic violence' and western hegemony in comparative education – the dangers of ahistoricism and positionality. *Comp Educ*. 2020;56(2):165–189. DOI: 10.1080/03050068.2019.1665268.
[17] Carter D, Warren R. Economic re-colonisation: Financialisation, indigeneity and the epistemic violence of resolution. *Polit Geogr*. 2021;84:102284.
[18] Chronaki A, Planas N, Svensson Källberg P. Onto/epistemic violence and dialogicality in translanguaging practices across multilingual mathematics classrooms. *Teach Coll Rec*. 1970;124(5):108–126.
[19] Cortés Gómez I. Antigypsyism as symbolic and epistemic violence in informative journalism in Spain, 2010–2018. *Crit Rom Stud (Online)*. 2020;3(1):4–25.
[20] Sims K. BRI as cognitive empire: Epistemic violence, ethnonationalism and alternative imaginaries in Zomian Highlands. *Singap J Trop Geogr*. 2022;43(3):309–324.
[21] Heleta S. Decolonisation of Higher Education: Dismantling epistemic violence and eurocentrism in South Africa. *Transform Higher Educ*. 2016;1(1):e1–e8.

[22] Neilson D. Epistemic violence in the time of coronavirus: From the legacy of the western limits of Spivak's 'can the subaltern speak' to an alternative to the 'neoliberal model of development.' *Educ Philos Theory*. 2021;53(8):760–765.

[23] Arkoun M, Lee, RD. *Rethinking Islam: Common Questions, Uncommon Answers*. Boulder, Colo.; Oxford: Westview Press; 1994.

[24] Jabiri, M. Abid. *Formation of Arab Reason: Text, Tradition and the Construction of Modernity in the Arab World*. I. B. Tauris in association with the Centre for Arab Unity Studies; 2011.

[25] Nasr, SH. *Knowledge and the Sacred*. Albany: State University of New York Press; 1989.

[26] Abou El Fadl K. *And God Knows the Soldiers: The Authoritatative and Authoritarian in Islamic Discourses*. Lanham, Md.: University Press of America; 2001.

[27] Sardar Z. *Postmodernism and the Other: The New Imperialism of Western Culture*. London; Chicago, Ill.: Pluto Press; 1997.

[28] Mernissi F. Scheherazade goes west: Different cultures, different harems. New York: Washington Square Press; 2001.

[29] Metelerkamp L, Schiffer E. Epistemic cartography: Evaluating Net-Map as a frontline tool for navigating informal knowledge networks. South Afr *J Environ Educ*. 2020;36(2). DOI: 10.4314/sajee.v36i1.11.

[30] Allen J, James AD, Gamlen P. Formal versus informal knowledge networks in R&D: A case study using social network analysis. *R&D Manag*. 2007;37(3):179–196.

[31] Reagans R, McEvily B. Network structure and knowledge transfer: The effects of cohesion and range. *Adm Sci Q*. 2003;48(2):240–267.

[32] Yoon W, Jeong J, Park KW. Informal network structure and knowledge sharing in organizations: An empirical study of a Korean paint manufacturing company. *Adm Sci*. 2021;11(2):1–18.

[33] Goldfarb B, Yan L. Revisiting Zuckerman's (1999) categorical imperative: An application of epistemic maps for replication. *Strateg Manag J*. 2021;42(11):1963–1992.

[34] Kamran AB, Abro B, Basharat A. Semantic Hadith: An ontology-driven knowledge graph for the Hadith Corpus. *Web Semant*. 2023;78:100797.

[35] Ta'a A, Shaari MS, Arif ASCM, Bakar MSA, Mahmad MA. Semantic approach for Al-Quran knowledge representation in Islamic knowledge management framework. *J Quranic Sci Res*. 2021;2(1):35–46.

[36] Beirade F, Azzoune H, Zegour DE. Semantic query for Quranic ontology. *J King Saud Univ-Comput Inform Sci*. 2021;33(6):753–760.

[37] Costantini S, Formisano A, Pitoni V. An epistemic logic for formalizing group dynamics of agents. *Interact Stud*. 2022;23(3):391–426.

[38] Cross V, Bathija V. Automatic ontology creation using adaptation. *Artif Intell Eng Des Anal Manuf.* 2010;24(1):127–141.

[39] Lenzerini M. Managing data through the lens of an ontology. *AI Mag.* 2018;9(2):65–74.

[40] Salatino A, Osborne F, Motta E. Ontology extraction and usage in the scholarly knowledge domain. arXiv; 2020. DOI: 10.48550/arxiv.2003.12611.

[41] Mohamed EH, Shokry EM. QSST: A Quranic semantic search tool based on word embedding. *J King Saud Univ-Comput Inform Sci.* 2022;34(3):934–945.

[42] Al-Twairesh N. The evolution of language models applied to emotion analysis of Arabic tweets. *Information (Basel).* 2021;12(2):84. Available at: https://doi.org/10.3390/info12020084.

[43] Jallad KA and Ghneim N. ArNLI: Arabic Natural language inference for entailment and contradiction detection. 2022. Available at https://doi.org/10.48550/arxiv.2209.13953.

[44] Munshi AA, Al-Sabban WH, Farag AT, Rakha OE, Al Sallab A, Alotaibi M. Automated Islamic jurisprudential legal opinions generation using artificial intelligence. *Pertanika J Sci Technol.* 2022;30(2):1135–1156.

[45] Abood RH, Tiun S. A comparative study of open-domain and specific-domain word sense disambiguation based on Quranic information retrieval. *MATEC Web Conf.* 2017;135:00071.

[46] Saad S, Bahari I. Axiomatic ontology learning approaches for English translation of the meaning of Quranic texts. *MATEC Web Conf.* 2017;135:00075.

[47] Jamal K, Kurniawan R, Batubara AS, Nazri MZA, Lestari F, Papilo P. Text classification on Islamic jurisprudence using machine learning technique. In: *4th International Conference on Computing and Applied Informatics*, 26–27 November 2019, Medan, Indonesia. *J Phys Conf Ser.* 2020;1566 012066. DOI: 10.1088/1742–6596/1566/1/012066.

[48] Al-Rumkhani A, Al-Razgan M, Al-Faris, A. TibbOnto: Knowledge representation of prophet medicine (Tibb Al-Nabawi). *Procedia Comput Sci.* 2016;82:138–142.

[49] Othman R, Tawil SFM. Ontological methodologies for counselling intervention: Do'a and Zikr Al-Mā'Thur Corpus. *Majallat Baghdād Lil-'ulūm.* 2021;18(2 Suppl.):856.

[50] Aboubacar S, Kisito KK, Traore Y. Towards an ontology for Islamic finance. *Int J Comput Trends Technol.* 2021;69(12):10–16.

[51] Keltoum B, Nabila N, Djamel M. Towards a reference ontology in Islamic finance and banking. In: *International Conference on Information and Communication Technology for the Muslim World.* 2018. DOI: 10.1109/ICT4M.2018.00023.

[52] Zouaoui S, Rezeg K. Islamic inheritance calculation system based on Arabic ontology (AraFamOnto). *J King Saud Univ-Comput Inform Sci.* 2021;33(1):68–76.

[53] Almeida B, Costa R. OntoAndalus: An ontology of Islamic artefacts for terminological purposes. *Semant Web.* 2021;12(2):295–311.

[54] Brachman RJ, Levesque HJ. Toward a new science of common sense. In *Proc AAAI Conf Artif Intell.* 2022;36(11):12245–12249. https://doi.org/10.48550/arxiv.2112.12754.

[55] Choi Y. The curious case of commonsense intelligence. *Daedalus* (Cambridge, Mass.). 2020;151(2):139–155.

[56] Hasselberger W, Lott, M. Where lies the grail? AI, common sense, and human practical intelligence. *Phenomenol Cogn Sci.* 2023 October 31:1–22.

[57] Zhu Y, Gao T, Fan L, Huang S, Edmonds M, Liu H, Gao F, Zhang C, Qi S, Wu YN, Tenenbaum JB, Zhu SC. Dark beyond deep: A paradigm shift to cognitive AI with humanlike common sense. *Engineering* (Beijing, China). 2020;6(3):310–345.

[58] Matuszek C, Witbrock M, Kahlert RC, Cabral J, Schneider D, Shah PA, Lenat DB. Searching for common sense: Populating CycTM from the web. In: *National Conference on Artificial Intelligence.* p. 1430–1435. https://people.cs.pitt.edu/~litman/courses/cs2710/papers/cyc2005.pdf.

[59] Meo T, Kim C, Raghavan A, Tozzo A, Salter DA, Tamrakar A, Amer MR, Weng P. Aesop: A visual storytelling platform for conversational AI and common-sense grounding. *AI Commun.* 2019;32(1):59–76. https://doi.org/10.3233/AIC-180605.

[60] McCarthy J. From here to human-level aI. *Artif Intell.* 2007;171(18):1174–1182.

[61] Hutson M. AI Takes on video games in quest for common sense. *Science* (American Association for the Advancement of Science). 2018;361(6403):632–633.

[62] Yu H, Zhao W, Zhao Q. Distributed representation learning and intelligent retrieval of knowledge concepts for conceptual design. *Adv Eng Inform.* 2022;53:101649.

https://doi.org/10.1142/9781800616295_0002

Chapter 2

Muslim Societies and the Rise of Artificial Intelligence: Impacts, Challenges, and the Way Forward

Muhammad Adil Iqbal[*,‡] and Najimdeen Bakare[†,§]

[*]*NUST Business School, National University of Sciences & Technology, Islamabad, Pakistan*

[†]*Department of International Relations and Strategic Studies, Faculty of Arts and Social Sciences, Universiti Malaya, Kuala Lumpur, Malaysia*

[‡]*m.adiliqbal@nbs.nust.edu.pk*

[§]*olaaayo@gmail.com*

Abstract

The ontology of artificial intelligence (AI) surpasses any denial. Its manifestation in all works of human existence is a testimony to the success of humanism and human intellect. While technology is nonreligious, it is not always culturally blind, especially when substantial scientific and technological interventions and inventions are products of certain regions of the world. The debate is not about who wins and is vanquished in the quest for AI; rather, it concerns how different societies, especially those outside of the West, embrace this unfolding reality. To this end, this chapter examines the correspondences and reactions of Muslim societies to the growing trend of AI. It particularly focuses on the impacts and challenges the face, and examines the way forward. Within the larger context of rejection and integration, the chapter addresses the reactions of Muslim societies when exposed to new technologies or manifestations of modernity. The chapter largely dwells on existing secondary data, which makes the chapter purely a qualitative epistemic venture.

1. Introduction

It goes without saying that the rise of artificial intelligence (AI) and its associated technologies is yet another human technological feat. Outer space, once considered beyond human reach, is no longer unattainable, as many modern issues are now being addressed through advanced technology. This, of course, leads to the conclusion that AI is a product of modernity that celebrates humanism and human intellect. Through the ages, the nature of human intellect has given rise to many questions and serious scholarly concerns. Epistemologically, it became a preoccupation for philosophers and those seeking to understand how the intellect is conceived [1], how it works, its limits [2], and its immateriality. For Aquinas, this immateriality is closely related to our power to make free choices, our capacity for self-knowledge, and our ability to think and reason abstractly [3] and shape the immediate and future world [4]. In the world of Islamic philosophy, human intellect is associated with *aql*, which in Arabic means "to prevent" or "to prohibit" undesirable and unwarranted things [5]. According to Ṣag̱hīr Ḥasan, *aql* is generally used in three senses: manners, universal judgment, and the soundness of the primary nature in man (faculty) [5]. During the heyday of Muslim philosophers, intellect was accorded the most profound intellectual scrutiny. Although there is no room in this study to elaborate on these streams of thought, we can nonetheless afford to entertain an idea from one among an ocean of thinkers of the past. Abu Bakr Muhammad ibn Yahya al-Sa'igh (d. 533/1138), known as Ibn Bajjah, was inspired by al-Farabi and was the teacher of Ibn Rusd and Ibn Tufayl. According to Ibn Bajjah:

> The intellect is the most important part of human body. In his opinion the correct knowledge is obtained through the intellect, which alone enables us to attain prosperity and to build character. Ibn Bajjah believes in the plurality of intellects and refers to the first intellect and secondary intellects. In his opinion, the human intellect is the remotest intellect and its existence is one with the insight which it receives from the first intellect [5].

Human faculty is considered intriguingly complex because of its capability to generalize experiences, work with abstract terms, draw conclusions from assumptions, and, above all, attend to complex phenomena beyond the comprehension of all other living species. Today, with the rapidity and intensity of AI technology, what was once solely a human endeavor is increasingly being extended to machines. Biliana Popova argues, "we are shifting authority back to the more knowledgeable, but unlike the middle ages when the knowledgeable were the religious scholars, now they are the machines [6]."

Inferring from Ibn Bajjah, intellect enables us to attain prosperity; this is certainly not untrue for what we expect from AI. In a survey of some 979 technology pioneers, innovators, developers, business and policy leaders, researchers, and activists, conducted by the Pew Research Centre in the summer of 2018, 63% of respondents said they are hopeful that most individuals will be better off overall in 2030; however, 37% expressed concerns about how advances in AI will affect what it means to be human, to be productive, and to exercise free will [7]. This line of thinking and apprehension is not new. Charles Rubin argues that, before the advent of AI, in both ancient and modern times, there have been many attempts geared at eliminating the need for human beings, or, specifically, leaving behind the miseries of human life for science and technology to address [8]. Indeed, AI draws its intelligence from the active intellect of humans who programmed the machine or nurtured it with complex, multifaceted knowledge, resulting in machine learning. Although Al-Farabi argues that active intellect is the source of prophetic knowledge, at this juncture we do not pretend or arrogate prophethood to humans, though we may somewhat subscribe to the kind of intellect Farabi associates with philosophers attained after discursive thinking, whereby they (the philosophers) accomplish synthesis between universal concepts [9]. AI today is unique because of the synthesis between universal concepts; therefore, what distinguishes it is its capacity to act extraordinarily intelligent.

The advent of AI must be contextualized within the larger canvas of how humans correspond with technology to exercise their intellect and thus improve their lives. In the world, with natural resources becoming more scarce and global temperatures rising at an exceedingly fast pace, the greatest objective for humanity today is to survive; any such future visions which can convincingly contribute toward the fulfillment of that objective should be welcomed, explored, and given a chance. Though, one may argue that such a future may not be true or universal given the asymmetric nature of power and technological disposition. Nonetheless, that future may arguably be costly, and it is unlikely that every political or religious ideology will survive to be a part of it. The increasing trajectory of Al also proves a point that the future to come, is now the present, concurrently the world should be prepared for future challenges, which may pose existential threats to our collective humanity.

Technology, like AI, may claim irreligiosity, but it is not culturally blind, especially when substantial scientific and technological interventions and inventions are products of certain regions of the world. When technology overlooks or is insensitive to cultures different from where it was created, a clash is likely. This is true for societies such as Muslim ones, where Islamic credo consciousness constitutes a form of cultural ontology. To this end, the chapter begins with a brief review of the scholarship on AI; it then moves to discuss the reactions of Muslim societies when exposed to new technology. This is done in the context of Muslim societies and modernity. The next part of the chapter delves into the attitudes and reactions of Muslim societies to the growing trend of AI. It addresses the impacts of AI technology on these societies in terms of correspondence challenges and examines how Muslim societies can best navigate their path while relating to the reality of AI.

2. Artificial Intelligence

The depth with which the combination of animal life and human intelligence converge to produce machines meant to ease human burdens, beginning with the evolution of mechanical calculators to computers, computing, and faster-than-brain computational speeds, is proof of what Charles considers the road to extinction [8]. The super-capacity of these machines suggests they are "capable of responding to stimuli in ways that are indistinguishable from human responses. At that point, we would be justified in calling the machine intelligent; we would have the same evidence to call it conscious that we now have when giving such a label to any consciousness other than our own" [8]. A broader discussion is necessary to explore the question of whether or not AI will lead to the extinction of man, especially regarding Charles' claims of "active intellect" above other creatures in terms of imaginative power or the Muslim belief that humans are the best (most honorable) creature (*ashraful makhluqat*) – an idea derived from numerous verses of the Qur'an, among which is "We have honoured the children of Adam, provided them with transport on land and sea, given them for sustenance things good and pure, and made them superior to a great number of Our creations" [10]. Nonetheless, scholars have established the nexus between AI, the propensity to resolve natural problems [11], and developing new technologies for crafting smarter responses to human issues [12].

Glaringly, the functionality of AI synchronizes with the understanding of intelligence as "superior understanding, sagacity, quality of being intelligent" [13]. In the context of intelligence and in a broader sense, AI represents "the study of the computations that make it possible to perceive, reason, and act" [14] or "the automation of intelligent behaviour" [15]. Given its non-human propensity, although inspired by human manipulation, AI has come to be defined as "non-human intelligence that is measured by its ability to replicate human mental skills, such as pattern recognition, understanding natural language (NLP), adaptive learning from experience, strategizing, or reasoning about others" [16]. In his seminal work published in 1968, Marvin Minsky asserts, "AI is the science of making machines do things that would require intelligence if done by men" [17]. This definition raises a number of questions, among which is: "Are humans intelligible enough to do things on their own, or what sort of intelligence do we possess to perform tasks, but are only relevant to machines?" With the exponential pace of AI, there have been many (psychological, ethical, legal, religious, and philosophical) concerns *vis-à-vis* the functionality of this new form of intelligence that was developed more than 60 years ago [18]. For example, AI algorithms can make discriminatory decisions that constitute racial, religious, and cultural prejudices or are deemed unfair by human judgement; this calls for AI regulation [19]. In contrast, Barendregt argues, "the knowledge that AI uses to describe the world around it has been selected and standardized by its human creators. All data therefore necessarily comes with a human bias, That is well known by now. We can't blame technology for certain racist or sexist outcomes, because it is humans feeding the machine with such data" [20]. To make sense of this debate, let us consider the prejudice of AI through the prism of ChatGPT. When quizzed on self-determination with regard to Israelis and Palestinians, the algorithms of ChatGPT blatantly downplayed Palestinian self-determination while promoting and justifying that of the Israelis. Such discrimination underscores the argument of Maria Stefania.

She posits that, with AI technologies, "government activities make our lives more secure, and do work to hinder criminal activities. However, these same technologies actively monitor and track common citizens, which constitutes a violation of individual privacy and could result in future discrimination based on religious beliefs" [21] and a new form of authoritarianism [22]. The skepticism attached to AI further enables thoughts about potential strategic instability between great military powers [23] (see also [24]) and the emergence of new threats to grapple with [12], as is the case with every new technological intervention. Such cynicism therefore suggests the imperative for trust-building and the development of high-level principles for AI [18] in a bid to avoid walking the path toward extinction [8].

3. Muslim Societies and Modernity

We consider AI a product of modern advancements and a technology that generates a clash between culturally situated visions of modernity. Echoing Margaret Werth, Stef Aupers argues, "that the scientific age resulted in an expansion of 'physical space' while 'soul space' has become increasingly marginalized" [25]. What this suggests is that, even when AI or internet technologies appear emancipating for some people, spurring a new kind of techno-(ir)religiosity, some technologies are considered a threat. At the core of the discourse are the different responses to modernity and its manifestations.

Shireen Hunter refers to modernity as "a philosophical approach to certainty that relies on reason rather than revelation" [26]. Interestingly, this underscores the discourse on the incompatibility of modernity and religion and further locates modernity within a non-spiritual clime [27]. According to Hunter, the physical and intellectual aspects of modernity evolve organically, hence its success. However, this organic process is disrupted and produces negative reactions in societies characterized by religiosity and dependence on revelation rather than reason [27]. Reinforcing Hunter, Mohammed Alassiri writes, "in a Muslim country, the acceptance or rejection of new ideas is often heavily related to religious views of these ideas [28]."

Most scholarship on modernity often traces its roots back to northwest Europe in the mid-eighteenth century. Such historical reductionism is contestable among those who view modernity not as conditioned by Western history but as a development, phenomenon, and epoch long experienced in non-Western societies prior to the Western Enlightenment. For instance, Marshall Hodgson suggested that "at the dawn of the modern era Islam was the most vital civilization in the world" and that "it held a hegemonic potential over East and West" [29]. Today, what may be considered (Western) modernity was once phenomenal to the Muslim world, be it the scientific and technological achievements of Muslims in Baghdad, Damascus, the Qurtubi/Cordoba city of Andalusia in Spain, the city of Bukhara in Uzbekistan, or modern Iran. Richard Bulliet writes:

> The flow of technology and ideas from the Islamic world to the West slowed and, in the past 600 years, has reversed. Academics and politicians still debate the reasons for and consequences of this decline in Islamic science and technology. The legacy of Islamic civilisation, though, remains with us in making possible Europe's own scientific and cultural renaissance [30].

Several challenges posed by modernity have received multiple responses, such as the Islamization of modernity and its byproducts [31]. In fact, in the opening page of his seminal work, Fazlur Rahman argues that "like all great religions, Islam has felt the impact of, and responded to, the manifold forces of modern life – intellectual, scientific and socio-political since the dawn of the impingement of modernity in Muslim society [32]."

The relative success of Islamization hinges on "intellectual *elan* and the specifically intellectual and spiritual issues it addressed. This awakening struck a new, powerful chord in the Muslim mind because intellectual issues had remained for centuries under a state of self-imposed dormancy and stagnation at the instance of conservative orthodoxy" [33]. Taking the argument of the clash between modernity and Muslim societies further is the inability of some Western commenters and scholars to concede that Islam is a civilizational faith, not reducible to mere religion but rather a way of life, and bestowed with a well-developed and comprehensive jurisprudential, economic, and political system [34]. That inability is deeply rooted in history, dating back to the epoch of the Roman Catholic Church's opposition to Islam until the emergence of

European Orientalist scholarship, followed by the European colonization of Muslim societies. While modernity and its attendant technologies are far from being labeled anti-human, analyzing the destructive consequences of modern technology from an Islamic perspective, Seyyed Hossein Nasr argues that "modern technologies have also replaced traditional methods of making objects of daily use. This replacement has serious consequences for the spiritual health of humanity [35]."

4. Muslim Societies and the Rise of Artificial Intelligence

Muslim societies are diverse and combine an enriching mix of culture, history, religiosity, and varying levels of technological advancement. Traditionally, prior to the incursion of European modernity and modernization in Muslim societies, clergies have been pivotal in educating, shaping, and influencing the perceptions of Muslims, not just on religious matters but also on mundane issues such as modernity and technology.

Since time immemorial, technology has not only been shaping human sociophysical space but has equally been influencing how humans perceive themselves. Technology, therefore, promotes a certain way of life and enables us to set some goals for our lives. Deductively, technology corresponds with religion. Both technology and religion deal with the same universe, and as a result, they have produced opposing epistemic communities. Technology, such as AI, can bring a great amount of ease and comfort into our lives and can enable us to forget at times that technology serves a commercial interest. Yet, despite its remarkable benefits, technology has never been insulated from bias and error. Understanding the impact of technology on social values and religious beliefs, as argued by Ziauddin Sardar, is becoming increasingly important as technology advances [36]. Today, AI has become a buzzword for advanced intelligence, performing tasks with greater accuracy. As a new technology, how well is AI technology received in Muslim societies? Is the relationship one of rejection, integration, contradiction, or congruity? The following discussion examines the correspondences and reactions of Muslim societies to the growing trend of AI.

4.1. *Spiritual, religious, and theological challenges*

While Islam approves and permits its adherents to engage in intellectual pondering, contemplation, and inner meditation, it cautions against thoughts that either tend to cause a creedal threat or disturb the credo foundation of being Muslim. For instance, the Islamic scripture Qur'an, in many instances, enjoins its readers to contemplate creation and immediate physical geography and, at one point, encourages the exploration of the outer space [37]. Yet, the same scripture and the complementary sayings of the prophet, Hadith, warn against some forms of thought that question and challenge the existence and integrity of God [38]. Inferably, Islam and the indelible legacies of Muslim scholars past and present demonstrate that attaining knowledge, crowned by intelligence, is fundamental to Muslim tradition; however, it should not come at the expense of endangering social space, causing mischief, spreading iniquities, and above all employing such intelligence for dismantling the credo foundation that coalesces society. In his groundbreaking work, Shāh Walī Allāh argues that such knowledge (intelligence) or acts constitute social sickness within the polity [39].

4.2. *Playing God*

The place of Allah in the Islamic concepts of divinity, theology, and eschatology is paramount to the beliefs of a Muslim. The credo foundation of Islam is Tawheed – the fixated belief in the oneness or unity of Allah. Theologically, the unity of God is further categorized into three elements, namely, Tawheed al-Rububiyyah (the Oneness of Divine Lordship), Tawheed al-Uluhiyyah (the Oneness of Divinity), and Tawheed al-Asma wa'l-Sifat (the Oneness of the Divine Names and Attributes). Among the 99 names and attributes of Allah are al-Qadir (the Omnipotent) and al-Alim (the All-Knowing). The representation of AI contradicts this aspect of Islamic creed. Presenting AI as all-knowing and omnipotent will certainly be a misplaced notion and rejected in most Muslim societies where religiosity continues to shape the public domain. Similarly, such representation of AI may be considered to threaten religion, especially regarding the sanctity of the Qur'an. For instance, many Muslims believe that the composition of the Qur'an is divine and was revealed to the Prophet Muhammad (SAW).

For Muslims, the composition of the Qur'an is a testimony to its beauty, complexity, and subtlety, clearly beyond the compositional abilities of any human. Therefore, any attempt to subject the Qur'an to the play of AI or reduce the scripture to the level of AI wound amount to sacrilege. Even among those who view AI as an enabler for understanding the Qur'an, it is imperative to seriously consider the cultural, historical, spiritual, and interpretive contexts of its revelation. This reinforces the argument that understanding the Qur'an is a major new grand challenge for computer science and artificial intelligence [40]. Religious interpretations necessitate not only language expertise but also historical, sociological, and theological understanding. Therefore, the growing proliferation of AI technologies available online, which cater to both religious and mundane matters affecting Muslims, may lead to mediocrity in the issuance of *fatwa*, or religious ruling. While such a ruling has traditionally fallen within the purview of Muslim scholars, supplanting them with AI may have wide ramifications, in terms of issuing swift *fatwa* and catering to people who would feel uncomfortable asking certain questions in public. Bart Barendregt, a professor of digital anthropology at Leiden University and principal investigator in "Toward an Anthropology of Everyday AI in Islam," hails AI with regard to Islamic principle of questioning:

> Think about issues of romance, intimacy, or sexuality and what a proper Muslim should do with those. Another success story is the spiritual counselling through apps and now chatbots, asking 'how to best do' questions... Muslims especially seem to make use of chatbots to get an instant answer for an increasingly complicated world, which also leaves their religion very fragmented and where no one is for sure which sources are authoritative [20].

Nevertheless, this may amount to challenging the established Islamic authority [41]. It can also undermine traditional learning methods, rupturing the long-established relationship between teacher and student [42]. Similarly, critics of AI see the possibility of oversimplification, misinterpretation, or wrong interpretation of religious beliefs, which are by definition nuanced. AI might unintentionally promote a worldview or moral stance that contradicts Islamic customs and beliefs. The role of AI in the interpretation of religious texts can be contentious [42]. For instance, while commenting on the reactions of

Muslims in Malaysia to the growing religious bots, Bart Barendregt observed:

> That the data these apps are fed with are not always necessarily sympathetic to their religion or may depict them in often stereotypical or outright orientalist ways. One of my colleagues in Kuala Lumpur, specialising in Sharia law was telling me that ChatGPT is an incredible source ... it helped him prepare classes on Islamic law, and produce slides on the topic. Yet, the software has enormous problems with coping with the classical Arab language of Quran and hadith in which it simply is less well trained. It also tends to look for data among preachers who tend to be more popular and mediagenic and therefore more cited, easily leading to an echo chamber of Islamic style [20].

In addition, ideological critiques of AI point to the fact that future generations of Muslims will be born into a different world, where the primary source of creativity would be generative AI. In such a future, how will future generations of Muslims understand and accept miracles, divine revelations, destiny, and afterlife? How will they take a leap of faith? Misguiding ill-prepared Muslims might be much easier in such a future scenario and could renew attempts to undermine Muslims' faith, thereby posing a potential challenge to the Islamic constructs of divinity, theology, and eschatology.

Irrespective of how critics perceive the potential manifestations of AI, especially in the realms of theology and eschatology, Bruce Watson cautioned against outright disapproval of technology that may purportedly be inimical to Islamic ethos. For him, "the main danger arises if Muslims accept the more extreme view of the difference of Islam and the insistence on establishing 'the third way'. If everything Western is to be discarded, then the creative and productive dynamism inherent in Islamic traditions will be suppressed yet again" [43]. To this end, the problem may not necessarily lie in the technology but rather in what the Muslim societies make of it in terms of serious epistemic engagement. Combating the potential "ideological transgression" of AI reminds one of Fazlur Rahman. For him, Muslim societies and Islam need "some first-class minds who can interpret the old in terms of the new as regards substance and turn the new into the service of the old as regards ideals" [44]. The foregoing reinforces the fact that "there are no elements in Islam which make it particularly antagonistic to modernity. Rather aspects of Islam are more compatible with foundational principles of modernity than some other religions [6]."

4.3. *Philosophical considerations*

Biliana Popova, in her phenomenal work, *Islamic Philosophy and Artificial Intelligence: Epistemological Arguments*, endeavors to understand AI through the prism of Islamic philosophical schools, including Mu'tazilite, Falsafa, the Ashari school, and Sufism. Her work reimagines history with a taste of philosophy. It goes beyond merely reducing AI discussions to mathematics or any of the pure and applied sciences. Epistemologically, using the tools of Islamic philosophy, Popova examines the questions of immortality, death, and the afterlife according to aforementioned Islamic philosophical schools. Popova refers to an ontological system developed by Ibn Bajja, al-Farabi and Ibn Rushd and argues:

> This system is constructed on the belief that the world is eternal, the Qur'an was created, which also aligns with the Mutazilite position and thus, normative logic and kulliyat (universal ethical principles) are possible only within a strict hierarchical system. If the First Principle, God, emanates being through the excess that is created through His cognition of Himself, then the world exists in an eternal cycle where the link with the active intellect is the one that converts spirit into matter and matter into spirit and through which humans can achieve immortality. This strongly relates to the futuristic dream of uploading consciousness and achieving immortality through AI, where matter will be overcome at last and humans will be able to live a virtual life without physical constraints [6] (p. 984).

If immortality were achieved, then what purpose would remain for the desires of life, movement, change, and *barzakh* – life in the grave, an intermediary stage between this life and another life in the Hereafter – and the continuation of afterlife? This all becomes irrelevant. However, this is not the message of the Holy Qur'an. Reality and the ultimate ontology are considered an afterlife provided by a "benevolent" God [6], which is fundamental to the Islamic belief system. On the other hand, there have been efforts to use AI technology to quench the centuries-old craving for immortality, involving the scientific enterprise, which will not only significantly advance human health systems, but will also find solutions to aging and possibly make human genes immortal. In addition, AI is tailored toward discovering the origins of human intelligence and consciousness [45]. Ahmed Belim argues "any new and seemingly mystical technology gradually deceives modern people into thinking that scientists have obtained, or will soon acquire, the ability to create living, animate beings, much like ancient people watching the magician of Pharaoh conjures up false serpents" [45].

Philosophically, another response of Muslims to AI, in today's context, is that we have not yet seen AI effectively equipped with consciousness. Once this is achieved, it will shake the very foundation of religion and present more intricate and unprecedented challenges to Muslim societies, which modern-day Muslims may not be fully aware of. Interestingly, what possibly could happen in the presence of a fully conscious superintelligence when AI is capable of understanding, analyzing, and is on a path to acquiring a body and mind of its own? Such features of AI nearly bring it to the level of another species, with similar or superior cognitive capabilities comparable to those of humans. Thus, effectively understanding AI from an Islamic perspective is a challenging and exhausting task; however, it is necessary. Without this progressive step, Muslims cannot truly understand, adopt, and adapt AI. Elmahjub's illustration of the Muslim world *vis-à-vis* AI reinforces this fear:

> The big challenge for countries in the Islamic World is to build AI systems that are aligned with their religious and cultural beliefs. Aligning AI systems with religious and cultural beliefs will ensure that these systems are more acceptable to the population. This is important because acceptance is a critical factor for successfully implementing any new technology. If AI systems are not aligned with religious and cultural beliefs, they may be perceived as a threat to local values and traditions [46].

The discourse of fear surrounding AI technologies in Muslim societies has a historical context. Long before the proliferation of AI, Ziauddin Sardar cautioned against unquestioningly embracing modern technology without considering Islamic norms [47]. Popova adds, "the ideologies and philosophies that underpin AI development and use from an Islamic perspective have yet to receive the attention they deserve [6]."

4.4. *Adaption*

The enormous benefits associated with AI technologies explain why experts in every field of knowledge are trying to integrate them into their work. While many in the developed nations have made significant advances in the process of adaption, Muslim societies tended to be left behind. Ana Khoirunnisa *et al.* argue that "Islam is a religion that accepts all forms of technological progress, including advances in artificial intelligence. However, in its use, Islam emphasizes that technology must be used wisely and must pay attention to the effects on human life and the environment" [48]. Any form of adaption, therefore, must align with the fundamental requirements of advancing human life and protecting the environment. This is reflected in the observation of Ezieddin Elmahjuba: "there is massive interest in many countries with predominantly Muslim populations to localize and promote the integration of AI technologies into their societal infrastructure" [46]. In fact, the interest in AI explicates the manifestation of the technology in developing Muslim societies in areas such as "smart cities, smart security systems, smart educational and medical devices, and even smart judges who can easily settle property disputes" [6].

Interestingly, AI is also gaining traction among religious authorities and Muslim clergies. AI facilitates many Islamic practices, including Islamic education, preaching, and Arabic learning. The current surge in global interest in AI has engulfed religious clerics in various parts of the Islamic world. Muslim clerics are now contemplating AI's possible assistance in using Islamic texts for issuing religious edicts. Such a desire to interact with global technological advances remains visible in many Islamic countries, such as Iran, as Muslims today seek to accelerate, progress, and modernize [49]. High-ranking religious clerics in Iran have expressed very positive views on using AI and are looking into effective ways of using this cutting-edge technology. On 17 November 2021, Iran's Supreme Leader Ayatollah Khamenei, in a meeting with young elites and top scientific talent, called AI an essential and future-shaping issue and emphasized the need for Iran to join the movement and become among the top 10 countries in the world of artificial intelligence [50]. In a similar context, in 2020, the first AI conference was also held in Qom, Iran [49]. AI is changing the way Muslims interact with religion, and today it is crucial for them to discuss their relationship with AI when it comes to faith [51].

AI appears to be shaping the role of Muslim clerics by influencing their authority in Muslim societies. However, AI cannot be considered solely responsible for this; rather, a process of scientific developments, and numerous other factors have effectively contributed toward shaping the role of Muslim clerics by influencing their authority in Muslim societies. Barendregt opines, "AI in itself often has all dimensions of becoming a religious cult, complete with ideas of salvation through big data – no theory needed, but enough data to set the truth free" [20].

Regardless of how AI is increasingly seductive, even amongst (traditional) Muslim scholars, it is difficult to foresee the acceptance of mechanized preaching in Muslim societies in the near future. The question is also whether Muslims in the future can delegate or outsource various Islamic rituals to AI through digital applications. Shaping a moderate religious discourse remains crucial, particularly after the events of 9/11. Muslim societies remain committed to their values and religious identity and are resistant to, and apprehensive of, radical changes. This is nicely articulated by Kunwar Khuldune Shahid using ChatGPT as an example:

> While ChatGPT has undergone supervised pre-training to generate 'appropriate' responses on contentious subjects, including religion, its evident bias when it comes to Islam is also an off shoot of its transformer architecture. This architecture limits the bot's generative ability to the available dataset, which it is then programmed to use in accordance with the pre-trained language guidelines. Even in the unlikely event that contrasting views were included in the dataset fed to Chat GPT on controversial issues, the algorithmic bias in favour of Islam was always going to be inevitable [52].

Shahid further states:

> This is because, where texts lambasting casteism in Hinduism, or fallacies of the Bible, are widely available on the internet – often written by members of the communities whose beliefs are being targeted – the unhinged criticism of Islam is predominantly limited to anti-Muslim fora likely to have been flagged in the pre-training phase of ChatGPT. This has resulted in an algorithmic bias not merely in favour of Islam, but in particular in favour of the majority Sunni sect within Islam [52].

4.5. *Educational challenges*

Concerns about an overreliance on increasingly powerful AI have triggered job loss fears across industries, even among notable AI and tech CEOs. However, there is some hope among religious leaders [53]. We should strive to embrace the conveniences and benefits emerging from AI in the fields of Islamic education, Arabic language learning, and Quranic recitation while maintaining the integrity of theological knowledge and not neglecting moral and ethical considerations. HadithGPT is a testimony to such an effort. This application uses hadiths to answer questions about Islam. Its comments are accompanied by a disclaimer [53]. AI can accelerate Islamic scholars' communication with the public and can further enhance Islamic education [49]. This can, in turn, provide them with a greater ability to address the concerns of Muslims and swiftly reconcile them with Islam. Young clerics can contribute to modernizing traditional ways of learning and education within Muslim societies. AI can assist in this connection by helping Muslim clerics in issuing guidance in an increasingly complex and intricate Muslim societies for creating a better social impact. AI heavily relies on English; however, in many Muslim societies, Arabic is fundamental to their identity. This presents a dilemma for Muslims in Arabic-speaking societies: choosing between a cutting edge of technology and essential cultural values [54]. AI can help in modernizing traditional religious seminaries. Omar Al-Ubaydli suggests:

> An AI bot can easily surpass a traditional scholar's abilities by translating seamlessly into any language – including sign language – and by instantly explaining things in a different way as many times as is necessary for the inquiring Muslim to understand the answer to their question, while providing full references in case of a desire for further reading [54].

Ways of feeding historical data into AI algorithms can be explored. This can also modernize traditional Islamic seminaries.

5. Conclusion: The Way Forward

We are being shaped to trust AI with solving the future challenges to humanity. We are still not sure whether or not it will be able to deliver beneficial knowledge and produce societal and civilizational goods. More Muslim philosophers and scholars should join the debate on AI development, especially since many Muslim countries are among the leaders in the advancement and use of AI and smart devices; Islamic philosophy may offer all the required theoretical frameworks and epistemological tools for a fruitful engagement with AI development. Human critical examination is always required when implementing AI outcomes in society.

In today's world, facing climate change and resource scarcity at an exceedingly fast pace, the greatest objective for humanity is to survive; any such future visions which can convincingly contribute to its fulfillment should be welcomed, explored, and given a chance. However, that future will cost us dearly, as not everyone and not every political or religious ideology will survive to be a part of it. Preparation must start now. We need an "all world approach" to face the future challenges to the very existence of humanity. Let us begin by developing consensus among people of faith, including Muslims.

References

[1] Sweeney M. Greek essence and Islamic tolerance: Al-Farabi, Al-Ghazali, Ibn Rush'd. *Rev Metaphys*. 2011;65(1):41–61.

[2] Cooper LN. Source and limits of human intellect. *Daedalus*. 1980;109(2):1–17.

[3] Wood A. Introduction. In: Wood A, editor. *Thomas Aquinas on the Immateriality of the Human Intellect*. Catholic University of America Press; 2020. p. 1–6. https://doi.org/10.2307/j.ctvt1sh42.5.

[4] Sternberg RJ. Human intelligence: The model is the message. *Science*. 1985;230(4730):1111–1118.

[5] Ma'sumi MSH. Ibn Bajjah on the human intellect. *Islam Stud*. 1965;4(2):121–126.

[6] Popova B. Islamic philosophy and artificial intelligence: Epistemological arguments. *Zygon*. December 2020;55(4): 977–995.

[7] Anderson J, Rainie L. Artificial intelligence and the future of humans. Pew Research Center. December 10 2018. https://www.pewresearch.org/internet/2018/12/10/artificial-intelligence-and-the-future-of-humans/.

[8] Rubin CT. Artificial intelligence and human nature. *The New Atlantis*. 2003;1:88–100.

[9] Ceylan Y. Some remarks on Al-Farabi's views on the relationship between philosophy and religion. *Islam Stud*. 1994. 33(1):77–89.

[10] Holy Quran, Surah Al-Isra, 17:70.

[11] Henley TB. Natural problems and artificial intelligence. *Behav Philos*. 1990;18(2):43–56.

[12] Kavanagh C. Artificial intelligence. In: Kavanagh C, editor. *New Tech, New Threats, and New Governance Challenges: An Opportunity to Craft Smarter Responses?* Massachusetts: Carnegie Endowment for International Peace; 2019.

[13] Harper D. Intelligence. Online etymology dictionary. Accessed September 28, 2016. http://www.etymonline.com/index.php?allowed_in_frame=0&search=intelligence.

[14] Patrick HW. *Artificial Intelligence*, 3rd edn. Massachusetts: Addison-Wesley Publishing Company; 1992.

[15] George FL, William AL. St eubblefield, *Artificial Intelligence: Structures and Strategies for Complex Problem Solving*, 3rd edn. Benjamin-Cummings Pub Co; 1997. Also Barr A, Feigenbaum EA, editors. *The Handbook of Artificial Intelligence*. Vol. 2. Stanford, California & Los Altos, California: Heuris Tech Press and William Kaufmann; 1982.

[16] De Spiegeleire S, Maas M, Sweijs T. What is artificial intelligence? Artificial intelligence and the future of defense: Strategic implications for small- and medium-sized force providers. Hague Centre for Strategic Studies; 2017.

[17] Minsky M. Matter, mind and models. In: Minsky M, editor. *Semantic Information Processing*. Cambridge, Mass: MIT Press; 1968.

[18] Rossi F. Building trust in artificial intelligence. *J Int Aff*. 2018;72(1):127–134.

[19] Etzioni A, Etzioni O. Should artificial intelligence be regulated? *Issues in Science and Technology*. 2017;33(4):32–36.

[20] Borges J. How AI bots are emulating Gods to provide answers to life and its problems. *MSN*. 2023 August. https://www.mid-day.com/sunday-mid-day/article/training-the-bot-to-become-shri-krishna-23292895.

[21] Cataleta MS. Humane artificial intelligence: The fragility of human rights facing AI. East-West Center; 2020.

[22] Ünver HA. Artificial intelligence, authoritarianism and the future of political systems. Centre for Economics and Foreign Policy Studies; 2018.

[23] Johnson JS. Artificial intelligence: A threat to strategic stability. *Strateg Stud Q*. 2020;14(1):16–39.

[24] Also see Garvey C. Artificial intelligence and Japan's fifth generation: The information society, neoliberalism, and alternative modernities. *Pac Hist Rev*. 2019;88(4):619–658.

[25] Aupers S. The revenge of the machines: On modernity, digital technology and animism. *Asian J Soc Sci*. 2002;30(2):199–220.

[26] Hunter ST. Can Islam and modernity be reconciled? *Insight Turkey*. 2009;11(3):1–12.

[27] Masud MK, Salvatore A. Western scholars of Islam on the issue of modernity. In: Masud MK, Salvatore A, van Bruinessen M, editors. *Islam and*

Modernity: Key Issues and Debates. Edinburgh University Press, Edinburgh; 2009. p. 36–54.

[28] Alassiri M. Evolution is a disguised friend of Islam. Nature. *Nat Hum Behav*. 2020;4:122. https://doi.org/10.1038/s41562-019-0771-7.

[29] Salvatore A. Tradition and modernity within Islamic civilisation and the West. In: Salvatore A, Masud MK, van Bruinessen M, editors. *Islam and Modernity: Key Issues and Debates*. Edinburgh University Press, Edinburgh; 2009. p. 3–35. http://www.jstor.org/stable/10.3366/j.ctv2f4vqw9.4.

[30] Bulliet R. *The Case for Islamo-Christian Civilization*. Irvington, NY: Columbia University Press; 2004.

[31] Sulayman A, Hamid A. *Islamization of Knowledge: General Principles and Workplan*. Herndon, VA: IIIT International Institute of Islamic Thought (IIIT); 1989.

[32] Rahman F. The impact of modernity of Islam. *Islam Stud*. 1966;5(2):113–128.

[33] Rahman F. Islamic modernism: Its scope, method and alternatives. *Int J Middle East Stud*. 1970;1(4):317–333.

[34] Khalil MI. Islam and the challenges of modernity. *Georget J Int Aff*. 2004;5(1):97–104.

[35] Nasr SH. Islam, Muslims, and modern technology. *Islam Sci*. 2005;3(2):27–46. https://cis-ca.org/_media/pdf/2005/2/A_imamt.pdf.

[36] Hamed K. The intersection of AI and Islam? Unveiling the anthropological insights. Universitas Islam Internasional Indonesia; 2023 May 17. https://www.uiii.ac.id/editorials/read/57351/the-intersection-of-ai-and-islam-unveiling-the-anthropological-insights.

[37] Holy Quran, Surah Al-Isra, 17:12.

[38] Khan MM. Beginning of creation - Sahih Bukhari. Vol. 4, Book 54, Number 496. https://www.iium.edu.my/deed/hadith/bukhari/054_sbt.html#:~:text=Allah's%20Apostle%20said%2C%20%22Satan%20comes,and%20give%20up%20such%20thoughts.%22.

[39] Allāh SW, The conclusive argument from God, Shāh Walī Allāh of Delhi's Ḥujjat Allāh Al-Bāligha, Translated by Marcia K. Hermansen. Islamabad: Islamic Research Institute; 2020.

[40] Atwell E, Brierley C, Dukes K, Sawalha M, Sharaf A-B. An artificial intelligence approach to Arabic and Islamic content on the internet. Leeds: I-AIBS Institute for Artificial intelligence and Biological Systems, School of Computing, University of Leeds; 2011 January.

[41] Bakare N. Religion and conflict in a globalised cyber sphere: Dynamics and implications. In: Adogame A, Olufunke Adeboye OA, Williams CL, editors. *Fighting in God's Name: Religion and Conflict in Local-Global Perspectives*. Lanham: Lexington Books; 2020. W. 81–106.

[42] Salvi D. Iran: Artificial intelligence in the ayatollahs' fatwas. PIME AsiaNews; 2023 September 9. https://www.asianews.it/news-en/Iran: artificial-intelligence-in-the-ayatollahs'-fatwas-59229.html#google_vignette.

[43] Watson IB. Islam and its challenges in the modern world. *Insight*. May 1997; 1(33):12.

[44] Rahman F. Islam and modernity: *Transformation of an Intellectual Tradition*. Chicago: University of Chicago Press; 1982.

[45] Belim A. Does artificial intelligence go against the principles of Islam? *The Invitation*. 2021 February 26. https://www.invitation-magazine.org/does-artificial-intelligence-go-against-the-principles-of-islam/.

[46] Elmahjub E. Artificial intelligence (AI) in Islamic ethics: Towards pluralist ethical benchmarking for AI. *Philos. Technol.* 2023;36,73. https://doi.org/10.1007/s13347-023-00668-x.

[47] Sardar Z. *Information and the Muslim World: A Strategy for the Twenty-First Century*. London: New York: Mansell; 1988.

[48] Khoirunnisa A, Rohman F, Azizah HA, Ardianti D, Maghfiroh AL, Noor AM. Islam in the midst of AI (artificial intelligence) struggles: Between opportunities and threats. *Int J Islam Stud.* 2023;35(1):1–5.

[49] Bozorgmehr N. 'Robots can help issue a fatwa': Iran's clerics look to harness AI. *The Financial Times*. 2023 September 24. https://www.ft.com/content/9c1c3fd3-4aea-40ab-977b-24fe5527300c.

[50] A scientific solution can be found for all the problems of the country. The Office of the Supreme Leader. 2021 November 17. https://www.leader.ir/en/content/25373/The-Leader-addressing-the-young-elites-and-top-scientific-talents.

[51] Bettiza S. God and robots: Will AI transform religion? *BBC*. 2021 October 21. https://www.bbc.com/news/av/technology-58983047.

[52] Shahid KK. Artificial intelligence and algorithmic bias on Islam. *The Free Thinker*. 2023 March 26. https://freethinker.co.uk/2023/03/artificial-intelligence-and-algorithmic-bias-on-islam/.

[53] Bhuiyan J. Are chatbots changing the face of religion? Three faith leaders on grappling with AI. *The Guardian*. 2023 April 7. https://www.theguardian.com/technology/2023/apr/07/chatgpt-artificial-intelligence-religion-faith-leaders.

[54] Al-Ubaydli O. The Gulf governments need to openly discuss the risks of artificial intelligence. *Al Arabiya*. 2023 May 10. https://english.alarabiya.net/views/2023/05/10/The-Gulf-governments-need-to-openly-discuss-the-risks-of-artificial-intelligence.

https://doi.org/10.1142/9781800616295_0003

Chapter 3

Leveraging Historical Responses and Islamic Perspectives for AI in 21st-Century Healthcare in Muslim Societies

Ajwah Nadeem, Noor Sabah Rakhshani, Kamran Aslam, and M. Imran Khan*

PHC Global (Pvt.) Ltd., Bahadruabad, Karachi, Pakistan

**imran@phcglobal.org*

Abstract

The chapter explores the complex historical, sociopolitical, and jurisprudential dynamics influencing artificial intelligence (AI) integration in global healthcare, with a particular emphasis on Muslim societies. Adopting a multi-scalar lens, it situates diverse stakeholders, including governments, Muslim scholars, and human–computer interaction developers, as pivotal agents influencing perceptions and uptake of advanced medical technologies. Through case studies on Islamic bioethics and culturally attuned AI solutions, it provides insights into the diverse mechanisms underlying the integration. The chapter aims to offer a multidisciplinary perspective to deepen understanding of the intricacies at play, with the firm belief that complexity has the potential to inspire innovative, creative, and cooperative approaches for ethically aligned, user-centered AI adoption as part of holistic healthcare solutions for diverse Muslim populations worldwide.

1. Introduction

Artificial intelligence (AI) is transforming healthcare through an array of technologies aimed at augmenting clinical decision-making, personalizing care, and improving operational efficiency [1]. Machine learning algorithms can analyze large datasets from electronic health records, medical imaging, genomics, and wearable devices to predict health outcomes and support diagnostic and disease management. Examples include algorithms that can interpret radiological images to identify pathological changes, optimize radiation therapy planning for patients suffering from specific cancers, or predict the onset of complications, such as sepsis, by monitoring vital signs. Beyond clinical applications, AI chatbots, robotic process automation, and logistics optimization algorithms are improving hospital workflows and aiding in administrative tasks such as scheduling appointments and coordinating care teams.

Healthcare stands unique in that adopting potentially life-saving technologies becomes indispensable, despite valid concerns around transparency, accountability, and equitable access. While regulatory checks are essential, resistance may impede patients' access to cutting-edge treatments. Thus, AI for healthcare necessitates a judicious approach: developing context-aware tools through multidisciplinary collaboration and thoughtful governance through effective policies that promote safe adoption while preventing harm, especially for vulnerable groups. However, the transformative potential, if harnessed prudently, makes AI integration in healthcare services not only inevitable but also ethically obligatory to expand treatment capabilities and reduce costs.

A comprehensive international patent analysis, conducted by Benjamens *et al.* [2] using the Espacenet database, reveals new insights into this trend. The results reveal a significant increase in healthcare-related AI patents, particularly after 2020, with China emerging as a front-runner.

The study identified certain medical specialties where AI's potential is most pronounced, correlating with the nature of the tasks involved. Radiology, cardiology, and oncology – known for their repetitive or data-heavy tasks – saw a high number of patents, reflecting AI's aptitude for automation. The utility of AI in analyzing medical images and videos extends across specialties, from radiology to surgery, including dentistry, ophthalmology, and emergency medicine. Dermatology and pathology also stand to benefit from AI applications in analyzing skin lesions and digitized slides in histopathology. In contrast, specialties such as psychiatry and neurology, which involve more interactive and creative tasks, might see fewer AI innovations. This variance in AI applicability across medical fields showcases the technology's potential and limitations.

AI for healthcare adoption in Muslim societies necessitates additional considerations given the interplay between religious beliefs, cultural traditions, and sociopolitical realities. Appraising AI while considering Islamic ethics is vital to ensure its responsible integration. Muslim societies encompass immense diversity across ethnicities, cultures, and sectarian affiliations. Various interpretations of Islamic scripture and jurisprudence coexist, ranging from literalist to syncretic approaches. Core beliefs may permeate institutions, yet localized expressions allow dynamic negotiations between Islamic identity and indigenous cultures.

Additional nuances emerge around theological orientations such as Sunni, Shia, and Sufi ideologies, each with distinct schools of thought. Gender dynamics also influence technological integration as women navigate an increasingly tense intersection of religious scriptures, cultural practices, and shifting norms. Furthermore, diasporic Muslim minorities in secular societies experience unique challenges in preserving their beliefs while assimilating. This plurality necessitates contextualizing AI adoption and galvanizing stakeholder participation to ensure physical, social, and mental well-being at both the individual and community levels.

This chapter explores the multifaceted dynamics shaping the integration of AI technologies within contemporary healthcare systems serving Muslim populations. The discussion commences by highlighting governments as pivotal actors in normalizing and catalyzing acceptance of these potentially disruptive innovations. Delving into the rich history of scientific advancements by pioneering Muslim scholars provides critical context, underscoring the congruence between Islam and technological progress. Case studies that analyze deliberations on modern bioethical dilemmas, such as organ donation and genetic testing, offer instructive insights into how Islamic jurisprudence navigates emerging technologies through its ethical paradigms. The proliferation of Islamic digital services, including fintech, serves as timely examples of how AI can align with religious values when thoughtfully designed.

The conversation culminates in tangible human–computer interaction (HCI) strategies to embed cultural nuances into AI systems, facilitating their adoption as user-centered tools for holistic health and well-being. This multilayered analysis aims to provide a textured appreciation of the diverse considerations shaping AI integration in Islamic healthcare milieus, spanning historical, sociotechnical, bioethical, and practical dimensions. By highlighting opportunities for developing culturally attuned AI, this chapter aspires to open constructive pathways for its responsible adoption as an integral component of comprehensive, ethically aligned healthcare solutions for Muslim societies worldwide.

2. Setting the Stage: Governments as Key Actors

In the examination of the reception and perception of disruptive healthcare technologies within Muslim societies, governments emerge as pivotal entities wielding significant influence. Their role transcends a mere reflection of public readiness; it encompasses a multifaceted approach. Through the strategic integration of AI into established patient care infrastructures, governments serve as agents in normalizing its utilization. This normalization, in turn, catalyzes the standardization and enduring integration of AI within healthcare systems. The multifaceted nature of governmental involvement is underscored by the formulation of discerning policies, targeted allocation of funds, the establishment of stringent regulatory frameworks, and the cultivation of dynamic public–private collaborations. Such top-down initiatives function not only to mitigate skepticism surrounding disruptive healthcare technologies but also to demystify AI by embedding it seamlessly into routine patient care. Consequently, this strategic incorporation ensures that AI becomes an intrinsic and commonplace element of citizens' healthcare experiences.

Many Muslim countries within the MENA region stand as exemplars of this proactive stance [3]. The UAE's Strategy for Artificial Intelligence [4], established as early as 2017, and Saudi Arabia's inauguration of its National Strategy for Data and Artificial Intelligence in 2020 [5] dovetail with broader development goals to diversify their economies from reliance on oil to becoming knowledge-driven. These efforts serve broader diplomatic objectives, including asserting regional leadership in technological innovation, establishing geopolitical standing within the Islamic world, and bolstering their roles in international health fora and policy-making bodies.

Similarly, the state-led Qatar Genome Program (QGP), piloted as early as 2015, defies the notion that AI in health is a recent phenomenon within Muslim countries. As a national AI-driven project, QGP focuses on identifying genetic variations that are either unique or prevalent in Qatar's 300,000-strong population [6]. This initiative, integrating genomic data with clinical databases, has significant implications for understanding disease prevalence, drug responses, and personalized medical treatments and preventive strategies. AI is indispensable to the project due to its capabilities in efficiently processing extensive datasets for sequencing and variant analysis, which are tasks that would otherwise be time-consuming and less thorough. Predictive analytics, employing neural networks and deep learning, are necessary for pattern recognition. Additionally, the application of AI in natural language processing (NLP) is crucial for extracting insights from scientific literature and clinical records to aid in the interpretation of genomic data. Cloud-based AI platforms facilitate global collaboration and data sharing. QGP's research in mapping the Arab genome provides valuable regional public health insights, e.g., their work in developing ancestry-specific genetic risk scores for coronary heart disease in Middle Eastern populations [7]. Efforts to establish an open disease genomics database further the understanding of health risks specific to the Arab population. These advancements, driven by AI's analytical capabilities, are instrumental steps toward developing indigenous medicine and contribute to a more globally representative body of medical research. AI's role is illustrated as critical in furthering healthcare beyond its often-sensationalized portrayals.

Transforming medicine is an ethical, epistemic, and practical imperative for publicly funded health systems. Seeking to dismantle lingering colonial structures that perpetuate health inequities, the effort aims to rectify the historical oversight of diverse genetic, epidemiological, and cultural contexts in health studies and interventions. AI can be an essential asset in reducing these disparities. For instance, the predominance of European genomes in key genomic databases, such as the Genome-Wide Association Studies (GWAS) Catalog, has led to a narrow understanding of diseases and treatment efficacy, often rendering medical solutions less effective for non-European populations, which is evident in some cancer and cardiovascular therapies and diabetes management protocols.

Over 50% of published GWAS studies focus on European genomes, followed by Asian studies at approximately 20%, compared to less than 1.5% from the Middle East, Africa, or Latin America [8]. Human genetic diversity varies greatly, both within and across geographies, with African genomes exhibiting the greatest diversity due to the presence of many ancient lineages not found elsewhere.

AI's proficiency in big data analytics facilitated recent initiatives, such as the COVID-19 Host Genetics Initiative, which identified critical loci associated with SARS-CoV-2 infection in Asian and Middle Eastern patients [9]. Initiatives such as the genomic programs of Qatar and Saudi Arabia can better and more quickly tailor precision medicine to enhance pharmacogenomic strategies, thanks to the use of AI.

The first large-scale survey of public attitudes toward genomic testing in the MENA region [10] commissioned by QGP offers critical insights that challenge mainstream fearmongering. Intriguingly, the survey revealed that practical barriers such as limited time and insufficient information, not attitudinal ones, were predominant concerns for over half of the respondents. An avenue for disseminating this information could be premarital genetic testing, a familiar concept in Qatar, where nationals are mandated by law to undergo carrier testing – a process in which individuals are tested to identify potential genetic disorders that could be passed on to offspring. This underscores the inevitable importance of developing localized, context-sensitive communication strategies and the inapplicability of a "one-size-fits-all" global strategy.

AI integration in healthcare systems extends beyond technical feasibility or philanthropic goals; adoption is shaped by broader government agendas. State-driven policies and ambitions inevitably influence whether and how emerging health technologies are leveraged. For example, the medical diplomacy initiatives of Muslim-majority nations stand to be enhanced through strategic AI adoption within healthcare delivery. Medical diplomacy refers to the strategic use of healthcare initiatives and expertise to advance geopolitical interests and the national agenda. Throughout the 19th and 20th centuries, humanitarian medical relief efforts, particularly by the Global North, laid the foundation for healthcare to be formally employed as a tool of soft power and diplomacy. With health initiatives providing visible platforms for states to demonstrate goodwill and progressiveness, medical diplomacy has become an appealing soft-power approach. It allows countries to advance their strategic interests and standing while framing interventions as benevolent and cooperative. The effectiveness of medical diplomacy as a foreign policy tool continues to be recognized and prioritized by nations worldwide [11].

Iran has actively leveraged medical diplomacy to build regional credibility, prestige, and influence over the past decades [12]. From 2007–2016, Iran constructed over 20 hospitals in Lebanon, four in Iraq, two in Afghanistan, and one in Syria, furthering its geopolitical footprint and projecting an image of benevolence and stability. In 2008, Iran reportedly completed 140 technical schools, 50 mosques, and 19 medical centers in Lebanon alone [13]. The adoption of AI in healthcare can further a country's soft power objectives by bolstering the efficacy, competitiveness, and prestige of its medical diplomatic efforts.

The adoption of AI is also indispensable in advancing universal health coverage (UHC) milestones in Muslim countries, which directly ties into donor expectations. The deployment of AI in healthcare transcends conventional medical practices, offering unparalleled precision, efficiency, and personalized care, which are essential factors in meeting UHC targets. This integration, therefore, is not merely a technological advancement; it is a critical step in fulfilling international health commitments, enhancing healthcare delivery, and ultimately increasing the lifesaving capabilities of these health systems.

3. Historical Context: Islamic Contributions to Science and Medicine

The rich history of scientific advancements in the Islamic world, particularly during the Islamic Golden Age, underscores the congruence of Islam with scientific inquiry, challenging cultural misconceptions regarding their purported incompatibility. Pioneering Muslim scholars include Al-Rāzī from Persia, a polymath in physics, chemistry, and medicine who produced seminal works such as *The Comprehensive Book of Medicine* [14]. This compendium, a culmination of his lifelong medical experiences and readings, which was later translated into Greek and Latin, showcases the advanced state of Islamic medical knowledge in the 9th century. Similarly, Al-Zahrāwī, the 10th-century surgeon from Córdoba, known as the "father of surgery," invented numerous surgical tools and authored *Kitab al-Taṣrif*, a seminal surgical guide [15].

In the 11th century, Ibn Sīnā (Avicenna) of Baghdad, a medical prodigy by eighteen, compiled the *Canon of Medicine*, a five-volume work that encapsulated contemporary medical knowledge and was celebrated in both the Islamic world and the West. Following him, Ibn Rushd (Averroës) in the 12th century wrote *Kulliyat*, a comprehensive medical encyclopedia. Additionally, physician Alauddin Ibn al-Nafīs, in the 13th century, discovered cardiac and pulmonary circulation and authored influential medical texts such as *Mu'giz al-Qanun*. The 14th century saw Serefeddin Sabuncuoğlu authoring *Imperial Surgery*, the first surgical atlas.

Twenty-first-century scholars, such as Fatima Al-Hayani and Seyyed Hossein Nasr [3], further emphasize the centuries-old tradition of integrating sacred and empirical knowledge, and its contribution to modern technological developments. This tradition, as illuminated by historian Robert Geraci, includes fascinating medieval Arab explorations into artificial life, reflecting the advanced conceptualizations of Islamic alchemy and philosophy. These explorations, often inspired by the quest to understand creation and life processes, contemplated the possibility of artificial life that might emulate divine creativity while acknowledging the ultimate supremacy of God's creative power. Such explorations, deeply anchored in Qur'anic teachings, not only affirm Islam's receptivity to complex scientific concepts but also pave the way for embracing contemporary healthcare innovations, positioning them as natural continuations of Islamic scientific curiosity.

Conversely, what is often perceived as Muslim reluctance toward technology and scientific progress is more accurately a cautious approach to Western science and its rationalist underpinnings. This perspective often overlooks the extensive tradition of Islamization of knowledge, a movement that emerged in the 20th century in response to the Enlightenment [16]. It advocates for the integration of faith and knowledge ("*ilm*"), a concept highly esteemed in Islamic scriptures, and calls for critical engagement with Western knowledge. Scholars within this movement, such as Ismail Raji al-Faruqi and Seyyed Hossein Nasr, have been instrumental in articulating a framework that harmonizes Islamic principles with contemporary scientific inquiry [17]. This critical engagement, far from rejecting scientific progress, encourages a thoughtful assimilation of technologies, including those in healthcare, through an Islamic lens, ensuring that advancements such as AI and genome editing are congruent with Islamic ethical paradigms and historical legacy.

4. Case Studies: Organ Donation and Genetic Testing in Islamic Bioethics

4.1. *Introduction to Islamic bioethics*

Islamic bioethics boasts a rich scholarly tradition, encompassing more than 5,000 articles in various international research databases. It engages the full spectrum of ethical quandaries associated with the advent of medical technology, advances in the life sciences, and the impact of modern technology and lifestyles on the environment. In its response to these ethical quandaries, Islamic bioethics captures both the human understanding of the divine expectations inherent in Islamic moral precepts and the aspirations of believers to preserve and implement these precepts [18].

Islamic perspectives on AI and bioethics highlight key considerations regarding human dignity, accountability, and social impacts. Bodily integrity and consent are crucial issues in biometric surveillance, robotic surgery, neural implants, and lab-grown organs, particularly when involving Muslim patients' biological materials and data. Scholars emphasize respecting patient privacy and autonomy while also recognizing communal obligations, given Islam's interdependent social ethics [19]. Intention (*niyyah*) underpins Islamic ethics; therefore, delegating morally consequential decisions to AI systems raises accountability issues. Programming cannot replicate human moral agency and the ability to evaluate the intentions behind actions. Scholars advocate human discretion in deploying AI, lest its probabilistic recommendations absolve responsibility. Islamic bioethicists also consider socioeconomic impacts, given Islam's commitment to human welfare and dignity.

Examining past and present medical innovations that have sparked ethical debates within Muslim societies provides insights into facilitating the integration of emerging biotechnologies such as AI. Two relevant case studies with rich scholarship and varied positions are organ donation and genetic testing.

4.2. *Organ donation*

The discourse on organ donation within Islamic jurisprudence distils valuable insights into the broader Islamic engagement with medical innovations, including the integration of AI in healthcare. At the core of this exploration lies a conundrum, as ancient as it is urgent: whether it violates divine rights over human bodies – a question that probes the boundaries between the sacred and the empirical. The debates surrounding bodily integrity, sanctity of life, and definitions of death within organ donation discourse reveal patterns and approaches that can shape integrative AI policies, offering lessons at the intersection of theology, technology, and the human condition.

There are three main scholarly views regarding organ donation: impermissible, conditionally permissible if lifesaving, and generally permissible if done properly [20]. This diversity stems from the different interpretations and weighing of scriptural sources and precedents. Scholars from the Indo-Pakistani subcontinent and those belonging to the Ḥanafī school typically advance the impermissible or contingently permissible views. Scholars in the Middle East, as well as those from *Shafi'ī* and *Shia* backgrounds, advance the permissible views.

The Quran affirms qualified ownership rights for humans over possessions and bodies; however, ultimate sovereignty belongs to *Allah*, who grants this trusteeship. Semantic analysis of the word "ownership" (*milkiyya*) in the Quran has led to the general conclusion that while humans can own material things, *Âllah* retains control over fundamental matters such as life, death, and sustenance. This has implications for debates such as organ donation, where human discretion over bodies is qualified by higher divine principles.

There are also differences regarding the nature of the soul and whether it departs only upon brain death or persists if the heart is beating. Since the Quran does not clarify the nature of the human soul (*ruh*) and is used to refer to broader integrative life functions, it is generally understood as an integrated personhood across physical, mental, and spiritual realms – the loss of which constitutes death. Scholars differ on whether the brain or the heart better represents this integrative function. But the soul's essence remains ambiguous in the scripture, allowing multiple interpretations to emerge.

A fatwa on organ donation issued by the Fiqh Council of North America (FCNA) exemplifies the complexity of Islamic fatwas and simultaneously reveals the potential of a multidisciplinary approach that incorporates diverse perspectives [21]. It involved presentations from various stakeholders, including organ donation professionals, donor families, clinicians, religious studies experts, social scientists, and chaplains, epitomizing holistic, direct engagement with the ethical complexities. The deliberative process also involved brainstorming effective communication strategies to convey the value of organ donation to Muslims, rooted in acknowledging religious controversies surrounding the practice. The process initiated mutual understanding, enabling Islamic jurists to become aware of the clinical and social aspects of the process, thereby grounding religious rulings in real-world contexts. While specific to diaspora Muslim populations, this template provides a valuable model for addressing complex bioethical issues comprehensively within Islamic law. It offers a strategic blueprint for other *fiqh* bodies across diverse Islamic traditions to adopt a similarly expansive approach. Such a method can enhance the relevance and acceptance of fatwas, particularly in the context of disruptive healthcare technologies, where an understanding of the interplay among religious, ethical, and scientific dimensions is crucial. By advocating for such an inclusive and adaptable strategy, we can foster a more universally relevant and accepted framework for addressing bioethical questions within Islamic law, even in regions with traditionally conservative interpretations.

FCNA's fatwa permits organ donation under specific conditions, such as prohibiting the sale of organs for material benefit, allowing only charitable donations, and restricting the donation of vital organs while alive to prevent the proximate cause of death. Furthermore, it mandates that deceased donations must occur after cardiac death determination, not brain death, and explicitly forbids the donation of reproductive organs.

Alternatively, the Islamic Fiqh Academy (IFA) of the Organization of Islamic Cooperation (OIC) and the Muslim World League (MWL) hold distinct positions on organ donation, particularly regarding brain death criteria [21]. The IFA-OIC's acceptance of both cardiac and irreversible brain death, with rigorous medical validation, and the IFA-MWL's distinction between brain and cardiac death, requiring consensus among three physicians, illustrate the nuanced ways Islamic jurisprudence engages with medical advancements. These positions underscore the intricate balance that Islamic bioethics seeks to maintain between religious doctrine and medical advancements, often resulting in diverse interpretations and applications across different Islamic judicial bodies. They underscore the importance of a deliberative fatwa process that accommodates various viewpoints.

The intricate fatwa process on organ donation within Islamic bioethics offers critical lessons for AI integration in healthcare. First, the principle of balancing the sanctity of human life with bodily rights is directly applicable to AI technologies such as robotic surgery. Such AI systems, while enhancing surgical precision and patient outcomes, must align with Islamic ethics by ensuring minimal invasiveness and upholding bodily integrity, as concerns have been raised regarding organ donation practices.

Second, diverse Islamic interpretations of death and the soul inform the ethical use of AI in critical care. For instance, AI-powered predictive analytics in intensive care units can support decision-making in end-of-life care. However, this technology must align with Islamic views on life termination, where debates on brain versus heart death criteria are pertinent. The use of AI here must respect Islamic understandings of the soul's departure, ensuring that technology supports, rather than overrides, the sanctity of human life.

The "net benefit over gross harm" argument in Islamic jurisprudence is particularly relevant to AI applications such as health data analytics. While there are privacy concerns and potential autonomy infringements in gathering patient data, the overarching benefits of AI in diagnosing diseases early and tailoring personalized treatment plans can be seen as outweighing these concerns. This parallels organ donation, where saving lives is deemed to supersede the violation of the body.

The principle of necessity in Islamic bioethics, which is crucial during medical emergencies, aligns well with the rapid integration of AI in responses to crises such as COVID-19. AI's role in accelerating drug discovery and vaccine development against COVID-19, by analyzing complex biochemical interactions and simulating the virus's structure, exemplifies this. AI-driven wearable devices and home monitoring systems, which provide vital patient data remotely, mirror Islamic jurisprudence's adaptability in emergent situations, akin to the modified rituals for handling the deceased during the pandemic. This adaptability is evident in the provision of alternative methods, such as *tayammum* (dry ablution) in place of conventional practices.

However, the application and interpretation of these principles can manifest diversely across Muslim geographies, revealing the contextual essence of Islamic bioethics. In Western Muslim diaspora contexts, organizations such as IIFA and ECFR demonstrate a greater inclination for collaboration with medical institutions. Nonetheless, the predisposition for straightforward dichotomies fails to capture the plurality across

Muslim-majority countries, where the pace and nature of adoption, while impacted by jurisprudential outlooks, defy facile categorizations. Undoubtedly, certain Muslim nations are spearheading AI integration in healthcare, whereas in other places the influence of traditional authority might delay AI's disruptive potential. This underlines the necessity for a nuanced understanding and application of these principles in line with varying cultural and governmental contexts.

4.3. *Genetic testing*

The debate surrounding DNA testing in Islamic jurisprudence, particularly in paternity cases, showcases the dynamic interaction between modern science and traditional Islamic law, offering valuable intermediary insights for AI adoption in healthcare within Muslim societies [22]. One stance advocates prioritizing DNA testing over traditional methods such as the "oath of condemnation" (*lian*), a procedure where a husband accuses his wife of infidelity without witnesses, leading to mutual oaths invoking divine retribution for falsehood. This perspective aligns with modern scientific approaches, viewing DNA as a reliable *sharīʼah*-based proof that can decisively establish or negate paternity.

In contrast, another group of scholars maintains the primacy of traditional methods. They emphasize the profound religious and legal implications of these traditional practices, such as irrevocably ending a marriage and absolving punishments related to false accusations or adultery. From this standpoint, the sanctity and trust embedded in marital relationships, as upheld in Islamic law, outweigh the empirical evidence provided by DNA tests. They point out that *Iian* serves a dual purpose, providing an opportunity to bypass strict punishments dictated for adultery in Islamic *fiqh* [23]. They also point out that DNA test results require scrutiny due to possible human error. This mirrors broader apprehensions within Muslim societies about technical errors and the need for rigorous validation of AI technologies. This underscores the need to demystify AI for Muslim societies, either through processes of co-creation or by adopting the language of Islamic ethical frameworks.

A third viewpoint considers DNA testing as a supplementary method to traditional oaths [24]. This perspective advocates for a complementary approach, where DNA testing can provide additional clarity; however, traditional oaths retain their significance and can be invoked when necessary. This approach represents a synthesis of traditional Islamic jurisprudence and contemporary scientific methods, acknowledging the roles of both in ethical decision-making. Representative of a nuanced attitude toward AI in healthcare, where technologies such as genome editing might initially be introduced as supplementary tools rather than primary decision-makers, this perspective aligns with Islamic principles of ethical decision-making.

Within certain medical contexts, AI's enhanced precision can be strategically used to belie conventional resistance to increasingly novel scientific technologies. Resistance to DNA testing for paternity verification is one such context. A common counterargument, heralded by Islamic scholars and equally salient in popular Muslim imagination, is the room for human error in conducting or interpreting tests; even though improbable, the error concerns sanctified matrimonial relationships. For many, the risk is not worth it. However, AI advancements, i.e., more accurate pattern recognition, automated and improved quality control checks, and more expansive database matching, can alleviate those fears. While concerns about algorithmic bias against Muslims, often seen as a continuation of human error, are generally valid, they are less pertinent in the specific context of DNA paternity testing. Strict data and protocol controls standardize the medical procedure, while human oversight adds accountability. So, in regulated settings such as DNA testing, bias is likely less prevalent than in mass-deployment applications. Similarly, the integration of AI-enhanced noninvasive prenatal testing (NIPT) within Muslim societies, particularly in light of the Islamic perspective on fetal ensoulment, represents a significant stride in prenatal healthcare [25,26]. Islamic jurisprudence, recognizing four distinct fetal development stages, places critical importance on the 120-day mark post-conception for ensoulment. Leveraging machine learning, NIPT emerges as a pivotal technology in this context.

Traditionally, women undergo diagnostic tests such as chorionic villus sampling between 11 and 14 weeks of gestation and amniocentesis after 15 weeks; both procedures entail risks of miscarriage that could raise ethical concerns if pregnancy termination is considered post-ensoulment. However, NIPT circumvents these risks by safely analyzing fetal DNA from maternal blood as early as 9 weeks, with results available by 11–12 weeks, thus aligning with Islamic ethical standards by providing critical data well before the ensoulment threshold. In Muslim societies, where consanguineous marriages are more prevalent and genetic screening is often mandated, AI-augmented NIPT offers substantial benefits. It ensures early detection of potential genetic disorders, facilitating informed decision-making at stages that are not in conflict with Islamic teachings on ensoulment.

Furthermore, the application of NIPT carries profound implications for abortion considerations in Islamic contexts. The diversity of fatwas on abortion within Islamic jurisprudence, addressing scenarios such as fetal anomalies or maternal health risks, reflects the complex ethical landscape surrounding this issue. By providing precise, early diagnostic results, AI-enhanced NIPT extends the window for decision-making regarding pregnancy termination, offering choices that might not have been available or viable within a religious ethical framework at later stages of gestation.

These cases demonstrate that constructive dialogue, grassroots outreach, and translating biomedical advances into Islamic ethical frameworks can prevail over initial hesitations. A similar cultural ambassadorship will be vital for emerging AI applications. Muslim bioethicists must be proactively engaged to shape AI governance in line with Islamic principles of human dignity, environmental stewardship, and trustworthy knowledge.

4.4. *Islamic scholars' attitude toward AI*

Our understanding of Islamic jurisprudence's response and attitudes toward AI is fragmented, as evidenced by the disparate findings of various surveys. These studies suggest a notable gap in knowledge about AI among Islamic scholars and leaders. This lack of comprehensive understanding leads to a cautious approach; they neither outright condemn AI due to insufficient knowledge nor fully embrace it with trust. In a study conducted by Vinichenko *et al.* [27], involving 58 Islamic religious leaders from the Spiritual Administration of Muslims of KHMAO-Yugra and the Republic of Tajikistan, a complex perspective on AI's societal impact emerged. They acknowledged AI's potential in enhancing efficiency across sectors, recognizing its alignment with contemporary human values. However, 54% express concerns about its cultural implications, fearing a disruption to traditional value systems.

Despite this, over half (51%) showed openness towards AI's integration in artistic domains, as illustrated by their acceptance of an android robot taking center stage in Stefan Kaegi's theatrical production, "The Sinister Valley" in Germany, instead of playwright Thomas Melle. In religious affairs, 79% see AI as beneficial. However, there is unanimity that AI cannot replicate the spiritual essence intrinsic to humans, echoing the Islamic bioethical focus on the soul (*ruh*).

Nawi *et al.* [28] add depth to this understanding through a survey of 37 Muslim experts. They find widespread support (95%) for ethical oversight of AI, with reservations about its role in religious teaching; this indicates a gap in knowledge and understanding of AI's diverse capabilities, especially in healthcare.

The anxiety related to AI in Muslim societies is not an isolated phenomenon. Rather, it is intertwined with broader concerns about rapid sociopolitical changes in our understanding of human biology and societal norms. Transhumanism, a movement that advocates enhancing human faculties and capabilities through advanced technologies, including AI, raises profound questions about the nature and future of humanity. This movement's emphasis on surpassing human biological limitations through AI-driven health interventions strikes a chord of apprehension, especially within the context of Islamic bioethics. For instance, the increasing visibility and discussions surrounding LGBTQ+ individuals in Muslim societies have sparked debates at the intersection of biology, identity, and religious ethics and doctrine. Similarly, transhumanism's promise of altering human capabilities through AI and other technologies brings to the forefront questions about what constitutes human nature and the ethical boundaries of modifying it.

Academic discourse reflects these anxieties and debates, focusing on how transhumanism's reproductive policies conflict with traditional ethical principles, treating humans as objects for technological advancement [29–32]. They delve into the ethical and philosophical implications of this movement, raising significant concerns over the spiritual and moral dimensions of human existence – aspects that transhumanism and its reliance on AI appear to overlook or undervalue.

Omar Suleiman, an influential figure among younger, diasporic Muslims due to his progressive stance and online presence, contributes to this discourse. As the founder of the *Yaqeen* Institute and listed in "The Muslim 500," he emphasizes technology's spiritual limitations and advocates for its selective adoption, balancing technological advancement with spiritual integrity [33]. His approach, mindful of eroding human capabilities, resonates with the broader Muslim society's cautious yet open stance toward AI, advocating for its use in a manner that complements human effort and spiritual values, rather than replacing them. This perspective from a prominent, internet-savvy scholar suggests a broader, more inclusive approach to AI, beyond mere refusal or acceptance.

It also aligns with the emerging concept of prayer bots [34], revealing a desire to leverage technology while preserving the core spiritual values and personal agency intrinsic to Islamic worship. Prayer bots, essentially software applications programmed to perform religious prayers or rituals, offer convenience and adhere to religious practices; however, they also raise significant questions within the Islamic context. The authenticity of a bot's actions, devoid of sincere human intent, is questionable in Islam, where intention holds paramount importance. Furthermore, the use of prayer bots highlights the nature of spiritual connections, given that direct human involvement and mindfulness are crucial in fostering a genuine relationship with the divine. Lastly, the Islamic emphasis on personal responsibility in worship challenges the delegation of religious duties to algorithms, highlighting concerns about agency and accountability in the digital age.

5. Innovation and Faith: The Rise of Islamic Digital Technologies

The apprehension toward AI in healthcare within Muslim societies is not due solely to a lack of technological adaptability. As of 2024, the global Muslim population is estimated at two billion [35], representing a significant market for digital Islamic services. The young, technologically literate demographic, with a median age of 23, is highly receptive to digital innovations that resonate with Islamic values. Deloitte's report [36] identifies two key consumer segments: "futurists" and "traditionalists." Futurists, who embrace both faith and modernity, are young, well-educated, and open to new ideas. They represent a significant portion of potential users for digital Islamic services. Traditionalists, conversely, are more conservative, value social harmony and long-standing traditions, and are less likely to adopt new technologies. Deloitte's 2014 analysis segments 40% of the Muslim consumer market as futurists – who blend faith with modernity, embodying young, educated, globally oriented, tech-savvy individuals – and 60% as traditionalists, who prioritize harmony, belonging, and adherence to collective traditions, typically over 35 years old. The diverse consumer behavior within the Muslim community shapes distinct market niches, highlighting the need for tailored engagement strategies attuned to the values driving diverse Muslim healthcare decisions. Some eagerly adopt AI's potential, while others weigh its disruption against communal traditions.

The dichotomy in these approaches is evident in the varying uses of technology for Islamic purposes. There is a significant demand for halal, organic food; and digital platforms play a crucial role in ensuring transparency and tracking across the supply chain. Digital Islamic media content also serves as a unifying force, addressing common values and targeting specific demographics. In addition, the concept of halal-friendly travel is gaining traction, with digital initiatives focusing on online booking, ratings, and accreditation. Mosque management is another area where technology is making inroads, with digital solutions for information services, sermon projections, and eco-friendly technologies. In the realms of Islamic art and design, finance, and education, digital platforms are growing, offering specialized services, access to Islamic funding, and online educational resources.

The integration of AI and blockchain in Islamic fintech exemplifies how disruptive technologies can align with religious principles and cater to the needs of Muslim societies. Islamic fintech leverages blockchain's decentralized and transparent attributes, aligning with Sharia principles that emphasize honesty and risk aversion. Blockchain is being explored for various applications in Islamic finance, including crowdfunding, microfinance, and managing Islamic philanthropy [37].

For instance, the Sukuk Network [38], which is a platform that leverages blockchain and smart contracts, adheres to Islamic principles by avoiding interest-based transactions and utilizes a machine-learning-based system to evaluate projects. This AI system thoroughly assesses various data points, including financial data and management information, to determine the creditworthiness and risks associated with these projects. Such a system highlights the potential for AI to bring about more informed, ethical decision-making in Islamic finance.

Similarly, the field of Islamic scholarship is undergoing AI-mediated transformation. The Natural Language Processing group at Leeds

University focuses on Quranic Arabic, employing AI to enrich the text with linguistic annotations and extract underlying knowledge [39]. This approach allows for a deeper understanding of the Quran, facilitating advanced reasoning and interpretation.

These examples demonstrate the potential for disruptive technologies to be embraced within Muslim societies. The key lies in developing these technologies with a clear understanding of Islamic values and the diverse needs of Muslim societies.

6. Practical Modifications: Human–Computer Interaction in Muslim Healthcare AI

Human–computer interaction is an interdisciplinary field that studies and designs interactions between users and computer systems, integrating principles from cognitive psychology, design, and ergonomics to create end products that are intuitive, accessible, and responsive [40]. Research in HCI in the context of public health and AI is not merely a field of academic inquiry; it unlocks creative, practical possibilities. It is an essential component of creating responsible AI that is people-centered. Merging empathy, innovation, and cultural sensitivity, HCI transcends mere functionality and aspires to foster meaningful ownership of the end product. It aims for technology to not only be used as a tool but also as a reflection of the community, echoing its diversity and aspirations. It promotes a much-expanded notion of design, positioning it as a powerful strategic and creative problem-solving methodology within the complex healthcare environment.

Human-centered design, a component of HCI, describes a process that begins and ends with accommodating the needs and desires of our end users – the patients, families, providers, and staff, each playing a part in the co-creation of healthcare. It requires an interrogation of one's own positionality, along with adopting an essentially iterative, thoughtful design approach. Islamic HCI is typically not centered in dialogues about creating inclusive AI for Muslim societies, which reflects a wider tendency to privilege critique over creative, practical adaptations that can be made to these technologies. Modern computational systems and their designs often reflect a secular user base, typically not factoring in faith-based perspectives. This trend likely stems from a Eurocentric view in science and technology, where faith, spirituality, and religion are often overlooked in favor of empirical evidence. Rifat *et al.* [41] have emphasized how this perspective tends to marginalize religious considerations in the field of HCI, giving rise to widely used standards such as Nielsen's Ten Usability Heuristics, Web Content Accessibility Guidelines, and User-Centered Design, which remain carelessly limited in their implementation within Muslim contexts. Highlighting this oversight, Genevieve Bell [42] advocates for integrating spiritual practices into technology. For instance, an AI-driven health application, meticulously designed with HCI principles, could embed Islamic dietary regulations and context-aware adaptations, offering a more holistic, faith-integrated user experience. Such an innovation not only aligns with the specific cultural and religious requirements of Muslim users but also enhances the user interface's accessibility and relevance, thereby advancing the priority of inclusivity in public health technology.

Though not devoid of studies on religion and spirituality, HCI research has predominantly focused on facilitating religious practices rather than delving into the everyday implications of religious beliefs. This gap, identified as "techno-spiritualism," reflects challenges including limited funding, the sensitivity of the subject, a perceived lack of scientific rigor, and risks inherent to such research. Notable strides have been made in understanding techno-spiritual practices in various religious contexts, including American Christian and Orthodox Jewish homes and within Muslim societies, both in the United States of America (USA) and in relation to Islamic institutions [43].

By embedding Islamic values into AI solutions, Muslim societies are provided with healthcare options that not only result in improved patient outcomes but are inextricably linked with their spiritual ethos and, therefore, take a holistic view of health beyond traditional biomedical body-centric approaches. Techno-spiritual designs in HCI can be numerous; for example, research conducted into designing eHealth for Muslim women who experience miscarriage recommended informational support that included religious explanations citing Prophet Muhammad's (peace be upon him) companions' experiences of miscarriage to encourage resilience and emphasized religious rewards in its mental well-being messaging [44].

Incorporating values into the design of healthcare AI innovations is crucial from the outset, rather than as an afterthought. As Knobel and

Bowker [45] suggest, values should be integrated into information technologies from the beginning. The concept of "cultural valence" in system design is equally important. Systems developed in one cultural context, such as the USA, should not impose their inherent values on users from different cultural backgrounds. For example, an American-designed online patient portal might intuitively align with American healthcare norms, but it could clash with the healthcare practices or patient-doctor interaction styles of non-American users. Pereira *et al.* [46] advocate for a design approach in HCI that focuses on the lives of the people using the technology rather than just the technology itself; e.g., an AI-powered health monitoring app solely focused on functionality might overlook Muslim users' daily lifestyle nuances, which will eventually deter its usability and adherence.

Organizational semiotics and the socially aware design approach advocate for a nuanced understanding of values in the context of interactive system design. Values are seen not as properties of individuals or objects but as elements of the dynamic relationship between them within a social context. This perspective shifts the focus from mere actions (doing/not doing) to the essence of existence (being/not being) in the realm of interactive AI systems. The "target user" methodology, which is deeply institutionalized within design thinking, often overlooks secondary populations that are indirectly affected by the AI intervention. For Muslims, the initial design and implementation of a medical AI system shape their inhibitions, perceptions, and interactions with the technology, regardless of whether they are the primary focus of the intervention. For instance, a clinical decision support system designed for oncologists may not initially have Muslim patients as its primary user base during development. However, the system's real-world adoption and recommendations influence Muslim communities' perceptions of and openness to embracing AI in cancer care.

The HCI literature is replete with alternative approaches that can be adapted for Muslim users. Friedman's value-sensitive design methodology, refined over two decades, is crucial for embedding ethical values into computer systems. Her practical guide [47] begins with pinpointing a value, technology, or context of use. It then involves identifying direct and indirect stakeholders, assessing benefits and harms for each group, and mapping these onto corresponding values. A deep dive into the conceptual investigation of key values and the identification of potential value conflicts is also integral to this process. By organizing the development process around values, the methodology reimagines it as a reiterative site of inquiry, actively preventing the accumulation of unrecognized biases.

Moreover, considering "non-use" in design is pivotal. For instance, an AI-driven health management app that respects prayer times or religious fasting in Muslim societies not only caters to active use scenarios but also thoughtfully integrates non-use or reduced-use periods. Such designs acknowledge and respect the rhythms of spiritual life. This approach is not only about technological functionality but also about addressing historical biases and fostering a sense of belonging.

Insights from Mustafa *et al.* [48] illustrate how the concept of *purdah* can be reflected in the design elements of healthcare technologies. For instance, respecting privacy can be operationalized by blurring or pixelating images of intimate body parts in educational materials, thereby aligning with the ethos of modesty and discretion. This approach also addresses the varied comfort levels of users, allowing them to control the visibility of sensitive information. Additionally, considering the limited personal physical space in homes available to women in the Global South, technologies should be designed to ensure that personal information is accessible only under conditions of physical privacy. This could involve user-controlled covered images on apps or websites, revealing content according to the user's comfort and privacy settings.

Furthermore, Islam's emphasis on the pursuit of knowledge offers a potent foundation for informative design in healthcare. Design strategies could integrate religious teachings on health, making technologies such as reminder apps for biennial pap smears or breast exams more resonant with Muslim women. Linking these reminders to religious narratives about the importance of healthcare could significantly enhance their effectiveness, compared to secular messaging.

The challenges of defending Islamic cultures and values, often misunderstood or negatively portrayed in the global media, also impact HCI research. Researchers and participants alike may face hesitation or feel compelled to neutralize or liberalize their descriptions of Islamic practices, thereby influencing both the reporting and interpretation of data.

Worth-centered design emphasizes the importance of identifying collective value in the design of interactive media, a principle that extends to public health AI and HCI [49]. This approach recognizes the collective worth of digital innovations, such as interactive fiction, computer games, and digital art, which contribute to societal enrichment and individual self-growth.

This approach underlines that participatory design is not only about direct community involvement but also entails a deep-seated sensitivity and willingness to engage with the community's values. It entails a commitment to extensive research into cultural discourse and religious practices. This responsibility lies primarily with creators, managers, and developers, who must cultivate openness and actively seek to understand the collective worth and cultural nuances of their target audience. Such a perspective shifts the emphasis from merely catering to individual needs to embracing a broader communal context; it adopts a value-driven, holistic lens. Furthermore, the question of when not to design or continue research is critical. Sometimes, the best solution might involve stepping back and acknowledging that certain technologies might not align with the core values of a society.

Edward T. Hall's cultural theory, as interpreted by Pereira *et al.* [46], offers insights into understanding Muslim societies as high-context cultures. in which much of the communication is implicit, relying on shared understandings and symbols rather than explicit verbal instructions. This implies that, in designing an AI tool for health education in these societies, implicit cultural knowledge and nonverbal cues should be heavily incorporated. Familiar cultural metaphors, stories, and proverbs should not only be incorporated into health communication but also into the promotional messaging of the AI tool.

7. Conclusion

Integrating AI into healthcare for diverse communities presents both opportunities and challenges. Equitable and culturally sensitive implementations require in-depth research into the nuanced perspectives of Muslim communities. This includes understanding their unique views on health, illness, and AI, alongside user preferences and accessibility concerns. Culturally tailored design and development are crucial and can be achieved through multidisciplinary collaborations involving AI developers, ethicists, religious scholars, and community representatives. Incorporating Islamic bioethical principles and robust evaluation methodologies is instrumental.

However, vigilance against algorithmic bias and fairness is essential. Rigorous testing, transparent data collection practices, and inclusive datasets representing Muslim populations are necessary. Ultimately, empowering communities is key. Educational programs and fostering local expertise in AI, data science, and bioethics within Muslim communities are crucial, alongside open dialogue and community participation in decision-making.

By pursuing these research avenues and prioritizing collaboration, critical reflection, and continuous learning, we can build a future where AI serves as a powerful tool for equitable, culturally attuned, and holistic healthcare for all. In this future, Muslim communities will actively shape their own well-being journey, ensuring that technology serves humanity with respect and inclusivity.

References

[1] Lim CP, Vaidya A, Jain K, Mahorkar VU, Jain LC, editors. *Handbook of Artificial Intelligence in Healthcare: Vol. 1 – Advances and Applications* [Internet]. Cham: Springer International Publishing; 2022 [cited 2023 November 16]. (Intelligent Systems Reference Library; Vol. 211). Available from: https://link.springer.com/10.1007/978-3-030-79161-2.

[2] Benjamens S, Dhunnoo P, Görög M, Mesko B. Forecasting artificial intelligence trends in health care: Systematic international patent analysis. *JMIR AI.* 2023 May 26;2(1):e47283.

[3] Al-Hayani FA. Islam and science: Contradiction or concordance. *Zygon.* 2005;40(3).

[4] UAE-National-Strategy-for-Artificial-Intelligence-2031.pdf [Internet]. [cited 2023 Nov 16]. Available from: https://ai.gov.ae/wp-content/uploads/2021/07/UAE-National-Strategy-for-Artificial-Intelligence-2031.pdf.

[5] Hassan O. Artificial intelligence, Neom and Saudi Arabia's economic diversification from oil and gas. *Polit Q.* 2020;91(1):222–7.

[6] Welcome to Qatar Genome Programme. Qatar Genome Programme [Internet]. [cited 2023 Nov 17]. Available from: https://www.qatargenome.org.qa/.

[7] Mbarek H, Ismail SI. Mapping the Arab genome. *Nat Genet.* 2022 Dec;54(12):1761–3.

[8] Dajani R, Mbarek H, Ismail SI, Awad A, Somai M. Overcoming Eurocentric bias makes for better science. *Med.* 2022 Dec 9;3(12):813–4.

[9] Niemi MEK, Karjalainen J, Liao RG, Neale BM, Daly M, Ganna A, *et al.* Mapping the human genetic architecture of COVID-19. *Nature.* 2021 Dec;600(7889):472–7.

[10] Abdul Rahim HF, Ismail SI, Hassan A, Fadl T, Khaled SM, Shockley B, *et al*. Willingness to participate in genome testing: A survey of public attitudes from Qatar. *J Hum Genet*. 2020 Dec;65(12):1067–73.
[11] Fidler DP. The globalization of public health: the first 100 years of international health diplomacy. *Bull World Health Organ*. 2001;79(9):842–9.
[12] Marrogi AJ. Medical diplomacy in achieving U.S. global strategic objectives. National Defense University Press, 2014.
[13] Dolatbandi AB, Kamrava M. Medical diplomacy and Iranian foreign policy. *Sociol Islam*. 2021;9(1):1–17.
[14] Khan MS, Nayab H. Digital health technologies and artificial intelligence in the Islamic world: Embracing the evolution in healthcare. *Journal of Islamic Governance*. 2021;6.
[15] Al-Khalili J. *The House of Wisdom: How Arabic Science Saved Ancient Knowledge and gave us the Renaissance* [Internet]. Penguin Publishing Group; 2012 [cited 2023 Nov 17].
[16] Rahman F. Islamization of knowledge: A response. *AJIS*. 1988 Sep 1;5(1):3–11.
[17] Furlow CA. The Islamization of knowledge: Philosophy, legitimation, and politics. *Soc Epistemol*. 1996 Jul 1;10(3–4):259–71.
[18] Shabana A. Bioethics in Islamic thought. *Religion Compass*. 2014 Nov;8(11):337–46.
[19] Rattani A. A critique of contemporary Islamic bioethics. *Bioeth Inq*. 2021 Jul;18(2):357–61.
[20] Padela AI. Islamic bioethical positions on organ donation and transplantation: Stressing rigor and caution in fatwa reviews. *Transplant Direct*. 2020 Aug;6(8):e586.
[21] Padela AI, Auda J. The moral status of organ donation and transplantation within Islamic law: The Fiqh council of North America's position. *Transplant Direct*. 2020 Mar;6(3):e536.
[22] Shabana A. Paternity between law and biology: The reconstruction of the Islamic law of paternity in the wake of DNA testing. *Zygon*. 2012 Mar;47(1):214–39.
[23] Shabana A. Islam, culture, and reprogenetics: Implementation of genetic and reproductive technologies in Qatar. *Muslim World*. 2022;112(3):286–310.
[24] Korbatieh S. Evidence laws in Sharia and the impact of modern technology and DNA testing. *Aust J Islam Stud*. 2020 Dec 6;5(3):4–29.
[25] Shabana A. Islamic ethics and the legitimacy of scientific innovation: Reproductive genetic counseling within the Muslim context. *Sociol Islam*. 2020 May 1;8(2):265–89.
[26] Haidar H, Rispler-Chaim V, Hung A, Chandrasekharan S, Ravitsky V. Noninvasive prenatal testing: Implications for Muslim communities. *AJOB Empir Bioeth*. 2015 Jan 2;6(1):94–105.

[27] Vinichenko MV, Chulanova OL, Vinogradova MV, Amozova LN. The impact of artificial intelligence on society views of Islamic religious leaders. *Eur J Sci Theol*. 2020. 16(3):67–77.

[28] Nawi A, Yaakob MFM, Ren CC, Khamis NY, Tamuri AH. A preliminary survey of Muslim experts' views on artificial intelligence. *Islāmiyyāt*. 2021 Nov 11;43(2):3–16.

[29] Soysal EK. The production of human reproduction: Impacts of Transhumanism's inconsistent reproductive policy on classical ethical principles. *Ilahiyat Stud*. 2023 Jul 31;14(1):9–50.

[30] Besnier JM. D'un désir mortifère d'immortalité. À propos du transhumanisme. *Cités*. 2013;55(3):13–23.

[31] Cruz ER. Giving birth, Transhumanism and human nature. *Revista de Filosofia Aurora* [Internet]. 2021 Aug 31 [cited 2023 Nov 17];33(59). Available from: https://periodicos.pucpr.br/aurora/article/view/28225.

[32] Can S. Critique of Transhumanism's concept of humans from the perspective of Islamic thought. *Ilahiyat Stud*. 2023 Jul 31;14(1):107–31.

[33] Yaqeen Institute for Islamic Research [Internet]. 2023 [cited 2023 Jun 16]. AI and ChatGPT: spiritual resilience and ethics. *Khutbah*. Available from: https://yaqeeninstitute.org/omar-suleiman/ai-and-chatgpt-spiritual-resilience-and-ethics-khutbah.

[34] Öhman C, Gorwa R, and Floridi L Luciano. Prayer-bots and religious worship on twitter: A call for a wider research agenda (April 01, 2019). Available at SSRN: https://ssrn.com/abstract=3831367 or http://dx.doi.org/10.2139/ssrn.3831367 [cited 2023 Jun 19]. Available from: https://papers.ssrn.com/sol3/papers.cfm?abstract_id=3831367.

[35] World Population Review. Muslim population by country 2024 [Internet]. Available from: https://worldpopulationreview.com/country-rankings/muslim-population-by-country. [Accessed 2024 Feb 1].

[36] Deloitte. The Digital Islamic Services landscape: Uncovering the Digital Islamic Services opportunity for the Middle East and the World. [cited 2023 Nov 10]. Available from: https://www.scribd.com/document/526355779/Deloitte-Me-Islamic-Digital-Services.

[37] Unal IM, Aysan AF. Fintech, Digitalization, and blockchain in Islamic finance: Retrospective investigation. *FinTech*. 2022 Nov 17;1(4):388–98.

[38] Sukuk Network [Internet]. 2023 [cited 2023 Jun 16]. A.I for rating Islamic Sukuk. Available from: https://www.sukuk.network/blog/more-about-us-1/ai-for-rating-islamic-sukuk-7.

[39] Atwell E, Brierley C, Dukes K, Sawalha M, Sharaf A. An artificial intelligence approach to Arabic and Islamic content on the internet. In: Proceedings of NITS 3rd National Information Technology Symposium; 2011.

[40] Sandamal H. Human computer interaction [Internet]. *Medium.* 2020 [cited 2023 Nov 9]. Available from: https://hansasandamal.medium.com/human-computer-interaction-cb0f7cc2cf23.
[41] Rifat MR, Peer F, Rabaan H, Mim NJ, Mustafa M, Toyama K, *et al.* Integrating religion, faith, and spirituality in HCI. In: CHI EA '22: Extended Abstracts of the 2022 CHI Conference on Human Factors in Computing Systems; 2022. p. 1–6.
[42] Bell G. No more SMS from Jesus: Ubicomp, religion and techno-spiritual practices. In: UbiComp 2006: Ubiquitous Computing. Orange County, California, USA: Springer; 2006 [cited 2023 Nov 17]. Available from: https://link.springer.com/chapter/10.1007/11853565_9.
[43] Bubandt N. Spirits as technology: Tech-gnosis and the ambivalent politics of the invisible in Indonesia. *Cont Islam.* 2019 Apr 1;13(1):103–20.
[44] Alqassim M, Pain H, Wolters M. Designing eHealth with Muslim women who have experienced miscarriage. Paper presented at: IslamicHCI: Designing with and within Muslim populations; 2020 Jul 23; [Accessed 2023 Nov 27]. Available from: https://web.lums.edu.pk/~IslamicHCI/papers/Designing%20e-health%20with%20Muslim%20Women%20who%20have%20experienced%20Miscarriage.pdf.
[45] Knobel C, Bowker GC. Values in design. *Commun ACM.* 2011 Jul;54(7):26–8.
[46] Pereira R, Cecília Calani Baranauskas M. A value-oriented and culturally informed approach to the design of interactive systems. *Int J Hum-Comput Stud.* 2015 Aug;80:66–82.
[47] Friedman B, Kahn PH Jr, Borning A. Value sensitive design and information systems. In: Zhang P, Galletta D, editors. *Human-Computer Interaction and Management Information Systems: Foundations.* Armonk: M.E. Sharpe; 2006. p. 348–372.
[48] Mustafa M, Zaman KT, Ahmad T, Batool A, Ghazali M, Ahmed N. Religion and women's intimate health: Towards an inclusive approach to healthcare. In: *Proceedings of the 2021 CHI Conference on Human Factors in Computing Systems* [Internet]. Yokohama Japan: ACM; 2021 [cited 2023 Nov 10]. p. 1–13. Available from: https://dl.acm.org/doi/10.1145/3411764.3445605.
[49] Camara F, Calvary G. Worth-centered design in practice: Lessons from experience and research agenda. In: Abascal J, Barbosa S, Fetter M, Gross T, Palanque P, Winckler M, editors. *15th Human-Computer Interaction* (INTERACT) [Internet]. Bamberg, Germany: Springer; 2015 [cited 2023 Nov 9]. p. 123–39. Available from: https://hal.science/hal-01492566.

https://doi.org/10.1142/9781800616295_0004

Chapter 4

How Artificial Intelligence is Changing Newsrooms

Subhra Priyadarshini

Nature Portfolio, Springer Nature, London, UK
s.priyadarshini@nature.com

Abstract

The use of artificial intelligence (AI) tools is changing how news is created, presented, disseminated, and consumed. This chapter discusses fast-evolving AI technologies, traces their origins in newsrooms across the world, and explores how societies are keeping pace with the dynamic realm of news.

In December 2022, a small newsroom in India's capital, Delhi, was abuzz with conversations around a new tool that produces coherent and grammatically perfect text when you ask it a well-framed, pointed question. The hour-long editorial meeting of reporters and editors, generally dedicated to discussing the big news stories of the day, was consumed by excited chatter around this new technological wonder. Is it a chatbot, or is it like Google or Siri? What kind of subjects is it well versed in – politics, sports, or finance? Can it produce a catchy, search-engine-friendly headline if we give it keywords? Can it write our emails or our social media posts?

Everyone had a question, and everyone felt the tool could make some bit of their repetitive work – structuring emails, sourcing a story, or writing a social media post – easier. A computational journalist in the team shared the results of her first experiments with the tool based on a large language model (LLM), a model fed with such massive amounts of data that it might be able to find a correct-sounding answer to almost every question asked. Other journalists tried to make sense of the concept behind the model but wanted to see its magic in action. The computational journalist, a frequent usherer of new and emerging technology into the newsroom, promised a demonstration in the next day's meeting.

The excitement of this conversation spilled into many successive meetings, with demonstrations of several free-to-use LLM tools that were flooding the market in quick succession. Newsrooms and other creative industries across the world were witnessing a similar surge of interest around the promise and future of generative artificial intelligence (gen AI), a kind of AI capable of producing original content.

Many media organizations were quick to jump on to the gen AI boom. Others were cautious about adopting the technology since they did not want to replace the qualities of human thinking, analysis, and emotive expression, all intrinsically connected to the pursuit of journalism, with machines. There were other ethical concerns to be considered, such as the copyright and privacy of the material on which the LLMs were trained, the authorship of the material they generated, and their inherent biases. Soon enough, for the first time in several years of using AI in various forms, newsrooms were formulating guidelines governing the use of AI.

Going by the interest it generated and by its quick adaptation and experimentation in the publishing industry, the gen AI boom has established itself as a significant milestone in the history of the use of AI technologies in newsrooms. However, it is not the first or only kind of AI being widely used across the media industry.

1. Introduction: A Brief History of AI in News Media

In the past few years, the landscape of news media has undergone a sudden and significant change, fueled by profound technological transformations in the field of AI, especially gen AI.

The proliferation of AI in journalistic endeavors reflects the broader digitization of media and its deep impact on public life. A paradigm shift toward applications, algorithms, and social media has fundamentally altered journalism as an institution. These changes have disrupted traditional business models and work routines in newsrooms. They have also created information channels beyond conventional news outlets. In this backdrop, the introduction of AI technologies marks an inflection point in the history of news media, both in transforming the presentation and business of news in the short term and in directing the future of the industry.

The use of AI for tasks that could easily complement journalism has been in practice since the mid-1990s. In 1958, American technology innovator IBM automated the process of extracting an abstract or summary from a research paper with an AI tool, a version of which IBM continues to develop to date to include new functionality [1].

However, the recent widespread use of AI tools in journalism mostly stems from advancements in natural language processing (NLP) and machine learning technologies in the early 2000s. AI and automation technologies were introduced into newsrooms in 2006, when Thomson Reuters started auto-generating their financial news stories [2].

In 2014, the news agency Associated Press used an Automated Insights platform called Wordsmith to generate snappy summaries of companies' quarterly earnings. By 2018, the agency was producing more than 3,700 stories on U.S. traded stocks – 10 times the number of stories they would normally produce. The volume and scale of this AI-augmented project were disruptive for the news industry.

In 2016, a Pulitzer-winning muckrake by the International Consortium of Investigative Journalists (ICIJ) – famously known as the Panama Papers [3] – used optical character recognition (OCR) algorithms to digitize text from 11.5 million leaked financial and legal records. The sheer magnitude of mining 2.6 terabytes of data to reveal how politicians, banks, criminals, and sports celebrities took advantage of the secrecy provided by tax havens, in some cases breaking the law, is considered a landmark in the history of investigative journalism.

Giving a face to the AI boom, AI news anchors made their debut in 2018, when China's state news agency Xinhua introduced a simulated version of one of its anchors to work round the clock, "reducing the cost of news production." Created using machine learning to mimic the voice, facial movements, and gestures of the broadcaster, it presented what the agency called a "lifelike image instead of a cold robot" [4]. Across Asia, a host of AI news anchors – India Today TV's "Sana," Odisha TV's "Lisa," Indonesian TV One's "Nadira," "Sasya," and "Bhoomi," Malaysian Astro Awani's "Joon" and "Monica," Kuwaiti Middle Eastern's "Fedha," and a Taiwanese FTV News weather presenter – have replaced real people in specific news bulletins ever since [5].

These were early adaptations that created sporadic yet significant changes in the way newsrooms were experimenting with AI. However, more recent advances in gen AI, promising to create fast original content, have had the deepest impact on the media industry. Gen AI is a class of AI systems capable of generating fresh content in a matter of seconds. It does not follow the rules or predefined instructions of traditional AI systems. Gen AI models are designed to learn patterns and generate content on their own in the blink of an eye.

The first use of gen AI dates to the 1960s, when chatterbots (later called chatbots) were introduced to provide quick custom replies based on the patterns they were trained to recognize in the input queries. In 1966, MIT Professor Joseph Weizenbaum released ELIZA, a computer program that emulated a Rogerian psychotherapist, a therapist that reflected on questions by turning them back at the patient. ELIZA was one of the earliest test cases for the Turing test, a test developed by computer scientist Alan Turing to test machine intelligence.

Gen AI continued to evolve but wasn't widespread up until 2014, when American computer scientist Ian Goodfellow proposed generative adversarial networks (GANs) that made it possible to create original content. GANs are the most common type of gen AI based on two neural networks – a generator and a discriminator – that work together. The generator creates data such as text or images, and the discriminator evaluates the generated content against a dataset of real-world examples. The two networks iteratively improve their performance through this adversarial process. The generator creates content that is increasingly difficult for the discriminator to distinguish from real data.

Then came the LLMs, a type of AI trained on massive datasets and capable of generating coherent and grammatically correct language. LLMs have significantly changed the way the news industry uses gen AI today. The much-used AI tool ChatGPT, developed by OpenAI, made its debut in November 2022, sparking what industry observers called the second most important disruption after the internet revolution. Other LLMs, such as Google's Bard, or deep-learning text-to-image models, such as DALL-E and Midjourney, quickly joined the repertoire of editorial experimentation tools. Within the span of a year, a December 2023 survey report by the Reuters Institute for the Study of Journalism [6] found that almost three-quarters of global newsrooms were convinced gen AI will help them do things more efficiently.

In the global media landscape, gen AI experiments have been aplenty – from creating bespoke texts that meet the content and style requirements of individual publishers to generating images and videos that complement and position the content for younger audiences surfing news on non-traditional news platforms, such as Instagram or TikTok. Gen AI has also been used in creating human-like voices for regular broadcasts or podcasts and newscaster avatars who can sit in when their human analogues are sick, sleeping, or on a holiday. The legacy processes of news gathering, dissemination, and audience engagement also benefit from integrating AI systems and protocols at every step. Newsrooms are using gen AI for greater efficiency in these complex processes or to handle monotonous office work so that journalists and editors can free up their time for more creative pursuits.

2. Current Use of AI Tools in Newsrooms

Gen AI has opened many possibilities for easily adaptable and implementable scenarios in the media industry. In the past decade, journalists have successfully employed machines or automation for computer-assisted reporting, computational or automated journalism, and data or algorithmic journalism. AI complements everyday newsroom operations by generating automatic texts or metadata, summarizing articles, making video/audio transcripts, detecting events in large datasets, or recognizing images.

Some of the functions of newsrooms have benefited more than others from the use of AI in recent years. The functions are explained using some illustrative examples.

2.1. *News gathering*

Sourcing news, or news gathering, is one of the most resource-intensive activities for traditional media houses. It is also one of the most important first steps in the production cycle of news. In a typical newsroom workflow, journalists get first-hand information or investigative leads from sources such as people in the know, credible organizations or institutes, congregations of experts such as seminars or conferences, and official reports and assessments. However, with resource-limited newsrooms cutting down on "leg work" and resorting to what is sometimes disparagingly referred to as "armchair journalism," the competition for exclusivity and accuracy of sources has peaked. This has necessitated the use of digital information and verification tools that journalists can safely and quickly use.

AI has made this process of "sniffing out news" easier with umpteen tools that can crawl the web to find specific information, analyze big data in seconds to point to newsworthy incidents, or uncover documents hidden in the deep web. It is possible, even for small newsrooms, to unearth untapped sources of news with relative ease.

Take for example Michigan Radio's tool "Minutes," which uses an innovative newsgathering application to make sure journalists can access autogenerated transcripts of city council meeting videos posted on video sharing services [7]. This allows the radio's reporters to quickly access the proceedings of meetings they cannot physically attend. The application not only automates transcription but also generates summaries of meetings and notifies journalists based on the occurrence of keywords of their interest.

The *Financial Times* (FT), UK, uses an algorithm that helps predict trending topics in news by tracking user preferences. The algorithm collects data on parameters reflecting how people interact with FT's content on the web. These data are sorted by topic through unsupervised machine learning approaches, plotted on a graph, and then processed to reduce bias in predicting how each data point will change over time. The patterns generated are interpreted by journalists to understand audience interest trends. FT tested this model successfully with developing news stories – such as COVID-19 and the Black Lives Matter movement – and directing editorial focus toward the trends [8].

In China, the news aggregator Toutiao has no staff writers on its rolls. It simply uses AI that can recommend relevant content and discard fake news or content not appropriate for its audience [9]. Many newsrooms use similar tools, such as Heliograf, News Tracer, or CrowdTangle, to keep abreast of breaking or trending news.

2.2. *News production*

The production of news involves many steps. From receiving the primary journalistic inputs, such as unedited text, audio, or video, to its final publication, production is a treatment-heavy, creative process. Most news content undergoes pruning, cleaning up, rewriting, structuring, styling, supplementing, or visualizing. Sometimes, summaries, analyses, and transcripts are made, for example, for stock market or sports commentaries or videos and podcasts. On most occasions, these steps need to be executed quickly to meet the daily deadlines of a news cycle without compromising on accuracy, clarity, or brevity. In essence, the process is rigorous and limited by time.

Newsrooms constantly strive to achieve the golden balance between efficiency, accuracy, and timeliness in this largely manual production process. AI tools are increasingly being experimented with to achieve this balance and make the production processes more agile and free of biases. Crime writing, for instance, has historically been thought to be time-consuming and susceptible to a journalist's internal biases. In April 2022, the *Toronto Star* started publishing autogenerated crime news [10] that scraped the Toronto Police Service's public crime records. The generated content followed a set format and left out any personal information. The newspaper very carefully tracked the content produced, made it clear that it was AI-generated, watched out for any trends in crime occurrences, and eliminated the scope for biases in reporting the occurrences.

Similarly, during Puerto Rico's hurricane season in 2023, the El Vocero de Puerto Rico newspaper created an AI-based weather bot system [11] that operated in real time to automatically pick weather updates from the National Hurricane Centre (NHC) and parse information relevant for generating hurricane news updates. This automated an otherwise manual process, where the reporter would have to continually refresh the NHC website to check for updates. The stories were originally written in English and were auto translated to Spanish by DeepL, an AI translation service. Before publication, each story was reviewed by a human. The team is now trying to create an open-source application that all newsrooms can use.

AI tools are also being used to add data visualizations to stories, adding an interactive element to text-based articles. Reuters has partnered with Graphiq, a semantic technology company, to provide their news agency customers access to data-driven interactive visualizations on a broad range of topics including financial news, sports, and entertainment, with data updating in real-time, which can be added to news stories [12].

2.3. *Fact-checking*

Though fact-checking has traditionally been part of the sub-editor's or editor's remit in the news production process, modern newsrooms have dedicated fact-checkers to vet the veracity of the news before it is published. The proliferation of fake news, misinformation, and disinformation has also made it an important part of the production of news. Fact-checkers and editors also form part of the human–machine handshake that is deemed mandatory for any autogenerated content to be published.

For example, in 2019, the UK-based fact-checking organization Full Fact collaboratively developed a software that automatically scans all forms of online content, largely related to claims made by politicians and public institutions. It extracts sentences, classifies, annotates, and filters them based on relevant criteria, and then matches them with previously fact-checked data to pinpoint any inconsistencies or false claims. This analysis is then made public, along with a report of the process used to verify the claims. This is the kind of fact-checking model that almost all news organizations now use, with some technical differences in the algorithms or statistics generated.

Fact-checking images, on the other hand, has been traditionally limited to using reverse image checks using search engines such as Google. Nowadays, AI tools are being used to detect deepfakes and other image-based AI-generated mis/disinformation. Free tools such as TensorFlow and PyTorch can deal with nearly all kinds of visual media to compare a real image/video with a suspected fake one and point out discrepancies. Image-based fact-checking tools such as Deepware focus primarily on spotting manipulations in human facial expressions. Some tools, such as Illuminarity, in addition to deepfake detection, can also identify which AI models were likely used to generate the deepfake. While all these tools have their margins of error, they offer promise for fact-checkers wanting to churn out quick rebuttals to fake images that spread like wildfire, stoked by social media.

Such misleading content generated by machine learning tools could have drastic implications, sometimes at a national level. In January 2020, the face-swapping app Zao met with massive public disapproval in China, leading the government to criminalize the use of AI to create misleading content [13]. Deepfakes or fake videos have also been a cause for concern, especially for celebrities and public personalities. Reuters and AFP are now using AI tools that their journalists can oversee to detect such fake videos and fake news.

2.4. *Content distribution and audience engagement*

Once news is published, disseminating it effectively for wide audiences is the next step. AI tools have revolutionized this aspect of media operations, generally portrayed in the public imagination by a hawker throwing a newspaper into one's house. With the massive increase in digital consumption of news, its distribution has seen a sea change.

AI tools have made it easier for media houses to distribute their wares and quicker for people to consume news. For instance, in 2023, Agência Pública, a Brazilian investigative journalism agency, added an AI reader [14] to their website that reads out up to 20-minute-long reviews of important developing stories each week. The audio is designed to sound human-like and is edited by a journalist before publication.

Media organizations employ several methods to understand the pulse of their audiences and tailor content according to what they want. Many organizations have fully or heavily automated this process of connecting with consumers.

In 2017, *The Washington Post* launched ModBot to automatically read users' comments on its website to determine if they meet quality standards or should be moderated. *The New York Times* also uses a machine-learning-based classifier to moderate comments on its site. The tool flags user generated content as "toxic," and an algorithm learns to classify future comments. Similarly, in 2021, a popular Finnish newspaper, *Helsingin Sanomat*, saw a spike in subscriptions when it employed an AI-based customer analysis tool [15] to track each customer's activity on their website, based on which they created customized user experiences.

AI based contextual analytics tools, which generate insights on content distribution on channels such as Google Discover, allow publications to understand their audience demographics and reach. Likewise, tools for automated content posting on social media channels and automated metatags reduce manual input, enabling faster engagement with audiences. Personalized recommendations of content based on browsing history are also increasingly being used to improve user satisfaction and retention. Some newsrooms use scripted social bots to automate the sharing of news stories [16]. Audiences and readers can also "speak" with conversational bots such as Politibot, which provides political news in Spanish [17]. There are bots to answer your queries about a specific news event with relevant content, such as the one deployed by the American news website Quartz. Readers can specify when they want to receive news briefings on topics of their interest with a Facebook Messenger chatbot, like the one *The Guardian* uses.

2.5. *Research and innovation*

New-age newsrooms are constantly experimenting with technology to figure out what works best for their content, serves their audiences better, or increases revenue. To keep pace with the market and be ahead of the competition in achieving any of these goals, visionary media companies are known to invest in technological experiments to create bespoke tools and programs that best serve their editorial content or businesses.

The Singapore Press Holding, for instance, has established an AI lab to integrate data-driven techniques into news collection, editing, and delivery. The team constantly innovates to personalize experiences for readers and consumers of its products. *The Washington Post*'s computational political journalism lab created reporting tools during the 2020 U.S. elections to bring its readers powerful data-driven storytelling and automated analysis.

The New York Times' research and development division used computer vision (a computer's ability to derive meaning from images) during sporting events of the 2020 Summer Olympics to measure athlete movements. They synchronized their photographers' cameras, machine learning, and computer vision to capture this live data that helped report parameters such as gymnasts' peak height, rotation, or speed. Two years before that, the newspaper's data science team also ran "Project Feels," which aimed to understand and predict the emotional impact of its articles via prediction algorithms with large amounts of crowdsourced readers' data.

Forbes Magazine, on the other hand, continuously innovates its core content management system using an AI tool called Bertie, named after the magazine's founder, Bertie Charles Forbes. Bertie provides their writers with a "bionic suit" capable of pulling up real-time trending topics to cover, recommending compelling headlines, and suggesting images relevant to the content.

The BBC News Lab also experiments with visualization on its Instagram account. Its innovators wanted to create something bespoke for younger audiences without burdening their social media managers with additional work. In 2020, they successfully created an in-house automation tool that could spin a comic animation graphical story from the text of a COVID-19 story.

3. Recent Trends in the Use of AI in News Media

In 2019, before the LLM boom, a London School of Economics-based think-tank POLIS and Google News Initiative conducted a survey [18] on the use of AI tools in 71 news organizations across 32 countries. They found that the use of AI-based tools had permeated every stage of news-gathering, news production, and news distribution. The general view in newsrooms was that AI assisted journalists in ways that made their work more efficient and data processing faster. Most newsrooms were using tools that helped automate processes such as translation, transcription, image recognition, filtering user-generated content, pattern recognition, content accessibility, generating templates or texts for articles, and summarizing large datasets. They also came in handy for curating and personalizing news, marketing content recommendations, fact-checking, and detecting fake news. This survey report and its successive annual iterations, which emphasize that AI is here to stay in newsrooms, serve as repositories of case studies and diverse views on the trends of AI use in global news media.

The researchers found that the factors influencing the use of AI in these processes were multi-pronged – they were not only financial and technological but also cultural and social. They recommended creating separate experienced and trained teams that focus on experimenting with the use of AI tools in newsrooms, especially in testing these tools for large data processing and pattern recognition.

As is common with any emerging technology, excitement comes with apprehension. A prevalent observation was that with the widespread use of AI, people working in newsrooms will need to be trained to adopt AI-based strategies or skilled people will need to be hired to drive AI-based journalism. This concern led to the apprehension that AI might result in journalists losing their jobs or that newsrooms might overhaul traditional workflows. Nothing so drastic has played out in the subsequent years, indicating that these apprehensions were, in part, indicative of the greater need for AI literacy in newsrooms.

In 2023, the Reuters Institute for the Study of Journalism dedicated a part of its wider study of newsrooms to the impact of using AI [19] on the production and consumption of digital media in six continents and 46 markets. The study considered the disparate conditions governing journalism in different parts of the world but still facing the common challenges of weak audience engagement and low trust in journalism.

This study reveals a prevailing skepticism among the public regarding algorithms deciding content presentation on search engines, social media, and other platforms. Specifically, less than one-third (30%) of respondents regarded the curation of news stories based on prior news consumption as a favorable method. This marks a decline of six percentage points from a comparable survey conducted in 2016. Despite this skepticism, users, on average, exhibited a slight preference for news selected through algorithmic means (30%), as opposed to editorial or journalist-driven curation (27%). This suggests that concerns regarding algorithms are embedded within the broader question of news curation mechanisms.

The study also identifies a decline in trust in news, reversing the gains observed during the peak of the COVID-19 pandemic in many countries. On average, 40% of the total sample expressed trust in news most of the time. The highest trust levels were recorded in Finland (69%), while Greece exhibited the lowest trust levels (19%), particularly following a year marked by contentious debates on press freedom and media independence.

Collectively, these findings point to the growing reliance of the public on social media and other traditionally non-news platforms. Alongside this, discontent prevails regarding the role of algorithms in driving news content, the veracity of such content (or misinformation), and the quality of associated debates (or participation). Platforms such as Instagram and TikTok, geared toward younger demographics with a focus on visual content, pose challenges for publishers, necessitating investments with uncertain returns in terms of traffic or revenue. The integration of AI and automation, however, holds promise for assisting publishers in navigating these platforms and cultivating deeper connections with audiences.

Against the backdrop of escalating production costs, diminishing revenues, waning public trust in journalism, and unpredictable traffic from established social networks, media entities confront mounting challenges in persuading audiences to subscribe to their content. These challenges are exacerbated by economic and political uncertainties, audience fragmentation, and disruptions from emerging platforms. The report anticipates substantial shifts in audience behavior driven by younger demographics, reflecting a preference for more accessible, informal, and entertaining news formats often delivered by influencers rather than traditional journalists on platforms such as YouTube, Instagram, and TikTok.

Consumers prefer not a greater quantity of news but rather news that may be relevant to them and might help them understand complex issues. The report posits that AI disruptions may create personalized yet potentially unreliable content. The responsibility of journalism lies in distinguishing itself from such content through accuracy, utility, and a humane approach. Interestingly, while audiences were ambivalent toward algorithms, they remained unconvinced that journalists and news organizations can surpass algorithmic capabilities in curating or summarizing important developments. The challenge, therefore, resides in reinstating relevance and trust by catering to the specific needs of audiences. Future relationships with communities will entail not only directing individuals to websites and apps crucial for business models but also outreach through alternative platforms and channels disseminating trusted information, the analysis suggests.

In another 2023 trend-spotting report, the Reuters Institute for the Study of Journalism surveyed 135 senior industry leaders from 40 countries and conducted 10 in-depth interviews across the print, digital, and broadcast media [6]. While most people thought that although gen AI will make news workflows easier and increase productivity, some thought it won't bring about any transformative change in the newsrooms. "When a greater proportion of stories are written by AI, news, analysis and on-the-ground reporting from humans will become more of a premium product," an editor working for a British legacy news organization was quoted as saying.

The report went on to caution, through a senior German publisher's observation, that gen AI will potentially impact workflows and back-office jobs in a big way but not in generating content. As discussed, almost three-quarters of those surveyed thought that gen AI will help newsrooms increase productivity and improve workflows without changing the essence of journalism. Just 21% said that gen AI will transform workflows and processes, fundamentally changing every role in the newsroom. Interestingly, 29% of news leaders reported that their organizations already have in place high-level principles to guide their AI plans, while 39% were working on developing such plans. Only 9% of leaders reported having training programs for staff already in place.

With the debate around the ethical and regulatory boundaries of AI-generated content surging in newsrooms across the world, the international non-profit Reporters Without Borders created the Paris Charter on AI in Journalism to ensure AI's ethical and responsible use [20]. The charter focuses on upholding journalistic ethics, preserving human decision-making in editorial processes, helping people distinguish between authentic and synthetic content, and actively participating in global AI governance. Newsrooms must prioritize originality, accuracy, and diverse opinions while using AI, the charter recommends. It also advocates for user choice in receiving AI-generated recommendations.

4. Challenges and the Way Forward

In July 2023, technology giant Google gave a sneak peek of a new AI tool called "Genesis" [21] to executives of three top US-based news publications – *The New York Times*, *The Washington Post*, and News Corp, owner of *The Wall Street Journal*. The tool is said to have the capability to process real-time events and data to create news articles. Google is pegging Genesis as a helpful and responsible personal assistant for journalists to automate tasks, allowing them to focus on other aspects of their work. Some executives expressed concerns about the implications of this AI tool, emphasizing the importance of human effort in creating accurate and compelling news stories and raising worries about how Genesis could impact journalistic integrity, *The New York Times* reported.

This is just an example of the caution that newsrooms are still exercising in fully embracing AI. Despite the offer of speed, scale, efficiency, and cost-effectiveness, the use of gen AI is fraught with several concerns. A global survey [22] of newsrooms in 2023 underscored that AI is not merely a futuristic prospect but is already effecting noteworthy changes within journalism. The survey also established the need for dedicated structures to explore gen AI, formulate industry-wide guidelines, and cautiously experiment with its integration into newsrooms.

Gen AI tools are known to "hallucinate," or spout nonsensical/inaccurate information based on the interpretation of the data they learn from [23]. Gen AI has the potential to generate realistic yet misleading content, such as deepfakes or automated, undetectable disinformation. Such misleading information gets prominently disseminated on social media platforms. Fed on limited data, gen AI also exacerbates issues of discrimination and bias and could amplify extreme speech or widen social inequalities.

Specific challenges come in the way of small or medium newsrooms in many Muslim countries while trying to adopt AI. A study in Pakistan [24], where many resource-starved media organizations are struggling to keep afloat, reports that journalists in the country's Urdu- and English-language dailies feel threatened and, therefore, resist the use of AI. They also feel that a lack of funding and poor AI and digital literacy among journalists, coupled with a wide digital divide, will not allow any significant automation in the country's newsrooms. A conversation with members of the Arab Reporters for Investigative Journalism (ARIJ) corroborated the limited use of AI in small and medium newsrooms in the Arab world due to the same reasons. They mentioned that poor data availability for machine learning in Arabic and non-customization for the cultures and backgrounds of Arab newsrooms were reasons for the poor uptake of AI. There are no active conversations in most Arab newsrooms about the implications and ethics of AI, especially since the Arab world is more conservative than other societies, according to ARIJ. One interviewee said AI is a "puzzle that lacks a lot of pieces" for Arab journalists. Most gen AI tools, lacking large training datasets either in the Arabic language or about the Arab world, display an inherent bias against these societies. For instance, querying Midjourney, Canva, or DALL-E for an image of an Emirati woman wearing an abaya generated a stereotypical image of a woman in black burqa or niqab, while in reality abaya fashion has undergone significant change, with women wearing colorful ones with designs. Therefore, ARIJ prefers to stay away from people's images and picks more general ones, such as buildings or cities, while using gen AI tools. To detect such biases in LLMs, reporters from ARIJ are collaborating with a team from the Australian Broadcasting Corporation (ABC) and Deutsche Welle (DW) to create a tool called BiasBlocker, an AI plugin that can identify and annotate bias in English and Arabic text. The Doha-based Al-Jazeera news network is also using AI, machine learning, and NLP to automate the process of identifying fake news, a major problem in Arab countries.

The AI "black box" [25], which refers to the unknown internal mechanism of such tools that developers often don't make public to protect their intellectual property, has also been flagged by industry insiders as a matter of concern.

With increased use, the reliability of AI tools has also come into question, alongside the ethical concerns related to their extensive data utilization for algorithmic training. The massive amounts of data on which open-source gen AI tools are trained pose a problem of privacy, fairness, and safety. Since early 2023, many organizations, such as The New York Times Company, Axel Springer, and Getty Images, have filed lawsuits against AI companies, including OpenAI, Microsoft, and Midjourney, for alleged copyright infringement and illegally training their LLMs on copyrighted content [26].

In the 2023 LSE-POLIS survey of newsrooms, the central question raised by journalists was how they might be able to integrate AI technologies while upholding the journalistic values of accuracy, fairness, accountability, and transparency. Media houses operate on readers' trust. The survey heard from newsrooms that readers' perceptions of AI-generated content may not be optimal, and therefore journalists and editors were skeptical of sweeping automation in the way they work, especially at a time when public trust in the media is not very high.

As an increasing number of gen AI tools invade the market and newsrooms find ways to integrate them into their processes, publishers are coming up with guidelines governing the use of AI. An analysis [27] of 52 such guidelines from publishers in Belgium, Brazil, Canada, Finland, Germany, India, the Netherlands, Norway, Sweden, Switzerland, the United Kingdom, and the United States reveals that the emphasis is on transparency and human supervision of AI-generated content. However, there are blind spots around technological dependency, sustainable AI, and inequalities in current AI guidelines, as the analysis points out.

Another key obstacle hindering AI development in news media is the intense competition for talent. It is difficult to attract technologically skilled individuals and to retain them, as newsrooms often provide lower salaries compared to the technology industry. The resulting brain drain impedes the integration of technologies in the news sector.

Despite some isolated efforts to create in-house innovation labs for AI experiments, the business models of most traditional and new-age media houses leave little room for diverting finances to either create such tools or buy them off the shelf. This challenge is even more pronounced for small newsrooms in the global south [24,28], which operate on tiny budgets and limited human resources and are not well poised to embrace technological changes. Most such newsrooms, therefore, are either not yet experimenting with the latest trends or making do with free-to-use and open-source tools to improve efficiency in their processes.

The most common fear among journalists, similar to other professionals facing a sudden spurt in automation in their industry, is that these tools may potentially replace humans. Journalists have had to make use of technologies forever. Nicholas Diakopoulos argues in his book, *Automating the News: How Algorithms are Rewriting the Media*, that given the intrinsically human nature of journalism, despite the numerous tasks amenable to augmentation by machines, this creative pursuit will continue to be led by humans [29]. Contrary to concerns about job displacement in journalism, he asserts that AI is, in fact, generating new employment and skilling opportunities.

A human–machine handshake is the way forward for newsrooms. Human-supervised automation and tools, which account for a human in the loop, will survive and find takers, as most media AI guidelines bear out [26]. After all, journalism, at its core, is not just about curating information or presenting it. The very essence of journalism lies in transforming this information to cater to human needs and sensitivities. That needs sentience, something that AI is yet to achieve.

References

[1] Sharath Kumar RK, Hosurmath M. Text summarization and visualization using IBM Watson Studio - IBM Developer. [cited 2024 Jan 3]. Available from: https://developer.ibm.com/patterns/text-summarization-topic-modelling-using-watson-studio-watson-nlu/.

[2] van Dalen A. The algorithms behind the headlines. *Journal Pract*. 2012 Oct 1 [cited 2024 Jan 3];6(5–6):648–58. Available from: https://doi.org/10.1080/17512786.2012.667268.

[3] ICIJ. A new ICIJ investigation exposes a rogue offshore industry. *ICIJ*. 2016 [cited 2024 Jan 3]. Available from: https://www.icij.org/investigations/panama-papers/new-icij-investigation-exposes-rogue-offshore-industry/.

[4] *Xinhua*. World's first AI news anchor makes "his" China debut. English.news.cn. [cited 2024 Jan 3]. Available from: http://www.xinhuanet.com/english/2018-11/08/c_137591813.htm.

[5] Kaur D. AI news anchors are on the rise. [cited 2024 Jan 3]. *Tech Wire Asia*. Available from: https://techwireasia.com/07/2023/ai-news-anchors-and-which-countries-has-them/.

[6] Cherubini F, Sharma R. Changing newsrooms 2023: Media leaders struggle to embrace diversity in full and remain cautious on AI disruption. Reuters Institute for the Study of Journalism; 2023 [cited 2024 Jan 3]. Available from: https://reutersinstitute.politics.ox.ac.uk/changing-newsrooms-2023.

[7] Dwyer D. Michigan Radio. 2021 [cited 2024 Jan 3]. Introducing Minutes, a new tool to keep track of local government in Michigan. Available from: https://www.michiganradio.org/station-news/2021-03-03/introducing-minutes-a-new-tool-to-keep-track-of-local-government-in-michigan.

[8] Gajtkowski A. Predicting FT trending topics. Identifying signals using time-series. FT Product & Technology. Medium. [cited 2024 Jan 3]. Available from: https://medium.com/ft-product-technology/predicting-ft-trending-topics-7eda85ece727.

[9] Zhang SI. The business model of journalism start-ups in China. *Digit Journal*. 2019 May 28 [cited 2024 Jan 3];7(5):614–34. Available from: https://doi.org/10.1080/21670811.2018.1496025.

[10] *Toronto Star*. Where old Toronto home break-ins were reported this week. [cited 2024 Jan 3]. Available from: https://www.thestar.com/news/gta/local-crime/where-old-toronto-home-break-ins-were-reported-this-week/article_c5be4f57-10d7-583d-9d9d-6d6e030a794b.html.

[11] *Associated Press*. AP case study, Newsroom: El Vocero de Puerto Rico. [cited 2024 Jan 3]. Available from: https://www.ap.org/wp-content/uploads/2024/02/ap-local-ai-el-vocero-oct-2023.pdf.

[12] Thomson Reuters. Reuters and Graphiq deliver interactive data visualizations to publishers. [cited 2024 Jan 3]. Available from: https://www.thomsonreuters.com/en/press-releases/2016/august/reuters-graphiq-interactive-data-visualizations.html.

[13] Reuters. China seeks to root out fake news and deepfakes with new online content rules. Reuters. [cited 2024 Jan 3]. Available from: https://www.reuters.com/article/us-china-technology/china-seeks-to-root-out-fake-news-and-deepfakes-with-new-online-content-rules-idUSKBN1Y30VU/.

[14] Agência Pública. Agência Pública lança leitura de reportagens por Inteligência Artificial. [cited 2024 Jan 3]. Available from: https://apublica.org/2023/10/agencia-publica-lanca-leitura-de-reportagens-por-inteligencia-artificial/.

[15] Google News Initiative. Case study: Google news initiative. Sanoma: Serving Subscriptions with the Help of Technology. [cited 2024 Jan 3].

Available from: https://newsinitiative.withgoogle.com/info/assets/static/docs/cs_gni_sanoma.pdf.

[16] Lokot T, Diakopoulos N. News bots. *Digit Journal*. 2016 Aug 17 [cited 2024 Jan 3];4(6):682–99. Available from: https://doi.org/10.1080/21670811.2015.1081822.

[17] Sánchez-González H, Sánchez-González M. Conversational bots used in political news from the point of view of the user's experience: *Politibot. Commun Soc*. 2020 [cited 2024 Jan 3]; Available from: https://repositorio.consejodecomunicacion.gob.ec//handle/CONSEJO_REP/2465.

[18] Beckett C. New powers, new responsibilities. A global survey of journalism and artificial intelligence. *Polis*. [cited 2024 Jan 3]. Available from: https://blogs.lse.ac.uk/polis/2019/11/18/new-powers-new-responsibilities/.

[19] Newman N. Overview and key findings of the 2023 digital news report. Reuters Institute for the Study of Journalism. [cited 2024 Jan 3]. Available from: https://reutersinstitute.politics.ox.ac.uk/digital-news-report/2023/dnr-executive-summary.

[20] Reporters Without Borders. RSF and 16 partners unveil Paris Charter on AI and Journalism. RSF. 2023 [cited 2024 Jan 3]. Available from: https://rsf.org/en/rsf-and-16-partners-unveil-paris-charter-ai-and-journalism.

[21] Mehra P. Google testing Genesis AI for journalists: A brief history of tech in the newsroom. [cited 2024 Jan 3]. Available from: https://www.techcircle.in/2023/07/25/google-testing-genesis-ai-for-journalists-a-brief-history-of-tech-in-the-newsroom.

[22] Beckett C and Yaseen M. Generating Change: A global survey of what news organisations are doing with AI. JournalismAI; 2023 [cited 2024 Jan 3]. Available from: https://www.journalismai.info/research/2023-generating-change.

[23] IBM. What are AI hallucinations? [cited 2024 Jan 3]. Available from: https://www.ibm.com/topics/ai-hallucinations.

[24] Jamil S. Artificial intelligence and journalistic practice: The crossroads of obstacles and opportunities for the Pakistani journalists. *Journal Pract*. 2020 Jul [cited 2024 Jan 3];15(10):1400–1422. Available from: https://doi.org/10.1080/17512786.2020.1788412.

[25] Bagchi S. *The Conversation* (repr. *Scientific American*). [cited 2024 Jan 3]. Why we need to see inside AI's black box. Available from: https://www.scientificamerican.com/article/why-we-need-to-see-inside-ais-black-box/.

[26] Panettieri J. Sustainable Tech Partner. 2023 [cited 2024 Jan 3]. Generative AI lawsuits timeline: Legal cases vs. OpenAI, Microsoft and more. Available from: https://sustainabletechpartner.com/topics/ai/generative-ai-lawsuit-timeline/.

[27] Becker KB, Simon FM, Crum C. Policies in parallel? A comparative study of journalistic AI policies in 52 Global News Organisations. *SocArXiv*; 2023 Sep [cited 2024 Jan 3]. Available from: https://osf.io/c4af9.

[28] Kothari A, Cruikshank SA. Artificial intelligence and journalism: An agenda for journalism research in Africa. *Afr Journal Stud.* 2022 Dec [cited 2024 Jan 3];43(1):17–33. Available from: https://doi.org/10.1080/23743670.2021.1999840.

[29] Diakopoulos N. *Automating the News: How Algorithms are Rewriting the Media.* Harvard University Press, Cambridge, MA, USA; 2019 [cited 2024 Jan 3]. Available from: https://www.jstor.org/stable/j.ctv24w634d.

Part II

Science and Technology

https://doi.org/10.1142/9781800616295_0005

Chapter 5

Fossil Fuel Decarbonization and Plastics-Waste Conversion to Hydrogen and High-Value Carbons: Pure Science Behind Two Emerging Disruptive Technologies*

Peter P. Edwards[†,§], Tiancun Xiao[†], Hamid A. Almegren[‡], Benzhen Yao[†], Michael Jie[ǁ], Daniel R. Slocombe[**], and Jon R. Dilworth[†]

[†]*University of Oxford and OXCCU, Begbroke Science Park, UK*

[‡]*King Abdulaziz City for Science and Technology, Riyadh, Kingdom of Saudi Arabia*

[ǁ]*Queen Mary University, London, UK*

[**]*Cardiff University, Cardiff, UK*

[§]*peter.edwards@chem.ox.ac.uk*

Abstract

Fossil fuels are renewable only over geological time scales. Their oxidation, via aerial combustion, in considerable amounts since the dawn of the industrial revolution has led to an accumulation of CO_2 in the

*Dedicated to the memory of Sir John Meurig Thomas, FLSW FRS.

atmosphere with an anthropogenic influence on the Earth's climate. We highlight here our innovations in the catalytic conversion or recycling of CO_2 captured from the air together with green or biogenic hydrogen to produce Sustainable Aviation Fuel (SAF). Releasing CO_2 back to the atmosphere following the combustion of SAFs recreates the natural carbon cycle and promises a net-zero future for aviation. We also highlight fossil fuels as potent, natural sources of sustainable hydrogen; so also, plastics-waste, now seen as an equally attractive anthropogenic source of clean hydrogen. This chapter reviews our advances in the microwave-initiated catalytic pyrolysis or "hydrogen-stripping" from fossil fuels and plastics-waste. This innovation is a rapid and highly-effective route to clean hydrogen and high-value solid carbon nanomaterials, in many cases accompanied by low- to zero-CO_2 emissions. Underpinning these advances are the remarkable physicochemical properties of mesoscale catalyst particles close to the Size-Induced Metal-Insulator Transition.

1. Preamble: Developing the KOPRC Ethos

The King Abdulaziz City of Science and Technology & Oxford Petrochemical Research Centre (KOPRC), the first of its type across the Arab world, was established in the Inorganic Chemistry Laboratory, Oxford University, in 2010 through generous funding from the Kingdom of Saudi Arabia. In 2015, KOPRC was designated a Centre of Excellence in Petrochemicals by the Kingdom. KOPRC has helped provide the scientific breakthroughs necessary to transition the world away from a linear carbon energy model to a truly circular carbon energy economy, where CO_2 emissions are captured and catalytically – converted using green hydrogen to carbon-neutral synthetic fuels. KOPRC also advanced an exciting vision for hydrogen-stripping from natural fossil hydrocarbons (e.g., methane) and plastic waste, identifying the latter as a valuable anthropogenic feedstock or resource to produce clean hydrogen and high-value nanocarbon materials using microwave catalysis – an entirely new field. Equally important, a total of 13 students – not only from Saudi Arabia but also from China, Malaysia, Pakistan, and India – were awarded higher degrees at Oxford University through the KOPRC initiative.

The three co-founders of KOPRC, Peter Edwards, Tiancun Xiao, and Hamid Almegren, were privileged to meet and collaborate with the Doyen of Global Warming Science, Sir John Houghton CBE FRS, who chaired or co-chaired the Scientific Assessments for the Intergovernmental Panel on Climate Change (IPCC) from its inception in 1988 until 2012. During that period, the IPCC reports were widely recognized as the most authoritative and comprehensive assessment of this complex but critically important scientific subject.

In 2009 in particular Peter Edwards, Tiancun Xiao, and Sir John together considered what contributions could – and should – physical scientists in KOPRC make to help find tangible solutions to global warming. Sir John gave Peter Edwards a copy of his classic book *Global Warming: The Complete Briefing* (Fig. 1) and highlighted his own thoughts on page 399 on that very subject: "None of us can argue that there is nothing we can usefully do [to counter global warming]". He further noted, "Edmund Burke, a British parliamentarian of 200 years ago, wisely proclaimed: '*No one made a greater mistake than he who did nothing because he could do so little.*'"

Hence, the founding vision and principle for KOPRC – "Pure Science, Applied to Issues of Global Warming" – was agreed upon in 2010 in discussions between the three co-founders, with the strongest support and encouragement from Prince Dr. Turki bin Saud bin Mohammed Al Saud, advisor at the Saudi Royal Court; Dr. Mohammed Ibrahim Al-Suwaiyei, (then) President of King Abdulaziz City for Science and Technology

Figure 1. The front page of the book presented to Peter Edwards in 2009 by Sir John Houghton CBE FRS.

(KACST); the late Dr. Jamie Ferguson of Oxford University Innovation; Professor Peter J. Dobson of the Begbroke Science Park, UK, and the (then) Oxford University Vice Chancellor Professor Andrew Hamilton FRS. Developing that mantra "Pure Science, Applied" was helped enormously by the fact Edwards, through his earlier research and collaboration [1,2] with Sir Nevill Mott CH FRS, had been constantly exposed to the view of the critical need for pure, underpinning fundamental science in order to advance technology.

A keen insight into Sir Nevill Mott's vision of the impact of pure science on technology can be seen in his observations [3] on the development of the modern solid-state electronics industry (Fig. 2):

> *The impact of solid-state electronics on our society has been enormous. It has given rise to whole new industries, new professions, new ways of production and new organizations. Moreover, unlike many industrial innovations, it depends to an exceptional extent on developments in pure, abstract science.*

We all, wholeheartedly, embraced the ethos that these generalizations are as true in the field of energy science and technology (i.e., fuel and power) as they have been in the development of modern semiconductor technology. Thus, the most disruptive technologies can surely *only* emerge from an understanding of, and developments in, pure science, some of

Figure 2. Professor Sir Nevill Mott CH FRS [3].

which may appear abstract. Areas of pure science in this chapter – some surely appearing abstract at first sight to a general readership – include, for example, the thermodynamics underpinning the synthesis of non-fossil, carbon-neutral hydrocarbon fuels made from *only* CO_2 and H_2; the quantum chemistry of bonding in, and catalytic activation of, the molecule CO_2; and the solid-state physics of the quantum-size phase transition from metal-to-insulator in an individual catalyst particle driven *solely* by the physical size of a particle.

We also gained inspiration for our research from the efforts of two Muslim scientific geniuses – Jabir ibn Hayyaan (known to the West under the name Geber, which is the medieval rendering of the Arabic Jabir) and Abu Bakr Muhammad ibn Zakariyya al-Razi (known to the West as Rhazi or Rhazes) – both "Makers of Chemistry" in the classical sense (Fig. 3) [4]. Jabir clearly recognized and enunciated the importance of experiments more than any other early chemist, *worldwide*, at that time, making noteworthy advances in both the theory and the practice of chemistry.

In relation to the magnitude of their scientific contributions, we need only quote from the classic text *Makers of Chemistry* by Eric John Holmyard [4] in his insightful statement: "By the efforts of Jabir and Razi, much of the vast accretion of unbridled speculation was cleared away, and chemistry began to take shape as a true science." From these two scientific geniuses, experimental fact was at last informed and understood through the beginnings and applications of reasonable theories – a completely new innovation in chemistry in that period.

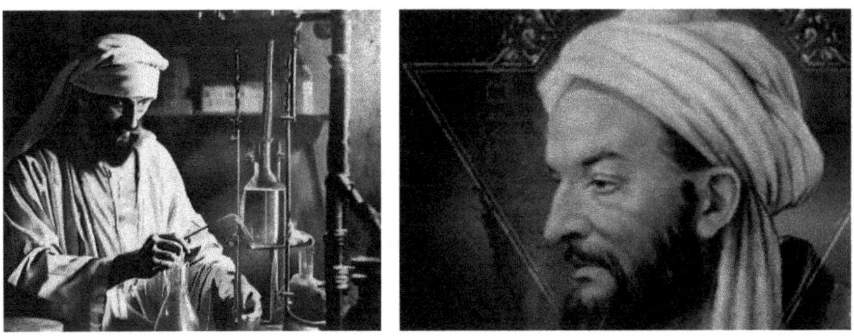

Figure 3. Left: Jabir ibn Hayyaan (known to the West as Geber, or Jabir). Right: Abu Bakr Muhammad ibn Zakariyya al-Razi (known to the West as Rhazes or Razi).

Source: Public domain.

In this overview, therefore, we concentrate on setting out some of the fundamental scientific principles and experimental studies that enabled the various KOPRC advances over the past decade or so. Readers will note that we only deal lightly with specifics of the emerging technological applications (except to highlight their potential universal applicability), knowing that a sound knowledge of the pure, underpinning science is surely the best possible preparation for any advance in disruptive energy technologies. As will also be evident, many such applications derived from these KOPRC advances are only in the early stages of technological development. We hope that this essay will highlight the great potential of this ethos, particularly in the new, emerging field of fossil fuel decarbonization for mitigating global warming.

2. Introduction

It is salutary to remind ourselves that despite decades of discussions and actions on climate change, global CO_2 emissions have marched inexorably upward, with emissions from burning fossil fuels climbing by some 1%, even in 2023. Notwithstanding the impressive growth and deployment of "renewables" (e.g., solar photovoltaics and wind power) over the past few decades, natural fossil hydrocarbons as fuels for power production continue to dominate the world's energy supply.

Just as the COP28 climate meeting agreed to transition away from fossil fuels, our global fossil fuel consumption is set to break records, with oil and gas production booming in many countries. Our present CO_2 emissions from burning fossil fuels have now reached a new record, highlighting how the goals of the Paris agreement to limit global warming are increasingly in jeopardy. The latest findings also project that the annual demand for fossil fuels, including natural gas, will keep rising until at least the end of the decade – most probably much longer. Thus, there appears little firm evidence to suggest that a global fossil fuel phase-out is on the immediate or intermediate horizon and, with it, any major reductions in CO_2 emissions. Moreover, these continuing trends surely speak volumes about the world's enduring and continuing appetite for fossil fuels. To understand this, one must remind ourselves that over the past century or so, humankind's progress has resulted in billions, worldwide, being lifted out of poverty. Much of that remarkable advancement must be traced back to the attraction, availability, and widespread utilization of fossil hydrocarbon fuels as the bedrock source of our global energy system.

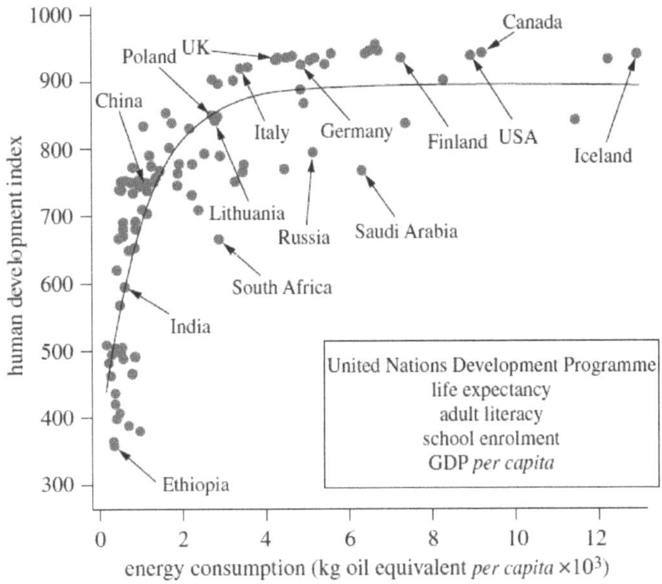

Figure 4. The human development index (HDI) plotted against the per capita energy consumption for 103 of the world's most populous nations.

Source: Used with permission of Elsevier Science & Technology Journals, from Kolasinki (2006) [5]; permission conveyed through Copyright Clearance Center, Inc.

In Fig. 4, we plot the UN Human Development Index (HDI) against the per-capita energy consumption of various countries, with energy expressed in units of kilogram equivalents of oil [5]. This UN HDI is a universally recognized measure of the "quality of life" in countries. It is abundantly clear that a universal curve is followed, with a higher standard of living found in countries that have a greater consumption of fossil fuels. The ready-access and increasing supply of energy for our complex way of life underpins the world's economic system and its growth. The fundamental challenge for all renewable energy sources, therefore, is to match this scale of this energy equivalent for human development using diffuse and non-dispatchable renewables, all at acceptable energy and monetary costs [6].

There are good reasons why fossil fuels have been (and continue to be) so effective in "fueling" humankind's development [7–9]: first; their large, intrinsic, stored chemical energy – contained entirely within C–H and C–C chemical bonds; second; their expansive resource base, allowing remarkable flexibility in use – from small-to-large-scale applications; and, finally, their general worldwide availability at (still) reasonable cost.

The primary fuels worldwide are coal, crude petroleum oil, and natural gas, which is largely methane (CH_4). Coal and petroleum are usually referred to as "fossil" fuels. This term is perhaps more picturesque than accurate, except that it is meant to indicate that these materials were once living matter.

In the classic 1966 text *An Introduction to The Study of Fuel*, J. C. Macrae [9] noted:

> *it is not too much to say that our whole industrial society is based upon the reactions*:

$$C + O_2 = CO_2 \tag{1}$$

$$H_2 + O = H_2O \tag{2}$$

However, it is now recognized that these and other emissions resulting from the aerial combustion of fossil fuels can degrade the environment to the extent of global warming and, perhaps, climate change [10].

Of course, the world is reconciled to reducing the use of fossil energy as much as possible. However, because of many challenges with the utilization of non-fossil renewable energy sources – which include the absolute need for 24/7/365 readily-available, dispatchable energy and cost and safety factors – this development will continue to take time.

While awaiting the necessary breakthroughs in the harvesting and storage of renewable energy, it is surely now imperative to advance CO_2 mitigation technologies applied to the continued use – in fact, the projected enhanced use – of fossil fuels. This, then, has been one of the major founding themes of KOPRC.

3. Fossil Fuel Decarbonization

Over two decades ago, in remarkable contributions, Meyer Steinberg and Chunshan Song [11] argued persuasively that to continue the use of fossil fuels as a universal energy source – while at the same time preventing CO_2 entering the atmosphere through their aerial combustion – our system must focus on two alternative approaches: to remove carbon *before* combustion or to remove carbon *after* combustion.

The first option, the removal of carbon prior to any fossil fuel combustion, requires the removal and sequestration of carbon either as gaseous CO_2 or as solid, elemental carbon. Through innovations at KOPRC, outlined in detail in the following, this fossil fuel decarbonization technology centers on the microwave-initiated, catalytic "hydrogen stripping" or "deep dehydrogenation" of fossil hydrocarbon fuels to produce high-purity hydrogen and only, or primarily, solid carbon nanomaterials (e.g., carbon nanotubes) as a highly attractive co-product. That process yields zero, or at least minimal, CO_2 emissions to the atmosphere.

The second option, the removal of carbon following the aerial combustion of fossil fuels, requires the sequestration of carbon only as gaseous CO_2. For this technology, one must utilize the process of carbon capture and, using green hydrogen from clean, renewable energy sources such as wind, solar, or even nuclear, synthesize "carbon-neutral fuels" [12] – or, in the current parlance, "net-zero carbon fuels" – as a natural alternative to "carbon-free fuels."

3.1. *Hydrogen from fossil fuels with zero or minimal CO_2 emissions*

A prescient initiative in 2003, led by teams at Oxford and Bath Universities (T. J. Mays), was the formation of the UK Sustainable Hydrogen Consortium (UKSHEC, Fig. 5), to advance research in many facets of hydrogen energy [13–17].

More recent research has highlighted the developing international activity in hydrogen technologies and fuel cells [18] in their important roles in decarbonizing "hard-to-decarbonize" major industries (e.g., steel manufacturing) and transport [19] and also in helping balance renewable energy systems [20].

Though hydrogen does not generate any CO_2 emissions directly when it is used in a multitude of applications, unfortunately, its current mass production process has a huge CO_2 footprint. The current worldwide process for producing hydrogen at industrial scale is via the so-called steam reforming of methane (SRM), inevitably leading to the reaction co-product, CO_2, which has routinely been vented into the atmosphere. The overall SRM reaction is:

$$CH_4 + 2H_2O = CO_2 + 4H_2 \tag{3}$$

Figure 5. The first UK initiative in hydrogen energy had a multi-disciplinary team with expertise across the scientific, technological, and socioeconomic facets of the subject.

The CO_2 emissions from hydrogen production through this route are obviously very large. Any attempt to decarbonize hydrogen production technology to mitigate global warming obviously requires that all the CO_2 produced through SRM must be sequestered [11].

Through KOPRC, we have advanced an alternative process for the large-scale production of hydrogen with zero or minimal CO_2 emissions; this is through the (non-combustion) catalytic "hydrogen stripping," or "deep dehydrogenation," of hydrocarbon fossil fuels [21]. For example, with methane, the hydrogen stripping process can be written as:

$$CH_4 = C + 2H_2 \tag{4}$$

Remarkably, as well as the application of microwave-initiated catalytic hydrogen stripping of natural gas, we have also discovered that when applied to the heavier natural fossil hydrocarbons (including, even, heavy crude oil), it leads to highly effective hydrogen, or hydrogen-rich gas

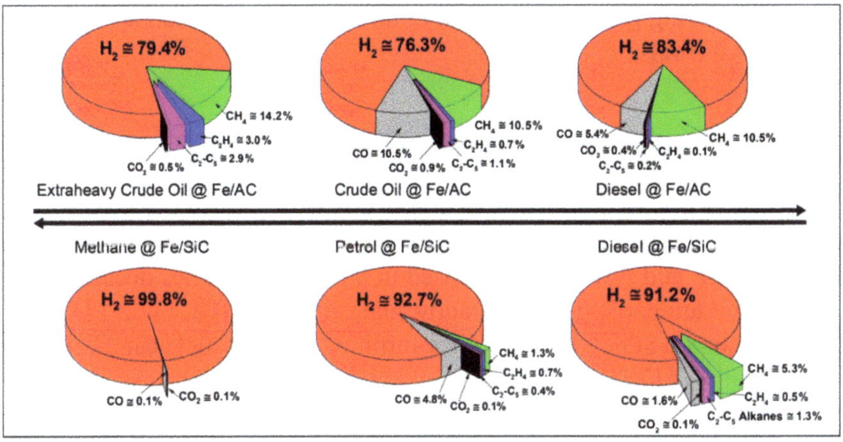

Figure 6. Fossil fuel decarbonization: Hydrogen stripping of a range of hydrocarbon fuels through microwave-initiated catalysis on supported iron catalysts.

Source: With permission of The Royal Society of Chemistry, from Jie *et al.* [21]; permission conveyed through Copyright Clearance Center, Inc.

production, leaving predominantly solid nanocarbon materials, again with no significant CO_2 emissions.

In Fig. 6, we show the results [21] of an investigation of the microwave-initiated catalytic hydrogen stripping of a variety of fossil fuels, ranging from methane to even crude oil; note, in particular, the high conversion of methane to hydrogen, exceeding some 99%!

It is important to recognize that both the gravimetric and volumetric densities of these hydrocarbon fossil fuels as hydrogen sources exceed the US Department of Energy "Performance Targets" for hydrogen storage materials [13].

Our recent advances also show that the microwave-initiated catalytic deep dehydrogenation of Saudi Arabian light crude oil yields hydrogen, hydrogen-rich "syngas" ($CO + H_2$), and valuable solid carbon nanomaterials, again with minimal CO_2 production [22]. In many cases, the major carbon co-product is again high-value carbon nanotubes.

Even putting aside the very considerable potential commercial value of these solid nanoscale carbon co-products, any carbon sequestration in this case obviously involves only *solid* carbon (Eq. 4). This will surely require much less energy and financial and environmental costs than sequestering gaseous CO_2 arising through the conventional combustion of fossil fuels.

3.2 *Turning atmospheric CO_2 into carbon-neutral or net-zero fuel*

The idea of synthesizing hydrocarbon fuels directly from only the feedstocks of CO_2 and water was proposed in pioneering studies decades ago, notably by Steinberg, Song, Muradov, and colleagues [11,23–25].

Three broad generic schemes for turning CO_2 into fuels can be envisaged as follows [7,8,12]:

(a) Probably the most familiar manifestation is in the production of biofuels formed in natural processes by extracting CO_2 from the atmosphere as part of the photosynthetic process, leading to plants, algae, or cyanobacteria. It is important to remind ourselves that the feedstocks – remarkably – are *only* CO_2 and H_2O, which are combined using chlorophyll to harvest the energy in sunlight and transform it into chemical energy in the form of carbohydrates in the resulting biomass material.

(b) A second possibility is a generic open-cycle process. There, CO_2 is captured, for example, from the flue-gas emissions of large industrial plants (e.g., power stations, steel and cement factories) and combined with renewable, green hydrogen to synthesize a hydrocarbon fuel. Rather than a genuine recycling process, this is perhaps better described as "CO_2 reuse." However, it might offer the potential of a notional reduction in CO_2 emissions.

(c) From a perspective of genuine sustainability, the third possibility – and surely the preferred option – is to source and recycle the CO_2 *only* by atmospheric extraction through the process known as direct air capture (DAC). In such a closed-cycle process, if only renewable energy and green hydrogen are used in any resulting hydrocarbon fuel production, this would lead to zero net release of CO_2 into the atmosphere. The resulting synthesized hydrocarbon would then be a carbon-neutral or net-zero hydrocarbon fuel.

The green hydrogen used for the hydrogenation of CO_2 in both (b) and (c) is usually assumed to be from the electrolysis of water with renewable energy [11,12]. Importantly, we also note that the hydrogen stripping of

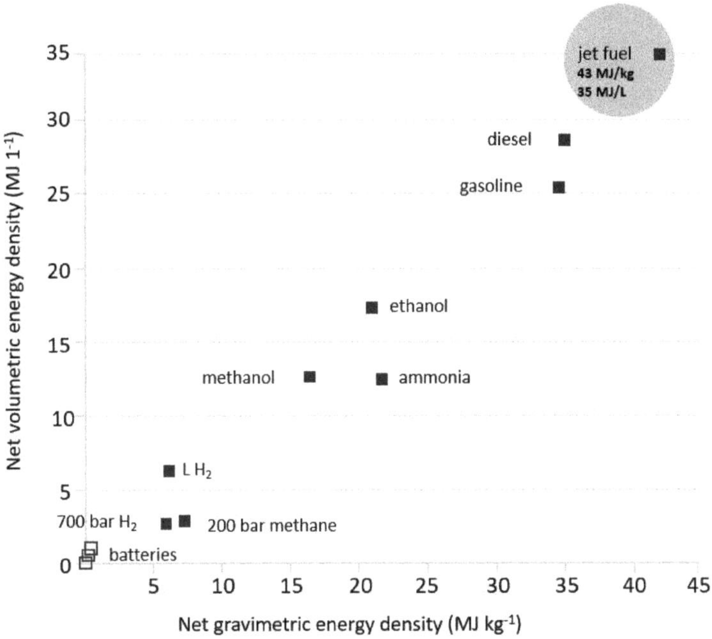

Figure 7. Net volumetric and gravimetric energy densities of various fuels and lithium-ion batteries. Note the remarkably high values of both energy densities for aviation jet fuel. *Source*: Courtesy of Andrew Symes.

natural hydrocarbons [21,22], outlined earlier in Section 3.1 – having minimal or no CO_2 emissions – could also be used in that context.

In terms of a target fuel, air travel has no realistic alternative, particularly for long-haul flights, but to retain the use of energy-dense liquid hydrocarbon fuels. The (net) gravimetric and volumetric energy densities of aviation jet hydrocarbon fuels (Fig. 7) illustrate their obvious attraction.

Similarly, the scale of currently increasing global CO_2 emissions means that the utilization of CO_2 to produce fuel is surely the only product that has the potential to match the necessary capacity between CO_2 emissions and utilization. Thus, a major focus was the development of a production process for so-called "sustainable aviation fuels" (SAFs): fuels made from only CO_2 and green hydrogen [11,12]. To make headway, one must examine the basis of the enabling Fischer–Tropsch process for hydrocarbon fuel synthesis through an understanding of the thermodynamics and kinetics of turning CO_2 into fuel.

3.2.1 *The general Fischer–Tropsch process*

The direct hydrogenation of CO_2 to a broad range of long-chain hydrocarbon fuels derives from the so-called Fischer–Tropsch synthesis (FTS) [27–30]. This process is a collection of successive chemical reactions that convert a mixture of carbon monoxide (CO) and hydrogen over a heterogeneous catalyst into target liquid hydrocarbons having the formula C_nH_m.

The FTS process itself is a well-established set of chemical reactions (first invented [27] in 1925) that have, in the past, been used to convert both coal and natural gas into liquid fuels [27–30]. It takes carbon-rich material – from whatever source – and, typically, reacts it with steam, producing a mixture of CO and H_2, known as syngas, which is then reacted over appropriate catalysts to produce hydrocarbons of the desired size (carbon number). For aviation fuel, these molecules should have between 8 and 16 carbon atoms in them.

The Oxford Advance [31], published in late 2020, revealed that by using specifically synthesized iron-based catalysts, CO_2 can be *directly, and in a one-step process,* hydrogenated to the necessary long-chain hydrocarbons in a single reactor. A schematic representation of that CO_2-FTS process [31] is given in Fig. 8.

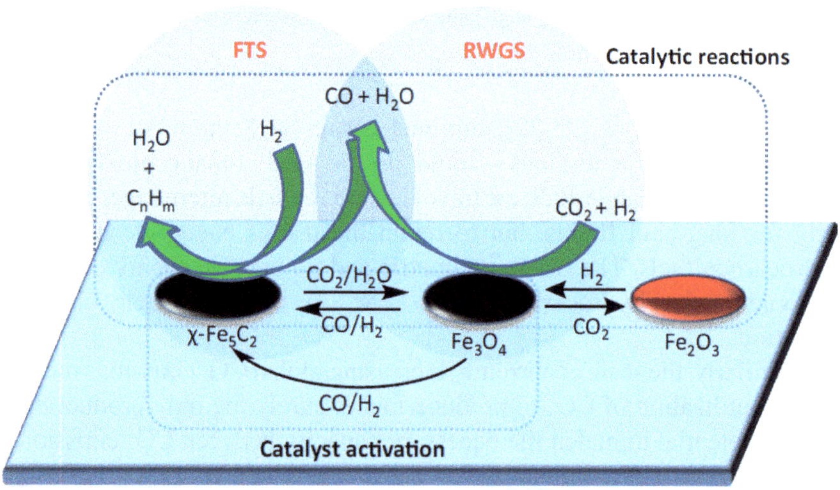

Figure 8. The CO_2 hydrogenation to jet fuel range hydrocarbons process through a tandem mechanism in which the so-called reverse-water gas shift reaction (RWGS) and Fischer–Tropsch synthesis (FTS) reaction are catalyzed by Fe_3O_4 and χ-Fe_5C_2, respectively. *Source*: Yao [29] CC BY 4.0 (https://creativecommons.org/licenses/by/4.0/).

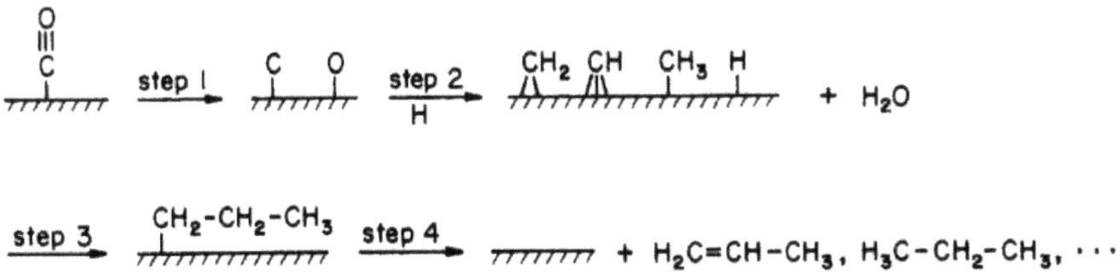

Figure 9. Schematic illustration of FTS, described as the reductive transformation of CO over a heterogeneous metal catalyst.

Source: Reprinted with permission from Zheng *et al.* [32]. Copyright 1988 American Chemical Society.

Understanding the full nature of this direct, one-step CO_2-FTS reaction is still a vast undertaking.

However, a mechanism [32] that nicely summarizes most of the current thinking of the FTS itself is one in which the CO_2 is first adsorbed onto the metal catalyst surface and then efficiently dissociated into CO (step 1 of Fig. 9). The subsequent growth of the hydrocarbon chain may be visualized as involving a repeated sequence in which hydrogen atoms are added to both carbon and oxygen (step 2); the C–O bond is thereby split and new C–H and O–H bonds are formed (the former as CH_2, CH, and CH_3 fragments; the latter as H_2O); the ensuing polymerization process (step 3) produces linear chain hydrocarbons of varying carbon number; leading ultimately to the desorption of the hydrocarbon fragments from the catalyst surface (step 4).

Any understanding of this fascinating but rather complex process must start with the overarching thermodynamics and kinetics of turning CO_2 into fuel.

3.2.2 *Thermodynamic considerations*

The C–O chemical bonds in CO_2 are very strong, as reflected in what is known as the thermodynamic standard Gibbs free energy of formation. In Fig. 10, we illustrate the Gibbs free energy of the formation of CO_2 on the left-hand axis (in units of kJ mol^{-1}) as compared to other molecules [7,8,14].

Clearly, CO_2, one product of the aerial combustion of hydrocarbons (Eq. 1), is a particularly stable molecule, as reflected in its large Gibbs free energy of formation of 394 kJ mol^{-1}. The very real challenge for any

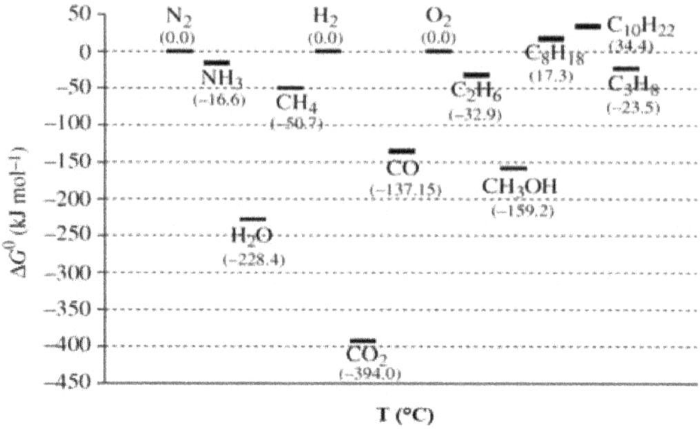

Figure 10. The Gibbs free energy of formation for various chemicals.

Source: Used with permission of The Royal Society from Jiang *et al.* [7,8]; permission conveyed through Copyright Clearance Center, Inc.

utilization and chemical conversion of CO_2 to hydrocarbon fuels will be the need for a substantial input of energy to break the C–O chemical bonds *and/or* the discovery of a highly effective catalyst for any chemical conversion.

In terms of thermodynamics, chemical reactions are driven by the differences in the Gibbs free energy of the reactants and the products [7,8,14]. CO_2 must therefore be combined with another chemical reactant molecule (in our case, H_2) with a higher Gibbs free energy shown in Fig. 10, which then gives up some of its intrinsic chemical energy embedded in its H–H bond to promote the formation of the required hydrocarbon energy carrier. However, thermodynamic arguments alone are not sufficient to overcome the great challenge of transforming CO_2 into a hydrocarbon fuel, such as SAF – the challenges are more likely to be kinetic in origin.

3.2.3 *Kinetics considerations*

As we have seen in the previous section, the main challenge for CO_2 as a chemical reactant is its rather low energy content, as reflected in its substantial Gibbs free energy of formation. This is in stark contrast, for example, to CO (Fig. 10). When energy-rich hydrogen is used as a co-reactant with H_2, the thermodynamics become much more favorable. However, a major barrier to overcome will be in the very first step of any transformation of CO_2; that is, the kinetic barrier associated with the initial interaction of CO_2 with a solid surface – typically, a metal catalyst surface. The challenge then centers on the design and synthesis of a suitable, high-performance catalyst required to initiate and advance the reaction. The universally accepted definition of a catalyst for any chemical process is that due to Wilhelm Ostwald [33] in terms of the concepts of chemical kinetics: *"A catalyst is a substance which affects the rate of a chemical reaction without being part of its end products."*

Any chemical reaction involving CO_2 and H_2 involves the breaking of C–O and H–H bonds between the constituent atoms and the formation of new C–H and H–O bonds in the product(s). As noted by Gerhard Ertl in his beautiful 2008 Nobel Lecture [34], this is about the transformation of energy. An energy diagram illustrating the progress of such a chemical reaction is shown schematically in Fig. 11.

Noting from Ertl [34], such a chemical transformation requires that a reaction's unique activation energy E^* (Fig. 11) must first be surmounted. This energy can be provided by the available thermal energy, kT, where k is the Boltzmann constant at T, the temperature of the reaction.

Importantly, not all molecular encounters – only a fraction, some ($\exp -E^*/kT$) – will be successful in overcoming the energy barrier E^* to effect the chemical transformation. How, then, can one achieve an

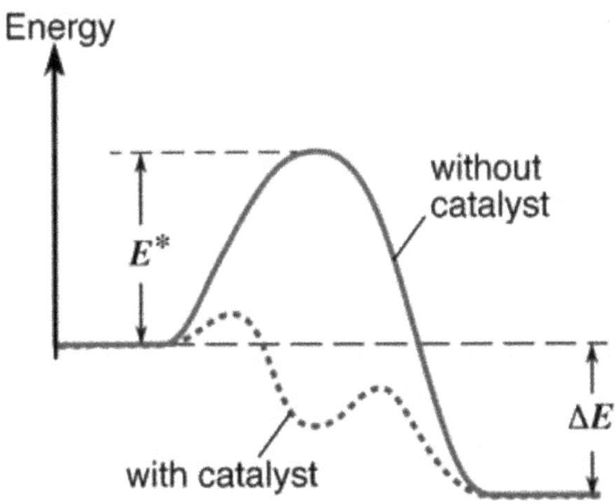

Figure 11. Energy diagram illustrating the progress of a chemical reaction both with and without a catalyst.

Source: Used with permission of John Wiley & Sons, from Ertl [34]; permission conveyed through Copyright Clearance Center, Inc.

increase in the reaction probability for a chemical reaction? This transformation can be achieved either by increasing the reaction temperature T or by lowering the activation energy E^*.

For the latter situation, this is provided by a catalyst which, through the formation of some sort of "intermediate" with the incoming reactant molecules, provides an alternative reaction path, as shown by the dashed line in Fig. 11. Clearly, this new reaction path now leads to a reduction in the activation barrier and a concomitantly higher overall reaction rate *at all temperatures*. In the final step, the resulting product molecules are then released from the catalyst, which is now available for subsequent reaction cycles [34].

In terms of the critically important intermediate state, upon approaching a metal catalyst surface, CO_2 may initiate the formation of new physical or chemical bonds to the surface catalyst atoms, whereby the chemical bond between the C and O atoms is weakened. This weakening of bonds, or in extreme cases bond breaking upon chemisorption to the metal surface of both CO_2 (and indeed H_2), is perhaps *the* most important function of a high-performance functioning catalyst.

To understand how this may take place, we need to have a cursory examination of the chemical bonding in CO_2 within a so-called "Walsh diagram" [35] of the molecule's orbital electronic energies (Fig. 12).

The electronic structure of CO_2 in its ground state may be represented by a so-called "molecular orbital diagram," as shown in Fig. 12. On the right-hand side are schematic drawings of the molecular orbitals of CO_2 in a sequence of increasing energy, as revealed by quantum-chemical calculations. The constituent atomic orbitals on the carbon and oxygen atoms, which are critically important in C–O bond formation, are the 2s and 2p orbitals.

CO_2 contains 22 electrons, of which 6 occupy the so-called "core" 1s orbitals. The remaining 16 (valence) electrons are distributed over various orbitals having either sigma (σ) or pi (π) symmetry.

Perhaps the two most important orbitals in the present context are the "highest occupied molecular orbital (HOMO)," labeled the $1\pi_g$ orbital, and the "lowest unoccupied molecular orbital (LUMO)," labeled the $2\pi_u$ orbital. The "activation" of an incoming CO_2 molecule by a metal catalyst surface involves a partial electron transfer from the occupied metal catalyst orbitals (usually the "band" orbitals in the metal) into the accessible unoccupied orbitals of the CO_2 molecule, that is, a process leading to the partial occupation of the LUMO [7,8,35]. The result is a highly significant

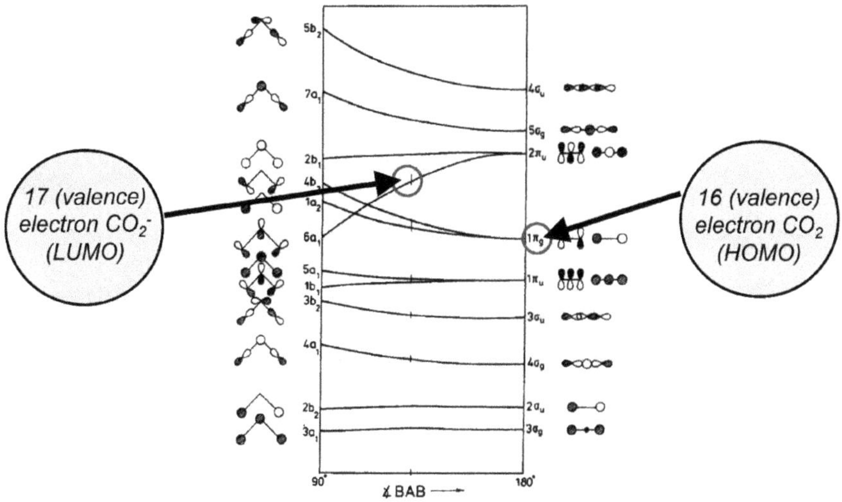

Figure 12. Bonding and the process of the activation/reduction of CO_2. The Walsh diagrams of CO_2 orbital energies in both linear and bent geometries are shown. The 17th valence electron represents the partial electron transfer from the metal catalyst surface to the CO_2 molecule, with this transferred electron density into the LUMO, leading to an effective bonding of the partially reduced CO_2 molecule (CO_2^-) and its "activation."

Source: Adapted from Freund and Roberts (1996). CC BY 4.0 (https://creativecommons.org/licenses/by/4.0/).

lowering of energy of this newly occupied orbital, as shown in Fig. 12, together with a pronounced bending of the CO_2 molecule, forming a thermodynamically metastable state. This electronic state of the slightly reduced CO_2 molecule is now perfectly suited – and perfectly activated – for the necessary subsequent chemical reactions with H_2 or any other co-adsorbed molecules. This "bent" (slightly reduced) CO_2 molecule is central to the understanding of the reactivity of CO_2 in providing the low energy pathway (Fig. 11) to its ultimate hydrogenation to hydrocarbon fuels.

The challenge, then, was to design and synthesize an inexpensive, abundant, and highly effective catalyst that can form this bent, catalytically activated CO_2 as a feedstock.

It was clear to us that any progress in using CO_2 to make SAF would only emerge through novel, innovative catalytic chemistry. We were able to announce such an advance in *Nature Communications* in late 2020 [31] with the synthesis of a high-performance iron-based catalyst.

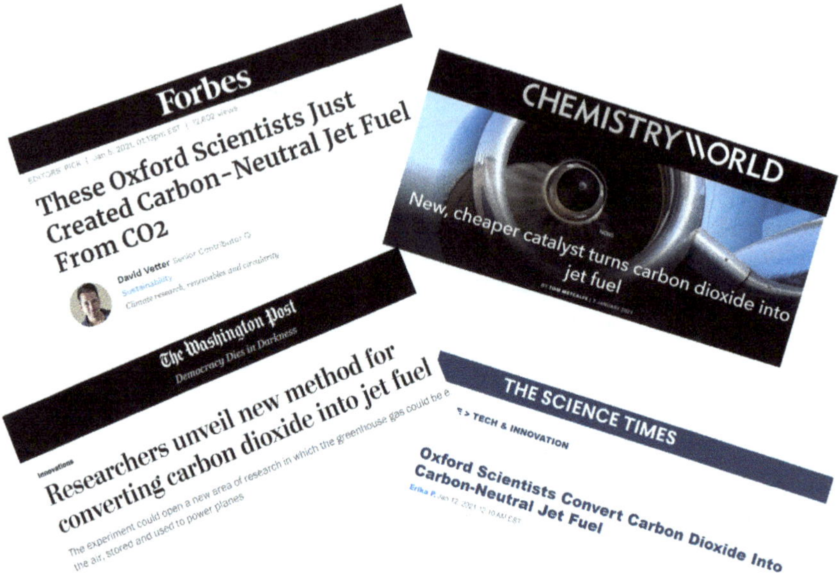

Figure 13. Representative examples of the worldwide media coverage of the Oxford/KOPRC advance published in *Nature Communications* in late 2020 [31].

That paper generated considerable worldwide interest (Fig. 13). It also led to the creation of a new Oxford spin-out company OXCCU (https://www.oxccu.com/), which last year completed a US$23 million funding round to commercialize a cost-effective route to SAF. Financial backers for OXCCU include the oil majors Saudi Aramco and Eni, as well as United Airlines, venture capital firms such as Clean Energy Ventures and Kiko Ventures, and the commodity trader Trafigura.

4. Plastics Waste: A Route to Clean Hydrogen and Carbon Nanomaterials

The OECD has reported that the global production of plastics reached 460mn tons in 2019. Almost three-quarters of that plastic ends up as waste – almost all destined for landfills. For the remainder, plastics transformation processes such as thermochemical pyrolysis, gasification, and incineration are now being targeted. However, a recent extensive life-cycle analysis [36] has shown that all of the current pyrolysis and chemical recycling processes for plastic waste emit large quantities of CO_2, as well as dangerous emissions, effectively negating the proposed – seemingly attractive – plastics recycling economy. This critical issue will become increasingly problematic as more plastic waste is targeted as a potential source of hydrocarbon fuels. Importantly, those authors concluded that any such plastic transformation processes, therefore, must also require the accompanying CO_2 separation, capture, and storage technologies to reduce greenhouse gas emissions from the processes in order to comply with carbon-neutrality targets [36].

Our basic philosophy was fundamentally different; it was to discover an effective catalytic "deconstruction" process to take advantage of the high-atomic-weight content of both hydrogen and carbon in the most widely used plastics. These waste materials, themselves, were then viewed as highly effective hydrogen storage materials as a source of both hydrogen and solid carbon [37]. As an example, the world's most widely used and produced plastic, polyethylene, contains some 14% hydrogen and 86% carbon (Fig. 14).

We then discovered that a microwave-initiated catalytic hydrogen stripping – or deconstruction – of these polymeric plastics rapidly yielded

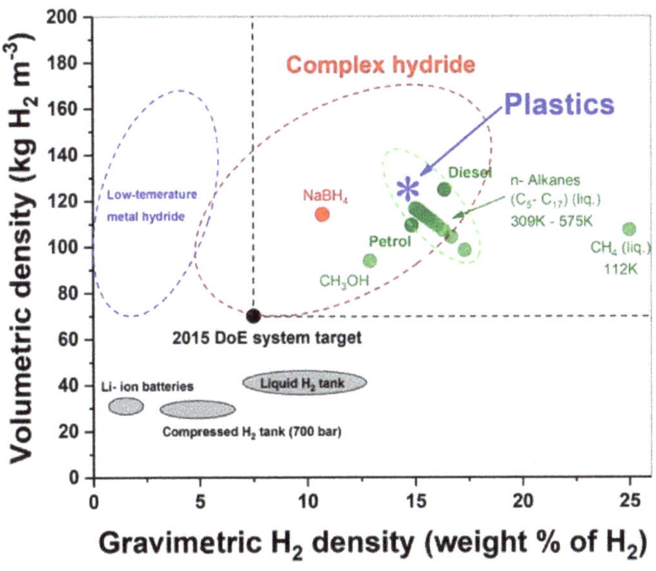

Figure 14. Plastics as hydrogen storage materials, highlighting their high intrinsic gravimetric and volumetric H_2 densities, including data for a range of solid state storage materials [37].

Source: Licence to publish granted by Nature Portfolio.

Figure 15. Some examples of the worldwide media coverage of the KOPRC advance in deconstructing plastic waste to H_2 and carbon nanomaterials [37]. That paper is ranked third among the articles of a similar age in *Nature Catalysis*.

hydrogen and solid carbon nanomaterials. This innovation, published in late 2020 in *Nature Catalysis* [37], built upon our earlier discovery of the highly effective microwave-catalyzed deconstruction of both hydrocarbon wax [38] and a variety of fossil fuels [21], but now applied to plastic waste. This approach, importantly, used abundant and inexpensive iron catalyst particles on an aluminum oxide (Al_2O_3) support. The innovation, again, generated significant worldwide interest [39,40] (Fig. 15).

It was clear that incident microwaves selectively – and very effectively – heat almost exclusively *only* the iron catalyst particles, with the bulk polymeric plastic materials being effectively transparent to microwaves. This microwave-initiated catalytic deconstruction provides a highly effective mechanism for the selective scission of C–H bonds in the polymeric plastics (Fig. 16).

A schematic representation [40] of the proposed mechanism for the conversion of plastics to hydrogen and carbon nanotubes is given in Fig. 17.

A major new initiative between the UK groups and Peak Sustainability Ventures in India (www.peakventures.in) is now urgently seeking to implement the large-scale upscaling of this process, not only as a solution

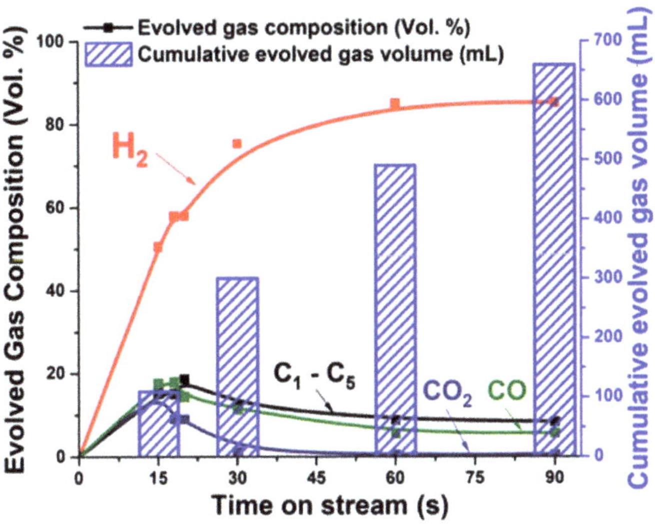

Figure 16. Microwave-initiated catalytic hydrogen stripping from polyethylene showing the large-scale evolution of hydrogen and minimal amounts of other products [37].

Source: Licence to publish granted by Nature Portfolio.

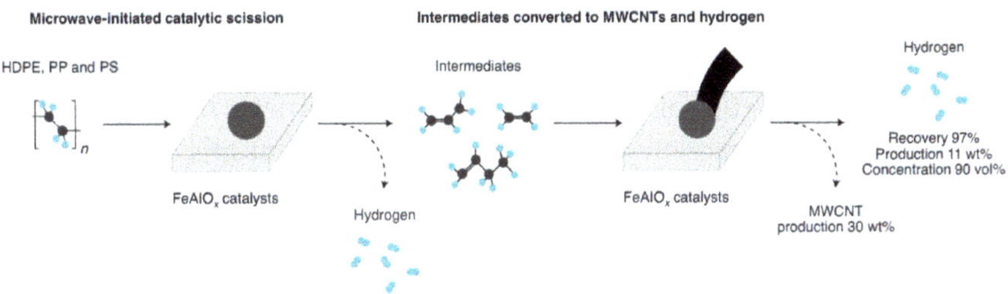

Figure 17. Proposed mechanism for the conversion of plastics to hydrogen and carbon nanotubes.

Source: Lopez and Santamaria (2020) [40]. Licence to publish granted by Nature Portfolio.

to the burgeoning plastic waste problem but also as a source of hydrogen and high-value carbon nanomaterials [41].

This is a perfect example of how we apply the scientific innovations developed under KOPRC to address real-world problems of society in a meaningful manner. This solution allows the safe disposition of plastic waste, which would otherwise find its way to the oceans or landfills, where they would degrade over decades at significant environmental cost. Rather, the approach is to convert them into useful materials such as hydrogen – for a multitude of applications – and solid carbon materials which have many uses to industry. For India, for example, it also accelerates its journey to reduce dependence on traditional fossil fuels and allow decarbonization of hard-to-abate sectors, such as steel and cement, where this hydrogen (and also the co-produced solid carbon) can be used to meet energy needs for cleaner manufacture of these critical materials [41].

The intention also is to help mount a similar effort in the Kingdom of Saudi Arabia and the UK, where (as in most countries) the majority of collected plastic waste is disposed in landfills or dumpsites [42].

5. An Important, Emerging Field in Energy Science and Technology: Microwave Catalysis

A major theme that has emerged from research at KOPRC is the remarkable ability of incident electromagnetic radiation in the form of microwaves to effect the rapid heating of supported and free iron catalyst particles (and indeed many other metal and other catalysts). This heating process leads to a rapid, highly effective catalytic C–H bond scission, both in a wide range of fossil hydrocarbon fuels (Fig. 6) and plastic waste (Fig. 16) to yield high-purity hydrogen and solid carbon nanomaterials. To understand the origins of this process, one must understand the fundamental electronic properties of typical catalytic metal particles of a few tens to a few hundreds of nanometers in size [43–50]. Within this size regime, these so-called "mesoscopic" catalyst particles are thus intermediate in size regime on the one hand, and the macroscopic bulk state of matter on the other. These particles challenge conventional thinking since it is *only* their characteristic physical size that governs both their physical and their chemical properties [44–49], and now including their unique and important catalytic properties.

There is much physical evidence, remarkably, to show that small isolated particles of "nominally" highly conducting metallic elements of the periodic table become non-conducting when their physical dimensions drop below a certain, critical size [43–51]. Importantly, the critical point for such a fundamental electronic transition appears to be within the regime of many operational heterogeneous catalysts. A schematic representation of the possible effects of the successive division or fragmentation of a single grain of a "nominally" metallic bulk catalyst particle is highlighted in Fig. 18.

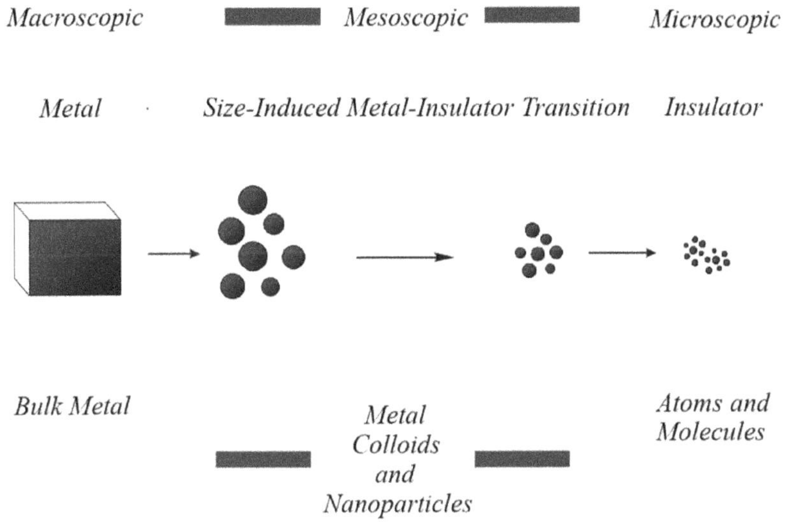

Figure 18. An adaptation of the successive division of a single grain of a (nominally) metallic element from the *macroscopic,* through the *mesoscopic*, and through to the *microscopic* regime.

Source: Edwards PP, *et al.* (1999) [46]; permission conveyed through Copyright Clearance Center, Inc.

Thus, the electronic properties of isolated small catalytic particles (typically with diameters, say, <500nm) are expected to be fundamentally different from those of the (parent) bulk metal. This arises from both classical and quantum size effects through the size-dependent phenomenon known as the size-induced metal–insulator transition (SIMIT), occurring entirely within a single grain of a nominally metallic element [43–55]. In broad terms, when the individual particle's size approaches, or is close to, the electron's characteristic (de Broglie) wavelength, the conditions for a SIMIT are fulfilled [47–55]. Remarkably, critically important measurements of individual particles for a range of metals with different sizes, ranging from the micron to the nanometer scale, show that the electrical conductivity *within* a particle is some seven to eight orders of magnitude *below* that of the bulk (parent) metal! [49–51].

To understand the SIMIT we must examine the evolution and consequences of this strongly size-dependent electronic structure of catalyst particles in the mesoscopic and microscopic regimes.

In bulk metals, the highest occupied electronic energy state resides at the Fermi Energy, E_F. Importantly, above E_F there exists an infinite number of infinitesimally separated (and empty) electronic energy levels, which can easily be populated for electronic conduction under the application of an applied electric field. In complete contrast, when a metal is sufficiently finely divided into mesoscopic or microscopic dimensions, the continuum of electronic energy levels now gives way to a manifold of discrete energy levels, with an average separation, δ_K, between levels of some E_F/N, where N is the number of atoms contained within a single metal particle. Critically, when δ_K, the so-called Kubo energy gap [54,55], becomes comparable to the (ambient) thermal energy, kT, the electronic energy levels of the particle now become discrete, rather than continuous. Even more striking, as noted by Professor Adrian Porch, is the occurrence of *any* transition or change whatsoever from a continuous – to a discrete – manifold of energy levels, which signals a major and fundamental, discontinuous transition in electronic properties [56].

Remarkably, then, this size-dependent process determines the fundamental metallic or insulating status of an individual particle [51]. A schematic representation of the size-dependent electronic structure of (nominally) metallic particles is given in Fig. 19.

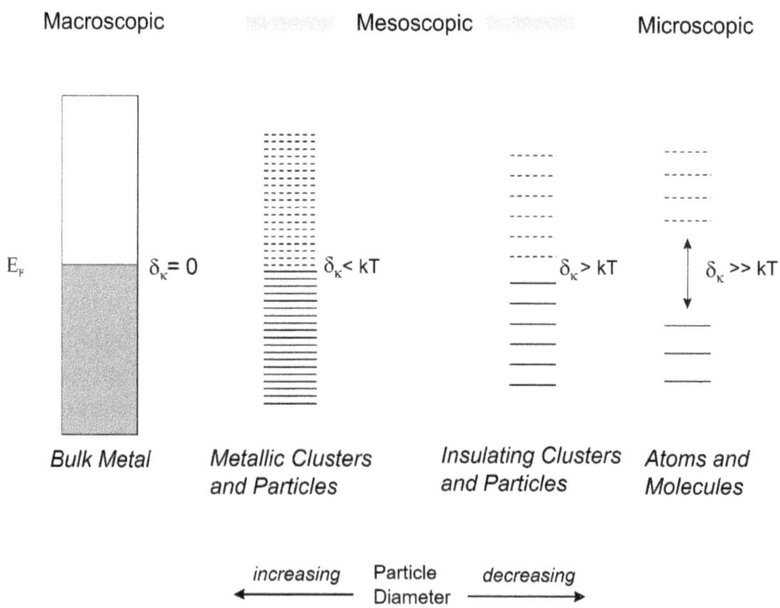

Figure 19. The size-induced metal–insulator transition: The evolution of the Kubo energy gap.

Source: Edwards PP, *et al.* (1999) [46]; permission conveyed through Copyright Clearance Center, Inc.

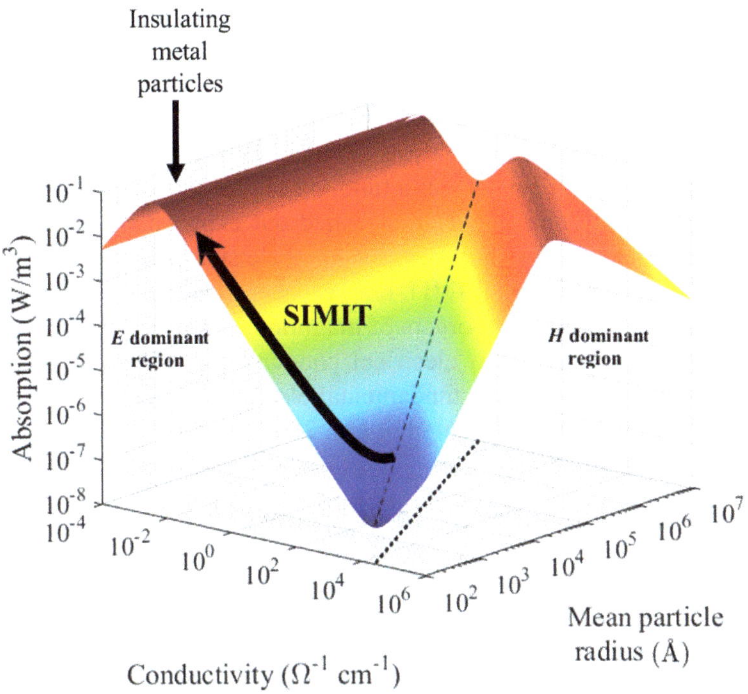

Figure 20. Electromagnetic absorption across the size-induced metal–insulator transition (SIMIT) in isolated particles.

Source: Used with permission of the Royal Society of Chemistry, from Porch *et al.* [58]; permission conveyed through Copyright Clearance Center, Inc.

Therefore, by varying *only* the physical size of an individual mesoscopic catalyst particle, remarkably, its electronic properties can be adjusted between the full extremes of a metal or an insulator [51].

We took this as sound evidence that our required and operational catalyst particles, with dimensions close to or below the SIMIT, would exhibit "non-metal," low-electrical-conductivity behavior, in stark contrast to their bulk, highly conducting parental "metals." Such mesoscopic catalyst particles (Fig. 19), we believed, would therefore have the remarkable ability to heat most effectively when placed in a microwave electric field.

That certainly turned out to be the case [21,36,37]. When visiting our KOPRC laboratory in 2015, Nobel Laureate Professor Roger Tsien, after being shown by Dr. Sergio Gonzalez-Cortes the instantaneous and large-scale evolution of H_2 from the fossil hydrocarbon wax under microwave catalysis conditions, exclaimed: *"Remarkable, Peter, and Colleagues: This must surely be a revolution for the rapid production of hydrogen!"* [57].

Our detailed theoretical analysis of the total electromagnetic absorption in typical catalyst particles as a function of electrical conductivity and mean particle radius had indeed confirmed our expectations and experimental findings [58]. Thus, as a catalyst particle size is reduced to a critical size so that it crosses the SIMIT, one sees a huge *increase* in microwave absorption (over some eight orders of magnitude), while at the same time there is a huge *decrease* in electrical conductivity within the particle. Paradoxically, this marks the fundamental electronic transition to *insulating metal particles*, as highlighted in Fig. 20!

6. Summary of KOPRC Achievements

6.1 *"Pure Science, Applied" in the emergence of disruptive energy technologies*

KOPRC advances at Oxford will be pivotal in resolving possible solutions to two of the greatest energy challenges our world faces in the 21st century.

First, the issue of global warming was highlighted over a decade ago to the three founders of KOPRC by Sir John Houghton (Fig. 1). Sir John's remarkable logical flow of ideas highlighted the need for practicing physical scientists and engineers, such as ourselves, to search for potential solutions. From those amazing and fruitful interactions with Sir John came the vision of "sustainably turning atmospheric CO_2 into fuel" using green hydrogen – the essence of advancing fossil fuel decarbonization science and technology to help mitigate global warming [11]. The target of a truly closed carbon cycle, a circular carbon economy has the advantage of not having to rely on a reduction of energy consumption, which as Professor Robert Schlögl [59] perceptively noted is, adverse to the trends in global population and the socio-economic pressure of all humans having the equal right of energy access.

Second, defining a new, exciting vision for plastic waste utilization – now recognizing it as a valuable anthropogenic resource or feedstock, particularly in renewable energy-scarce countries for the transition to a hydrogen-based economy. This is also a sounding call for governments and politicians not to forget that the world is also in the midst of a plastic waste crisis. As perceptively noted by Susan Goldberg of *National Geographic* [60], *"Some people deny climate change, but there are no ... plastic deniers. The problem's in plain sight."*

6.2 *Education, learning, and training of young people through "Pure Science, Applied"*

The various KOPRC advances in modern energy science and technology have been highlighted in this chapter. An equally important aim – again advanced from the outset by the founders of KOPRC and senior KACST management – was that the Oxford Centre of Excellence should be the fulcrum for a vision of "Education, Learning, and Training Through Research" for both undergraduate and graduate students from the Kingdom of Saudi Arabia, and indeed beyond, through masters' and DPhil degrees at Oxford. We are particularly proud that a total of some 13 students, not only from Saudi Arabia but also from China, Pakistan, India, and Malaysia, have now graduated through their research carried out in KOPRC since 2011.

Our hope was always that these students would return to the Kingdom of Saudi Arabia and their respective home countries and take a prominent part in helping their country's scientific endeavors through their broad experience and new connections in energy science. That has definitely been the case.

As the world searches for a wholly renewable energy future, Saudi Arabia and many other countries are of course striving to diversify in order to secure their future prosperity. The Kingdom's effort to become a knowledge-based economy is spearheaded by KACST, its national science agency, which was responsible for implementing the National Science, Technology and Innovation Policy (NSTIP). The ambitious KOPRC initiative launched by KACST and Oxford University in 2010 has undoubtedly and significantly expanded the country's scientific reach and endeavors.

We are proud that a number of our graduated students (Fig. 21) are now part of that vision to create new ideas and innovations in the Kingdom, and indeed beyond. We believe that their experience in KOPRC is an exemplar of the kind of curiosity-driven "Pure Science, Applied," that inspires young people to ask fundamental questions – across both

Figure 21. Our Oxford/KOPRC students from KACST in Saudi Arabia.

science and technology – and engage in humankind's energy future. Above all else, their education, learning, and training have been built on the power of curiosity, one of humankind's greatest assets.

Acknowledgments

We are truly grateful to the late Dr. Jamie Ferguson of Oxford University Innovation for his friendship, his invaluable professional guidance, and his steadfast support throughout this entire venture. Thanks also to Dr. Phil Clare of Oxford Research Services, who helped establish the agreement for cooperation, and the late Professor Roger Ainsworth (Master of St. Catherine's College, Oxford), Sir David King, and Sir Chris Llewellyn Smith for their strong support in the early days of KOPRC. As noted in Section 1, we thank Senior Managers at KACST and, most notably, Prince Dr. Turki bin Saud bin Mohammed Al Saud, advisor at the Saudi Royal Court, for continuing and steadfast support and encouragement. The authors also thank EPSRC (Grant EP/N009924/1), Rolls Royce, and Merton College for financial support.

We sincerely thank all colleagues who appear in the reference list, as well as Andrew Symes and Alan Aubrey (OXCCU), Anthony Strong and

Emmanuel Raptakis (OUI), Samir Shah (Peak Sustainability Ventures), Gari P. Owen (Annwvyn Solutions), Peter J. Dobson and Jinghai Li (Chinese Academy of Sciences) for their invaluable input to our research and its up-scaling development. Peter Edwards particularly thanks Professor Adrian Porch, Cardiff University, for introducing him to the potential applications of microwaves in the activation of heavy hydrocarbons, a theme developed and advanced (as noted in Section 5) with the arrival at KOPRC of Dr. Daniel Slocombe from Cardiff. He also thanks Professor Gerhard Ertl for a most illuminating exchange on the fundamental steps of catalytic activation and reaction at metal surfaces.

A special word of sincere thanks goes to Mrs. Linda Webb for her superb professionalism and support in helping all aspects of KOPRC, in particular her work in organizing the four KOPRC (KACST-Oxford Petrochemical) Forums (https://koprc.kacst.gov.sa/events/event-list.html) and her support to our DPhil students throughout and for her outstanding efforts in helping us in assembling this chapter.

And finally, for all of these advances (and adventures), we owe the greatest debt of gratitude to our dear colleague, the late Sir John Meurig Thomas, FLSW, FRS; from its very conception, Sir John was the strongest possible supporter and friend of KOPRC. It is a fitting tribute to Sir John's relentless pursuit of knowledge that he was a co-author in the two major papers in late 2020 in *Nature Catalysis* and *Nature Communications*, published just before and then just after his death in November 2020 – that form the basis of this entire chapter. This surely demonstrates Sir John's long-held passion of the necessity of scientific endeavor to address humankind's energy challenges – through "Pure Science, Applied."

After submission of our manuscript, we became aware of the excellent review by Li, H. Expanding plastics recycling technologies: chemical aspects, technology status and challenges. *Green Chemistry*. 2022; 24: 8899-9002.

References

[1] Edwards PP. The enquiring chemist. In: Davis EA, editor. *Nevill Mott – Reminiscences and Appreciations*. Taylor and Francis Ltd; 1998. p. 252–56.

[2] Edwards PP, *et al*. The insulator-superconductor transformation in Cuprates. *J Supercond*. 1998;11:151–154.

[3] Mott NF. Memories of early days in solid state physics. *Proc R Soc Lond A*. 1980;371:56–66.

[4] Holmyard EJ. *Makers of Chemistry*. Oxford at The Clarendon Press, Oxford, England; 1931. p. 41.

[5] Kolasinki KW. Frontiers of surface science. *Curr Opin Solid State Mater Sci*. 2006;10:129.

[6] Pearson RJ. Private communication.

[7] Edwards PP, *et al*. Turning carbon dioxide into fuel. *Phil Trans R Soc A*. 2010;368:3343–3364.

[8] Yao B, *et al*. Thermodynamic study of hydrocarbon synthesis from carbon dioxide and hydrogen. *J Greenhouse Gas Sci Technol*. 2017;7:942–957.

[9] Macrae JC. *An Introduction to the Study of Fuel*. Amsterdam: Elsevier; 1966.

[10] Houghton, SJ. *Global Warming: The Complete Briefing*. 5th edn. Cambridge University Press, Cambridge CB2 8BS, England; 2015.

[11] Steinberg M. Fossil fuel decarbonization technology for mitigating global warming. *Int J of Hydrogen Energy*. 1999;24(8):771–777; Song, C. CO_2 conversion and utilization. American Chemical Society Symposium Series 809. Washington DC; 2001.

[12] Pearson RJ, *et al*. Energy storage via carbon-neutral fuels made from CO_2, water and renewable energy. *Proc IEEE*. 2012;100(2):440–460.

[13] Grochala W and Edwards PP. Thermal decomposition of the non-interstitial hydrides for the storage and production of hydrogen. *Chem Rev*. 2004;104(3):1283–1316.

[14] Edwards PP, *et al*. Hydrogen energy. *Phil Trans R Soc A*. 2007;365:1043–1056.

[15] Sartbaeva A, *et al*. Hydrogen nexus in a sustainable energy future. *Energy Environ Sci*. 2008;1:79–85.

[16] Edwards PP, *et al*. Hydrogen and fuel cells: Towards a sustainable energy future. *Energy Policy*. 2008;36(12):4356–4362.

[17] Ekins P, editor. *Hydrogen Energy; Economic and Social Challenges*. London: Earthscan; 2010.

[18] Thomas JM, *et al*. Decarbonising energy: The developing international activity in hydrogen technologies and fuel cells. *J Energy Chem*. 2020;51:405–415.

[19] Alvera, M. *The Hydrogen Revolution*. Marco Alvera Hodder Studio; 2021.

[20] Llewellyn Smith, SC. University of Oxford, Large-scale electricity storage, Royal Society report. 2023 Sep. https://royalsociety.org/-/media/policy/projects/large-scale-electricity-storage/V1_Large-scale-electricity-storage-report.pdf?la=en-GB&hash=90BC8F8BCBC2A34431B6CF9DD80A8C9D.

[21] Jie X, *et al*. The decarbonisation of petroleum and other fossil hydrocarbon fuels for the facile production and safe storage of hydrogen. *Energy Environ Sci*. 2019;12:238.

[22] S. Aldrees, *et al*. Unpublished observations.

[23] Steinberg M and Cheng HC. Modern and prospective technologies for hydrogen production from fossil fuels. *Int J Hydrogen Energy*. 1989;14:797–820.

[24] Muradov NS. How to produce hydrogen from fossil fuels without CO_2 emission. *Int J Hydrogen Energy*. 1993;18(3):211–215.
[25] Muradov NS. Low to near-zero CO_2 production of hydrogen from fossil fuels, *Int J Hydrogen Energy*. 2017;42(20):14058–14088.
[26] Chen L, *et al*. Ternary NiMo-Bi liquid alloy catalyst for efficient hydrogen production from methane pyrolysis. *Science*. 2023;381:857–861.
[27] Fischer F and Tropsch H. *The Synthesis of Petroleum at Atmospheric Pressures from Gasification Products of Coal*. Brennstoff-Chemie. 1926;7:97–104.
[28] Crawford SR and Rideal EK. The mechanism of the synthesis of hydrocarbons from water gas. *J Chem Soc*. 1939:1604.
[29] Hermann WA. Organometallic aspects of the Fischer-Tropsch synthesis. Angew. *Chem. Int. Ed*. 1982;21(2):117.
[30] Klerk AD. *Fischer-Tropsch Refining*. Wiley-VCH Verlag GmbH & Co.; 2011.
[31] Yao B, *et al*. Transforming carbon dioxide into jet fuel using an organic combustion-synthesized Fe-Mn-K catalyst. *Nat Commun*. 2020;11: 6395.
[32] Zheng C, Apeloig Y and Hoffmann R, Bonding and coupling of C_1 fragments on metal surfaces. *J Am Chem Soc*. 1988;110:749–774.
[33] Ostwald W. Physik, Z. 1902;3:313; Ostwald W, Ann Naturphil. 1910;9:1.
[34] Ertl G. Reactions at surfaces: From atoms to complexity (Nobel lecture). *Angew Chem Int Ed*. 2008;47:3524–3535.
[35] Freund HJ and Roberts MW. Surface chemistry of carbon dioxide. *Surf Sci Rep*. 1996;25:225–273.
[36] Kwon S, *et al*. Nonviable carbon neutrality with plastic waste-to-energy. *Energy Environ Sci*. 2023;16:3074–3087.
[37] Jie X, *et al*. Microwave-initiated catalytic deconstruction of plastic waste into hydrogen and high-value carbons. *Nat Catal*. 2020;3:902–912.
[38] Gonzalez-Cortes S, *et al*. Wax: A benign hydrogen-storage material that rapidly releases H_2-rich gases through microwave-assisted catalytic decomposition. *Nat Sci Rep*. 2016;6:35315.
[39] Whipple, T. *The Times* (London), Saturday 2020 Oct 17.
[40] Lopez G and Santamaria L. Microwaving plastic into hydrogen and carbons. *Nat Catal*. 2020;3:861–862.
[41] Shah, S. Peak ventures. www.peakventures.in. Private communication.
[42] Almadhi A, *et al*. Moving from linear to circular economy in Saudi Arabia: Life-cycle assessment on plastic waste management. *Sustainability*. 2023;15(13):10450.
[43] Edwards PP and Sienko MJ. What is a metal? *Int Rev Phys Chem*. 1983;3(1):83–137.
[44] Harrison MR and Edwards PP. Electrons in small metallic particles. In: Edwards PP, Rao CNR, editors. *The Metallic and Nonmetallic States of Matter*. Taylor and Francis, London EC4A 3DE, England; 1985. p. 389.

[45] Edwards PP. Divided metals. In: *Proceedings of the Indian National Science Academy Golden Jubilee Symposium on Solid State Chemistry*. New Delhi; 1986. p. 265–291.

[46] Edwards PP, *et al*. On the size-induced metal-insulator transition in clusters and small particles. In: Raithby PR, Braunstein P, editors. *Metal Clusters in Chemistry*. Wiley-VCH, D-69469 Weinheim, Federal Republic of Germany; 1999. p. 1454–1481.

[47] Rao CNR, *et al*. Metal nanoparticles and their assemblies. *Chem Soc Rev*. 2000;29:27–35.

[48] Rao CNR, *et al*. Size-dependent chemistry: Properties of nanocrystals. *Chem Eur J*. 2002;8(1):29–35.

[49] Edwards PP, *et al*. The size-induced metal-insulator transition in mesoscopic conductors. In: Alexandrov AS, Demsar J, Yanson IK, editors. *Molecular Nanowires and Other Quantum Objects*. NATO science series, 148. Dordrecht: Springer; 2004. p. 39–341.

[50] Edwards PP and Thomas JM. Gold in a metallic divided state – From Faraday to the present day nanoscience. *Angew Chem Int Ed*. 2007;46(29):5480–5486.

[51] Marquardt P, *et al*. Microwave absorption by small metal particles. *Phys Letts*. 1986;114(1):39–42.

[52] Nimtz G, *et al*. Size-induced metal-insulator transition in metals and semiconductors. *J Crystal Growth*. 1988;86(1):66–71.

[53] Marquardt P, Nimtz G. The size-induced metal-insulator transition and related electron interference phenomena in modern microelectronics. In: Rössler, U. (eds) *Festkörperprobleme 29*. Advances in Solid State Physics, vol 29. Springer, Berlin, Heidelberg; 1989.

[54] Kubo R. Electronic properties of metallic fine particles I. *J Phys Soc Jpn*. 1962;50:975–986.

[55] Perenboom JAAJ, *et al*. Electronic properties of small metallic particles. *Phys Rep*. 1981;78(2):173–292.

[56] Porch A. (Cardiff University). Private communication.

[57] Tsien R. 2015. https://www.nobelprize.org/prizes/chemistry/2008/tsien/facts/.

[58] Porch A, Slocombe DR and Edwards PP. Microwave absorption in powders of small conducting particles for heating applications. *Phys Chem Chem Phys*. 2013;15:2757–2763.

[59] Schlogl R. Chemical energy storage. EPJ Web Conf. 2017;148:00015:1–14.

[60] Goldberg S. The plastics apocalypse. *National Geographic*. From the editor, June 2008.

https://doi.org/10.1142/9781800616295_0006

Chapter 6

Waste to Value Technology: The Key Enabler for Sustainability in Muslim Societies

Erfan Ibrahim

CEO & Founder, The Bit Bazaar LLC, Corona, California, USA

erfan@tbbllc.com

Abstract

This chapter describes a disruptive technology that can address the rapidly growing challenges of global waste disposal in a time of climate change. Waste disposal is a significant contributor to greenhouse gas emissions from human activities that drive climate change. A detailed technical and financial model is presented for a commercially viable, scalable waste management technology that can address the waste disposal problem in Muslim societies while creating well-paying jobs, producing valuable fuel and generating carbon credits to help meet the net zero targets for 2035 and 2050. This waste management model is presented as part of a comprehensive vision for a "smart community" of the future that can adapt to the effects of climate change while reducing greenhouse gas emissions for environmental protection.

1. Introduction

The Organization of Islamic Cooperation (OIC) has 56 member countries, covering an area of 31.92 million square kilometers and with a cumulative population of 1.98 billion people (24% of the global population) [1,2]. These 56 nations contain the majority of the largest Muslim societies in the world. A major exception is India, which has over 200 million Muslims but is not part of the OIC.

The per capita fossil fuel consumption of most OIC member states is generally lower than that of developed nations in Europe, Asia, North America, and Oceania, and their per capita consumption based carbon footprint is generally at par with Intergovernmental Panel on Climate Change (IPCC) targets for the 21st century [3]. Despite this, many of these OIC member states are unfortunately experiencing the most serious effects of climate change (e.g., higher average temperatures, floods, cyclones, and droughts) because of their locations on the planet.

A transition from the fossil-fuel-based economies of OIC member states today to nuclear and/or renewable energy is not only exorbitantly expensive and time-consuming, but it will also not result in any appreciable change in the global carbon footprint by 2050. This is because the seven major global economies of the world (the United States, China, the European Union, Russia, India, Brazil, and Japan) generate 63% of total annual atmospheric greenhouse gas (GHG) emissions [4] and their contribution has been growing over the past few years after a steady decline in the first two decades of this century [5].

This increase in annual greenhouse gas emissions across the seven major economies of the world is occurring despite the large-scale implementation of solar and wind technology to power the electric grid, the execution of extensive energy efficiency projects in buildings and industrial processes to reduce per capita energy consumption, and the gradual shifting from coal to natural gas as the primary fuel source for heat and power generation. Growing demand for energy (80% of which is still derived from fossil fuel combustion [6]) to support industrial, commercial, and residential sectors in these seven large global economies is the primary driver behind their rising contribution to annual greenhouse gas emissions into the Earth's atmosphere.

The dilemma for OIC member states is how to mitigate the adverse effects of climate change in their regions, given that their overall contribution to atmospheric greenhouse gas emissions is too small to reverse the growing global trend.

One effective way to address this dilemma is for OIC member states to adapt to the effects of climate change rather than trying to find ways to lower their energy sector's carbon footprint to mitigate its effects. Climate change adaptation can be successfully accomplished through building resilient communities that have a local supply chain for electricity generation and transportation fuel, leveraging abundant water resources without just relying on precipitation, developing robust local food production capabilities instead of importing food, and reusing natural resources to reduce dependence on both local and global mining.

OIC member states can build these resilient "smart communities" that: rely on a distributed electric grid with sufficient diversity in clean energy resources to minimize outages during high-impact weather events (e.g., small modular nuclear reactors, solar, wind, geothermal, and small hydro); leverage large fresh water supplies by desalinating seawater and/or purifying brackish water from aquifers with reverse osmosis technology to reduce reliance on lakes, rivers, and streams that depend on unpredictable levels of precipitation; electrolyze water to produce hydrogen that can be used to generate peak power for the electric grid and power trucks/vehicles using fuel cell technology; leverage vertical farming techniques in greenhouses to grow fruits and vegetables locally and avoid the deleterious effects of crop destruction in traditional land-based farming from parasite infestations and/or high-impact weather events; and develop waste-to-value plants for efficient recycling of carbonaceous waste to enable a circular economy.

This chapter outlines a disruptive waste management technology that can form the basis of a circular economy for natural resources in future "smart communities" that can be implemented in OIC member states to build resilience against climate change. A case study is presented for OIC member states to show the potential of this disruptive waste management technology to:

- eliminate dumping of waste in open pits;
- eliminate the incineration of waste;
- improve air, soil, and water quality, and minimize the amount of waste going to a landfill;
- maximize the recycling of waste;

- produce renewable natural gas for transportation and/or process heat;
- generate CO_2 credits from sequestered carbon in ash and collection of CO_2 emissions from the plant; and
- establish renewable identification number (RIN) credits from renewable natural gas.

The waste that can be processed using this technology includes any carbonaceous waste, such as municipal solid waste (MSW), mixed plastic waste (MPW), sewage sludge, medical waste, used tires, and agricultural residue. The focus of this study is on MSW processing.

2. Waste Management Technology Overview

Traditional methods of waste management include:

- partial dewatering of sewage sludge using aeration ponds and metallic and/or polymer coagulants;
- biological and chemical treatment of the coagulated sewage sludge to reduce pathogens and toxicity;
- mixing of partially dewatered and treated sewage sludge with food waste before landfilling;
- sorting of curbside collected MSW at transfer stations to remove recyclables;
- transporting unrecyclable MSW to an incinerator for combustion and/or landfilling;
- collecting medical waste from hospitals and clinics to be vitrified thermally and subsequently landfilled;
- transporting tire waste to an incinerator for combustion or delivering to a landfill for long term storage; and
- combusting agricultural residue at the farm and disposal of the residual ash at a landfill.

A society with a growing population is not sustainable if it generates massive quantities of non-recyclable waste, which requires a landfill for long-term storage. The valuable raw materials from finished goods in one lifecycle must be reclaimed for the next lifecycle to maintain a local supply chain for construction materials and raw materials for manufactured goods (circular economy).

Additionally, waste cannot be incinerated at scale because it produces massive quantities of CO_2, fly ash, bottom ash, dioxins, and furans, which are harmful to humans, animals, and plant life. Fly ash from the flue gas of an incinerator is classified as hazardous material and requires storage in a landfill with a proper liner. It can be as much as 15%–25% by weight of the incinerated solid waste [7]. Pyrolysis of mixed solid waste or sewage sludge produces tarry gases and char mixed with ash, which are difficult to clean and use in commercial applications. Plasma torches require high maintenance, produce significant quantities of volatilized heavy metals, and require massive quantities of power to operate, making them uneconomical to operate for large-scale waste remediation.

The only commercially feasible option for low-carbon waste remediation today is to gasify carbonaceous waste (e.g., MSW, sewage sludge, medical waste, agricultural waste, and tire waste) to produce syngas (H_2 and CO) which can then be utilized to generate either liquid fuels such as diesel, jet fuel, and naphtha via the Fischer–Tropsch process or renewable natural gas through a methanation process. The portion of liquid fuels or renewable natural gas derived from biogenic materials in waste is considered renewable and earns RIN credits in the market.

The recyclable materials from the waste emerge from the bottom of the gasifier, along with some inert ash. The gasification process has a limited carbon footprint, as it involves the production of some CO_2 during the pyrolysis and combustion stages. Nevertheless, the overall greenhouse gas emissions from a gasification plant are significantly lower than those from an incinerator, and there is negligible dioxin or furan production. Additionally, the calorific value of the waste is sufficient to provide the energy for process heat and electricity generation in a gasification plant, making it self-sustaining.

The amount of ash generated in a gasification plant, which requires landfilling, is approximately 9.8% by weight of the initial waste processed [8]. This is 39%–65% of the weight of the ash produced by an incinerator during the combustion of the entire waste. As a result, gasification is the most sustainable, economical, and environmentally friendly option for waste remediation, supporting a circular economy today.

3. Gasification/Methanation Process Overview

Gasification and methanation have been well-established industrial processes for decades. Gasification of coal has produced synthesis gas (H_2 and CO) for commercial use since the mid-19th century [9].

Over the past several decades, gasification of MSW, MPW, wood waste, agricultural residue, and sewage sludge has produced syngas for electricity generation and for process heat globally. These plants were developed to support the electricity and process heat requirements of industry.

Gasification of carbonaceous waste involves five basic steps following general sorting to remove easily identifiable recyclable and inert materials (e.g., glass, metal, dirt, and ceramic) [10]:

- Drying – excess water is removed from the waste (down to 10–15% moisture content).
- Pyrolysis – waste is heated in the absence of oxygen up to 350–450°C to break it down to charcoal (carbon + inert ash) and tarry gases (carbon-based and inorganic volatile compounds).
- Combustion – a portion of the waste is combusted to increase the operating temperature of the gasifier to as high as 800–1,000°C.
- Cracking – the extremely hot temperature from combustion cracks the tarry gases into gases of lower molecular weights (including H_2 and CO) and activates the charcoal.
- Reduction – carbon dioxide and water combine with activated charcoal to produce more H_2 and CO (the main ingredients of syngas).

The syngas coming out of the gasifier is hot and has several impurities in it. These impurities include particulate matter, carbon dioxide, water vapor, hydrogen chloride, hydrogen sulfide, and ammonia. The syngas undergoes a series of dry and wet filtration processes to remove these impurities, resulting in a gas stream containing only H_2 and CO at a lower temperature.

The purified syngas can then be put through a methanation process where the carbon monoxide and carbon dioxide react with hydrogen from syngas to produce methane gas (a renewable natural gas) and water vapor by two exothermic chemical reactions (the Sabatier process) [11]:

- $CO + 3H_2 \rightarrow CH_4 + H_2O$ (−206 KJ/mole)
- $CO_2 + 4H_2 \rightarrow CH_4 + 2H_2O$ (−165 KJ/mole)

The renewable natural gas is dried and stored for use as fuel for transportation, electricity generation, or process heat. Some of the purified syngas from the gasification system is combusted in a combined heat and power (CHP) engine to generate onsite electricity along with rooftop solar panels in a microgrid for the plant's internal power requirements, making the overall plant energy self-sufficient.

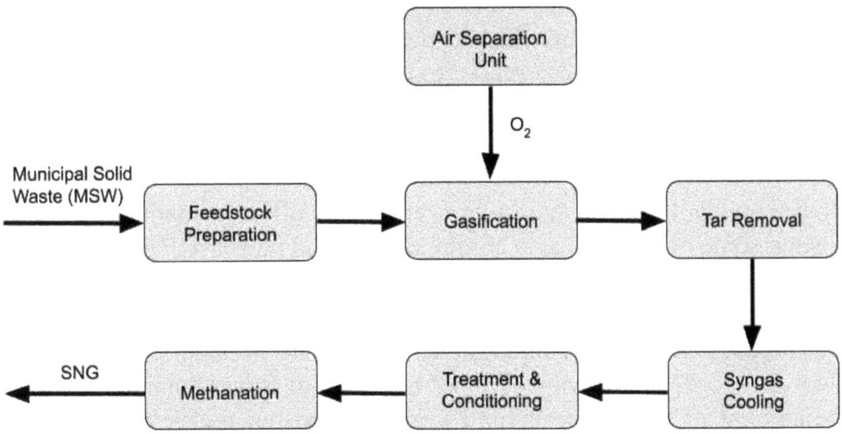

Figure 1. Gasification and methanation process flow diagram.

Figure 1 shows a schematic diagram of a commercially viable advanced gasification/methanation technology process.

Gasification technology has several benefits, including being readily permitted, reducing landfill volumes, being scalable, producing green renewable energy, and reducing GHG emissions.

4. Gasification/Methanation Plant Technology Overview

Waste is transported to the plant facility via curbside collection or a transfer station on trucks and stored onsite. An automated process tears open the waste bags and crushes, shreds, and cuts all the waste into small pieces before sorting through the waste using AI based pattern recognition technology and removing clearly distinguishable recyclable and inert materials such as glass, metal, ceramics, dirt, and hazardous substances. The presorted waste is then placed on a moving belt where teams of general workers remove additional recyclable and inert materials that the sorting machine may have missed. Powerful magnets are used to pull out ferromagnetic particles from the waste stream after the manual sorting process is complete. The waste can be mixed with mixed plastic waste particles in a predefined ratio to increase the calorific value and then enters a briquetting system where the waste particles are dried down to 10% overall moisture content and compressed into 25 mm × 25 mm residual derivative fuel (RDF) briquettes. The gasification plant is set up in a modular design.

Excess water from the waste stream in storage, sorting, and drying processes is recycled and used in the gasifier. The water vapor in the methanation process is also reused to conserve water.

If the calorific value of the RDF exceeds 17.5 MJ/kg due to its carbon content, then approximately 321 m^3 of renewable natural gas can be produced from the gasification/methanation process from each metric ton of RDF. The plant can operate in an energy self-sufficient manner by combusting some of the syngas in combined heat and power (CHP) engines to generate the required electricity and process heat for its operation. This is a key requirement for plant resilience in a time of climate change when the electric grid can be vulnerable to high-impact weather events. Note, the use of some of the syngas from the gasifier to power the plant reduces the amount of renewable natural gas produced per metric ton of RDF processed from 321 m^3 down to 257 m^3.

5. Four-Module Gasification/Methanation Plant Case Study

The proposed gasification/methanation plant will operate four modular gasification/methanation lines, each processing 6.76 metric tons of RDF per hour, to process a total of 27.04 metric tons per hour of RDF for 24 hours per day and 329 days per year, resulting in a total of 213,508 metric tons of RDF processed annually. The plant site will be 50,000 square meters and have easy access to a major roadway, storm drainage, and a supply of fresh water (piped or from an underground aquifer). There is no electric grid tie.

Total forecasted annual global MSW generation from 4.3 billion urban residents is projected to be 2.1 billion metric tons by 2025 [12]. Table 1 provides the detailed mass and energy characteristics of the sample MSW for the four-module gasification/methanation plant, based on global MSW data.

Table 2 provides detailed mass and energy characteristics of the sample MPW for the four-module gasification/methanation plant, based on global MPW data [13].

Table 1. MSW characterization.

Municipal Solid Waste (MSW)	% Composition in MSW	Moisture Content (%)	Daily Weight Wet (Kg)	Daily Weight Dry (Kg)	High Heating Value (MJ/Kg)	High Heating Energy Available from Waste Type (MJ)	High Heating Value (MSW) Dry Weight MJ/Kg	% Inerts (Wet Waste)	% Renewable Energy
Food Waste	29.33%	76.44%	347,235	81,809	18.61	1,522,458			
Paper	11.33%	6.00%	134,135	126,087	16.28	2,052,692			
Cardboard	5.67%	5.00%	67,127	63,770	16.28	1,038,180			
Plastics	12.00%	2.00%	142,067	139,226	41.80	5,819,627			
Textiles	2.00%	10.00%	23,678	21,310	18.61	396,580			
Rubber	1.00%	2.00%	11,839	11,602	23.26	269,865			
Leather	1.00%	10.00%	11,839	10,655	23.26	247,836			
Yard Waste / Agricultural Residue	14.67%	51.73%	173,677	83,834	15.11	1,266,728			
Wood	2.00%	20.00%	23,678	18,942	18.61	352,515			
Glass	5.00%	2.00%	59,195	58,011	0	0			
Metals	4.00%	8.00%	47,356	43,567	0	0			
Dirt, Ceramic, Ash & Hazardous Materials	12.00%	8.00%	142,067	130,702	0	0			
Total	100.00%	33.31%	1,183,891	789,514		12,966,481	16.42	21.00%	55.12%

Table 2. MPW characterization.

Mixed Plastic Waste (MPW)	% Composition in Mixed Dry Plastic Waste	Total Plastic Waste with 10% Inerts (Kg)	Total Plastic Waste Dry Weight - No External Inerts (Kg)	High Heating Value of Plastic Waste Type (MJ/Kg)	Mass of Plastic Waste Type (Kg)	Heating Energy Available from Plastic Waste Type (MJ)	Avg. Heating Value of Mixed Plastic Waste (MJ/Kg)
Low Density Polyethylene (LDPE)	23.00%	11,839	10,655	43.34	2,450.65	106,211.32	
High Density Polyethylene (HDPE)	19.00%	11,839	10,655	47.39	2,024.45	95,938.82	
Polypropylene (PP)	14.00%	11,839	10,655	47.56	1,491.70	70,945.35	
Polyvinyl Chloride (PVC)	6.00%	11,839	10,655	21.00	639.30	13,425.32	
Polystyrene (PS)	9.00%	11,839	10,655	42.95	958.95	41,186.96	
Polyethylene tetraphthalate (PET)	10.00%	11,839	10,655	22.00	1,065.50	23,441.03	
Wax Mix	19.00%	11,839	10,655	46.55	2,024.45	94,238.28	
Total	100.00%	11,839	10,655		10,655.02	445,387.09	37.62

The average calorific value of the MSW is 16.42 MJ/Kg with 33.31% moisture content and 21% inert materials. The average calorific value of the MPW is 37.62 MJ/Kg with 0% moisture content and 10% inert materials. The briquetting system will combine the MSW RDF with the MPW RDF in a 100:1 ratio by weight. The combined RDF briquette with 10% moisture content and 5% inert materials will be 20.67 MJ/Kg. This exceeds the 17.5 MJ/Kg threshold to generate 257 m^3 of renewable natural gas at standard temperature and pressure (STP) per metric ton of RDF gasified. The daily RDF intake of the plant will be ~649 metric tons, with a total calorific value of 13,411,870 MJ.

The plant will operate on a 24/7 schedule, with 329 days of operation per year for 25 years. It will employ a total of 100 people, including executive management, administrative staff, engineers, technicians, general workers, drivers, and security personnel. The plant site will have waste and product storage capacities of two weeks each. This will ensure a high availability factor for the plant and resilience against high-impact weather events, waste supply/product pickup delays due to strikes, labor shortages, or other unforeseen circumstances.

6. Gasification/Methanation Plant Financial Overview

The annual gross revenue for the four-module gasification/methanation plant includes:

- gate fees of US$5 per wet metric ton of MSW received at the plant site;
- US$15.00 per MMBTU (27.97 m^3 at STP) of renewable natural gas produced;
- 12.98 RIN credits per MMBTU of natural gas from renewable waste resources (food waste, garden trimmings, and wood waste);
- US$3.00 per RIN credit;
- US$100 per metric ton of CO_2 credits earned from carbon sequestered in the plant.

The average annual salary plus benefits for personnel is estimated to be US$40,000; the total payroll will amount to US$4,000,000 per year.

The services, general, and administrative expenses (SG&A) and other operating cost data were provided by an established gasification

Table 3. Technical and economic analysis of a four-module gasification/methanation plant.

Global MSW+MPW Gasification Plant Strawman Technical Specifications	Values
Annual MSW supply (wet metric tons)	389,500
Plastic : MSW wt. ratio	1.00%
Annual mixed plastic supply (with 10% inerts)	3,895
# of days of operation per year	329
Daily MSW (wet metric tons)	1,183.89
MSW moisture content (%)	33.31%
MSW wt. % inerts	21.00%
Daily MSW (dry) metric tons	789.51
Daily MSW (dry without inerts) metric tons	540.90
Daily MSW RDF (with 10% moisture content and 5% inerts) metric tons	**636.35**
Daily MSW RDF calorific value HHV (GJ)	12,966.481
Daily mixed plastic waste (metric tons)	11.84
Mixed plastic waste % inerts	10%
Mixed plastic waste moisture content (%)	0%
Daily mixed plastic waste without inerts (metric tons)	10.66
Daily mixed plastic waste RDF with 10% moisture content and 5% inerts (metric tons)	**12.54**
Daily calorific value of mixed plastic waste RDF HHV (GJ)	445.39

Total daily RDF intake MSW + plastic (metric tons)	**648.88**
Total RDF calorific value (HHV basis) (GJ)	13,411.87
Average HHV of RDF (GJ/ton)	20.67
Hourly feed rate of RDF	27.04
# of gasification modules	4.00
Hourly feed rate per module	6.76
Yield of SNG/RNG per ton of RDF (m^3)	257.40
Calorific value of SNG/RNG (MJ/m^3)	35.196
Estimate of daily SNG/RNG production (m^3)	167,023
Calorific value of daily estimate of SNG/RNG LHV (MJ)	5,878,535
Annual output of SNG/RNG (MMBTU)	1,833,211
Net plant efficiency (%)	43.83%

Economic Analysis	
Total plant CAPEX with 10% contingency	$300,000,000
Equity investment (30%)	$90,000,000
Debt financing (70%)	$210,000,000
Annual inflation rate (%)	3.00%

(*Continued*)

Table 3. *(Continued)*

Revenue	Values
Tipping fee rate ($/metric ton)	$5.00
Annual revenue from tipping Fees ($)	$1,947,500
SNG/RNG Price ($/MMBTU)	$15.00
Annual revenue from SNG/RNG Sales ($)	$27,498,170
% Energy from biogenic sources	53.29%
RIN credits per MMBTU from biogenic sources	12.98
RIN credit price ($)	$3.00
Annual revenue from RINs credits ($)	$38,039,438
Annual ash to be landfilled – 17% of RDF processed (metric tons)	36,292.10
Carbon content in ash (%)	25.99%
Annual CO_2 credits from sequestered ash (metric tons)	34,522.28
CO_2 credit price ($/metric ton)	$100.00
Annual revenue from carbon credits from landfilled ash ($)	$3,452,228
Annual CO_2 sequestered from gasification, methanation & CHP engines (metric tons)	180,988
Annual revenue from sequestered carbon from gasification, methanation, & CHP engines ($)	$18,098,800
Total Annual Gross Revenue ($)	$89,036,136

Costs for Year 1	Values
Annual salary ($)	$40,000
Number of employees	100
Annual payroll ($)	$4,000,000
Plant site area (sq. meter)	50,000
Monthly land lease rate ($/sq. meter)	$1.20
Annual land lease Cost ($)	$720,000
SG&A ($/MMBTU)	$1.57
SG&A ($)	$2,878,142
Insurance ($/MMBTU)	$1.57
Annual insurance ($)	$2,878,142
Maintenance ($/MMBTU)	$0.55
Annual maintenance ($)	$1,008,266
Utilities ($/MMBTU)	$4.18
Annual utilities ($)	$7,662,823
Ash disposal ($/metric ton)	$5.00
Annual ash disposal Cost ($)	$181,460
Total OPEX ($)	$19,328,833

Table 4. Financial summary of four-module gasification/methanation plant.

Financial Summary	Year 1	Year 2	Year 3	Year 4	Year 5
EBITDA ($)	**$69,707,302**	**$71,820,121**	**$73,996,325**	**$76,237,815**	**$78,546,549**
Annual interest rate (%)	10.00%	10.00%	10.00%	10.00%	10.00%
Debt ($)	$252,000,000	$235,200,000	$219,520,000	$203,840,000	$188,160,000
Annual interest paid ($)	$25,200,000	$23,520,000	$21,952,000	$20,384,000	$18,816,000
Annual debt reduction ($)	$16,800,000	$15,680,000	$15,680,000	$15,680,000	$15,680,000
Annual debt payment ($)	$42,000,000	$39,200,000	$37,632,000	$36,064,000	$34,496,000
Annual depreciation schedule (25 yrs)	$12,000,000	$12,000,000	$12,000,000	$12,000,000	$12,000,000
EBT ($)	$15,707,302	$20,620,121	$24,364,325	$28,173,815	$32,050,549
Corporate tax rate (%)	25.00%	25.00%	25.00%	25.00%	25.00%
Annual tax ($)	$3,926,826	$5,155,030	$6,091,081	$7,043,454	$8,012,637
Net income ($)	$11,780,477	$15,465,091	$18,273,244	$21,130,361	$24,037,912
Cash in bank	$23,780,477	$51,245,568	$81,518,811	$114,649,172	$150,687,084
Financial Summary	**Year 6**	**Year 7**	**Year 8**	**Year 9**	**Year 10**
EBITDA ($)	**$80,924,545**	**$83,373,882**	**$85,896,698**	**$88,495,199**	**$91,171,655**
Annual interest rate (%)	10.00%	10.00%	10.00%	10.00%	10.00%
Debt ($)	$172,480,000	$156,800,000	$141,120,000	$125,440,000	$109,760,000
Annual interest paid ($)	$17,248,000	$15,680,000	$14,112,000	$12,544,000	$10,976,000
Annual debt reduction ($)	$15,680,000	$15,680,000	$15,680,000	$15,680,000	$15,680,000
Annual debt payment ($)	$32,928,000	$31,360,000	$29,792,000	$28,224,000	$26,656,000
Annual depreciation schedule (25 yrs)	$12,000,000	$12,000,000	$12,000,000	$12,000,000	$12,000,000
EBT ($)	$35,996,545	$40,013,882	$44,104,698	$48,271,199	$52,515,655
Corporate tax rate (%)	25.00%	25.00%	25.00%	25.00%	25.00%
Annual tax ($)	$8,999,136	$10,003,470	$11,026,175	$12,067,800	$13,128,914
Net income ($)	$26,997,409	$30,010,411	$33,078,524	$36,203,399	$39,386,741
Cash in bank ($)	$189,684,493	$231,694,904	$276,773,428	$324,976,828	$376,363,569

technology vendor from the UK. The monthly land lease rate is nominally set at $1.20 per square meter per month. Plant site size is 50,000 square meters. The annual lease rate for the plant site is $720,000. Plant site should be located enroute to a major landfill in an industrially zoned area.

The inflation rate is estimated at 3% annually. For a shorter equity payback period, the plant investment cost of $300,000,000 can be covered by 30% equity partner investments (and/or government grants) and 70% debt financing from banks. The annual interest rate for the loan is estimated at 10% The corporate tax rate is estimated at 25%.

Table 3 provides the complete technical and financial overview of the 4-module gasification/methanation plant.

Based on these assumptions, the 10-year cash flow for the 4-module gasification/methanation plant in Table 4 indicates a return on equity period of 3–4 years and a full return on investment (ROI) period of 8–9 years (with no tax or other governmental/financial institution incentives).

7. Application of the Gasification/Methanation Plant Model to OIC Member States

At a global level, 2.1 billion wet metric tons of MSW generated per year by 8.1 billion people on the planet will require (2,100,000,000/389,500) = 5,392 gasification/methanation plants with four modules each.

This number of plants would require a global capital investment of $5,392 × US$300,000,000 = US$1.6 trillion (~1.48% of global GDP [14]).

The per capita cost for implementing this disruptive waste management technology globally will be US$1.6 trillion/0.0081 trillion = US$200!

Based on the generic case study for a commercially viable four-module gasification/methanation plant described above, this model can easily be applied to the 56 OIC member states to determine how many such plants will be needed to process the MSW in each country based on the specific characterization of their MSW and MPW (Tables 1 and 2) and the detailed technical/financial model in Table 3.

Since the total investment for a four-module gasification/methanation plant is known, the total investment required to design, build, commission, and operate the requisite number of plants in each OIC member state to meet their MSW generation needs can be determined. Table 5 provides a sample of four large Muslim nations.

Table 5. Waste characterization and plant economics for four OIC member states.

	Indonesia	Pakistan	Egypt	Malaysia
Population	273,800,000	231,400,000	109,300,000	33,570,000
Daily MSW production (Kg/day)	0.69	0.4	0.82	1.17
# of days per year	365	365	365	365
Total MSW generated (metric tons)	68,956,530	33,784,400	32,713,490	14,336,069
GHG emissions from MSW (metric tons of CO_2 eq/metric ton of MSW)	0.649	0.649	0.649	0.649
GHG emissions from MSW (metric tons of CO_2 eq)	44,752,788	21,926,076	21,231,055	9,304,108
Moisture content (%)	33.30%	28.65%	37.68%	32.10%
% inerts	12.60%	28.00%	3.00%	7.70%
Calorific value (MJ/Kg)	21	14.28	25.37	22.97
% Renewable energy	48.04%	62.00%	47.00%	52.66%
Dry waste (metric tons)	45,994,006	24,105,169	20,387,047	9,734,191
Dry waste without inerts (metric tons)	37,305,483	14,645,537	19,405,642	8,630,313
Amount of RDF (metric tons)	43,888,803	17,230,044	22,830,167	10,153,310
Total calorific value of waste (MJ)	9.64494E+11	3.44222E+11	5.17219E+11	2.23594E+11
Average calorific value of RDF (MJ/Kg)	21.98	19.98	22.66	22.02
RNG/SNG potential in country (MMBTUs)	413,313,111	162,260,134	214,998,059	95,616,552
Wholesale price of RNG/SNG ($/MMBTU)	$15.00	$15.00	$15.00	$15.00

RIN credits	2,577,251,932	1,305,804,656	1,311,617,160	653,564,756
Wholesale price of RIN ($)	$3.00	$3.00	$3.00	$3.00
CO_2 credits from sequestered carbon in ash (metric tons)	7,099,979	2,787,339	3,693,282	1,642,521
CO_2 credits from sequestered plant CO_2 emissions (metric tons)	37,204,005	14,605,699	19,352,855	8,606,837
CO_2 credit price ($/metric ton)	$100.00	$100.00	$100.00	$100.00
Tipping fees for MSW ($/metric ton)	$5.00	$5.00	$5.00	$5.00
Revenue potential from gasification of MSW ($)	$18,706,633,550	$8,259,541,727	$9,628,003,533	$4,491,558,724
# of 4-modules gasification plants required	206	81	107	48
CAPEX for plants	$61,668,184,941	$24,209,945,639	$32,078,682,508	$14,266,421,819
Per capita investment ($)	$225.23	$104.62	$293.49	$424.98

As Table 5 indicates, there are significant variations in the per-capita MSW generation in each country and its composition, which will alter how many plants will meet the MSW processing requirements. OIC member states with higher-moisture-content MSW and/or a higher percentage of inert materials will require fewer plants (less RDF), whereas those with lower-moisture-content MSW and a lower percentage of inert materials (more RDF) will require more plants.

Additionally, these total plant cost estimates will be significantly higher than the actual investment required because the cost model does not assume any economies of scale from mass production of the major portions of the gasification and methanation modules in each country using prefabrication, as well as savings in engineering, procurement, and construction costs from building several plants in each country simultaneously.

Nevertheless, even without the expected savings at scale, this model offers a reasonable per-capita cost for implementing the gasification/methanation technology for waste management in each of the 56 OIC member states. The gasification/methanation plants will produce significant quantities of renewable natural gas to meet domestic natural gas needs in each country while generating CO_2 and RIN credits to meet the IPCC net zero targets for 2035 and 2050.

8. Conclusion

A disruptive waste management technology has been described that can help Muslim societies become more resilient to the effects of climate change while protecting their environment, creating well-paying job opportunities for their citizens, generating new revenue streams for economic prosperity, and meeting IPCC greenhouse gas emission targets for 2035 and 2050. The per capita investment in the technology is well within the range of traditional waste management service costs over a 1–3 year period, and the 8–9-year payback period on the capital investment is reasonable compared to other large infrastructure projects that typically require 15–20 years. The governments of OIC member states are strongly encouraged to consider this disruptive waste management technology and develop plans for its phased implementation through public–private partnerships that can minimize financial risks and maximize benefits to their citizens.

Acknowledgments

The author wants to thank Ms. Anam Siddiqui of Riverside, CA, USA, The Bit Bazaar LLC (TBB) student intern, for her research work that produced the valuable references in this chapter and her assistance in the final editing. The author also wishes to thank Mr. Andrew Blume of Laguna, CA, USA, a TBB contractor, for creating the gasification/methanation process diagram in the chapter and validating renewable natural gas, RIN credit and CO_2 credit pricing from industry for the financial model presented in this chapter.

References

[1] WorldData.info. Members of the OIC: Organization of Islamic Cooperation. Available from: https://www.worlddata.info/alliances/oic-islamic-cooperation.php.

[2] Organization of Islamic Cooperation. History. Available from: https://www.oic-oci.org/page/?p_id=52&p_ref=26&lan=en.

[3] Organization of Islamic Cooperation. OIC environment report, 2021. Statistical, Economic and Social Research and Training Centre for Islamic Countries (SESRIC). 2021. Available from: https://sesricdiag.blob.core.windows.net/sesric-site-blob/files/article/805.pdf.

[4] Paddison L, Choi A. As climate chaos accelerates, which countries are polluting the most? *CNN*. 2023 Dec 1. Available from: https://www.cnn.com/interactive/2023/12/us/countries-climate-change-emissions-cop28/.

[5] Emissions Database for Global Atmospheric Research (EDGAR). GHG emissions of all world countries: 2024 report. Available from: https://edgar.jrc.ec.europa.eu/report_2024.

[6] Foster S, Elzinga D. The role of fossil fuels in a sustainable energy system. *United Nations UN Chronicle*. 2015 Dec; No. 3, Vol. LII. Sustainable Energy. Available from: https://www.un.org/en/chronicle/article/role-fossil-fuels-sustainable-energy-system.

[7] United States Environmental Protection Agency (EPA). Energy recovery from the combustion of municipal solid waste (MSW). Last updated 2023 Jun 7. Available from: https://www.epa.gov/smm/energy-recovery-combustion-municipal-solid-waste-msw.

[8] National Energy Technology Laboratory (NETL). Major gasification solid byproducts. Available from: https://netl.doe.gov/research/Coal/energy-systems/gasification/gasifipedia/solid-byproducts.

[9] Pereira EG, Martins MA. Gasification technology. Encyclopedia of sustainable technologies. 2017. Available from: https://www.sciencedirect.com/science/article/abs/pii/B9780124095489101332?via%3Dihub.
[10] All Power Labs – Carbon negative power & products. How we get there: The five processes of gasification. Available from: https://www.allpowerlabs.com/gasification-explained.
[11] Styring P, Rackley S. Sabatier reaction. Negative emissions technologies for climate change mitigation. *Encyclopedia of Sustainable Technologies*. Elsevier; 2023. Available from: https://www.sciencedirect.com/topics/earth-and-planetary-sciences/sabatier-reaction.
[12] Hoornweg D, Bhada-Tata P. What a waste: A global review of solid waste management. *Urban Development Series Knowledge Papers*, no. 15. The World Bank; 2012 Mar. https://documents1.worldbank.org/curated/en/302341468126264791/pdf/68135-REVISED-What-a-Waste-2012-Final-updated.pdf.
[13] Bodzay B, Banhegyi G. Polymer waste: Controlled breakdown or recycling? *International Journal of Design Sciences and Technology*; 2017;22(2):109–138. Available from: https://www.researchgate.net/figure/Typical-composition-of-plastic-waste-within-MSW-12_tbl2_320142206.
[14] Dyvik EH. Global GDP – statistics & facts. Statistica. 2023 Dec 18. Available from: https://www.statista.com/topics/7747/gross-domestic-product-gdp-worldwide/#editorsPicks.

https://doi.org/10.1142/9781800616295_0007

Chapter 7

Toward a Geospatial and Temporal Experience of Islamic Architecture: Caravanserais of Anatolia

Güzden Varinlioğlu[*,†,§,¶] and Özge Börekçi[‡,|]

[*]*Department of Architecture, University of Liverpool, Liverpool, UK*

[†]*Department of Architecture, Massachusetts Institute of Technology, Cambridge, USA*

[‡]*Department of Informatics, Faculty of Architecture, Istanbul Technical University, Istanbul, Turkey*

[§]*guzden.varinlioglu@liverpool.ac.uk*

[¶]*guzden@mit.edu*

[|]*borekcio@itu.edu.tr*

Abstract

Caravanserais, one of the important representations of Seljuk Islamic architecture, not only embody functionality, such as facilitating trade and travel, but also exhibit the aesthetic and cultural characteristics of Islamic architecture. This research aims to examine this unique example of Islamic architecture and its temporal changes by creating precise spatial data using digital tools. The research presents a systematic, parametric, and digital compilation of information obtained from previous studies on caravanserais, cross-checked with information obtained on-site.

1. Introduction

The ancient landscapes of Anatolia, situated at the crossroads of civilizations and the easternmost point of the famous Silk Road, face risks from unplanned invasive restorations, natural decay, and neglect. As the monetary value of these heritage sites is prioritized and unplanned adaptive reuse takes precedence, the threats to archeological sites in this historically rich region demand urgent attention to safeguard their heritage. The visibility of endangered heritage stands as a crucial factor in safeguarding these assets. Academic research on Anatolian archeological sites has the potential to elevate their visibility; however, obstacles arise from the complexities involved in such scholarly pursuits. The wealth of information available, although valuable, is often disparate and outdated, complicating efforts to effectively showcase and protect these invaluable historical sites.

Caravanserais in Anatolia were integral to facilitating trade and communication along ancient routes. Strategically positioned, they served as vital rest stops for travelers and merchants, offering accommodation, food, and shelter. Their locations were meticulously chosen to optimize accessibility and safety, fostering the flow of goods and ideas across the region. The construction dates of caravanserais in Anatolia vary, as they were built over centuries, with some dating back as far as the 11th century during the Seljuk period and continuing through the Ottoman era. Caravanserais, built by the Anatolian Seljuks in the 13th century, are among the most important commercial structures in the Islamic world. These structures, located on the Silk Road, served not only as commercial buildings but also as architectural legacies, integrating defense and accommodation functions. They bear significant traces of the sociocultural and economic life of their time.

Caravanserais are significant structures of Anatolian heritage and serve as a good example of the preservation challenge they face. Various researchers have documented these structures by different names, leading to fragmented records that hinder a comprehensive understanding of their significance in Anatolian history. The absence of current and comprehensive studies obstructs access to accurate and precise information crucial for the preservation and appreciation of these unique cultural assets. This chapter explores the challenges of documenting archeological sites in Anatolia, particularly dealing with outdated and incomplete information. Through an exploration of the challenges faced in preserving Anatolian heritage, we aim to shed light on the necessity of comprehensive and updated studies to ensure the safeguarding and promotion of these invaluable cultural treasures for future generations.

Although many studies have been carried out on Anatolian Seljuk caravanserais in order to record and analyze this special heritage, Erdmann's research in 1961 remains the key study [1]. A much more recent example is Acun's collection of articles on the Seljuk caravanserais [2]. Architectural historian Ayşıl Tükel Yavuz devoted her academic career to analyzing many architectural and cultural aspects of this unique heritage. Many academic studies have been published on this subject [3,4]. Another researcher, the historian Özergin [5], focused on the importance of the Anatolian trade routes during the Seljuk period and recorded architectural/identical information about many caravanserai structures along this route. In Hillenbrand's study [6], the architectural characteristics and functional phenomena of caravanserais in the Islamic world are examined. These studies range from on-site examinations of architectural features to compilations of literature and mappings of these historical structures, illuminating their spatial representations across Turkey.

Comprehensive academic studies on Seljuk caravanserais began in 1961, with Erdmann's [1] focus being on the architectural features and classification of Anatolian Seljuk caravanserais based on on-site examinations. Other scholars, including Özergin [5] and İlter [7], expanded on this work by creating catalogs, bibliographies, and studies of both Seljuk and Ottoman caravanserais. More recent work, such as Tuncer's index in 2007 [8], compared and processed caravanserais using large-scale maps to enhance their spatial representation.

Together, the studies on Seljuk caravanserais also form a comprehensive corpus, offering architectural, historical, archeological, and spatial information about these unique structures. Yavuz's [4] comprehensive analysis emphasized the diversity and vast influence of caravanserais on Anatolian Seljuk architecture, particularly in terms of scale. This analysis focused on their architectural intricacies and functions within their context, as well as their roles in providing shelter and defense. Redford [9] highlighted the significance of caravanserais spread across a wide geographical area during the Seljuk period. He viewed them as a key factor in settlement development, evaluating their social-historical contexts and emphasizing the need for further archeological investigations to unveil their deeper historical significance.

In Anatolian Seljuk heritage studies, certain caravanserais have been classified in various ways: "invisible structures" or "newly added" [1], "deteriorated over time" [10], "repaired" [10], "lost" [11], "having unknown locations" [8], or "vanished completely" [12]. These classifications highlight the need for a comprehensive database detailing Caravanserai's spatial characteristics and historical evolution, essential for understanding Islamic architecture. However, issues such as limitations in resources, professional restrictions, and the lack of cultural importance ascribed to the field of heritage often hinder efforts to visually present data and conduct studies that reveal their temporal and spatial contexts in three-dimensional (3D) formats.

1.1. *Problem definition*

Unplanned restoration or adaptive reuse, natural deterioration, and neglect threaten archeological sites in Anatolia, the easternmost point of the Silk Road. Through a comprehensive literature review and on-site observations conducted as part of the study, the existence of numerous caravanserais left unprotected and neglected in terms of conservation has been observed. These caravanserais (or "hans" in Turkish) are gradually losing their significant architectural and historical elements, such as ornaments and inscriptions, and face extinction due to various environmental factors that cause a loss of structural integrity and destruction over time. Further, additional changes made during the restoration of privately owned and refunctionalized caravanserais, as well as their unconscious use, may threaten the authentic features of these heritage sites. The visibility of heritage at risk is important in mitigating these threats. While academic studies on archeological sites in Anatolia hold promise for increasing visibility, this potential is diminished by the complex, dispersed, and outdated nature of the available information and documentation. The existence of the same caravanserais, documented under different names by various researchers, along with a lack of current and comprehensive studies, makes it difficult to obtain precise and accurate information about these unique heritage structures.

1.2. *Research questions*

The responsibility for documenting Anatolian Seljuk caravanserais is distributed among various disciplines, including architecture, archeology, and architectural history, with the information being influenced by temporal changes in these structures across different time periods. Thus, this study, taking a multifaceted approach, aims to answer the following questions:

- What is the best approach to evaluating the accuracy of the data when identifying Anatolian Seljuk caravanserai structures?
- What are the most suitable technological tools for determining the geographical distribution of Anatolian Seljuk caravan routes based on available data sources?
- What are the potential limitations and challenges associated with using technologies for compiling and disseminating data on Anatolian Seljuk caravan routes and caravanserais?

1.3. *Methodology*

It is of great importance to model this heritage in a virtual environment based on its geographical and geo-temporal documentation, including architectural features, location, and historical and archeological elements, for the protection and promotion of national heritage. Therefore, within the scope of this research, the aim is to design and implement a modeling, visualization, and experimentation system that is repeatable, sustainable, and efficient in terms of labor and time. Conducting secondary research on the existing literature constitutes the first step in the data collection phase of the project. At this point, taking a geographical approach helped avoid overlapping data sources and eliminate unnecessary data. Later, during the field studies, the approach involved creating spatial, visual, and three-dimensional data related to the structures. The final stage involved simulating visual data and integrating the obtained data with the website.

1.4. *Chapter in brief*

In this chapter, the early efforts to document caravanserais in Anatolia from the Seljuk period are presented. The study of Seljuk caravanserais underwent systematic compilation, employing a nonlinear documentation approach that facilitated precise information gathering through field studies along specific routes in Anatolia, as part of the Sustainable Information Lifecycle of Kervansaray (SILK) project. The SILK project encompasses multiple stages of making Anatolian caravanserais visible: mapping their architectural heritage; documenting them through photogrammetry; revitalizing these buildings using digital reconstruction models; raising public awareness among local people; and creating immersive, virtual tours for the public. Thus, this chapter provides information about compilation, documentation, and dissemination efforts for mapping the caravanserais by examining the development of urbanization in Anatolia, utilizing mapping tools to reveal caravanserai networks, and presenting the current status through generated visual, 3D, and digital models.

2. Scope

This section examines the spatial-commercial routes of Anatolian Seljuk caravanserais, drawing attention to their historical and geographical importance. The locations of Seljuk caravanserais in Anatolia are shown on the map, highlighting those revisited during the project (Fig. 1).

Anatolia, also known as Asia Minor, connects to Asia and Europe by land and to Africa by sea. It is strategically located at the crossroads of the

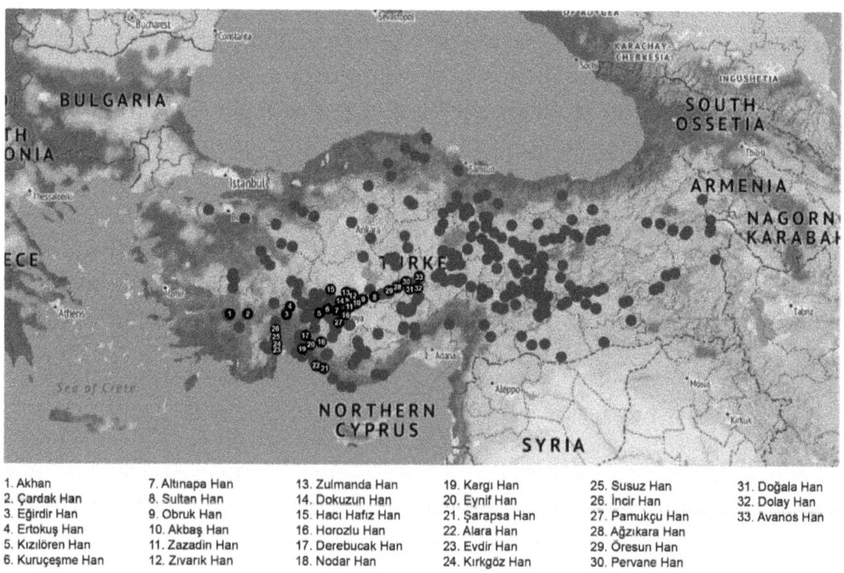

Figure 1. Black markers shows the Seljuk caravanserais in Anatolia studied during the field surveys.

world's wealthiest routes, roads, and tracks. These roads have fostered connections between both individuals and societies through interactions which would not have been nearly as fast or easy without such development. Roads play an important role in both material and information transportation. The following archeologists have researched the connections between Anatolia and Eastern Europe: French [13] studied the Roman Empire's road networks; Preiser-Kapeller [14] researched Byzantine road networks, and Orbis [15] developed an online system to simulate movement along Roman road networks. These very few studies demonstrate the incompleteness of the examination of Anatolia's connections to the East.

2.1. *The Silk Road*

The Silk Road was a network of routes that connected Eastern, Central, and Western Asian societies to the Mediterranean. These caravan routes, including those through Anatolia, represented the ancient world's leading long-distance communication networks. ICOMOS' thematic work on the Silk Road routes extends to Antalya on the East–West axis. However, Turkey's Silk Road routes in Anatolia, which are as yet only on the project's temporary list, are not included in this comprehensive study [16]. Other studies related to these trading centers include Ottoman-era bedestens (covered markets), hans, and arastas (bazaars) [17]; urban networks and spatial hierarchies in Seljuk Anatolia [18]; and marine archeology and ancient trade routes in the Mediterranean [19]. The Anatolian Seljuk period (1077–1308) is remarkable for its intense construction activity and the rapid development of trade networks. During this period, the need to ensure the security of developing trade networks and the demand for accommodations available within a reasonable daily travel distance contributed to the development and widespread adoption of the unique architectural typology of caravanserais [20]. This architectural typology, originating from Central Asia, is also referred to as "ribat" or "han" in official correspondence. Caravanserais were established to provide links and security between commercial or transportation centers. Over time, they contributed to the formation of a functioning commercial network throughout Anatolia. Caravanserais function as independent structures; however, a holistic evaluation of their location along particular routes, distances to other caravanserais, ports, and/or settlements, as well as their relationship with the topography, has the potential to reveal different information about the period.

Although the caravanserais of the Anatolian Seljuk Period have been studied across various disciplines such as history, art history, economic history, architectural history, and cartography, there remains an important gap in the literature regarding an interdisciplinary and multidimensional approach to systematically analyzing the network of caravanserais. Additionally, a comprehensive approach to mapping these networks in terms of temporal and spatial coordinates has been limited to local studies.

In addition to serving as nodes within an emerging transportation network, caravanserais functioned as interaction spaces where elements from settled and nomadic life converged [21]. These representative structures of Anatolian trade routes exhibit a developed architectural style that continues to be visible in the urban networks of Antalya, Konya, Akşehir, Sivas, and Kayseri. These types of structures were primarily designed to provide temporary accommodation for travelers, riding animals, and goods while also allowing for human interaction. The focus of studies on these architectural structures has been on their typological similarities, despite being built in different periods. Other important considerations included the geographical layer (such as topography, slope, and access to water) where they are located, as well as the distances between them.

In recent years, there has been a growing interest in digital heritage preservation within the Muslim world, with several notable endeavors standing out alongside the research presented in this chapter. An exemplary initiative is the digitization of ancient manuscripts and texts, which has been undertaken by institutions such as the Qatar Digital Library and the Digital Library of the Middle East. These projects aim not only to preserve invaluable cultural and historical artifacts but also to make them accessible to a global audience, fostering greater understanding and appreciation of Islamic heritage. Additionally, advancements in 3D scanning and modeling technologies have facilitated the documentation and virtual reconstruction of significant architectural heritage across the Muslim world. Projects such as the Virtual Reconstruction of Palmyra in Syria [22] exemplify the innovative use of digital tools for recreating and preserving architectural heritage under threat from conflict, urbanization, or natural degradation. These initiatives not only safeguard the physical remnants of the past but also offer immersive experiences that allow viewers to explore and engage with history in unprecedented ways. Furthermore, collaborative efforts among academia, government agencies, and cultural institutions have resulted in the creation of comprehensive digital archives and databases dedicated to preserving and disseminating knowledge about Islamic art, architecture, and cultural heritage. Platforms such as ARCHNET, an online resource focusing on Islamic architecture and urbanism, serve as invaluable repositories of information, fostering scholarly research and public engagement with Islamic heritage on a global scale. Through these multifaceted initiatives, the Muslim world continues to harness the power of digital technologies to safeguard its rich cultural legacy for future generations.

3. Methodology

In the pilot project, where the locations of Seljuk structures along the Silk Road were transferred to a mapping system, the geographical information system (GIS), the data obtained from rapid and detailed modeling using photogrammetric techniques formed the basis of the digital data pool. The research, summarized in Fig. 2, was conducted in three stages: data collection and compilation, the creation of a parametric and systematic document, and the integration of the data into a website for accessibility and visibility.

Figure 2. The framework of research conducted on Anatolian caravanserais.

3.1. *The process of collecting and compiling the data*

The data collection phase was based on both a literature review encompassing a wide range of academic publications, maps, and web-based archives, as well as fieldwork along the caravanserai route covering Turkish cities such as Denizli, Burdur, Antalya, Isparta, Aksaray, Konya, and Nevşehir. After an examination of the changes in temporal and spatial information of the caravanserais, a comprehensive database was created following a visual survey that confirmed the current information gathered at the sites.

3.1.1. *Compiling existing resources*

Caravanserais, also known as "han" in Turkish, served as resting places for travelers during their journeys. Ideally, they were located at intervals of approximately 30–40 km, equivalent to one day's journey. According to the Old World Trade Routes (OWTRAD) project [23], there are 154 Seljuk caravanserais at intervals between Denizli and Doğubeyazıt. Among the many studies conducted on caravanserais are Branning's popular work on Turkish hans [11] and Acun's [2] compilation book on caravanserais, as well as research and theses on Anatolian caravanserais [5,24–47]. These provide some, but incomplete, work related to the transfer to the GIS [32,35,46].

The studies within the scope of the research begin with the compilation of information on Seljuk period caravanserais in Anatolia from the mentioned sources to create a han database for subsequent use. To maintain the integrity of the data in the lists resulting from these scans, lists from all sources were cross-checked. While conducting the literature review phase of the project, the focus was on verifying the accuracy of the existence and locations of the caravanserais. After the cross-checking process, the coordinates of the hans that had been identified were manually checked and verified using satellite images. Afterward, wide-ranging information about the hans was obtained from various sources, including academic articles, books, maps, website databases, archives, and theses (Fig. 3).

The literature review of the sources has been designed to cover areas such as architecture, archeology, and architectural history. In addition, architectural-historical information, such as hans' construction period, preservation status, materials used, and plan types, was also included in the literature review. As noted by researchers such as Branning [11],

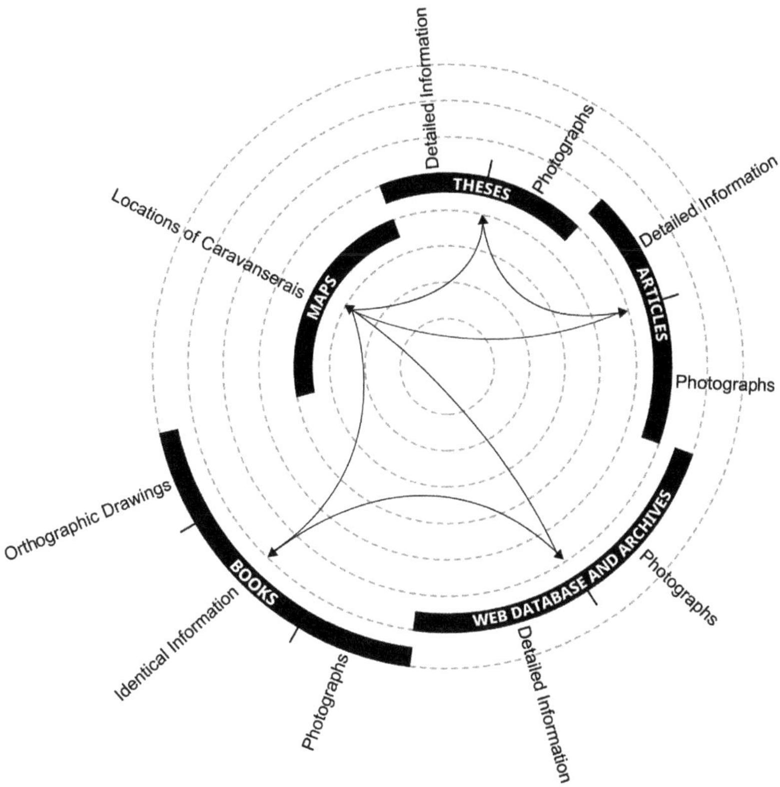

Figure 3. Resources used in the scope of the SILK Road project.

Yavuz [4], and Erdmann [1], caravanserais were built according to four general plan types: open plans, open courtyards, closed central spaces, and mixed plans. The next phase involved obtaining plans, sections, and view documents of rectangular architectural building examples for each scheme.

Map resources [4,8,10,48] also served as the basis for the literature review. In particular, the following two sources were used: a map obtained from the Çevre ve Kültür Değerlerini Koruma ve Tanıtma Vakfı – ÇEKÜL (Foundation for the Promotion and Protection of the Environment and Cultural Heritage) – containing the locations and names of the hans, and a map study on Anatolian caravanserais from Istanbul Technical University (ITU). For the course, the ÇEKÜL map [48: p. 1] was divided into nine regions, and the students involved in the project were asked to

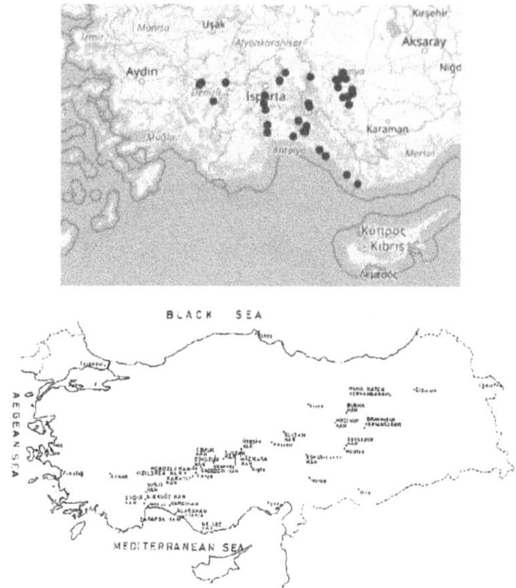

Figure 4. Above: Mapping work in Zone 2. Below: Yavuz's Map.

Source: Used with the permission of Brill, from Yavuz, Ayşil Tükel. (1997) [4]; permission conveyed through Copyright Clearance Center, Inc.

compile archeological and historical data for each region using various sources containing the mapping studies (Fig. 4). Zones were based on the criteria that each covered a similar numbers of caravanserais and included those on a specific route. These maps [4: p. 80, 8: p. 28, 10: p. 103, 48: p. 1] are insufficient in terms of digitized data for all Anatolian hans, and as such they only serve as a guide for the literature review. The mapping work in Zone 2, which includes the provinces of Isparta, Denizli, Konya, and Antalya in southern Turkey, within the scope of the course is shown as an example in Fig. 4.

Old photographs and detailed information regarding the preservation status, plan type, location, and construction period of hans were obtained from academic articles and theses. Cross-checking was needed because the hans were known by different names, their conservation status varied over time, and their locations are only approximations. The information obtained in the fields of architectural history and archeology was checked against web-based archives and databases, with the ARCHNET and SALT archives being especially valuable in this regard. As an example, old photographs of Sultan Han, obtained from ARCHNET [49–51] and SALT [52–54] archives, are shown in Fig. 5.

Figure 5. Old photographs of Sultan Han from the ARCHNET (top) [49–51] and SALT (bottom) [52–54] archives.

Academic books on Anatolian caravanserais and the Silk Road have been crucial to the literature review phase for obtaining comprehensive information. The research involved a wide range of publications and multilingual resources and utilized academic books, articles, and conference papers authored by scholars from various disciplines, including architectural historians, archeologists, art historians, and architects.

During the data collection process, approximately 169 academic resources were reviewed. At the end of the process, data collected from a total of 322 caravanserais were transferred to the database. In particular, the information from book sources contributed to deepening the scope of the database, both quantitatively and qualitatively. For example, in Özergin's book [5], there are 132 listed caravanserais, while in İlter's book on Seljuk and Anatolian caravanserais [7], 28 are listed; these provide identical information, including the names, locations, and construction dates, thus validating the details.

On the other hand, art historian Erdmann's book [1], which is the first important compilation on Anatolian caravanserais, and the book titled

Rumselçuk Caravanserais of Anatolia [10], which contains studies by architectural historian Johansen, are two important sources that contributed to the project in terms of context and process. Caravanserai listings were found in books written in various languages; consequently, compilations by Acun [2], İlter [7], and Özergin [5] were cross-checked with Erdmann's studies [1]. Moreover, Johansen's field studies [10] focusing on caravanserais in southwestern Anatolia provided details of the structures themselves and their context, with photographs and 2D and 3D drawings, which informed the route chosen for subsequent field studies carried out for the project.

Tuncer's book [8], published by Türkiye Cumhuriyeti Vakıflar Genel Müdürlüğü (Republic of Türkiye General Directorate of Foundations), contains detailed information about caravanserais in Anatolia, including maps and contextual features. He also reserves a section for "*Adresi Bilinmeyen Hanlar*" (Caravanserais with Unknown Locations) while compiling information on caravanserais, inspiring the methodology for classification in the current research project.

3.1.2. *Collecting data through fieldwork*

The fieldwork undertaken significantly contributed to obtaining modern spatial and visual data for the research, which aims to document, make visible, and disseminate the complex cultural heritage inherent in caravanserais.

The first fieldwork in April 2023 covered a total distance of 1,000 km across Denizli, Eğirdir, Konya, Manavgat, Antalya, and Denizli. This field study involved taking photographs of the structures using photogrammetry in order to produce 3D visualization data about the caravanserais in southwest and central Anatolia (including Akhan, Çardak, Dokuzun, Eğirdir, Ertokuş, Eynif, Hacı Hafız, İncir, Horozlu, Kargı, Kızılören, Kuruçeşme, Sultan, Obruk, Zazadin, and Zıvarık). A route was created to include Nevşehir for the second field study, which took place in June 2023 and aimed to collect the missing photogrammetry data from the first field study. In particular, Derebucak, Nodar, and Kulak Murat Han were visited, which were locations that lacked precise location data in the sources but included approximate information and images to indicate their location. Through the field study, their exact locations were found and visual data were collected.

In total, 29 caravanserais located in the southwestern and central parts of Turkey were visited: Akhan, Çardak, Eğirdir, Ertokuş, Kızılören, Kuruçeşme, Sultan, Obruk, Zazadin, Zıvarık, Dokuzun, Hacı Hafız, Horozlu, Derebucak, Kargı, Eynif, Şarapsa, Alara, Evdir, Kırkgöz, Susuz, İncir, Pamukçu, Ağzıkara, Öresun, Pervane, Doğala, Dolay, and Avanos. Of these, 24 were used to create 3D models, and 26 featured 360-degree videos in these field studies. The exact location of one of the three caravanserais whose estimated locations were described in the publications was obtained by using image and text references in the literature and contacts made with locals. However, only approximate locations of the other two were obtained due to the limitations of the field study, including the locals' lack of awareness of this heritage, insufficient information in the literature, and time constraints.

3.2. *Geotemporal database on existing resources*

The systematic data preparation phase took place in the GIS environment. The comprehensive data collected on the Anatolian Seljuk caravanserais and the current data obtained on-site through field studies were systematically compiled in the Quantum Geographical Information Systems (QGIS, qgis.org/en/site/) interface. GIS is the information technology infrastructure necessary for the provision, storage, processing, accessibility, utilization, and updating of geographical data. In the project, GIS was chosen as the suitable option for storing and processing geographical data derived from literature reviews and fieldwork. The foundation of the database, based on the location data of caravanserais, was established using the QGIS program. In addition to data operations, establishing a sustainable workflow for accessibility, database updates, and remote work was critical. The easy integration of QGIS with common data formats such as Excel spreadsheet (XLS) and comma-separated values (CSV) enabled a sustainable and systematic workflow for the project. The data operations using GIS within the scope of the research are explained in four main phases: a parametric analysis, data classification, updating the data with fieldwork results, and integrating the current database with the website.

Based on the existing published literature, an analysis was conducted to collect geographic data, store them in the GIS system, and create digital 3D models of architectural elements for the architectural heritage of Anatolian caravanserais.

The data classification was conducted in an Excel document stored on Google Drive to enable remote and collaborative work. Afterward, the Excel file containing the data was adapted to the QGIS environment as a CSV file for use in future studies. First, the information obtained through the literature review was entered into the appropriate fields of the data structure. Then, the data classification process specific to the project was conducted, as described in the following section.

3.2.1. *Data classification*

Based on the data structure introduced by the GIS system, the following information was transferred to the database: coordinates, orientation, description, construction date, plan type, related publications, and modeling aids such as plans and sections for the caravanserais. At this stage, it is important to layer the data by accuracy levels as indicated in the literature. Approximately 58 caravanserais' locations can be identified with the naked eye in systems such as Google Earth and Maps, which are similar to the GIS system; however, the exact coordinates of many caravanserais are unknown. At this stage of the research, a classification method was developed to integrate the caravanserais' locations into the GIS system.

3.2.1.1. Classification of caravanserais according to accuracy levels

While the findings about the location of the caravanserais were being processed into the data set, four levels – Level 1, Level 2, Level 3, and Level 4 – were proposed relating to the accuracy of the data. These accuracy levels were determined such that Level 1 represented the highest and Level 4 the lowest. Level 1 describes the hans where accurate information about its existence and coordinates, photographs, and architectural and historical information can be accessed from various sources. Level 2 includes the hans whose information can be accessed from one or more sourccs, but the information obtained cannot be confirmed, and Level 3 includes the hans that are known as "lost" in the sources; there is estimated or approximate information regarding their locations, although it is likely that the structures are no longer intact. Level 4, which expresses the lowest level of data reliability, consists of hans whose existence cannot be definitively demonstrated in the sources. For each level, one han

Table 1. Accuracy levels of location data: sample caravanserais.

Primary Name of Han	Region	Level of Confidence	Explanation
Sultan	Sultanhanı, Aksaray	L1	Visible on Google Earth, listed by the Ministry of Culture and Tourism
Zulmanda	Altınekin, Konya	L2	Exists but cannot be documented
Kıreli	Hüyük, Konya	L3	Listed as a lost caravanserai
Akören	Akören, Konya	L4	Some written sources can be considered proof of existence of the caravanserais or other caravanserais in this region

was selected as an example and shown in Table 1. The longitude–latitude information of the hans represent precise data for the caravanserais in L1, whereas for other caravanserais, this information shows the district centers or approximate locations as described in the literature.

3.2.1.2. Classification of caravanserais according to their plan types

In this research, before the fieldwork, classification was conducted based on the types of structures. The plans, sections, elevation drawings, and old photographs in the literature were examined. Afterward, the caravanserais were classified into four plan types according to the presence of covered sections, courtyards, exclusive courtyards, and concentric/mixed plans. In addition to this main classification, a sub-classification was made based on the presence and size of extra spaces. The classification of over 51 caravanserais was added to the database under the "Plan Types" heading. During the fieldwork, unique architectural and contextual features of hans were examined on-site.

3.2.1.3. Adding project-specific columns to the data structure

In addition to the established data structure specific to the research, the data classes "Plan Type," "Preservation Status," "Inscription," and "Building Material" were added. The classes mentioned for the Kargı Han data selected as the sample are shown in Table 2.

Table 2. Project-specific data classes for four caravanserais.

Primary Name	Preservation Status	Plan Type	Building Material	Inscription
Kargı	Restoration process of the building has been initiated	OC (Open Courtyard Plan)	Rubble stone and face stone	Does not feature inscriptions
Şarapsa	Restored	C (Covered Plan)	Smooth-cut stone, aggregate stone, square-cut limestone, rubble stone, and plaster	There are two inscriptions: one over the main door and the other over the mosque door
Kuruçeşme	Restored	COC (Covered Section with Courtyard Plan)	Spolia material	Inscription on the portal to the covered section
Alara	Restored	CON (Concentric Plan)	Carefully joined and finely-hewn limestone blocks, pitch-faced stones, rubble stone, and mortar	A square inscription above the entrance crown door

3.2.2. *Updating the data set with fieldwork*

The data set created in QGIS was updated with findings from the fieldwork. The findings and contributions of the field studies to the research can be examined under two headings, as follows.

3.2.2.1. Accessing the accurate location information of caravanserais (level of confidence)

During the fieldwork in April, discoveries were made at the L2-, L3-, and L4-level caravanserais in Isparta, Antalya, and Konya. The coordinates of these structures were recorded in the field and then entered into the data set. Findings in these studies were obtained from the caravanserais of Derebucak Han, Nodar Han, and Kulak Murat Han. These three are classified according to their locations within the context of caravanserai plan types.

3.2.2.2. Improving data set with visual-3D materials and content

During the fieldwork in cities such as Isparta, Konya, Antalya, and Nevşehir, photographs of each caravanserai were taken, and 360-degree videos were recorded for creating photogrammetry models and virtual tours. The tour details and models were shared on the project's social media accounts, and later, links to published models and videos were added to the data set for dissemination and published on the website. Şarapsa Han was chosen as the sample in order to explain the integration between the website and visual 3D materials. The virtual 3D content of Sarapsa Han is shown in Fig. 6.

3.3. *Dissemination of the updated data set on the website*

By disseminating spatial, visual, and 3D data about caravanserais on the website, the aim is to increase awareness by making the Seljuk heritage corpus more accessible. While selecting the data classes for publication,

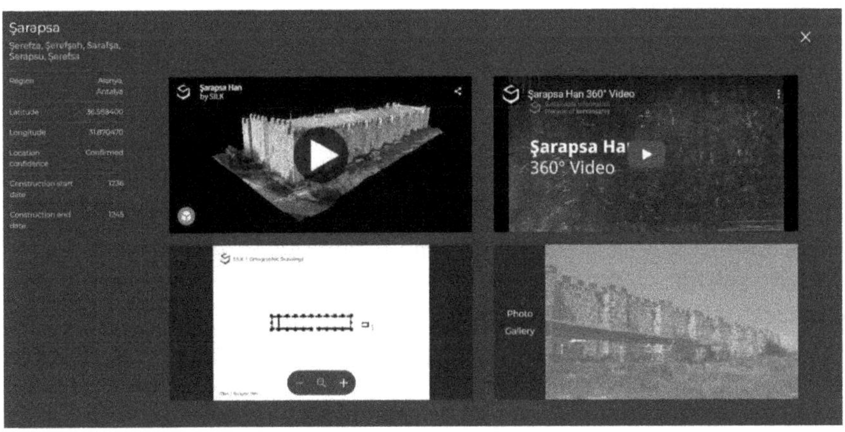

Figure 6. Virtual 3D content of Şarapsa Han (makingindigital/SILK).

Table 3. Data classes in terms of common and memorable data classes.

Common for All Caravanserais	Memorable
• Zone	• Sketchfab photogrammetry model
• Primary name	• Sketchfab reconstruction model
• Region	• 360-degree videos
• Longitude	• Orthographic drawings
• Latitude	• Icon/Thumbnail photographs
• Level of confidence	• Old photographs

we considered two criteria: being memorable for potential users and stakeholders and having features in common with all caravanserais. While the publication of the classes common to all caravanserais serves to create a general view of these structures, the visual and 3D data make them more memorable. The data classes integrated with the website are shown in Table 3.

Among the above-mentioned classes, the primary names, regions, coordinates (longitude-latitude), and levels of confidence are presented both as text and on the map. The results of the photogrammetric documentation were disseminated through Sketchfab, and the 360-degree videos were shared on YouTube; additionally, embedded links to the project's website at makingindigital/SILK are presented to potential users. Two different methods were developed to publish 2D materials with copyright problems. The plan of the caravanserais was redrawn based on the reference images obtained for the orthographic drawings. In addition, while it is possible to compare the size of the caravanserais spatially with their plan drawings prepared at the same scale, architectural elements such as plan type, roof-wall connection elements, and openings can be easily read in the published plans. Icon photographs were generated using an AI filter. The architectural features of the buildings formed the basis for selecting the icon photographs. Old photographs were also published, along with their sources. In Fig. 7, the integration of caravanserai information with the website is demonstrated through the Figma and Code interfaces.

The SILK website was developed using PHP because it is well-known, open source, and freely available. The data for each site were originally collected in spreadsheet format, and an admin panel was developed to enable uploading to the MySQL database. Again, PHP was the

Zone	Primary Name	Other Names	Region	Start Date	End Date	Latitude	Longitude	Location Confidence	Location Explanation
West	Güllük	Güllik	Korkuteli, Antalya			37.02043	30.51207	L4	Not Accurate
West	Hacı Hafız	Bahri	Selçuklu, Konya	1201	1225	38.128725	32.495258	L1	Accurate
West	Han		Merkez, Uşak			38.76242	29.21119	L4	Not Accurate
West	Ibradi	Koca, Oluk, Tolga	İbradı, Antalya			37.09596	31.59553	L4	Not Accurate
West	Iney	Inay, İnay	Ulubey, Uşak			38.42794	29.21358	L4	Not Accurate
West	İkinci Pazarcık	Bıçkıcı Köprüsü, Gazipaşa, Selinus, Silinti	Gazipaşa, Antalya			36.29079	32.29187	L4	Not Accurate
West	İshaklı	Sultandağ, Sahipata, Saipat	Sultandağı (İshaklı)	1249		38.532608	31.228325	L1	Accurate
West	Kadın	Raziye Sultan	Kadınhan, Konya		1223	38.24015	32.20992	L1	Accurate
West	Karasunkur	Vakıf, Karasungur, Yeni, Kara-sunkur	Merkez, Denizli	1249	1250	37.78370085(	29.09634935!	L4	Not Accurate
West	Kargı		Manavgat, Antalya	1236	1246	37.00454	31.38019	L1	Accurate
West	Kırgız	Dağbeli, Bademağacı	Döşemealtı, Antaly			37.20191	30.49401	L4	Not Accurate
West	Kırkgöz		Döşemealtı, Antaly:	1236	1246	37.11116	30.58556	L1	Accurate
West	Kızlar		Alanya, Antalya			36.54444	31.9954	L4	Not Accurate
West	Korkuteli		Korkuteli, Antalya			37.06624765!	30.196035967	L4	Not Accurate
West	Köprü Suyu	Aspendos, Belkıs	Serik, Antalya	1019		36.91436	31.16306	L3	Low Accuracy
West	Küçük Yenice		Korkuteli, Antalya			37.01309	30.48561	L4	Not Accurate
West	Nodar	Rodar	Akseki, Antalya			37.1751	31.93693	L2	High Accuracy
West	Ortapayam	Kireçli	Akseki, Antalya			37.31940580(	31.463700563	L2	High Accuracy
West	Oymapınar	Homa	Manavgat, Antalya			36.87963	31.52003	L4	Not Accurate
West	Sertavul		Mut, Mersin	13thcentury		36.8808	33.27901	L2	High Accuracy
West	Sultanönü	Taş	Tepebaşı, Eskişehir			39.89562	30.53	L4	Not Accurate
West	Şarapsa	Şerefza, Şerefşah, Sarafşa, Serapsu, Şerefs	Alanya, Antalya	1236	1245	36.5884	31.87047	L1	Accurate
West	Tahtalıbeli		Korkuteli, Antalya			37.03637	30.39528	L4	Not Accurate
West	Taş	Bedesten	Merkez, Bayburt			40.26093	40.22662	L4	Not Accurate

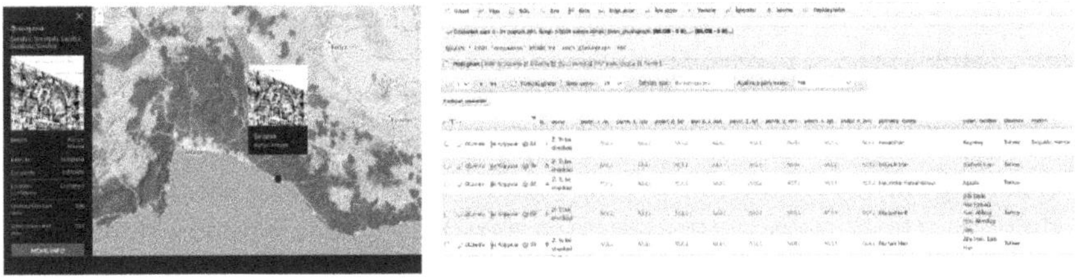

Figure 7. Integration of caravanserai data (Şarapsa Han) with website (Figma and Code interfaces).

technology of choice. To represent the locations of the sites, Stadia map tiles from the Stadia Maps website (stadia.com) were preferred over other map providers, such as Mapbox, due to their simpler API, and minimal preparation requirement. A compromise was reached to host all the images the team collected, and it was decided to store them on Google Drive, allowing the team to gather imagery progressively without the necessity of uploading to databases. However, latency in Google APIs can cause a slight drop in performance. Finally, Bootstrap was used to enable easy development of user interface elements for both large- and small-screen devices, such as mobile phones and tablets.

4. Results

The research began with implementing the literature review, followed by completing the website integration. In Table 4, the flow and sub-headings that were followed during the research process are summarized as follows: data collection and compilation, data analysis, and publication of the updated data set on the website. In addition, the numerical data obtained during the research process provides an idea of the study's broad scope.

The compilation of existing data on the Seljuk caravanserais involved reviewing approximately 169 academic publications, consisting of books, articles, theses, conference papers, maps, and web-based archives. The existing literature was used to create the main framework of the database. The final form of the database emerged from the fieldwork conducted in April and June 2023. In this fieldwork, 29 caravanserais were visited, resulting in 3D models and a total of 26 360-degree videos.

Table 4. Three main headings of the research and the outputs.

Main Headings of the Research	Related Subheadings	Outputs/Findings
Collecting and compiling the data	Literature review	Approximately 169 publications consisting of books, academic articles, theses, conference papers, maps, and web-based archives were reviewed.
	Collecting data through fieldwork	In total, 29 caravanserais were visited, out of which 24 provided 3D models and 26 were featured in 360-degree videos.
Creating parametric/ systematic data	Parametric analysis	The data structure was used in the GIS environment to collect and store information regarding the caravanserais.
	Data classification	The locations of 58 caravanserais are exactly known. The locations of 29 caravanserais are known with high precision, while 9 are known with low precision. There is no accurate information about the location or existence of 226 caravanserais.
		Orthographic drawings of 27 caravanserais were created.
		Research-specific data classes were added: "Plan Type," "Preservation Status," "Inscription," and "Building Material."
Dissemination of the updated Data set on the website		The data of 322 caravanserais in Anatolia were shared on the website.

In the second stage, which included parametric analysis and data classification, all obtained data were entered into the database for cross-checking. In addition to examining the accuracy of the data, a grading method was used to measure the accuracy of spatial data to prevent location-related data losses and guide future studies. Thus, the exact locations of 58 caravanserais are now known. Of these, 29 locations are known with high precision, while 9 are known with low precision. There is no accurate information available regarding the location or existence of an additional 226 sites.

In the last stage of the research, which is the dissemination of data, the spatial data of Seljuk caravanserais were shared using a real map base. The temporal changes in the buildings were revealed using old photographs obtained from web-based archives and academic publications, while the current conditions of the structures examined on site during the field studies were also made public through 360-degree videos. Of the 29 caravanserais visited during field studies, 24 had their architectural features and context conveyed through 3D models and representative 2D plans created via the photogrammetry method. The 3D models can not only be examined in 360 degrees on the website but also offer users a VR experience, provided they have the necessary equipment.

The approach adopted in this research, in which a systematic spatial database was prepared, can be continued with further studies that could add information on both known and newly discovered caravanserais from various literary sources. To support such research, a sustainable data layout is now in place, designed using GIS. In addition, dissemination efforts could involve making future research studies on Anatolian Seljuk caravanserais available to potential stakeholders and website visitors.

5. Conclusion

In conclusion, this chapter breaks new ground in realizing its mission of bringing to life the Islamic architectural heritage of Anatolia, with a particular focus on the Anatolian Seljuk period. The research aims to develop a highly accessible system that provides an enriching experience, utilizing technological tools to transcend traditional learning methods and enable students to interact with and appreciate the rich representation of Anatolian Islamic architecture and the region's historical treasures within its cultural fabric. However, embarking on this ambitious journey, the project faces challenges arising from the linguistic complexity of Turkish and the scarcity of resources available in widely accessible languages. The recognition of these obstacles underlines the need for concerted efforts to overcome language barriers and compile accurate information, especially regarding the iconic heritage of the Anatolian Seljuk period. This chapter, focusing on the literature review at the initial stage of research, illuminates the key role of obtaining and compiling precise information. Given the recognized lack of complexity and accuracy in existing sources, it is critically important for the research to remain committed to addressing historical nuances and subtleties. This implies that a rigorous approach is required to lay the foundations of a comprehensive knowledge base. Such a base is vital to the success of the immersive experience that the research aims to deliver, as a result of extensive fieldwork. As the research progresses through the complex geography of the Anatolian Seljuk heritage, its efforts in compilation mark a significant step toward unraveling the mysteries of the past. The SILK project strives not only to create a fascinating encounter with history through scientific pursuit but also to overcome linguistic barriers and make the experience accessible to a diverse audience. The first phase of SILK, detailed in this book chapter, sets an optimistic tone for further exploration of the architectural treasures of Anatolia, promising a future in which the magnificent legacy of the Anatolian Seljuk period can be fully appreciated by a global audience.

Acknowledgment

The academic research of Dr. Varinlioglu is supported by the Fulbright Visiting Scholar Program, TUBITAK 2219 International Postdoctoral Research Programme, and the Chevening Abdullah Gül Oxford Centre for Islamic Studies Fellowship (OCIS). The SILK project, the subject of this chapter's research process, was carried out under the sponsorship of the U.S. Mission Turkiye Grant, grant number STU-15022IN0044, with Dr. Varinlioglu as the principal investigator, partnering with Prof. Nagakura from the MIT Department of Architecture and the MISTI Global Seed Funds. The fieldwork covering a part of the Anatolian Seljuk caravanserai network/route was carried out with the permission of MoCT. We gratefully acknowledge the in-kind support provided by local governments and Suna & İnan Kıraç Akdeniz Medeniyetleri Araştırma Merkezi (AKMED) during the fieldword.

We would like to thank academic advisors Prof. Tim Williams for sharing the data set, Prof. Scott Redford for providing published and unpublished papers, Prof. Peter Frankopan for providing ideas, Prof. Takehiko Nagakura at MIT for his endless support, and Prof. Adeel Malik at the University of Oxford for his unwavering support. Finally, we thank the fieldwork of 2023 team members, İrem Ercan, Hilal Kaleli, Baver Bekiroğlu, Sepehr Seyedian Choubi, Müge Berat Özteker, Han Tu, Xiaoyun Zhang, Beril Toper and Tomoko Nagakura, as well as the software development and website design team Koen Maes, Kaya Oğuz, Kaan Özer and Doruk Türkmen for their efforts during the SILK project.

For further information, check out the website at https://makingin-digital.com/silk.

References

[1] Erdmann K, Erdmann H. *Das Anatolische Karavansaray des 13. Jahrhunderts*. Berlin: Verlag Gebr. Mann; 1961.

[2] Acun H, editor. *Anadolu Selçuklu Dönemi Kervansarayları*. Ankara: T.C. Kültür ve Turizm Bakanlığı Kütüphaneler ve Yayımlar Genel Müdürlüğü; 2007.

[3] Tükel Yavuz A. *Anadolu Selçuklu Hanları ve Posta-Menzil-Derbent Teşkilatları*. Prof Doğan Kuban'a Armağan. 1996; p. 25–38.

[4] Yavuz AT. The concepts that shape Anatolian Seljuq Caravanserais. *Muqarnas*. 1997;14:80–95.

[5] Özergin KM. Anadolu'da Selçuklu Kervansarayları. Tarih Dergisi. 1965;15(20):141–70.

[6] Hillenbrand R. *Islamic architecture: form, function, and meaning*. Edinburgh: Edinburgh University Press; 1994.

[7] İlter İ. *Tarihi Türk Hanları*. Ankara: Karayolları Genel Müdürlüğü Matbaası; 1969.

[8] Tuncer OC. *Anadolu Kervan Yolları*. Vakıflar Genel Müdürlüğü Yayınları; 2007.

[9] Redford, Scott Caravanserais, Roads, and Routes in Seljuk Anatolia. In: Vandeput, L., Baird, D., Görkay, K., Haldon, John, Massa, M. and Mitchell, S. (eds.), *Pathways of Communication: Routes and Roads in Anatolia from Prehistory to the Seljuk Period*. Cambridge: Cambridge University Press. (Forthcoming).

[10] Johansen EM. *Rūmselçuk Caravanserais of Anatolia*. Narayana Press; 2016. Available from: https://books.google.com.tr/books?id=ePJinQAACAAJ.

[11] Branning K. The Seljuk Han in Anatolia. 2001. Available from: http://www.turkishhan.org/.
[12] Ünal RH. Doğu Anadolu'da Bilinmeyen Üç Selçuklu Hanı. *Sanat Tarihi Dergisi*. 1983;2(2):106–18.
[13] French D. *Roman Roads and Milestones of Asia Minor: 1 The Pilgrim's Road*. Vol. 105. BAR International Series 105; 1981.
[14] Preiser-Kapeller J. Calculating the middle ages? The project "Complexities and Networks in the Medieval Mediterranean and Near East" (COMMED). *Medieval Worlds*. 2015;(2):100–27.
[15] Scheidel W. ORBIS: The Stanford geospatial network model of the Roman world. Princeton/Stanford working papers in classics paper; 2015. Available from: http://dx.doi.org/10.2139/ssrn.2609654.
[16] Williams T. The silk roads: an ICOMOS thematic study. ICOMOS; 2014. Available from: http://openarchive.icomos.org/id/eprint/1487/.
[17] Akar T. Osmanlı Kentinde Ticari Mekânlar: Bedesten-Han-Arasta-Çarşı Mekânları Literatür Değerlendirmesi. *Türkiye Araştırmaları Literatür Dergisi*. 2009;7(13):267–92.
[18] Özcan K. Anadolu'da Selçuklu Kentler Sistemi ve Mekânsal Kademelenme. *METU J Fac Archit*. 2006;23(2):21–61.
[19] Robinson D, Wilson A. Introduction: Maritime archaeology and the ancient economy. In: *Maritime Archaeology and Ancient Trade in the Mediterranean*. Oxford: Oxford Centre for Maritime Archaeology; 2011. p. 1–10.
[20] Aslanapa O. Orta Çağda Türklerin İleri Bir Sosyal Yardım Müessesesi: Kervansaraylar. *Türk Kültürü*. 1963;1(5):26–30.
[21] Cezar M. Türk Tarihinde Kervansaray. In *Ankara*; 1976.
[22] Bobou O, Kristensen NB, McAvoy S, Raja R. Archive archaeology in palmyra, Syria a new 3D reconstruction of the tomb of Ḥairan. *Digit Appl Archaeol Cult Herit*. 2020;19:e00164.
[23] T. Matthew Ciolek. Old World Trade Routes (OWTRAD) project. T. Matthew Ciolek; 1999. Available from: http://www.ciolek.com/owtrad.html.
[24] Önge M. Caravanserais as symbols of power in Seljuk Anatolia. In: Osmond J., Cimdina A. (eds.). *Politica*. Pisa: Edizioni Plus — Pisa University Press; 2007. p. 49–69.
[25] Akalın FB. *Malatya İli Battalgazi İlçesi Kervansaray Mekanının Seramik Enstalasyon Çalışmalarıma Etkisi*. Kayseri: T.C. Erciyes Üniversitesi; 2010.
[26] Avcı O. *Anadolu Selçuklu Devlet Adamlarının Yaptırdıkları Kervansaraylar*. Eskişehir: Eskişehir Anadolu Üniversitesi; 2019.
[27] Aycibin S. *Anadolu Kervansaraylarının Tarihsel ve Mimari Gelişimi, Kervansaray Yapılarının İşlevlendirilerek Yeniden Kullanımı*. İstanbul: T.C. İstanbul Ticaret Üniversitesi; 2018.
[28] Aydoğdu M. *Anadolu Selçuklu Kervansarayları Üzerine Bir İnceleme*. Fırat Üniversitesi; 2003.

[29] Boz M. *XIII-XV. Yüzyıllarda Anadolu Kentleri ve Kentliler*. Kırklareli: Kırklareli Üniversitesi; 2014.
[30] Denknalbant A. *Anadolu Selçuklu Kervansaray Mescitleri*. İstanbul: İstanbul Teknik Üniversitesi; 2004.
[31] Eraybat GF. *Tarihi Konaklama Yapılarının Doğuşu, Gelişimi ve Günümüzde Çağdaş İşlevle Değerlendirilmesi: Edirne Rüstempaşa Kervansarayı Örneği*. Edirne: Trakya Üniversitesi; 2011.
[32] Ertepınar Kaymakcı P. Geoarchaelogical Investigation of Central Anatolian Caravanserais Using GIS. Ankara: Middle East Technical University; 2005.
[33] Gerçek M. *İşlevini Yitirmiş Kervansarayların, Günümüz Otel Yapılarına Dönüştürülmesindeki Mekansal Sorunlar*. İstanbul: Haliç Üniversitesi; 2010.
[34] Güler M. Han El *Bağrur Kervansarayı'nın Restitüsyonu*. Ankara: Gazi Üniversitesi; 1994.
[35] Hosseini Jahanabad H. *The Impact of Trade on the Transformation of Transport Routes in Anatolia: A Historical-Spatial Analysis*. İstanbul: Istanbul Technical University; 2015.
[36] Kılıç B. *Orhan Cezmi Tuncer'in Türk-İslam Sanat Tarihine Katkıları*. Çorum: Hitit Üniversitesi Sosyal Bilimler Enstitüsü; 2015.
[37] Köroğlu RE. *Batı Anadolu'da Kervansaraylar ve Bu Kervansarayların Anadolu Ticari Hayatındaki Yeri ve Önemi (1071–1308)*. Kafkas Üniversitesi; 2021.
[38] Kutlu M. Seljuk *Caravanserais in the Vicinity of Denizli: Han-Abad (Çardakhan) and Akhan*. Ankara: Bilkent University; 2009.
[39] Önge M. Restoration of Zazadin Han a 13th century Seljukid Caravanserai near Konya. Ankara: METU; 2004.
[40] Özcan K. *Anadolu'da Selçuklu Dönemi Yerleşme Sistemi ve Kent Modelleri*. Konya: Selçuk Üniversitesi; 2005.
[41] Özen İ. *Antalya-Burdur Kervan Yolu Üzerinde Yer Alan Anadolu Selçuklu Kervansaraylarının Taçkapı Süsleme Programları*. Isparta: Süleyman Demirel Üniversitesi; 2012.
[42] Şahin E. *Structural Analyses and Assessment of Historical Çardak Caravanserai in Denizli*. Izmir: Izmir Institute of Technology; 2019.
[43] Şahin M. *Anadolu Selçuklu Dönemi Mimarisi Mekan Tipolojisi Bağlamında Malatya Hekimhan (Taşhan) Kervansarayı Üzerine Bir İnceleme*. Kayseri: Erciyes Üniversitesi; 2016.
[44] Sevimli EE. *Konya'daki Kadınhanı Kervansarayı'nın Devşirme Malzemeler Üzerinden Değerlendirilmesi*. İstanbul: Marmara University; 2019.
[45] Taştan A. Türkiye Selçukluları Zamanında Tokat ve Çevresindeki Kervansaraylar. Tokat: Gaziosmanpaşa University; 2010.
[46] Telci A. *Türkiye'deki Ticaret Yolları Üzerinde Bulunan Han ve Kervansarayların Fotogrametrik Belgelenmesi ve Coğrafi Bilgi Sistemine Entegre Edilmesi*. Konya: Selçuk University; 2011.

[47] Tursun A. *Akören Ağzı*. Konya: Necmettin Erbakan Univeristy; 2020.
[48] ÇEKÜL. İpek Yolu-Kültür Yolu. Available from: https://www.cekulvakfi.org.tr/haber/ipek-yolu-kultur-yolu-haritasi-yayimlandi.
[49] ARCHNET. Grand portal of Seljukian Khan called Sultan Khan on royal post road from Ephesus to Persia. Fine Arts Library, Harvard College Library; 1887. Available from: https://www.archnet.org/sites/4017?media_content_id=8249.
[50] ARCHNET. General view of the Sultan Khan as it was in 1887. Note the stone ribs of the collapsed vault in the background. Fine Arts Library, Harvard College Library; 1887. Available from: https://www.archnet.org/sites/4017?media_content_id=8252.
[51] ARCHNET. Interior of the main hall of the Sultanhani. Fine Arts Library, Harvard College Library; 1887. Available from: https://www.archnet.org/sites/4017?media_content_id=8257.
[52] SALT. Sultanhan Kervansarayı – Caravansary of Sultanhan. IFEA; 1960. Available from: https://archives.saltresearch.org/handle/123456789/8246.
[53] SALT. Aksaray Sultanhan'ın kışlık bölümünün taç kapısı – Portal of winter section of Aksaray Sultanhan. Available from: https://archives.saltresearch.org/handle/123456789/78594.
[54] SALT. Sultanhan Kervansarayı ana girişinin yanındaki oyuk detayı – Caravansary of Sultanhan. Detail of a lateral niche, next to the main portal. IFEA; 1960. Available from: https://archives.saltresearch.org/handle/123456789/7632?locale=tr.

Part III

Health and Education

https://doi.org/10.1142/9781800616295_0008

Chapter 8

The Great Promise and Potential Perils of Genome Editing for the Islamic World

John Parrington[*,§], Ali Alhoshani[†], and Ali Hanbashi[‡]

[*]*Department of Pharmacology, Medical Sciences Division, University of Oxford, Oxford, UK*

[†]*Department of Pharmacology and Toxicology, College of Pharmacy, King Saud University, Riyadh, Kingdom of Saudi Arabia*

[‡]*Department of Pharmacology, College of Pharmacy, Jazan University, Jazan, Kingdom of Saudi Arabia*

[§]*john.parrington@worc.ox.ac.uk*

Abstract

Genome editing is a revolutionary new technology that makes it possible for the first time in history to precisely edit the genomes of the living cells of practically any species, including humans. This technology looks set to transform medical research, clinical medicine, and agriculture. However, major challenges remain in terms of efficacy and safety, and genome editing also raises many ethical issues. Here, we introduce this exciting new technology and examine the huge potential of genome editing for human advancement while considering potential perils with reference to the Islamic world and Islamic ethics.

1. Introduction

Occasionally, a scientific discovery is made whose future impact on society is likely to be so immense that even an abundance of superlatives may not do it full justice. Genome editing already looks set to be such a discovery. In contrast to previous genetic engineering approaches, the power of genome editing lies in four key features [1]. First, this approach can be applied to practically any cell type from any plant or animal species, ranging from bacteria to humans. Second, it can precisely target any region in a genome, thus providing a means to either completely abolish the function of a gene or subtly modify it by introducing a mutation. Third, the efficiency of gene targeting is extremely high. Fourth, the tools for the newest type of genome editing are simple to prepare, being well within the power of anyone with molecular biology skills, reagents, and equipment. This explains why laboratories across the world are adopting this technology, whether to study bacteria, plants, or human cells in culture. But from the point of view of genetic modification of life, perhaps the most revolutionary aspect of genome editing is the ease with which it can be applied to a fertilized egg.

Because of this, it is now possible to create a gene-edited mouse in several months, as opposed to a couple of years for previous approaches [2]. And unlike such approaches, genome editing can be applied to the fertilized eggs of other mammalian species; therefore, over the past few years, it has been used to create genetically modified rabbits, goats, and monkeys. Referring to the technology, Nobel Prize winner David Baltimore has said, "These are monumental moments in the history of biomedical research. They don't happen every day" [3]. In plants, this approach has generated modified versions of species such as wheat, rice, potatoes, and tomatoes [4]. "We are talking about bringing products to market in five to ten years," Neal Gutterson, vice president at Pioneer Hi–Bred, part of DuPont's chemicals and biotech seed business, has commented. "That is a pretty […] good timeline compared to other technology" [5].

Such are the possibilities; however, the new technology raises all sorts of questions about safety and ethics, and whether the perceived benefits of genome editing outweigh potential risks. In terms of basic research, there are ethical questions about the types of experimental animals that are likely to be created, as well as their health and well-being. Such issues of animal welfare are also relevant to the use of genome editing in agriculture, with the additional element of food quality and safety. For clinical medicine, genome editing offers the possibility of a truly precise gene therapy for the first time, but here too there are issues of safety to consider. Finally, perhaps the most controversial aspect of genome editing is the fact that it can potentially be used to edit the genome of a human embryo, with all the ethical issues that this raises.

Although the genome-editing revolution is a recent event, much of the science underlying it dates back decades. What sparked the revolution was the recognition that a number of previous discoveries could be combined to form a new technology that may be considered a very precise pair of "molecular scissors." Importantly, these scissors can not only cut a gene at a specific location but also guide other tools to modify it in various ways.

The discovery that a break in the DNA double helix inside a living cell can lead to precise modifications of that part of the genome was first made in the late 1990s by Maria Jasin and colleagues at the Memorial Sloan Kettering Cancer Center, New York, USA. Jasin's main interest was in understanding how such breaks play a role in tumor formation [6]. An interesting side aspect of this study was the discovery that if such a break in the DNA occurs in a normal cell, the DNA can be repaired in two ways: either by connecting the two broken ends together – but in such a clumsy manner that this adds or deletes DNA sequence – or more accurately by the process of homologous recombination, which restores the correct sequence [7].

Jasin's findings showed that if a way were found to accurately create a break in the genome at a specific place, the cell's own repair machinery would then create a mismatch join that could result in incapacitation of the gene or, if a suitable complementary piece of DNA were available, a substitution that would create a subtle modification. The only problem was that, at the time, no obvious way of creating a sequence-specific DNA break was known.

2. CRISPR/CAS

In fact, more than a decade would pass before such a tool became available. The cutting system that has proven so revolutionary is known as CRISPR/CAS9 (Fig. 1). The first part of the name comes from the acronym "clustered regularly interspaced short palindromic repeats," while

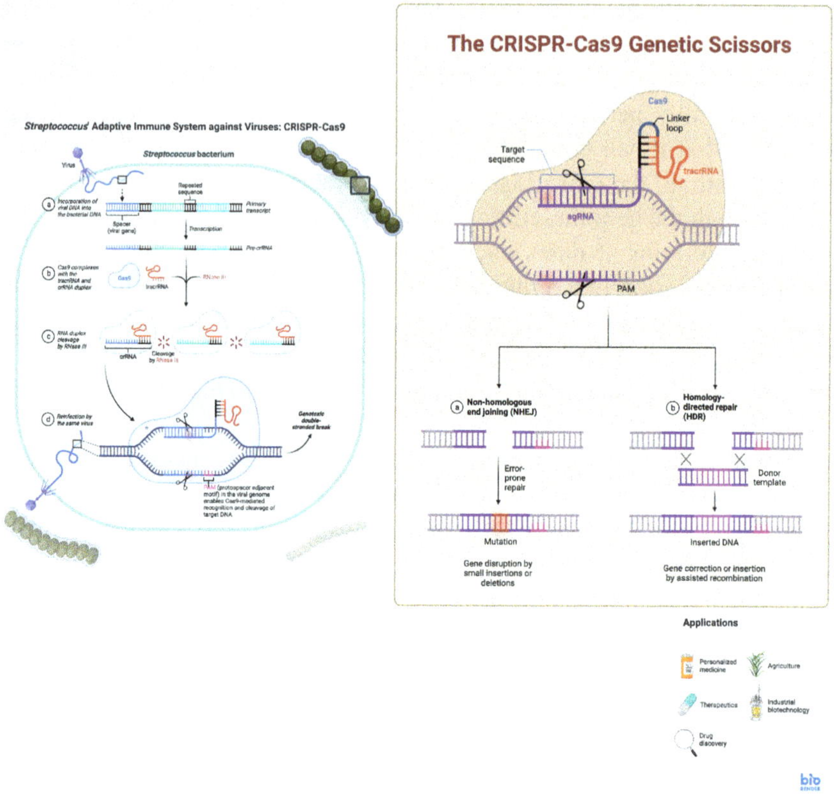

Figure 1. Left: CRISPR sequences in bacteria are separated by unique spacers derived from viruses. CRISPR-associated (CAS) endonucleases recognize the sequence of the spacer. If a virus with the stored genetic sequence infects the bacteria, CAS proteins cut the viral genome and destroy it. Right: CRISPR/CAS can be used to create breaks in the DNA of a living cell at any part of its genome. This triggers either non-homologous end joining to produce a gene knockout or homology directed repair, which can be used to subtly modify the DNA sequence or introduce transgenes into the genome. (BioRender.com.)

CAS9 is the name of the enzyme that cuts the DNA. The CRISPR repeats have been known since 1987, when they were first observed in the genome of the human gut bacterium *E. coli* by Yoshizumi Ishino and colleagues at Osaka University, Japan. It was over a decade later, in 2002, that Ruud Jansen and his colleagues at Utrecht University in the Netherlands made a breakthrough by showing that the sequences were nearly always found next to protein-coding CAS genes that had a similar structure to enzymes interacting with DNA. The researchers concluded that this association suggested a "functional relationship" existed between the CAS genes and CRISPR sequences, but the role of this relationship remained unclear [8].

Three years later, in 2005, several research groups independently discovered that the CRISPR spacers closely resembled the DNA of bacteriophages, a type of virus that infects bacteria. Then, Eugene Koonin, an evolutionary biologist at the National Center for Biotechnology Information in Bethesda, Maryland, USA, suggested that bacteria use CAS enzymes to grab fragments of DNA from viruses [9]. They then insert the viral DNA fragments between their own CRISPR sequences. Later, if a virus of the same type comes along, the bacteria can use CRISPR to recognize the invader. Our own immune system remembers past infections and rapidly responds if they reappear – which is why we are generally only infected once by viruses such as chicken pox; similarly, bacteria possess an analogous system via CRISPR.

What remained unclear was the underlying mechanism of this defense system. The big breakthrough on this front was made by Jennifer Doudna of the University of California, Berkeley, and Emanuelle Charpentier of Umea University, Sweden. Doudna and Charpentier showed that CRISPR operated by producing an RNA copy of a viral DNA, and this "guide RNA" then directs the CAS enzyme to a specific site in the viral genome, which is cleaved. The revolutionary aspect of this discovery was not only that it provided the mechanism of a key process in microbes, but it also suggested the system could be adapted to engineer genes. For Doudna and Charpentier recognized, "[n]ot only were we able to work out how it worked, we were able to reprogramme it to recognise new DNA sequences. If it could be made to work in eukaryote systems – plants and animals – then you'd have a system where you could effectively decide where to produce a double-stranded break in that cell's genome" [10].

The most straightforward way of using genome editing is to create a "knockout" cell or organism. The way this works is that, when an enzyme cuts DNA at a specific sequence, the cell responds by seeking to repair the break. But when this happens, the repair is often imprecise. If this were to occur in a gene coding for a protein, it could disrupt the genetic code and ensure that the protein is not produced. However, a segment of DNA identical to the one surrounding the cutting site but with a subtle difference, such as a mutation or a fluorescent tag, can also be introduced into a cell alongside CAS9 and the guide RNA. In this case, the cell's own natural homologous recombination mechanisms create this more subtle change.

In its different forms, CRISPR is already showing huge potential in basic biomedical research, agriculture, and clinical medicine. So, let us now discuss these in turn, beginning with the use of genome editing to generate animal models for studying diseases.

3. Biomedical Research

Genome editing can be used to edit the genomes of both mammalian and non-mammalian species. The latter possess particular features that make them valuable for research purposes [11]. With their short lifespans and large numbers of offspring, fruit flies and worms have been particularly suitable for genetics because it is possible to dose them with radiation or mutagenic chemicals and then screen the resulting offspring for specific characteristics of the mutant forms [12]. For studies of embryogenesis, the fact that fly and worm embryos develop outside their mother makes them much more amenable to study than those of mammals in their mother's womb. The former is also true of the zebrafish embryo, yet being a vertebrate, it shares many specific features of development with mammals. That zebrafish embryos are transparent is important because it allows sophisticated imaging approaches to be used to study what happens at the molecular level inside the cells of a living embryo [13].

Undoubtedly though, one of the principal ways that genome editing will affect biomedical research is through its capacity to precisely modify the genomes of a range of mammals. Despite the importance of research in worms, flies, and fish, major differences exist between mammals and other multicellular organisms. Such differences include not only the development of the mammalian embryo inside the mother's womb but also the particular challenges posed by maintaining a constant body temperature in a warm-blooded animal. In addition, among mammals, there has been a trend in some species toward larger brains and a greater emphasis on learning over instinct, with this feature being particularly pronounced in the primate group to which our own human species belongs [14].

Genome editing has greatly accelerated the generation of genetically modified mice for developing and testing new therapies for the treatment of diseases. Such diseases can include those caused by viruses, bacteria, or other pathogens, but they also encompass single-gene disorders, such as sickle cell anemia or cystic fibrosis, and even cancer. A key aspect of modern medicine is its arsenal of drugs – generally, small-molecular-weight chemicals that can either be ingested or injected and produce a beneficial effect on the body. Because drugs may not be as effective as hoped, or have adverse side effects, testing of new drugs on animals prior to their use in human clinical trials is a vital part of drug development [15]. Such testing allows the clinical usefulness of a drug as well as its potential for adverse side effects to be assessed. Testing can be carried out on an unmodified animal if the aim is purely to assess the potential toxic effects of a drug. However, given that the point of drugs is to treat disease, an important aspect of drug testing in animals should also be to test the capacity of a drug to relieve the symptoms or, even better, remove the underlying cause of an illness. In this respect, knockout mice and those with more subtle genetic alterations are important disease models, both for better understanding the biological basis of a disease and as living organisms in which drugs can be tested [16].

Yet, there are also some limitations to the usefulness of the mouse as a model for understanding certain aspects of human disease [17]. For instance, many potential drugs for brain disorders have been tested successfully in mice, only to prove ineffective in subsequent human trials. One new development is the use of genome editing to generate genetically modified primates for use, particularly in neuroscience. For while human brains are particularly large and complex compared to the size of our bodies, this is only the culmination of a trend in primates as a whole [18]. As such, primates offer an excellent model for studying the human brain and its various functions. Of particular interest are brain regions such as the prefrontal cortex, critical for many higher human brain functions, which are not well developed in mice. In contrast, the monkey prefrontal cortex is closer in size and structure to our own [18]. Another aspect of primates that makes them potentially better models for studying human brain disorders is the similar ways in which we and other primates interact with the world around us. So, while rodents primarily rely on smell to navigate their way around, primates, including humans, are far more dependent on visual cues. This similarity makes it easier to devise tests to assess primate behavior that have relevance for those used on humans [19].

That genome editing can be employed in primates was demonstrated in January 2014 by Weizhi Ji and colleagues at the Yunnan Key Laboratory of Primate Biomedical Research in China. They used CRISPR to knock out the genes coding for the PPARγ and RAG1 proteins in monkeys, initially targeting the genes in fertilized monkey eggs before implanting the gene-edited embryos into surrogate mothers [20]. Two resulting offspring had knockouts in the genes. PPARγ regulates metabolism, while RAG1 is involved in immunity, and the researchers are now investigating what effects the loss of these genes has upon metabolism and immunity. Ji's team subsequently targeted dystrophin – the gene defective in people with Duchenne's muscular dystrophy – in monkeys, and found that this caused severe muscle degeneration similar to that observed in humans with this condition [21]. As such, this could be important for studying this disease in a species closely related to humans.

However, the real interest in genetically modified primates lies in their use as a tool for studying brain disorders. With this in mind, scientists at the McGovern Institute in Boston, USA, have been using CRISPR to create genetically modified monkeys [22]. Because primate species are very social with highly structured communication patterns, they should offer a valuable new route for assessing the genes involved in social interactions. The aim is first to attempt breeding monkeys with a condition similar to autism spectrum disorder and then to move on to schizophrenia and other disorders. Such primate models will be important for understanding not only the basic biology of mental disorders but also for testing new drugs.

4. Agriculture and Farming

Another sphere of life – agriculture and farming – is already becoming a hot new area for the application of genome editing. One way that genome editing of plants has already demonstrated its potential is in combating disease. Potato blight is a fungus notorious for its role in the Great Famine that devastated Ireland in the late 1840s [23]. Today, blight remains a major problem for potato farmers. Recently, however, Jonathan Jones and colleagues at the John Innes Centre in Norwich, UK, used genome editing to create a GM potato resistant to the fungus [24]. To do this, the researchers introduced a genetic polymorphism, found in a blight-resistant wild potato from South America, into the popular Desiree variety.

There are already moves to use genome editing to introduce disease resistance mutations into several other crop plants. A team led by Caixia Gao at the Institute of Genetics and Developmental Biology in Beijing recently produced wheat resistant to a fungus called powdery mildew, one of the major pests of the world's top food source [25]. The researchers deleted genes in the wheat genome coding for proteins that block defense mechanisms against the mildew. This proved to be a particular challenge since the wheat genome contains three copies of most of its genes. Yet, using CRISPR, Cao reported that, "we now caught all three copies, and only by knocking out all three copies can we get this [mildew]–resistant phenotype" [25]. Meanwhile, a team led by Daniel Voytas of the University of Minnesota in Minneapolis, USA, recently used CRISPR to create plants that are resistant to geminiviruses – a common crop pest that infects plants ranging from beans to beetroots [26]. Such developments hold great potential for commercial importance, as plant viruses cause enormous losses in worldwide crop production each year.

A particularly beneficial development for human health could be the use of genome editing to create crops that don't trigger dangerous food allergies. A common one is an allergy to peanuts. A recent study of American children found that peanut allergies have risen threefold, from 0.4% in 1997 to 1.4% in 2010 [27]. The anaphylactic shock that can result from such an allergy can prove fatal. Acute attacks can be treated with adrenaline; however, there have been cases of children dying even after receiving multiple injections [28]. Because of this, there is a growing interest in engineering peanuts, so they do not trigger an allergic response. Analysis of peanut proteins has identified seven that can cause an allergy [28]. An important question is whether genome editing can now be used to delete or modify the genes coding for these proteins in the peanut genome.

Genome editing may also aid in the development of crops capable of withstanding the extremes of temperature, drought, wind, and snow that are predicted and are increasingly becoming apparent effects of global warming as it leads to increased instability in the Earth's atmosphere [29]. To deal with such extreme changes, scientists may need to do more than tinker with existing crop plants; instead, a major transformation of their basic biology may be required. With this in mind, Daniel Voytas, working with researchers at the Rice Research Institute in Los Baños, Philippines, aims to rewrite the physiology of rice by focusing on the process of photosynthesis [30]. This is the cellular mechanism common to all plants that traps energy from the sun and uses it to convert carbon dioxide and water into glucose, serving as the first step toward producing the other complex molecules of life. Photosynthesis can occur either as the C3 form, found in rice, wheat, and other grain-producing plants, or the more complex C4 form, common to plants such as corn and sugarcane [31]. The two types are distinguished by the initial molecule formed, with either a 3-carbon or 4-carbon sugar being produced. An important difference between the two processes is that C4 photosynthesis is far more efficient at high temperatures and dryness. So, if a way were found to create C4 versions of rice and wheat, their yields could be increased in regions becoming hotter and drier due to climate change [32].

One example of the way that genome editing is being applied to livestock comes from a recent study in which scientists used this technology to produce Brazilian Nelore cattle with increased muscle mass. This study, led by Scott Fahrenkrug of the University of Minnesota, in collaboration with the Roslin Institute in Scotland and Texas A&M University, introduced a mutation found in Belgian blue cattle, hulking animals that provide unusually large amounts of prized, lean cuts of beef, into rangy Nelore cattle, which are heat-tolerant [33]. The mutation, which inhibits production of a muscle-suppressing protein, myostatin, increases muscle mass, and its introduction into Nelore cattle results in animals that produce large amounts of quality meat and can be kept in hot countries, such as Brazil, unlike the Belgian blues.

Despite the potential political obstacles that may lie ahead for the practical application of genome editing in farming, Scott Fahrenkrug believes the technology represents the future of agriculture. As he puts it, "People will say to me, 'You realize this changes everything, don't you?' Because it does. The genome is information. And this is information technology. We have gone from being able to read the genome to being able to write it" [33]. In fact, it is because of such unprecedented power to manipulate life that the impact of genome editing looks set to permeate every facet of society in the future, as seen by the impact this technology is already having on another key area of our lives: clinical human medicine.

5. Clinical Medicine

Since genome editing is so new, its full potential as a therapeutic strategy in humans is still only at the first stages of assessment; yet, there are already highly promising signs [34]. Two main approaches are being pursued. First, cells are taken from an individual, modified, and then replaced inside that individual's body. Although this is much easier to achieve in a controlled fashion, it does limit this approach to only a few cell types, such as those in the bone marrow; consequently, this reduces the types of diseases that can be treated to those affecting the blood or immune system. Second, genome editing is being employed to target cells located within the body, such as those in the lungs of someone with a condition like cystic fibrosis, or in the muscles of someone with a disorder like Duchenne's muscular dystrophy. Although the second type of approach opens up the possibility of using genome-editing technology to modify practically any type of genetic disease, technically, this approach is considerably more challenging.

The first animal study to demonstrate the clinical potential of genome editing was carried out by Jinsong Li's team at the Shanghai Institute for Biological Sciences. In December 2013, they used CRISPR to target a mutant gene in a mouse model of cataract formation [35]. These mice have a mutation in the CRYGC gene which codes for the cystallin protein, a key component of the eye lens. Such mice develop cataracts at an early age; however, when genome editing was used to correct the CRYGC mutation in the fertilized eggs of this mutant, a third of the offspring grew up free of cataracts. Li acknowledged that the efficiency of the technique was low "and, for clinical purpose, the efficiency should reach 100 percent."

A limitation of Li's study was that the correction of the mutation was carried out in an embryo, not in an adult animal. However, such an employment of genome editing in an adult mouse was achieved shortly afterwards by Daniel Anderson and colleagues at the Massachusetts Institute of Technology, who reported in March 2014 that they had "cured" mice of a rare liver disorder [36]. The disorder in this mouse model was caused by a mutation in the gene coding for a liver enzyme called FAH, which breaks down the amino acid tyrosine. In this disorder, which affects about 1 in 100,000 people, the faulty enzyme leads to a buildup of tyrosine in the liver, which eventually causes hepatic failure. The only available treatments in humans involve a low-protein diet and a drug called NTCB, which inhibits tyrosine production; however, these measures are only partially effective. To treat the disorder in mice, Anderson and his team injected CRISPR/CAS9 constructs into the animals' blood supply under high pressure. These were subsequently taken up by the liver, leading to a correction of the gene defect in some cells of that organ. While only 1 in 250 cells were corrected, it still allowed the corrected healthy liver cells to proliferate and replace diseased ones. This was sufficient to cure the disease, allowing the mice to survive after being taken off the NCTB drug.

One of the most well-known single-gene disorders of the brain is Huntington's disease [37]. This dominant disorder affects a relatively large number of individuals – 12 in every 100,000 people in Britain. The condition typically starts with twitching and mood swings, but rapidly progresses to full-scale dementia and death, generally in middle age. And because sufferers may already have children before they begin to show symptoms, the disease is passed down through the generations. The identification of the genetic defect underlying Huntington's disease in 1993 – a decade before the completion of the Human Genome Project – was a triumph of modern genetics [38]. This showed that affected individuals have a defect in a gene that was named Huntingtin. This gene has a DNA sequence, CAG, at its start that is repeated around 17 times in normal individuals. Since each CAG codes for the amino acid glutamine, a typical individual will have 17 glutamine amino acid units at the start of the Huntingtin protein. However, faulty DNA replication can cause the CAG repeats to expand, and if a person inherits 36 or more, they will succumb to Huntington's disorder. The reason is that the extra glutamines lead to the Huntingtin protein forming aggregates, which cause the cells in which this occurs – particularly neurons – to dysfunction.

Initially the identification of the Huntingtin gene defect was greeted with hope for a cure. Unfortunately, all it has meant is that people at risk can now undergo a genetic test that reveals how many CAG repeats are present in their Huntingtin gene. This is obviously welcome news if it indicates that an individual is free of risk and can also help those hoping to have children. However, given that a positive result is effectively a death sentence, it is not surprising that most people at risk choose not to take the test.

Recently, there has been a glimmer of renewed hope for those with Huntington's disease, following a study by Nicole Déglon and colleagues at the University of Lausanne. They infected two groups of healthy adult mice with a virus expressing the mutant Huntingtin gene. One group was also injected with a virus expressing the CAS9 enzyme and a guide RNA targeting the Huntingtin gene. Déglon believes that what her team found is "remarkably encouraging," as, after only three weeks, the two groups of mice showed a striking contrast. While those treated only with the mutant huntingtin showed large amounts of protein aggregation in their brain cells, those with the mutant protein and the CRISPR treatment had almost none – the genome editing had prevented the expression of almost 90% of the mutant Huntingtin [39].

Such studies show the potential of genome editing for correcting mutations in rare single-gene disorders. In addition, an exciting aspect of this technology is the possibility of using it to treat more common human diseases, such as cancer. This disorder can either be caused by the loss of function of an inhibitory tumor-suppressing gene or by the activation of an oncogene, both of which can lead to abnormal cell growth and tumor progression [40]. Recent studies have shown that in a human population, many different gene mutations seem to be involved in driving the progression of a particular type of cancer. So, for instance, a recent investigation of women with breast cancer showed that in 50 such cases, over 1,700 mutations were detected in their tumors, most of which were unique to each individual [41]. The increasing ability to rapidly sequence the whole genome of a patient's cancer and compare that to their normal genome – so-called "cancer genomics" – means that it is becoming possible to pinpoint the exact molecular cause of a cancer in an individual [42]. But such genetic diversity also poses problems for standard drug therapy. However, with genome editing, it should be possible to correct the specific cancer-causing defects in a tumor, whether this be due to the loss of tumor-suppressor genes or the activation of oncogenes. Indeed, recently, scientists at the Walter and Eliza Hall Institute of Medical Research in Melbourne targeted and killed human lymphoma cells by using CRISPR to knock out a gene essential for the survival of these blood cancer cells [43].

Genome editing also offers a potential way to combat many types of viral infections. The Hepatitis C virus (HCV) is a bloodborne virus spread through needle sharing in intravenous drug use, poorly sterilized medical equipment, and transfusions [44]. An estimated 130–150 million people worldwide are infected and chronic carriers of HCV. Because the virus does not cause any obvious initial symptoms, infected individuals often go undetected for many years. However, over time, HCV can cause chronic scarring of the liver and cirrhosis, which can ultimately lead to liver failure or cancer. The genome of HCV is composed of RNA, not DNA. It is different though from retroviruses such as HIV which also have an RNA genome, as in the latter case, the RNA is converted into DNA by the viral enzyme reverse transcriptase, which can then integrate into the host genome located in the nucleus of the cell. In contrast, the HCV RNA genome remains in the host cell's cytoplasm, where it is replicated to produce more copies and infectious viral particles.

The fact that HCV is an RNA virus suggested that it might be impossible to target it by genome editing. However, recently, a team led by David Weiss and Arash Grakoui at Emory University achieved this goal by using a modified form of the CAS9 enzyme. This modified CAS9 uses a guide RNA to find its target in the HCV RNA genome, but instead of cutting the RNA, it creates a roadblock that prevents its replication. Weiss, Grakoui, and their colleagues found that, after introducing the modified CAS9 and its guide RNA into human liver cells in culture, these cells became resistant to infection by HCV [45]. The researchers believe their findings might eventually be used to treat chronic HCV infections. And given that viruses that have a much more acute effect on human health and survival such as the Influenza or Ebola viruses also have an RNA genome, this strategy may have much wider applicability.

Such are the possibilities of genome editing for direct treatment of both the genetic basis of disease and that caused by infectious agents. Yet, some major obstacles remain. One is that the efficiency and accuracy of the technology still need considerable improvement before it can be cleared for routine human use. However, given the speed of development of the technology, it is quite likely that such problems will eventually be ironed out. A more fundamental obstacle is getting the genome-editing tools into the cells of the tissues or organs to be treated [46]. This has been a major challenge for previous attempts at gene therapy. At the heart of the problem is the fact that cells are enclosed by a protective membrane that acts as a barrier to large molecules such as proteins or nucleic acids such as DNA and RNA. An additional obstacle is delivering genome-editing tools to the tissue of interest without them being degraded in the process by the body's natural defense mechanisms.

Due to these challenges, the diseases most likely to be initially treated using genome editing will be those affecting tissues that are most accessible or can even be removed from the body and then replaced once the genetic defect is corrected. Diseases that affect blood cells generally fall into the latter category. This includes the red blood cells that carry oxygen around the body and the white cells that make up our immune system, as both cell types originate from stem cells in the bone marrow. A sample of bone marrow can be removed from the patient, the cells within it treated, and put back in to repopulate the blood with corrected cells [47]. Potential treatable disorders in this category include different forms of leukemia as well as sickle cell anemia and thalassemia, which affect the red blood cells' oxygen-carrying capacity, and severe combined immune disorder. Indeed, recently, the U.S. Food and Drug Administration approved the first clinical CRISPR/CAS9 treatment for sickle cell anemia and thalassemia [48].

Although CRISPR/CAS9 genome editing is being investigated to treat a variety of diseases in children and adults, a far more controversial area is the use of this approach in human embryos. The use of genome editing in human embryos for research purposes, to study the role of genes in human embryo development, is already being pursued in several laboratories around the world. In December 2018, Jiankui He of the Southern University of Science and Technology in Shenzhen, China, announced that he had used CRISPR to modify human embryos that were then implanted into their mother and later born as female twins [49]. He claimed to have edited to delete the CCR5 gene which codes for a coreceptor required for HIV entry into cells, as the father was infected with HIV and could have passed the virus on to his offspring. It became clear that he had not obtained official ethical approval for this experiment and had misled the twins' parents regarding the potential risks associated with such genetic modifications. Because he acted in an unethical and unsafe manner, Jiankui He was sentenced to three years in prison; he was recently released and is now seeking to rebuild his career.

6. Basis of Ethics in Islamic Societies

To discuss Islamic thought and opinion concerning genome editing, it is useful to first explain the foundations of Islamic ethical theory [50]. This approach is used by Muslim scholars when there is no obvious solution for certain unprecedented situations, as in the case of genome editing, which is not addressed in the Holy Scripture (Quran) or the practices and teachings of the Prophet (peace be upon him) (with Sunnah being the practice of the Prophet (*pbuh*), while Hadith is a record of his teachings as recalled by his contemporaries and passed down through generations), the sources of Islamic jurisprudence.

Uṣūl al fiqh, or the principles of Islamic jurisprudence, is defined as the systematic approaches and principles by which Muslim scholars rationalize new rulings that have not been previously addressed. Concepts of *ijmā`* refer to the consensus of past Muslim scholars regarding a particular issue at a particular time, and *qiyas* refer to analogical reasoning, which are the concepts most commonly used to deal with ethical challenges. However, new ethical issues challenge Muslim scholars to not rely on previous strategies but rather seek novel solutions to public debates. Within this context, Muslim scholars construct their decisions based on the principle of *maqāṣid al sharī `a*, the purposes of the law [50].

Maqāṣid al sharī `a* consists of *dīn* (religion), *nafs* (life), *nasl* (progeny), *`aql (intellect), and *māl* (wealth). Any ethical solution should be built on these principles, in addition to *qiyās*, *`urf* (custom), *istiḥsān* (juristic preference), *istiṣḥab* (presumption of continuity), and *maṣlaḥa mursala* (considerations of public interest). Derived from these principles, *qawā`id fiqhiyya*, or the Islamic legal aphorisms, refer to a body of abstract rules which are derived from the detailed study of *fiqh* (jurisprudence) itself.

7. Islam and Genome Editing in Humans

Such principles can be applied to the case of the genome-edited Chinese twins. It might, for instance, be argued that the intention of using CRISPR for such genome editing was for the good purpose of protecting the newborn twins from HIV infection transmission from their HIV-infected father. In this respect, the principle of *yaqīn* (certainty) is relevant, in that the use of CRISPR should only have occurred after all safety measures had been taken into consideration and monitored by the legal and medical authorities in the country where the clinical intervention was performed. An evidence-based approach should have been applied in this situation to ensure that all safety concerns have been satisfied. Moreover, this principle obliges users of the CRISPR approach to ensure that its use is in accordance with what it has been licensed for and that no further experimentation occurs unless approved by the researcher's safety and institutional review board committees or their equivalent. Regarding the case of the Chinese twins, it is clear that this principle was not satisfied, and there is no certainty about the safety or absolute efficiency of this intervention as carried out.

The principle of *darar* (injury) also relates to the positive and negative effects on the patient and the community that could occur because of using CRISPR. The risk–benefit balance should be measured accurately by professional experts. Any harm or injury should be fully explained to the patients, and their consent should be obtained before any procedure is performed. This principle was clearly not fulfilled in the case of the Chinese twins, as the benefit is not clearly greater than the potential harm. The parents did not provide their informed consent since the full extent of the risks to the twins and their progeny is not yet understood.

Through the principle of *darūra* (necessity), all alternatives to CRISPR should have been discussed with the prospective parents, and the choice of genome editing as the best strategy should have been discussed and agreed to by scientists independent of the study. In fact, in this case, there were more established and proven safe alternatives to protect future children from HIV transmission from the father than via genome editing of human embryos.

According to the principle of *`urf* (custom), the social context of using any contemporary technology should also have been taken into consideration. According to this principle, CRISPR should have been appropriately introduced to the local community and population. This could have been accomplished through a series of educational lectures provided for the public to explain the CRISPR technology along with its risks and benefits to the community so that the public can be prepared for this novel technology and facilitate its use in the future. This principle was clearly not satisfied in the case of the Chinese twins, as neither the Chinese nor the global community were informed about the plan to use such an approach.

Given the uncertainties and risks attached to human germline genome editing, it is unlikely that either international law or Islamic ethics will be prepared to sanction the use of this approach for clinical purposes in the foreseeable future.

CRISPR technology can be applied in humans to both somatic cells and germline cells, which include egg, sperm, and embryos. While germline gene editing is problematic for both the scientific and religious communities with regard to issues related to safety and permanent genetic changes to future generations, somatic cell genetic modifications that only affect the patient could be permissible from the Islamic point of view. These would modify certain genes to treat a particular disease, as part of a normal medical procedure for which the patient or their legally authorized representative would provide informed consent, and these genetic modifications would not be transferred to their offspring.

8. Islam and Genome Editing in Agriculture

The debate among Islamic scholars about genome editing as applied to agriculture is more advanced than in medicine because genetic modification of crops and farm animals for purposes of food production (popularly known as GM foods) has been carried out for several decades. While CRISPR technology represents the most recent approach to such genetic modification, previous developments have raised issues of safety, ethics, and religion, which have been discussed globally and specifically by Islamic scholars [51].

For instance, in 1998, at a seminar in Kuwait organized by the Islamic Organization for Medical Sciences, the Islamic Fiqh Academy, the World Health Organization's Eastern Mediterranean Regional Office, and the Islamic Educational, Scientific and Cultural Organization (ISESCO), a group of Islamic scholars concluded that although there are many potentially justified fears about possible harmful effects of GM food technology and GM food products on human beings and the environment, there are no laws within Islam that prohibit the genetic modification of food crops and animals. Notably, scientists in Islamic countries such as Egypt and Indonesia (the latter having the world's largest Muslim population) have been actively manipulating plant genes in various ways. Thus, in 2003, the Indonesian Ulemas Council (MUI) approved the importation and consumption of GM food products [52].

A leading expert on the interpretation of the Quran in light of recent advances in GM technology is Ibrahim Syed, an Islamic cleric and the President of the Islamic Research Foundation International, an amalgamation of different Islamic religious groups. According to him, the verse in the Quran forbidding human beings from defacing God's creation "cannot be invoked as a total and radical ban on genetic engineering [...] If carried too far, it would conflict with many forms of curative surgery that also entail some change in God's creation" [53]. In line with this, Syed stated that African and Asian countries with large Muslim populations should "reject the propaganda of extremist groups" campaigning against genetic engineering and instead embrace them wholeheartedly.

Another Islamic scholar, Fatima Agha Al-Hayani, has argued that Muslims should ensure that genetic modification "may remain mercy-driven" and promote righteousness. She believes that GM food technology has the potential "to carry Allah's work, alleviate hunger and suffering, secure justice and equity for everyone," and because of this, Muslims "must keep up with the new research and discoveries and make connections within the scientific fields" [54]. However, not everyone within the Islamic world holds such a positive view of GM technology. For instance, in a letter written in October 2006 to the British government by Majid Katme, on behalf of the United Kingdom Islamic Medical Association (UKIMA), Katme quoted copiously from the Quran to the effect that there is no need for genetic modification of food crops because Allah created everything perfectly and human beings do not have any right to manipulate anything that Allah has created using His divine wisdom [51]. Katme also stated that the Quran contains several verses, prohibiting man from tampering with Allah's creations and ended the letter by emphasizing the position of members of UKIMA that there are no benefits that would accrue to Britain from GM food production.

Such points of view predate the development of CRISPR technology. One major difference between this technology and previous approaches to genetical engineering is the potential for extreme precision in the genetic changes made using CRISPR. Such is this precision that it has been compared to the types of mutations that occur in nature. As such, an interesting question for future Islamic debate might be whether this makes it different from previous approaches in terms of the concept of Allah's creation and what this means.

9. CRISPR and Halal Food Certification

One other interesting application of CRISPR technology in terms of food production is its potential as a means of carrying out molecular analysis of halal food products [55].

"Halal" means permissible by Islamic law, and halal food is permitted for consumption by Muslims. It is based on the dietary standards outlined in the Quran and Hadith and derived from the practices of the Prophet Mohammad, Ijma, and Qiyas [56]. To qualify as halal, the food must not consist of or have been in contact with prohibited animals or their by-products. To be considered halal, the permitted animals must also be slaughtered according to Islamic law. In Islam, all food is permissible, except pork, carnivorous animals, birds of prey, land animals without external ears, animals that died before slaughtering, and food dedicated to someone other than Allah.

Halal food businesses have expanded rapidly across every continent due to the rise in the Muslim population worldwide, which is projected to reach 2.2 billion by 2030 [57]. Muslim consumers depend on halal certification and labeling before consuming a product because halal is otherwise difficult to verify as it cannot be determined based on the odor, texture, or taste of the food. As well as its uses in genomic editing, the CRISPR system has been adapted for other applications, such as the detection of nucleic acids. CRISPR-associated proteins, such as CAS12, were found to have indiscriminate single-stranded DNA cleavage activity, and this led to signal production in the presence of target sequences [58]. This offers a strategy for molecular-based diagnostic tools with improved specificity, sensitivity, and speed.

CRISPR/CAS12 has been successfully used in halal food authentication through the design of guide RNAs specifically targeting the cytochrome b gene of pork mitochondrial DNA [59]. The presence of pork was determined using fluorescence analysis. This approach makes it possible to identify pork meat traces in chicken, beef, and lamb products. The assay takes only 30 minutes and can be carried out with inexpensive and easily available equipment and reagents. These advantages make this assay feasible for onsite detection in a standard biomedical laboratory.

10. Conclusion

Genome editing, particularly that employing the revolutionary new CRISPR technology, looks set to transform not only biomedical research but also clinical medicine and agriculture. CRISPR technology has the potential to transform biomedical science and clinical medicine, providing new ways to understand, diagnose, and treat diseases. It could also radically improve food production and even scientific certification of halal food, which is important for Muslims. The newfound ability to genetically modify crops and farm animals to make them more resistant to a rapidly changing climate is particularly pertinent to Islamic societies facing acute challenges in food production that are linked to global warming. However, while genome editing offers a plethora of methods to disrupt current human society in exciting and positive ways, it also raises many issues of safety and ethics. In this chapter, we have particularly focused on such issues from the perspective of Islamic thought and opinion.

References

[1] Riordan SM, Heruth DP, Zhang LQ, Ye SQ. Application of CRISPR/Cas9 for biomedical discoveries. *Cell Biosci.* 2015;5:33. DOI: 10.1186/s13578-015-0027-9.

[2] Aida T, Imahashi R, Tanaka K. Translating human genetics into mouse: The impact of ultra-rapid in vivo genome editing. *Dev Growth Differ.* 2014;56:34–45. DOI: 10.1111/dgd.12101.

[3] Maxmen A. Easy DNA editing will remake the world. Buckle up. Wired; 2015. http://www.wired.com/2015/07/crispr-dna-editing-2/.

[4] Weeks DP, Spalding MH, Yang B. Use of designer nucleases for targeted gene and genome editing in plants. *Plant Biotechnol J.* 2015. DOI: 10.1111/pbi.12448.

[5] Regalado, A. DuPont predicts CRISPR plants on dinner plates in five years. *MIT Technol Rev.* 2015. https://www.technologyreview.com/2015/10/08/109790/dupont-predicts-crisprplants-on-dinner-plates-in-five-years/.

[6] Prakash R, Zhang Y, Feng W, Jasin M. Homologous recombination and human health: The roles of BRCA1, BRCA2, and associated proteins. *Cold Spring Harb Perspect Biol.* 2015;7:a016600. DOI: 10.1101/cshperspect.a016600.

[7] Marx V. Genome-editing tools storm ahead. *Nat Methods.* 2012;9:1055–1059. DOI: 10.1038/nmeth.2220.

[8] Jansen R, Embden JD, Gaastra W, Schouls LM. Identification of genes that are associated with DNA repeats in prokaryotes. *Mol Microbiol.* 2002;43:1565–1575.

[9] Zimmer C. Breakthrough DNA editor born of bacteria. *Quanta Mag.* 2015. https://www.quantamagazine.org/20150206-crispr-dna-editor-bacteria/.

[10] Connor S. The more we looked into the mystery of Crispr, the more interesting it seemed. *The Independent.* 2013. https://www.independent.co.uk/news/science/the-more-we-looked-into-the-mystery-ofcrispr-the-more-interesting-it-seemed-8925328.html.

[11] Ma C. Animal models of disease. *Mod Drug Discov.* 2004. http://pubs.acs.org/subscribe/journals/mdd/v07/i06/pdf/604feature_ma.pdf.

[12] Algar J. What do we have in common with worms and flies? Our genomes. *Tech Times.* 2015. http://www.techtimes.com/articles/14346/20140828/what-do-we-have-in-commong-with-worms-and-flies-our-genomes.htm.

[13] Hove JR. In vivo biofluid dynamic imaging in the developing zebrafish. *Birth Defects Res. Part C Embryo Today Rev.* 2004;72:277–289. DOI: 10.1002/bdrc.20019.
[14] Dunbar RI, Shultz S. Understanding primate brain evolution. *Philos Trans R Soc Lond Ser B, Biol Sci.* 2007;362:649–658. DOI: 10.1098/rstb.2006.2001.
[15] Experimenting on animals. BBC. 2014. https://www.bbc.co.uk/ethics/animals/using/experiments_1.shtml.
[16] Melina R. Why do medical researchers use mice? Live Science. 2010. http://www.livescience.com/32860-why-do-medical-researchers-use-mice.html.
[17] Zaragoza C. et al. Animal models of cardiovascular diseases. *J Biomed Biotechnol.* 2011;2011:497841. DOI: 10.1155/2011/497841.
[18] Teffer K, Semendeferi K. Human prefrontal cortex: Evolution, development, and pathology. *Prog Brain Res.* 2012;195:191–218. DOI: 10.1016/B978-0-444-53860-4.00009-X.
[19] Mitchell JF, Leopold DA. The marmoset monkey as a model for visual neuroscience. *Neurosci Res.* 2015;93:20–46. DOI: 10.1016/j.neures.2015.01.008.
[20] Niu Y. et al. Generation of gene-modified cynomolgus monkey via Cas9/RNA-mediated gene targeting in one-cell embryos. *Cell.* 2014;156:836–843. DOI: 10.1016/j.cell.2014.01.027.
[21] Chen Y. et al. Functional disruption of the dystrophin gene in rhesus monkey using CRISPR/Cas9. *Hum Mol Genet.* 2015;24:3764–3774. DOI: 10.1093/hmg/ddv120.
[22] Dougherty E. From genes to brains: How advances in genomics are changing the study of neuroscience. McGovern Institute for Brain Research at MIT. 2014. https://mcgovern.mit.edu/2014/12/06/from-genes-to-brains/.
[23] Irish potato famine. The History Place. 2000. https://www.historyplace.com/worldhistory/famine/index.html.
[24] GM potato 'immune to blight. *The Telegraph.* 2014. https://www.telegraph.co.uk/news/science/10643226/GM-potato-immune-to-blight.html.
[25] Talbot D. Chinese researchers stop wheat disease with gene editing. *MIT Technol Rev.* 2015. https://www.technologyreview.com/2014/07/21/111563/chinese-researchers-stop-wheat-disease-with-gene-editing/.
[26] CRISPR cripples plant viruses. *Nature.* 2015;526:8–9.
[27] Ward A. Progress in peanut allergy trials raises hopes. 2015. https://www.ft.com/content/4c4bedaa-18da-11e5-a130-2e7db721f996.
[28] Novella S. CRISPR and a hypoallergenic peanut. *Neurologica.* 2015. https://theness.com/neurologicablog/crispr-and-a-hypoallergenic-peanut/.
[29] Lopez-Arredondo D, Gonzalez-Morales SI, Bello-Bello E, Alejo-Jacuinde G, Herrera L. Engineering food crops to grow in harsh environments. F1000Research. 2015;4:651. DOI: 10.12688/f1000research.6538.1.

[30] Rotman D. Why we will need genetically modified foods. *MIT Technol Rev*. 2013. https://www.technologyreview.com/2013/12/17/112585/why-we-will-need-genetically-modified-foods/.

[31] Gowik U, Westhoff P. The path from C3 to C4 photosynthesis. *Plant Physiol*. 2011;155:56–63, DOI: 10.1104/pp.110.165308.

[32] Pollack A. By 'editing' plant genes, companies avoid regulation. *The New York Times*. 2015. https://www.nytimes.com/2015/01/02/business/energy-environment/a-gray-area-in-regulation-of-genetically-modified-crops.html.

[33] Regalado A. On the horns of the GMO dilemma. *MIT Technol News*. 2014. https://www.technologyreview.com/2014/09/02/74158/on-the-horns-of-the-gmo-dilemma/.

[34] Xiao-Jie L, Hui-Ying X, Zun-Ping K, Jin-Lian C, Li-Juan J. CRISPR-Cas9: A new and promising player in gene therapy. *J Med Genet*. 2015;52:289–296. DOI: 10.1136/jmedgenet-2014-102968.

[35] Grens K. CRISPR for cures? The Scientist. 2013. https://www.the-scientist.com/crisprfor-cures-38297.

[36] Trafton A. Erasing a genetic mutation. *MIT News*. 2014. https://news.mit.edu/2014/erasing-genetic-mutation.

[37] Huntington's disease. *NHS Choices*. 2015. https://www.nhs.uk/conditions/huntingtonsdisease/.

[38] Thomson EA. Huntington's disease gene is found. *MIT News*. 1993. https://news.mit.edu/1993/huntington-0331.

[39] Armitage H. Gene-editing method halts production of brain-destroying proteins. *Science News*. 2015. https://www.science.org/content/article/gene-editingmethod-halts-production-brain-destroying-proteins.

[40] Cancer facts and figures. *American Cancer Society*. 2014. https://www.cancer.org/research/cancer-facts-statistics/all-cancer-facts-figures/cancer-facts-figures-2014.htm.

[41] DNA of 50 breast cancer patients decoded. *Science Daily*. 2011. https://www.sciencedaily.com/releases/2011/04/110402163425.htm.

[42] Jamieson NB, Chang DK, Biankin AV. Cancer genetics and implications for clinical management. *Surg Clin North Am*. 2015;95:919–934. DOI: 10.1016/j.suc.2015.05.003.

[43] New genome-editing technology to help treat blood cancers. *Science Daily*. 2015. http://www.sciencedaily.com/releases/2015/03/150312202211.htm.

[44] Lee SH. et al. New data and an old puzzle: The negative association between schizophrenia and rheumatoid arthritis. *Int J Epidemiol*. 2015. DOI: 10.1093/ije/dyv136.

[45] Keener AB. Delivering the goods: scientists seek a way to make CRISPR-Cas gene editing more targeted. *Nature Medicine*. 2015; 21:1239-41. DOI: 10.1038/nm1115-1239.

[46] Kamimura K, Suda T, Zhang G, Liu D. Advances in gene delivery systems. *Pharm Med* 25; 2011:293–306. DOI: 10.2165/11594020-000000000-00000.

[47] Fischer A, Hacein-Bey-Abina S, Cavazzana-Calvo M. Gene therapy of primary T cell immunodeficiencies. *Gene*. 2013;525:170–173. DOI: 10.1016/j.gene.2013.03.092.

[48] Lovelace Jr BA, Kopf M. FDA approves cure for sickle cell disease, the first treatment to use gene-editing tool CRISPR. *NCB News*. 2023. https://www.nbcnews.com/health/health-news/fda-approves-cure-sickle-cell-disease-firsttreatment-use-gene-editing-rcna127979.

[49] Lei R, Qiu R. Ethical and regulatory issues in human gene editing: Chinese perspective. *Biotechnol Appl Biochem*. 2020;67:880–891. DOI: 10.1002/bab.2032.

[50] Al-Balas QAE, Dajani R, Al-Delaimy WK. The ethics of gene editing from an Islamic perspective: A focus on the recent gene editing of the Chinese twins. *Sci Eng Ethics*. 2020;26:1851–1860. DOI: 10.1007/s11948-020-00205-5.

[51] Omobowale EB, Singer PA, Daar AS. The three main monotheistic religions and gm food technology: An overview of perspectives. *BMC Int Health Hum Rights*. 2009;9:18. DOI: 10.1186/1472-698X-9-18.

[52] Muslim council approves GM foods. *The Jakarta Post*. 2003. https://www.agbioworld.org/biotech-info/religion/muslim-council.html.

[53] Syed IB. Genetic engineering: 21st century's frontier science. Islamic Research Foundation International, Inc.

[54] Al-Hayani FA. Biomedical ethics. Muslim perspectives on genetic modification. *Zygon*. 2007;42:153–162.

[55] Kua JM, Azizi MMF, Abdul Talib MA, Lau HY. Adoption of analytical technologies for verification of authenticity of halal foods - a review. *Food Addit Contam Part A Chem Anal Control Expo Risk Assess*. 2022;39:1906–1932. DOI: 10.1080/19440049.2022.2134591.

[56] Regenstein JM, Chaudry MM, Regenstein CE. The Kosher and Halal food laws. *Compr Rev Food Sci Food Saf.* 2003;2:111–127. DOI: 10.1111/j.1541-4337.2003.tb00018.x.

[57] Adekunle B, Filson G. Understanding Halal food market: Resolving asymmetric information. *Food Ethics*. 2020;5:1–22.

[58] Chen JS. et al. CRISPR-Cas12a target binding unleashes indiscriminate single-stranded DNase activity. *Science*. 2018;360:436–439. DOI: 10.1126/science.aar6245.

[59] Wu Y. et al. CRISPR-Cas12-based rapid authentication of halal food. *J Agric Food Chem*. 2021;69:10321–10328. DOI: 10.1021/acs.jafc.1c03078.

https://doi.org/10.1142/9781800616295_0009

Chapter 9

Digital Technologies for Improving Pregnancy Care

Jane E. Hirst

The George Institute for Global Health, Imperial College London, UK

j.hirst@imperial.ac.uk

Abstract

Reducing maternal mortality remains a global challenge. Weaknesses in health systems are an important contributor to deaths around the world. Digital technologies could accelerate progress and support maternity services worldwide. Many digital innovations have been developed and implemented in maternity services. These target: the end users themselves (i.e., the pregnant woman and her family) to improve health knowledge and health-seeking behaviors; the primary and secondary care health workers in the community to support decision-making, scheduling, and referrals; and the health system and health management supporting the tracking of births and deaths. This chapter outlines the case for digital health innovations to support pregnancy and maternity services through a series of case studies, considering the potential advantages and challenges of scale-up. While the examples presented are not specific to Muslim populations, they have potential relevance for the challenges faced in Muslim countries worldwide.

1. Introduction

The WHO estimated in 2020 that 287,000 women died during pregnancy, childbirth, or within the six weeks after birth [1]. Maternal mortality is reported as deaths per 100,000 live births in a given population for a given time (the maternal mortality ratio, MMR). While efforts to reduce maternal mortality have been called for since the 1980s, it was only in 2000, when the Millennium Development Goals (MDGs) were agreed upon, that improving maternal health received global attention, with one of the eight goals (MDG5) focused only on maternal health [2]. This indicator aimed to reduce maternal mortality by 75% between 1990 and 2015, with sub-indicators on access to antenatal care and comprehensive reproductive health services. Although progress was made, with an overall reduction in MMR from 339 in 2000 to 227 in 2015, reductions were uneven, and many countries failed to reach their MDG target. Thus, in the era of Sustainable Development Goals (SDGs), reducing maternal mortality remains part of the "unfinished agenda." Health SDG target 3.1 aims to reduce the global MMR to less than 70 by 2030 [3]. Disturbingly, the 2022 report from the WHO showed that the world is off track to reach this target, with progress in reduction having nearly completely stalled since 2016 (MMR 223 in 2020), and in some countries getting worse [4]. In 2023, Dr Tedros Ghebreyesus, Director General of the World Health Organization noted [1],

> In the first five years of the Sustainable Development Goals, maternal mortality barely declined, if at all. Put simply, we are way off track to achieve the SDG target on maternal mortality. On current trends, more than one million additional maternal deaths will occur by 2030.

The number of women who die during pregnancy or childbirth is a direct reflection of health system functioning, or lack thereof, and the socioeconomic, nutritional, and security situations of the women and communities accessing the system [5]. Nowhere in health are the differences in outcomes between high-income and low-income countries starker. In Sub-Saharan Africa, the lifetime risk of maternal death is 1 in 40, compared to a risk of 1 in 16,000 in Australia and New Zealand [1]. The medical reasons why women die have been known for decades. Low-cost and scalable interventions exist to prevent most of these deaths. The WHO and other groups have released comprehensive guidelines regarding the content, timing, and quality of care needed to prevent maternal and perinatal deaths [6]. However, implementation and universal coverage of quality, timely, and affordable maternal care remain challenging [7].

The digital revolution has changed how we live our lives and how the healthcare system functions. There is hope that digital solutions can democratize access to healthcare and improve the quality of service provision globally. However, digital solutions can only augment and not replace a dysfunctional health system [8]. Many digital interventions have been developed to improve maternal and perinatal outcomes around the world, with the promise of helping revive stalled progress in maternal mortality reduction in hard-to-reach populations and providing cost-effective, high-quality care for all [9]. However, the evidence base for most interventions remains weak, with challenges in interoperability, technology infrastructure, and sustainability.

In 2021, the WHO released its global strategy on digital health [10] and in 2023 revised its classification of digital interventions, recognizing the wide range of functions that information technology systems can address, including mobile health solutions, the Internet of Things, big data, and generative AI [11]. The swift need for updates reflects the speed of technological developments in this area. The WHO classification considers digital interventions across three axes:

(1) the health system challenges they are addressing (for example, challenges in information access, accountability, access efficacy, and quality of care);
(2) who the digital intervention targets (the person, healthcare worker, health system management, or data services);
(3) the services and application types themselves (e.g., point of service, health system/provider administration, registries and directories, data management services, and surveillance and response).

The WHO also highlights the need for equitable, interoperable, affordable, scalable, and sustainable systems that respect individual rights to privacy [10].

Within maternity services, several interventions have been developed to address different health system challenges, targeting different health system challenges and the users of the health system using different application types.

We present five case studies of digital interventions in different stages of development and implementation from around the world. These examples have been selected either because the author has been personally involved in their development, providing first-hand insights and reflections, or to illustrate the potential and pitfalls of large scale-up. While digital interventions can be developed by the industry or the health sector itself, we focus on those that have published evaluations of their development, acceptability, feasibility, and/or effectiveness.

2. Case Study 1: Messages to Support Health Promotion: The Kilkari Program of India

2.1 *Digital health interventions to support women*

Kilkari is one of the largest maternal mobile messaging programs in the world, which was designed with BBC Media Action and the Ministry of Family Health and Welfare of India and is implemented across 13 states in India [12,13]. It is an example of a "direct-to-beneficiary" program, designed to close gaps in access and health knowledge among disadvantaged populations. The program sends weekly pre-recorded calls to new and expectant mothers and their families from the fourth month of pregnancy until one-year postpartum 14. It delivers reproductive, maternal, neonatal, and child health information directly to subscribers' phones.

In the first five years of its implementation (2016–2020), Kilkari reached over 10 million women. Unlike other large-scale direct-to-beneficiary mobile programs, the Kilkari Impact and Evaluation group has published detailed and critical evaluations of the reach and impact of the program on behavior change and health outcomes [12,14].

Part of the Kilkari implementation was evaluating the effect on health outcomes using an individually randomized trial in Madhya Pradesh [15]. The investigators set out to assess whether the Kilkari messaging program could improve the rate of breastfeeding as the primary outcome, with the secondary outcome being the use of modern contraceptive methods at one-year postpartum. Outcomes were assessed by a survey administered to women and their husbands at the end of the study [14].

The study team enrolled 5,095 women at baseline, with 2,695 randomized to receive the Kilkari intervention and 2,400 to usual care. At one-year follow-up, data were available for 2,349 women in the intervention group and 2,049 in the usual care group, with 346 and 326 women lost to follow-up, respectively. Although Kilkari did not improve breastfeeding, the uptake of reversible modern contraception improved by 12% from 31.1% to 38.5% (RR 1.12, 95% confidence interval 1.03–1.21). Access to modern reversible contraception, including intrauterine devices, oral contraceptive pills, emergency contraceptive pills, implants, and injections, is a key pillar in reducing maternal mortality. Preventing unwanted pregnancies, promoting birth spacing, and preventing pregnancies in women who may have medical complications all directly contribute to reducing maternal mortality. This will reduce the need for abortions (safe or unsafe), as well as give women and families choices over when is the best time for them to have more children. This improvement was noted particularly in women who delivered a male child (reflecting the entrenched cultural preference for boys in many parts of India) and those from the most disadvantaged groups. Significant improvements in other reproductive, maternal, neonatal, and child health outcomes were not observed.

The authors reflect on the penetration of the intervention, with a large number of the pre-recorded calls unanswered or only listened to for a few seconds [13]. They also reported that in their population, while household-level mobile access was near universal, only 48% of women owned their own phones. This meant that the messages may not have reached the woman, which needs to be a consideration in future planning. It was also noted that while the program can the knowledge and health-seeking behaviors of pregnant and postpartum women, this alone is not enough without health system improvements at the health facility and other levels. The Kilkari program is impressive in its reach and rapid scale-up, demonstrating the importance of government ownership and funding for sustainability; however, it also highlights the limitations of a direct-to-beneficiary messaging service as a standalone intervention.

3. Case Study 2: Self-Monitoring for Remote Management: The GDmHealth Program, UK

Gestational diabetes mellitus (GDM) affects around 1 in 6 pregnancies worldwide. If left untreated, it can increase the risk of complications for the baby (stillbirth, abnormally high birth weight, birth injury from shoulder getting stuck during vaginal delivery and obstructed labor, and low sugar after birth) and the mother (high blood pressure, birth trauma, caesarean section, and longer-term risk of type 2 diabetes) [16]. Management involves tailoring diet and exercise to prevent peaks in blood glucose, and if this is not successful, medications such as insulin or metformin are prescribed. To determine if glucose control is adequate, women are recommended to perform home blood glucose monitoring [17]. For most women, this involves a fingerstick blood sample tested using a handheld glucose meter. The National Institute of Clinical Excellence (NICE) in the UK recommends a minimum of four fingerstick tests per day: fasting and one hour each after breakfast, lunch, and dinner [18]. Results were traditionally documented in a paper diary, which was brought to the next antenatal appointment with a member of the diabetes in pregnancy team. Glucose monitoring and review is a significant burden for many women, as well as taking up a large amount of clinicians' time. Digital glucose monitoring holds promise to improve the patient experience; however, evidence suggests that its ability to improve outcomes or save time and money was lacking [19].

In response to this challenge, a team at the University of Oxford and the Oxford University Hospitals NHS Foundation Trust, a large referral hospital in the South East of England, developed a remote glucose monitoring and management system known as "GDm-Health" [20].

After training on finger prick glucose testing and general education around GDM and diet, women install a free app on their smartphone (iOS or Android). The app contains useful information about GDM, as well as a digital diary where users can record all their glucose readings. The glucose meters recommended for use with GDm-Health are Bluetooth enabled, meaning that after performing the fingerstick test, the result appears in the app. In the app, women can label the glucose value with respect to mealtime, dietary notes, and any medication taken and doses. Women can view their readings in tabular or graphical form. The app is linked to a secure hospital-specific website where registered clinicians can review each patient's results and communicate with the patient via a messaging system within the app. Women can also request a phone call with a diabetes midwife if they are experiencing any difficulties.

The system was co-designed and iteratively refined with 50 women [20] and then assessed in a pilot randomized controlled trial of 200 women, comparing compliance with monitoring and outcomes in those using traditional paper-based monitoring versus GDm-Health [21]. While no differences in clinical endpoints were demonstrated in this small trial, satisfaction with care and satisfaction with the diabetes team were higher in the GDm-Health group [22]. The system was acquired by a biotech company in 2018 and subsequently scaled across around half of the maternity hospitals in England. During the COVID-19 pandemic, the system proved highly valuable when there was a sudden shift to remote consultations in antenatal care to protect women.

A further advantage of the GDm-Health system is the large volume of data on intermittent fingerstick monitoring being generated, compared to traditional paper-based monitoring. This opens the possibility of streamlining care, identifying those at risk of selected adverse outcomes, and gaining new insights into the different phenotypes of GDM [23].

A group from Sensyne Health and the Department of Engineering Sciences at the University of Oxford developed the first data-driven model to help risk-stratify women and babies. The first algorithm to be developed (SYNE001) could predict which women were likely to need escalation to medication treatment within the next week [24]. This could potentially help with scheduling clinics and targeting care. Other algorithms have been developed using AI to predict primary caesarean section and the likelihood of blood glucose readings exceeding the target in the next 7 or 14 days [25]. Further research has been conducted to investigate the minimum number of glucose readings needed to decide whether to change or escalate care.

In many areas of the world, multiple daily self-glucose testing is not possible. This is primarily because of the expense of the glucose test strips for the portable meters (approx. £1 each). Using AI to help target limited resources could improve the care women receive in a cost-effective and sustainable way. Although these and other developments are not yet available outside of research studies, the use of data from personal sensors and monitors could significantly improve care quality and outcomes for women with GDM and their babies around the world.

For women with type 1 diabetes who are pregnant, digital technologies have already revolutionized the standard of care. Women with type 1 diabetes are at much higher risk of adverse outcomes compared to those with GDM, with the risk of stillbirth in women with type 1 diabetes four to five times that of women without diabetes, and over 60% of babies born large for gestational age [26]. Sadly, in the past 20 years in the UK, there have been few improvements in these adverse outcomes for this group of women. The landmark CONCEPPT trial published in 2017 has improved outcomes, with a digital innovation developed to support glucose monitoring outside of pregnancy [27]. CONCEPPT compared a digital continuous glucose monitoring (CGM) system to traditional fingerstick testing of glucose. CGM devices provide real-time information on interstitial glucose levels in the dermis, which closely reflect circulating glucose levels in the blood. A small device is stuck to the woman's upper arm or abdomen. The device contains a small filament that is inserted into the subdermal space and continuously provides readings, which are converted by a digital receiver into glucose readings in mmol/L or mg/dL depending on the user's preference. In this high-risk cohort, the authors demonstrated improved glucose control (measured as the proportion of time spent within the target glucose range) reduction in large for gestiatonal age babies (from 69% to 54%) and decreased need for neonatal intensive care. Despite the higher cost of CGM, these benefits translate into a net saving within the NHS environment where the study was undertaken. As a result of this trial, NICE and NHS England have made CGM available to all pregnant women with type 1 diabetes in pregnancy [18]. Encouragingly, in the National Diabetes in Pregnancy Audit, similar benefits have been shown in real-world practice outside the clinical trial environment since this technology was introduced.

Despite these major advances in diabetes in pregnancy technology, many challenges remain. These systems have been developed in high-income settings, and low-cost alternatives are not yet available for disadvantaged women living across low- and middle-income settings. It is also not certain how or when CGM technologies will be recommended to replace fingerstick testing for all pregnant women with diabetes. Currently, the only evidence is for type 1 diabetes. However, there are ongoing trials to assess its applicability for other types of diabetes. Ultimately, as the devices become cheaper, the technologies could be available more widely. In the meantime, finding ways to provide quality care at the lowest cost using fingerstick testing will be the priority for most obstetricians and diabetes physicians around the world.

3.1 *Digital health interventions to support health workers*

A key role of digital health interventions is to directly support health workers and improve the quality and organization of their work. These interventions can create person-centered health records to allow longitudinal tracking of individuals and health indicator data collection and management; provide healthcare worker decision support; support telemedicine (remote consultations); improve healthcare provider communication and referral coordination; scheduling and activity planning; healthcare provider training; prescription and medication management; and laboratory and imaging management and financial transactions.

4. Case Study 3: SMARThealth Pregnancy: Improving the Detection, Referral, and Management of High-Risk Pregnancy Conditions in Rural India

An example of a system that was co-developed with community health workers in rural India is the SMARThealth Pregnancy (SHP) system. SMARThealth stands for the systematic appraisal, referral, and management system and was developed by the George Institute for Global Health in India in 2012 to improve screening for cardiovascular disease risk factors in the adult population living in rural communities in India [28]. The system has subsequently been developed and adapted for a number of other conditions and geographies, namely for mental health [29], diabetes, tuberculosis, and HIV screening in other states in India, Indonesia, Thailand, China, and Myanmar [30,31].

The system trains frontline health workers (known as ASHA in India) to perform screenings and basic point-of-care tests in people's homes or at local health clinics to identify those at higher risk of disease. Results are entered into a secure Android app equipped with a clinical decision support algorithm to recommend guideline-based care. If any risk factors are detected, the algorithm may provide simple lifestyle advice (e.g., quitting smoking, eating more fruits and vegetables) or refer the patient to the local primary healthcare doctor. The doctor has a complementary app that notifies them of who has been screened and who has been referred for review. This app also contains a decision support algorithm incorporating local prescribing guidelines and referral to secondary care when indicated.

In 2017, ASHA workers who were using the SMARThealth (SH) system for cardiovascular diseases asked whether they could also use it for pregnant women, noting that rates of complications during pregnancy and after birth were high. It is well recognized that medical complications such as GDM and preeclampsia, which occur during pregnancy, are markers of risk for the development of diabetes or hypertension in the months and years immediately after birth [32,33]. This is important because death from premature cardiometabolic diseases, including heart attacks, strokes, diabetes, and their associated complications, is highly prevalent among women both in India and globally. Being able to detect high-risk women early and implement preventative treatments could save lives and prevent individual suffering and economic loss to families and communities.

Using the MRC framework for the development of complex interventions [34], we embarked on a process to identify the key priorities regarding high-risk pregnancy conditions for ASHAs and pregnant women in two rural settings in India [35]. We also began discussions around the potential to integrate non-communicable disease screening, referral, and management into antenatal and postnatal care in India [36]. From these consultations and conversations with higher-level policymakers, clinicians, and NGOs, it became clear that there was an urgent need to improve high-risk pregnancy detection and care in many parts of rural India, and post-natal follow-up was not yet formalized for high-risk women, with many in rural areas unaware of their risk and receiving no screening after birth. The key high-risk conditions identified were anemia, GDM, and preeclampsia.

The SHP platform was developed and tested through a pilot cluster trial across two districts: Guntur in Andhra Pradesh, South India, and Jhajjar in Haryana, North India [37]. A cluster trial was chosen as the intervention, which is a health system-level intervention, involving ASHAs and PHC doctors and the communication between them. Within these districts, two primary health centers (PHCs) were selected and randomized to either receive the SHP intervention or usual care, and 50 ASHA workers were trained to use the SHP intervention. Across both sites, 200 pregnant women were enrolled and followed up from 28 weeks of pregnancy until 6 weeks after birth. Those in the intervention group were assessed by their ASHA four times for anemia, hypertension, and diabetes, with a guideline-based referral. The primary outcome of this trial was feasibility and acceptability.

The trial ran between 2019 and 2020, and while some of the postnatal follow-ups were affected by the first COVID-19 lockdown, the results were extremely encouraging. The intervention was highly valued by the ASHA workers and women and was considered feasible given their workload. Strikingly, the rate of anemia at 70% in the locations of the pilot study was higher than expected. The rates of GDM and preeclampsia at 4% were, however, lower than expected from published rates across India [37].

The SHP platform is currently being assessed to see whether it can improve clinical outcomes in a major cluster randomized trial in Telangana and Haryana [38]. Based on feedback from the pilot study, the intervention has been modified to include more assessments during pregnancy, and follow-up has also been extended until one year postpartum. Follow-up postpartum assessments are designed to be timed with the national infant immunization schedule, as this will be a time of contact between women and the health system. The primary aim of the trial is to determine whether the SHP system can improve rates of anemia at 12 months after birth in women and improve postnatal follow-up after a high-risk pregnancy case.

As of January 2024, close to 3,500 pregnant women have been recruited from 30 PHCs across the two states. The trial is expected to be complete by mid-2025.

5. Case Study 4: Supporting Community Health Worker Education: Could Large Language Model Chatbots Hold the Key?

Remaining up-to-date with clinical practice guidelines is challenging for all clinicians. Through qualitative work with the SHP trial, the ASHA workers stated they would like to know more about common pregnancy complications as women frequently ask for their advice.

As part of the Gates Grand Challenges Equitable AI solutions funding, we have been co-developing a chatbot based on Indian guidelines for ASHAs to support their day-to-day tasks. The platform uses the ChatGPT application programming interface (API), and rather than creating answers from the World Wide Web, it is limited to an "encyclopedia" of 20 relevant clinical guidelines.

In parallel with the technical development, we have also developed a clinical validation pipeline. We conducted two workshops to identify a list of 180 priority questions that ASHA workers would like to have answered and then sought "ideal" answers from 14 community medicine doctors and obstetricians in India to train the model with two or three answers per question. We then combined these answers through a workshop with doctors and ASHA workers into a gold-standard list to train the chatbot.

The chatbot then generated answers, which were scored by doctors on accuracy, appropriateness for ASHAs and completeness [39]. A retrieval-augmented generation (RAG) pipeline was chosen for traceability to source material, scalability across vast knowledge bases, and seamless adaptability to evolving clinical guidelines.

The early pre-clinical validation of the chatbot is ongoing. Before testing in a clinical environment, several ethical and technical challenges need to be addressed. These challenges are not unique to the SHP chatbot. In 2024, the WHO released guidance on the ethics and governance of artificial intelligence for health, with a focus on guidance on large multi-modal models (LMMs), which are a form of generative AI and have been adopted faster than any other consumer application. Like ChatGPT, these mimic human communication, with responses that can appear human-like and authoritative [40]. The key concerns around the use of generative AI in healthcare are legal issues, the accountability of the models, and the possibility that the models could "hallucinate." Further concerns exist about bias (stemming from the training data and responses) and automation of health worker behaviors, which could unquestioningly follow the chatbot's advice. There are also concerns around accessibility and affordability, with "offline" solutions for areas with low bandwidth or poor mobile coverage, or those lacking smartphones. There are also concerns around data ownership and privacy. The SHP chatbot does not record any patient information and sits as an add-on program within the main SHP window. However, there is always a threat of cyberattack for any digital platform.

By developing the SHP chatbot in close dialogue with end-users (ASHAs), other health workers, health system managers, and policymakers, we are striving to demonstrate a practical clinical application that will provide benefits without unintentional harm.

5.1 *Digital health interventions to support health systems*

Digital tools are being used across a wide number of areas to support health system management and support personnel. The WHO Digital Interventions Classification highlights eight areas [11], all of which have relevance to maternity care. First, systems can support human resource management, listing health workers, monitoring performance, recording ongoing training, and credentialing and managing other activities. Digital tools can also be used as part of supply chain management, ensuring timely delivery of the right commodities to the right place, and managing cold chains and procurement. Systems are also useful for public health event notification and tracking infectious outbreaks or other notifiable conditions.

The fourth area of digital innovations to support health systems is of relevance to pregnancy services: civil registration and vital statistics. In high-income countries, over 90% of births are registered, compared to Sub-Saharan Africa, where less than 50% are registered [41]. These discrepancies can be even more stark within countries, with births occurring in rural areas and at home often not recorded. Registration of deaths is also extremely challenging for maternity services. As stated in the introduction to this chapter, global progress is compared using the MMR; however, for many of the poorest performing countries, this number is an estimate from representative smaller surveys, such as Demographic Health Surveys (DHS), or modeling exercises [1]. Recording stillbirths and newborn deaths is especially challenging in many settings. The definition of stillbirth is a baby born with no signs of life at or greater than 28 weeks of gestation, or 1 kg [42]. However, in many high-income countries, babies born after 20, 22, or 24 weeks will be counted as stillborn. Recording stillbirths is often overlooked in birth and death certifications, meaning that the burden of this condition cannot be measured, nor can the effects of interventions be assessed.

The final areas where digital tools are used to support health system management relate to finance and accountability, equipment and asset management, facility management, and person-centered health certificate management.

6. Case Study 5: ULTRA: A Low-Cost Digital Record System to Count All Births in Sub-Saharan Africa

Recording birth outcomes is essential for civil registration, monitoring health outcomes, identifying problems, and monitoring the impact of interventions. While comprehensive electronic medical record (EMR) systems are widely used in hospitals in urban centers and high-income countries to record birth outcomes along with other parts of the patient record, such systems are cumbersome, expensive, and out of reach for many in low-income settings.

Across most birthing units globally, a paper birth register is maintained by midwives, usually recording at a minimum the woman's name, the date of delivery, the outcome of the delivery (live birth or stillbirth), the weight and sex of the baby, and any complications. These large books have functioned well for decades; however, extracting data from these paper records is slow, and storage can be challenging due to their large size. Benchmarking unit performance or identifying units that are outliers can be a slow and laborious process, and much of these data are never looked at again [43]. Compounding this, a high proportion of births in some settings take place in the community or at home, and these births may never be recorded at all. For example, only 50% of births in Ethiopia take place in health facilities [44]. With the rapid increase in mobile phone ownership and network coverage, there exists potential for a handheld birth registration tool that could streamline birth registration and be agnostic to the birth setting.

A scoping review in 2022 identified 21 studies describing 15 digital solutions for collecting birth data in the delivery room [43]. These studies demonstrated that digital data collection is feasible and acceptable to healthcare providers and is preferred over paper-based records. However, it was noted among the studies that few of the interventions considered issues around interoperability or how the intervention could integrate into existing health information systems. Recording births in the community and hospitals was also not commonly done, with only one study from Ethiopia reporting this function [45].

Researchers at the University College Cork (Ireland), the Kilimanjaro Medical Centre (Tanzania), and the University of Oxford have been working closely with health workers and health policymakers since 2021 to develop a low-cost handheld digital tool to record all births [46]. The system (known as Ultra) uses the DHIS-2 platform, an open-source electronic medical record platform used by many low- and middle-income countries, for mobile devices. The clinical content of the tools was directly incorporated from the paper-based records used in Kilimanjaro district. Challenges the team has faced include limited internet coverage in many of the hospitals and a very large number of smaller primary care clinics (known as pharmacies) conducting antenatal and some delivery care in this setting. It has also been challenging, as health policymakers would like Ultra to record all antenatal and postnatal data, as well as intrapartum progress and events in addition to birth outcomes. Though technically possible, the issues related to data security, storage, and training will be greater if the intended use is for a low-cost EMR system. The Ultra team has demonstrated good acceptability and feasibility (unpublished data) and is now exploring paths to wider scale-up in Tanzania and other East African countries.

7. Conclusions

Digital innovation holds great promise for addressing the stubborn challenge of reducing deaths in childbirth and beyond. As the case studies outline, this ranges from innovations aimed at pregnant women themselves, increasing their knowledge and health-seeking behaviors (Kilkari), to enabling remote management of complex conditions such as diabetes (GDm-Health). The potential for digital tools to improve health workers' knowledge, skills, and ability to provide evidence-based care continues to grow. The SHP program illustrates how clinical decision support is being used in rural settings to improve high-risk pregnancy care and is exploring how LLMs can be used to improve community health workers' education and knowledge. Finally, systems that support the health system by digitally recording all births and deaths will greatly help managers and supervisors understand their population and disease burden and be responsive to health system shocks and challenges.

Two major challenges exist across all these and many other systems not discussed here. The lack of interoperability between digital platforms can mean that the same health worker will have to use multiple apps for different health conditions, fragmenting the clinical care record and potentially causing more confusion and data loss. Many digital health platforms are developed by third-party commercial providers and tech companies, and protecting their proprietary IP may limit interoperability. Recognizing this problem, some countries such as India have published detailed digital health strategies, including pathways for official adoption by the government and integration into a larger EMR platform [47].

A second major challenge is ensuring that these interventions are financially viable and sustainable. While some interventions could streamline care provision (e.g., GDm-Health can reduce the number of in-person clinic visits), cost savings are rarely realized in practice. The remote management system still requires several hours of work each week by the midwife, doctor, or diabetes nurse, reviewing the remote monitoring and providing advice. At this time, automated or AI-generated advice directly to the patient has not been licensed for clinical use. In other settings, investment by ministries of health and governments to establish and maintain digital systems is essential for sustainability. This is emphasized by the WHO in their guidance on digital interventions. Without this support, digital innovations will only be accessible to those with private insurance or independent means, further widening gaps in equity in maternity services around the world.

A further challenge is to ensure that AI-based tools do not entrench or worsen existing social biases. As AI systems are trained on existing datasets, biases within these will only be amplified as future iterations of AI are trained on the original outputs. A relevant example of this for maternity care is around gender-specific roles in society and gender bias. Ideally, new technologies should aim to be gender-transformative.

8. Future Directions

As the sophistication of digital interventions continues to increase rapidly, it is essential that these devices be developed within a regulatory framework that protects the rights of the individual and mandates a rigorous pathway to certification for clinical use. For new drug development, this pipeline is well established: from phase 1 human trials, all the way to post-market phase 4 trials to monitor potential effects when used in clinical practice. A similar pipeline is essential now, particularly in developing and testing generative AI tools for clinical use.

For all the promise of digital interventions for maternity care, they must be part of comprehensive health system-strengthening interventions if they are to contribute to real gains in maternal mortality reduction. The future for digital tools to improve outcomes in pregnancy is exciting. The challenge will be ensuring this is done equitably and that it reaches those most in need.

References

[1] WHO. Trends in maternal mortality 2000 to 2020: Estimates by WHO, UNICEF, UNFPA, World Bank Group and UNDESA/Population Division. Geneva: World Health Organization; 2023.

[2] UN. United Nations Millennium Declaration. New York: United Nations; 2000.

[3] UN. The Sustainable Development Goals Report (special edition). New York: United Nations; 2023.

[4] Zarocostas J. Global maternal mortality rates stagnating. *Lancet*. 2023;401(10377):632. DOI: 10.1016/S0140-6736(23)00385-9.

[5] Souza JP, Day LT, Rezende-Gomes AC, *et al.* A global analysis of the determinants of maternal health and transitions in maternal mortality. *Lancet Glob Health.* 2024;12(2):e306–e16. DOI: 10.1016/S2214-109X(23)00468-0 [published Online First: 20231206].

[6] WHO. WHO Labour Care Guide. Geneva: World Health Organization; 2021.

[7] Vogel JP, Pujar Y, Vernekar SS, *et al.* Effects of the WHO labour care guide on cesarean section in India: A pragmatic, stepped-wedge, cluster-randomized pilot trial. *Nat Med.* 2024. DOI: 10.1038/s41591-023-02751-4 [published Online First: 20240130].

[8] WHO. WHO Guideline: Recommendations on Digital Interventions for Health System Strenghthening. Geneva: World Health Organization; 2019.

[9] Hod M, Divakar H, Kihara AB, *et al.* The femtech revolution—A new approach to pregnancy management: Digital transformation of maternity care—The hybrid e-health perinatal clinic addressing the unmet needs of low- and middle-income countries. *Int J Gynaecol Obstet.* 2023;163(1): 4–10. DOI: 10.1002/ijgo.15032 [published Online First: 20230808].

[10] WHO. Global Strategy on Digital Health 2020–2025. Geneva: World Health Organization; 2021.

[11] WHO. Classification of Digital Interventions Services and Applications in Health: A Shared Language to Describe Uses of Digital Technology for Health (second edition). Geneva: World Health Organization; 2023. https://www.who.int/publications/i/item/9789240081949#:~:text=The%20WHO%20Classification%20of%20digital,needs%20and%20advance%20health%20goals.

[12] Mohan D, Bashingwa JJH, Scott K, *et al.* Optimising the reach of mobile health messaging programmes: An analysis of system generated data for the Kilkari programme across 13 states in India. *BMJ Glob Health.* 2022;6(Suppl 5). DOI: 10.1136/bmjgh-2022-009395.

[13] Bashingwa JJH, Mohan D, Chamberlain S, *et al.* Assessing exposure to Kilkari: A big data analysis of a large maternal mobile messaging service across 13 states in India. *BMJ Glob Health.* 2021;6(Suppl 5). DOI: 10.1136/bmjgh-2021-005213.

[14] LeFevre AE, Shah N, Scott K, *et al.* The impact of a direct to beneficiary mobile communication program on reproductive and child health outcomes: A randomised controlled trial in India. *BMJ Glob Health.* 2022;6(Suppl 5). DOI: 10.1136/bmjgh-2022-008838.

[15] LeFevre A, Agarwal S, Chamberlain S, *et al.* Are stage-based health information messages effective and good value for money in improving maternal newborn and child health outcomes in India? Protocol for an individually randomized controlled trial. *Trials.* 2019;20(1):272. DOI: 10.1186/s13063-019-3369-5 [published Online First: 20190515].

[16] *National guidelines for diagnosis & management of gestational diabetes mellitus.* Maternal Health Division Ministry of Health and Family Welfare,

Government of India; 2014. https://nhm.gov.in/images/pdf/programmes/maternal-health/guidelines/National_Guidelines_for_Diagnosis_&_Management_of_Gestational_Diabetes_Mellitus.pdf.

[17] Saravanan P, Diabetes in Pregnancy Working Group, Maternal Medicine Clinical Study Group, *et al*. Gestational diabetes: Opportunities for improving maternal and child health. *Lancet Diabetes Endocrinol*. 2020;8(9):793–800. DOI: 10.1016/S2213-8587(20)30161-3 [published Online First: 20200818].

[18] NICE. NG3: Diabetes in pregnancy: Management from preconception to the postnatal period. 2022.

[19] Ming WK, Mackillop LH, Farmer AJ, *et al*. Telemedicine technologies for diabetes in pregnancy: A systematic review and meta-analysis. *J Med Internet Res*. 2016;18(11):e290. DOI: 10.2196/jmir.6556 [published Online First: 2016/11/09].

[20] Mackillop L, Loerup L, Bartlett K, *et al*. Development of a real-time smartphone solution for the management of women with or at high risk of gestational diabetes. *J Diabetes Sci Technol*. 2014;8(6):1105–14. DOI: 10.1177/1932296814542271 [published Online First: 2014/07/07].

[21] Mackillop L, Hirst JE, Bartlett KJ, *et al*. Comparing the efficacy of a mobile phone-based blood glucose management system with standard clinic care in women with gestational diabetes: Randomized controlled trial. *JMIR Mhealth Uhealth*. 2018;6(3):e71. DOI: 10.2196/mhealth.9512 [published Online First: 2018/03/20].

[22] Hirst JE, Mackillop L, Loerup L, *et al*. Acceptability and user satisfaction of a smartphone-based, interactive blood glucose management system in women with gestational diabetes mellitus. *J Diabetes Sci Technol*. 2015;9(1):111–5. DOI: 10.1177/1932296814556506 [published Online First: 2014/10/30].

[23] Hirst JE, Loerup L, Mackillop L, *et al*. Digital blood glucose monitoring could provide new objective assessments of blood glucose control in women with gestational diabetes. *Diabet Med*. 2016;33(11):1598–99. DOI: 10.1111/dme.13035.

[24] Velardo C, Clifton D, Hamblin S, *et al*. Toward a multivariate prediction model of pharmacological treatment for women with gestational diabetes mellitus: Algorithm development and validation. *J Med Internet Res*. 2021;23(3):e21435. DOI: 10.2196/21435 [published Online First: 20210310].

[25] Lu HY, Ding X, Hirst JE, *et al*. Digital health and machine learning technologies for blood glucose monitoring and management of gestational diabetes. *IEEE Rev Biomed Eng*. 2023. DOI: 10.1109/RBME.2023.3242261 [published Online First: 20230207].

[26] Murphy HR, Howgate C, O'Keefe J, *et al*. Characteristics and outcomes of pregnant women with type 1 or type 2 diabetes: A 5-year national

population-based cohort study. *Lancet Diabetes Endocrinol.* 2021;9(3):153–64. DOI: 10.1016/S2213-8587(20)30406-X [published Online First: 20210128].

[27] Feig DS, Donovan LE, Corcoy R, *et al.* Continuous glucose monitoring in pregnant women with type 1 diabetes (CONCEPTT): A multicentre international randomised controlled trial. *Lancet.* 2017;390(10110):2347–59. DOI: 10.1016/S0140-6736(17)32400-5 [published Online First: 20170915].

[28] Praveen D, Patel A, Raghu A, *et al.* SMARTHealth India: Development and field evaluation of a mobile clinical decision support system for cardiovascular diseases in rural India. *JMIR Mhealth Uhealth.* 2014;2(4):e54. DOI: 10.2196/mhealth.3568 [published Online First: 2014/12/08].

[29] Maulik PK, Tewari A, Devarapalli S, *et al.* The systematic medical appraisal, referral and treatment (SMART) mental health project: Development and testing of electronic decision support system and formative research to understand perceptions about mental health in rural India. *PLoS One.* 2016;11(10):e0164404. DOI: 10.1371/journal.pone.0164404 [published Online First: 20161012].

[30] Peiris D, Praveen D, Mogulluru K, *et al.* SMARThealth India: A stepped-wedge, cluster randomised controlled trial of a community health worker managed mobile health intervention for people assessed at high cardiovascular disease risk in rural India. *PLoS One.* 2019;14(3):e0213708. DOI: 10.1371/journal.pone.0213708 [published Online First: 20190326].

[31] Praveen D, Patel A, McMahon S, *et al.* A multifaceted strategy using mobile technology to assist rural primary healthcare doctors and frontline health workers in cardiovascular disease risk management: Protocol for the SMARTHealth India cluster randomised controlled trial. *Implement Sci.* 2013;8:137. DOI: 10.1186/1748-5908-8-137 [published Online First: 2013/11/25].

[32] Bellamy L, Casas JP, Hingorani AD, *et al.* Type 2 diabetes mellitus after gestational diabetes: A systematic review and meta-analysis. *Lancet.* 2009;373(9677):1773–9. DOI: 10.1016/S0140-6736(09)60731-5.

[33] Brown MC, Best KE, Pearce MS, *et al.* Cardiovascular disease risk in women with pre-eclampsia: Systematic review and meta-analysis. *Eur J Epidemiol.* 2013;28(1):1–19. DOI: 10.1007/s10654-013-9762-6 [published Online First: 2013/02/09].

[34] Skivington K, Matthews L, Simpson SA, *et al.* A new framework for developing and evaluating complex interventions: Update of Medical Research Council guidance. *BMJ.* 2021;374:n2061. DOI: 10.1136/bmj.n2061 [published Online First: 20210930].

[35] Nagraj S, Kennedy SH, Norton R, *et al.* Cardiometabolic risk factors in pregnancy and implications for long-term health: Identifying the research priorities for low-resource settings. *Front Cardiovasc Med.* 2020;7:40. DOI: 10.3389/fcvm.2020.00040 [published Online First: 20200320].

[36] Nagraj S, Hinton L, Praveen D, *et al*. Women's and healthcare providers' perceptions of long-term complications associated with hypertension and diabetes in pregnancy: A qualitative study. *BJOG*. 2019;126(Suppl 4):34–42. DOI: 10.1111/1471-0528.15847 [published Online First: 20190816].

[37] Nagraj S, Kennedy SH, Jha V, *et al*. SMARThealth pregnancy: Feasibility and acceptability of a complex intervention for high-risk pregnant women in rural India: Protocol for a pilot cluster randomised controlled trial. *Front Glob Womens Health*. 2021;2:620759. DOI: 10.3389/fgwh.2021.620759 [published Online First: 20210528].

[38] Hirst JE, Votruba N, Billot L, *et al*. A community-based intervention to improve screening, referral, and follow-up of non-communicable diseases and anaemia amongst pregnant and postpartum women in rural India: Study protocol for a cluster randomised trial. *Trials*. 2023 [published Online First: 12 Julyy 2023].

[39] Ghadban YA, Lu H, Adavi U, *et al*. Transforming healthcare education: Harnessing large language models for frontline health worker capacity building using retrieval-augmented generation. *medRxiv*. 2023:2023.12.15.23300009. DOI: 10.1101/2023.12.15.23300009.

[40] WHO. Ethics and Governance of Artificial Intelligence for Health. Guidance on Large Multi-Modal Models. Geneva: World Health Organization; 2024.

[41] Shonchoy W. Birth registration, child rights and local governance in Bangladesh. In: Faguet JP, Pal S, editors, *Decentralised Governance: Crafting Effective Democracies Around the World*. London: LSE Press; 2023.

[42] Blencowe H, Cousens S, Jassir FB, *et al*. National, regional, and worldwide estimates of stillbirth rates in 2015, with trends from 2000: A systematic analysis. *Lancet Glob Health*. 2016;4(2):e98–e108. DOI: 10.1016/S2214-109X(15)00275-2 [published Online First: 2016/01/19].

[43] Cansdale LG, Kelly G, Khashan A, *et al*. Use of mHealth tools to register birth outcomes in low-income and middle-income countries: A scoping review. *BMJ Open*. 2022;12(10):e063886. DOI: 10.1136/bmjopen-2022-063886 [published Online First: 20221012].

[44] UNICEF. Maternal and newborn health coverage database: UNICEF; 2022 [cited 2024]. Available from: https://data.unicef.org/topic/%20maternal-health/antenatal-care/. [Accessed 2024 Feb 5].

[45] Little A, Medhanyie A, Yebyo H, *et al*. Meeting community health worker needs for maternal health care service delivery using appropriate mobile technologies in Ethiopia. *PLoS One*. 2013;8(10):e77563. DOI: 10.1371/journal.pone.0077563 [published Online First: 20131029].

[46] Woodworth S, Mmbaga B, Nyka G, *et al*. ULTRA: An electronic birth registry for the Kilimanjaro region. AIS Electronic Library (AISeL); 2022.

[47] India Go. National Digital Health Mission. New Delhi: Ministry of Electronics & Information Technology, Ministry of Health & Family Welfare, National Health Authority, Government of India; 2020.

https://doi.org/10.1142/9781800616295_0010

Chapter 10

How the COVID-19 Pandemic Impacted Learning in Islamic Countries

Shahid Jameel*

Oxford Centre for Islamic Studies;

Green Templeton College, University of Oxford, Oxford, UK

shahid.jameel@oxcis.ac.uk

Abstract

A post-mortem of the societal impacts of the COVID-19 pandemic shows reversals in gains made in education and learning across the world. The Program for International Student Assessment (PISA) 2018 and 2022 reports offer unique pre- and post-pandemic views of that. This chapter examines 13 Islamic countries that participated in PISA to evaluate the pandemic's impact. These Islamic countries showed encouraging pre-pandemic trends but poor resilience during the pandemic, the key reasons being extended school closures and a digital divide. Disadvantaged students in Islamic countries displayed better resilience than their peers in other countries, as well as the advantaged students in their own countries. Girls outperformed boys across all Islamic countries

*Disclaimer: This study is based on publicly available data. It represents the author's own interpretations and opinions, which do not necessarily reflect the views or opinions of any organization or institution with which he may be associated. These views are based on individual perspectives, beliefs, and experiences. The author acknowledges that differing opinions and interpretations may exist and encourages open and respectful dialogue on the topics discussed. Readers should exercise critical thinking and consider multiple sources of information when forming their own opinions and making decisions.

but failed to show resilience during the pandemic. As in the developed world, immigrant students performed better than their non-immigrant peers in Islamic countries with large expatriate populations, but not in countries with a smaller fraction of expatriates. Islamic countries can learn from the PISA 2022 report and adopt best practices to build resilient education systems.

1. Introduction

The devastating COVID-19 pandemic registered over 700 million confirmed cases and about 7 million deaths [1], with both numbers likely to be underestimates. Besides affecting health systems worldwide, it impacted economies, livelihoods, and all aspects of life, including education. Lockdowns and school closures became necessary to limit the spread of infection and protect the vulnerable. The resulting impact on education, though significant, is only now beginning to be understood at the regional, national, and global levels. A UNESCO report [2] critically examined the promises of digital distance education against what was actually delivered during the pandemic, especially between early 2020 and the end of 2022. According to this report:

> Although connected technology supported the continuation of education for many learners, many more were left behind. Exclusion soared and inequities widened. Achievement levels fell, even for those with access to distance learning. Educational experiences narrowed. Physical and mental health declined. Privatization accelerated, threatening education's unique standing as a public good and human right. Invasive surveillance endangered the free and open exchange of ideas and undermined trust. Automation replaced human interactions with machine-mediated experiences. And technology production and disposal placed new strains on the environment.

Even though the UNESCO report relied on different types and sources of data, it was missing one key piece of evidence: a quantitative (and objective) assessment of learning during the pandemic across multiple countries. This has now been provided by the Program for International Student Assessment (PISA) 2022 Survey, the results of which were released in December 2023.

The PISA [3] is a global standardized measure of mathematics, reading, and science comprehension among 15-year-olds, which is conducted every three years and serves as an indicator for the quality of education. About 80 countries that are members of the Organisation for Economic Co-operation and Development (OECD) [4], as well as several others, participate in this global assessment. The 2022 survey was the eighth such assessment and the first one conducted after the pandemic; the previous one was in 2018. This allows the first quantitative assessment of the pandemic's impact on learning across the participating countries. There are two other international student assessments: Trends in International Mathematics and Science Study (TIMSS) for fourth and eighth graders [5] and Progress in International Reading Literacy Study (PIRLS) for fourth graders [6]. However, neither offers a pre- and post-pandemic comparison. While TIMMS was carried out in 2019 and 2023, the latter results are not yet available; PRILS was carried out in 2016 and then again in 2021 during the pandemic.

This chapter examines the PISA 2022 survey to understand the pandemic's impact on learning in Islamic countries. The Organisation of Islamic Cooperation (OIC) [7] and its statistics arm, SESRIC, [8] also published an informative report on the socioeconomic impacts of the pandemic in Islamic countries in March 2022 [9]. However, this is also based on data from before and during the pandemic, and it lacks the benefit of a globally aligned post-pandemic assessment. The limitation of this study is that its analysis is based on data from only 13 out of the 57 OIC countries[1] that participated in the PISA surveys in both 2018 and 2022. All of these are high- and middle-income countries. Still, it is hoped that the data will shed light on how the pandemic impacted learning in Islamic countries within a broader global context.

2. Learning Across the Economic Landscape

The PISA test scores measure the "quality" of education using a standardized global format. It is generally agreed that average learning outcomes correlate positively with a country's per capita GDP and its expenditure

[1] The Islamic countries/regions that took part in PISA are: Albania, Brunei, Indonesia, Jordan, Kazakhstan, Malaysia, Morocco, the Palestinian Authority, Qatar, Saudi Arabia, Türkiye, the UAE, and Uzbekistan.

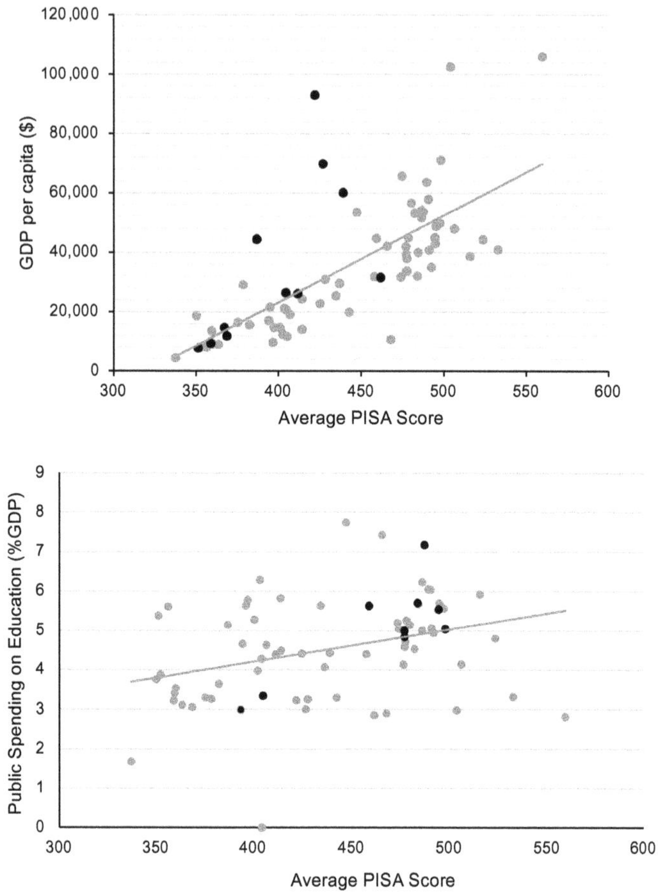

Figure 1. Correlation between quality of education (measured as PISA scores) and the country's per capita GDP or the country's public spending on education (expressed as percent of GDP) for all countries in PISA 2022. The Islamic countries are shown as black dots, others as grey dots. The trendline showed a positive correlation with $R^2 = 0.51$ (top) and $R^2 = 0.12$ (bottom).

on education [10]. When the average PISA scores[2] were plotted against either the per capita GDP [11] for the country or its public expenditure on education [12], there was a positive correlation at a cross-sectional level (Fig. 1). The correlation was stronger for a country's per capita GDP than its public expenditure on education.

[2] This is the average of mean scores for science, mathematics, and reading skills for each country in 2022.

There are several factors that affect both education expenditure and outcomes, and this correlation cannot be taken to imply causation. Indeed, the scatterplots show that, despite a broad positive correlation, there is substantial variance from the trendline. This means that a country's economy or its public expenditure on education alone is not responsible for the quality of its education. Beyond public expenditure, a much larger share of education-related expenditure is shared by households in high-income countries. Singapore highlights this better than any other country. Its average score of 560 (OECD average: 478) is the highest among all measured countries; while its per capita GDP, at US$106,032, is also one of the highest, its public spending on education, at 2.81% of GDP, is one of the lowest.

3. Learning and Pandemic Resilience

Several Islamic countries, especially those in the Middle East and North Africa, made significant progress in literacy rates over the preceding generation but still lagged behind the West and several other parts of the world [13]. In Islamic countries, the number of years spent in school increased from 5.2 years in 2000 to 7 years in 2017; however, it remained below the average of 7.7 years for non-Islamic developing countries and 12.6 years for developed countries [9]. In 18 Islamic countries, children attended school for less than five years, and in 13 of these countries, the literacy rates were below 50% [9].

For the 13 Islamic countries included in PISA 2022, the average scores were lower than the average OECD scores across the three skills. While the OECD average scores for mathematics, reading, and science were 472, 476, and 485, respectively, those for Islamic countries were 396, 382, and 403, respectively. Students in Singapore performed the best on these tests, with scores approximately 75–100 points higher than the OECD average. Singapore also accounted for 44.5% of students in the upper quartile in at least one subject (OECD average: 13.7%). Students from East Asian countries/regions, such as Taiwan, Hong Kong, and Macao, also registered high scores.

All 13 Islamic countries had a mean performance and share of top performers that were below the OECD average. Türkiye was the best-performing Islamic country for all three skills, with mathematics, reading, and science scores of 453, 456, and 476, respectively, and accounted for 7.3% of top performers. The lowest average scores were for Jordan in mathematics [361], and for Uzbekistan in reading [336] and science [355]. At least 6 of the 13 Islamic countries had fewer than 1% top performers but more than 50% low performers.

In consecutive PISA assessments up to 2018, the OECD average score did not change by more than four points in mathematics or five points in reading. However, in PISA 2022, it dropped by almost 15 points in mathematics and about 10 points in reading compared to PISA 2018. This is the pandemic's global impact; however, the decline began well before the pandemic. Pre-pandemic decennial trends were more favorable for Islamic countries, which showed an improvement of 6–11 points across the three skillsets, while the OECD average declined by 4–7 points during the same period. However, when their 2018 and 2022 scores were compared to account for the pandemic years, Islamic countries showed average drops in scores similar to other countries in the assessment. When viewed in terms of percentage, this reverse in the gains made during the pre-pandemic years is more pronounced for Islamic countries, where average scores ranged from 75 to 95 points lower than those of the OECD.

Figure 2 shows a comparison of the 2018 and 2022 average PISA scores for 11 Islamic countries.[3] There are two categories of Islamic countries: those with significant declines in post-pandemic scores, and others with less than a 5% change or an increase in post-pandemic scores. The former category included Albania (−30%), Malaysia (−16.5%), Jordan (−10.2%), Indonesia (−9.3%), and Morocco (−8.7%). Conversely, Kazakhstan (+7%), Qatar (+6.3%), and Brunei Darussalam (+3.8%) showed an increase in their average post-pandemic scores.

School closures were common during the pandemic. Among the PISA 2022 countries, school closures ranged from as little as 6 weeks (in Iceland and Switzerland) to as high as 81 weeks (in Panama) [14]. Schools remained closed in Islamic countries for an average of 27 weeks. This was longer than the global average of 22 weeks, as well as the average duration for low-income countries (23 weeks), middle-income countries (24 weeks), and high-income countries (10 weeks) [14].

Almost all OIC countries offered at least one remote learning modality, with television and online platforms being most popular. More interactive technologies suffered from poor penetration in lower-income countries and in rural areas. Compared to the global average, OIC countries on average

[3] The Palestinian Authority and Uzbekistan were excluded due to a lack of 2018 scores.

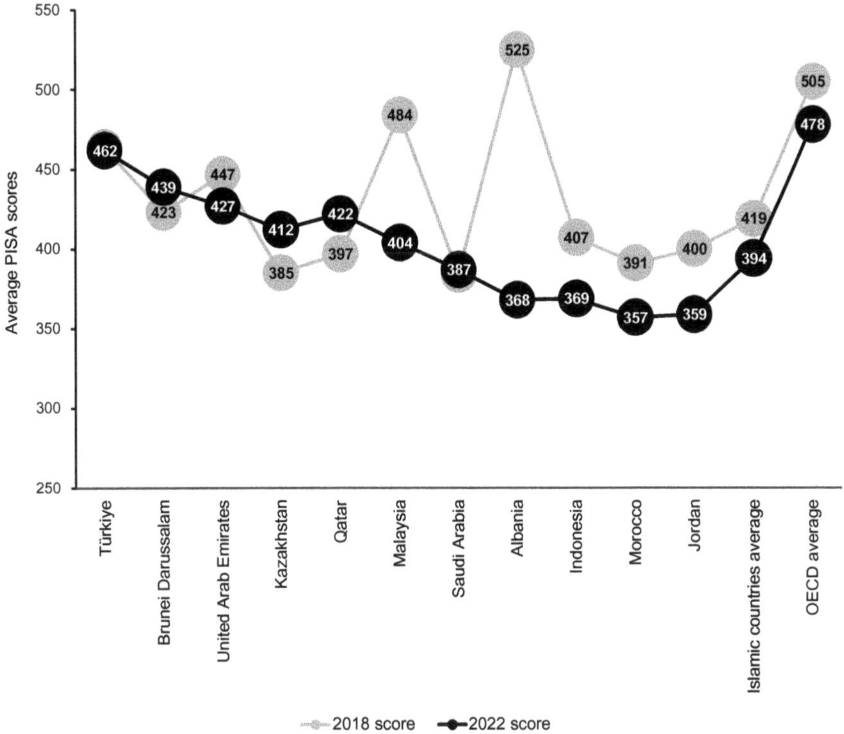

Figure 2. The 2018 and 2022 average PISA scores for 11 Islamic countries are shown along with the average for all Islamic and OECD countries. The score for each country is an average of the mean values for mathematics, reading, and science scores. For Jordan, only the mathematics scores are used. The numbers within the circles are the average scores.

had lower rural electrification, mobile phone subscriptions, computer ownership, and home internet access [9]. In UNICEF's Remote Learning Readiness Index, of the 27 OIC countries analyzed, 8 were above-average, 6 were average, and 13 were below-average [15].

To test whether student performance correlated with the duration of school closures, either the average PISA 2022 test scores or the differences in pre-pandemic and post-pandemic test scores for each country were plotted against the duration of school closures for that country. A negative correlation was observed between the length of school closures and PISA 2022 average scores, when all tested countries were included in

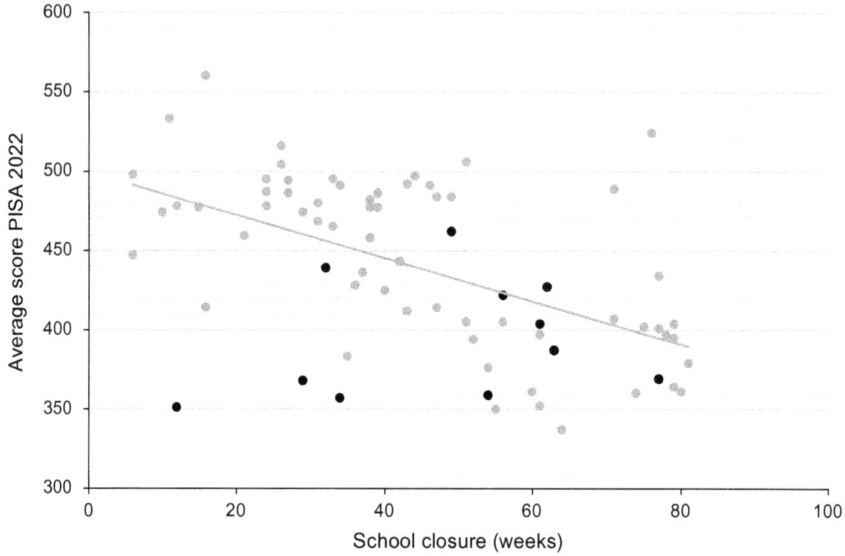

Figure 3. The averages of mean scores for mathematics, reading, and science in PISA 2022 for each country were plotted against the duration of school closure for that country. The trendline showed a negative correlation with $R^2 = 0.28$. The Islamic countries are shown as black dots, others as grey dots.

the analysis (Fig. 3). However, there was no significant correlation when only the 13 Islamic countries were considered. Further, no correlation was observed between the duration of school closures and the change in test scores from 2018 to 2022 (plots not shown).

4. Education, Equity, and the Pandemic

The PISA report also addressed equity by comparing the mathematics scores of advantaged students, defined as those with household incomes in the highest quarter for their country, to the scores of disadvantaged students, defined as those with household incomes in the lowest quarter for their country. Across the OECD countries, socio-economically advantaged students scored 93 points more than their disadvantaged counterparts. This performance gap was greater than 93 points in 22 countries/regions and 50 points or fewer in 13 countries/regions. For the 13 Islamic countries, the average performance gap between advantaged and disadvantaged students was 56 points, which is about half of the OECD average, indicating better equity within these Islamic countries.

Following the pandemic, the average scores for advantaged and disadvantaged students in OECD countries fell by 10 and 17 points, respectively, and for the Islamic countries, by 15 and 8 points, respectively. Thus, while advantaged students in Islamic countries were as vulnerable as those in OECD countries, disadvantaged students in Islamic countries appeared to be more resilient. Further, among the disadvantaged students, 13.4% in Islamic countries scored in the top quartile in mathematics, compared to 10.2% in OECD countries. This suggests that, compared to their peers in OECD countries and among the advantaged students in their own countries, disadvantaged students in the assessed Islamic countries displayed better resilience.

Is this systemic or individual resilience? To understand this, the difference in mathematics scores for PISA 2022 and PISA 2018 for students in each Islamic country was plotted against the per capita GDP of that country (Fig. 4). The scores for both advantaged and disadvantaged students showed a positive correlation with the country's per capita GDP, albeit with a wide variance. This suggests that, while overall economic prosperity may be one factor contributing to resilience, expectedly, there

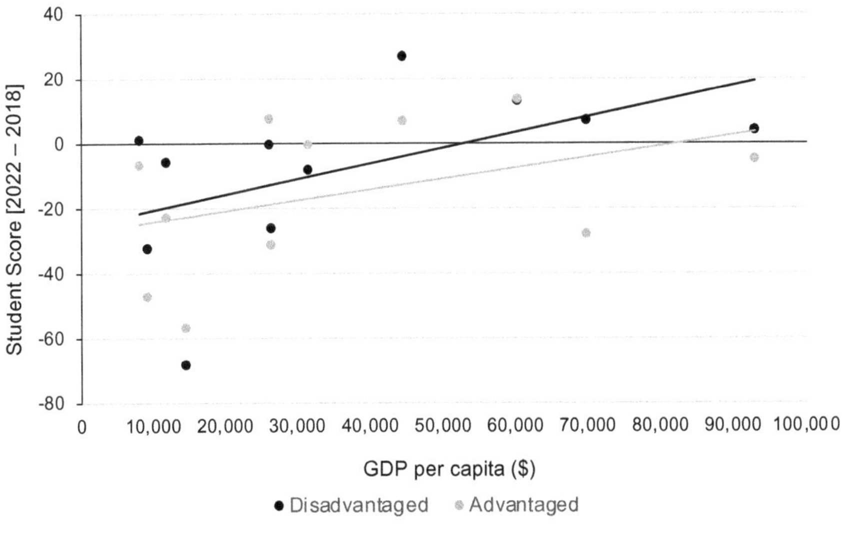

Figure 4. The difference between PISA 2022 and PISA 2018 mathematics scores for advantaged and disadvantaged students in 11 Islamic countries (no 2018 data for the Palestinian Authority and Uzbekistan) was plotted against their per capita GDP. A negative score indicates that performance declined during the pandemic; a positive score indicates improvement. $R^2 = 0.16$ for advantaged students; $R^2 = 0.26$ for disadvantaged students.

are other factors at play as well. This could also be a limitation of the low number of countries involved in this analysis (only 11).

It is also possible that the better performance of disadvantaged students in Islamic countries compared to the OECD average is an artifact of the inclusion of only high- and middle-income Islamic countries in the assessment.

5. Gender and Pandemic Resilience

When the PISA 2018 results were segregated by gender across the OECD countries, boys performed better in mathematics by 9 points, girls were better at reading by 24 points, and there was no difference in the science scores – on average, girls did better by 5 points. However, in Islamic countries, girls outperformed boys in all three skills – mathematics by 6 points, reading by 34 points, and science by 15 points – on average by 18 points.

But the pandemic abolished gains made by girls across the OECD countries, with an average reversal of 10 points: from −5 (i.e., girls ahead by 5 points) to +5 (i.e., girls falling behind by 5 points). In the Islamic countries, the average score reversal was by 20 points (−18 to +2; Fig. 5). Surprisingly, girls in the three richest Islamic countries showed the largest post-pandemic reversal in average test scores: Qatar by 43 points (−23 to +20), Saudi Arabia by 32 points (−15 to +17), and the UAE by 31 points (−23 to +8).

The pandemic exposed gender bias, with girls falling behind more than boys. As girls remained at home due to school closures, their household work burden may have increased, thereby reducing their available study time. A UNICEF report highlighted that 5- to 14-year-old girls spent 40% more time doing housework than boys [16]. In all the tested Islamic countries, girls outperformed boys on all test scores, which is an indication of the absence of bias in the educational system and the historical opportunities available to them. However, the pandemic affected the performance of girls in Islamic countries more than that of boys, which may reflect socioeconomic and cultural attitudes toward education. Since the largest performance drops for girls were in the richest Islamic countries, additional household work would hardly be a convincing explanation. The reasons are likely to be multifactorial, not amenable to analysis with this dataset; however, they remain important and should be analyzed by authorities in the concerned Islamic countries, whose expenditure on education is 3–5% of GDP and 9–19% of total government spending [12].

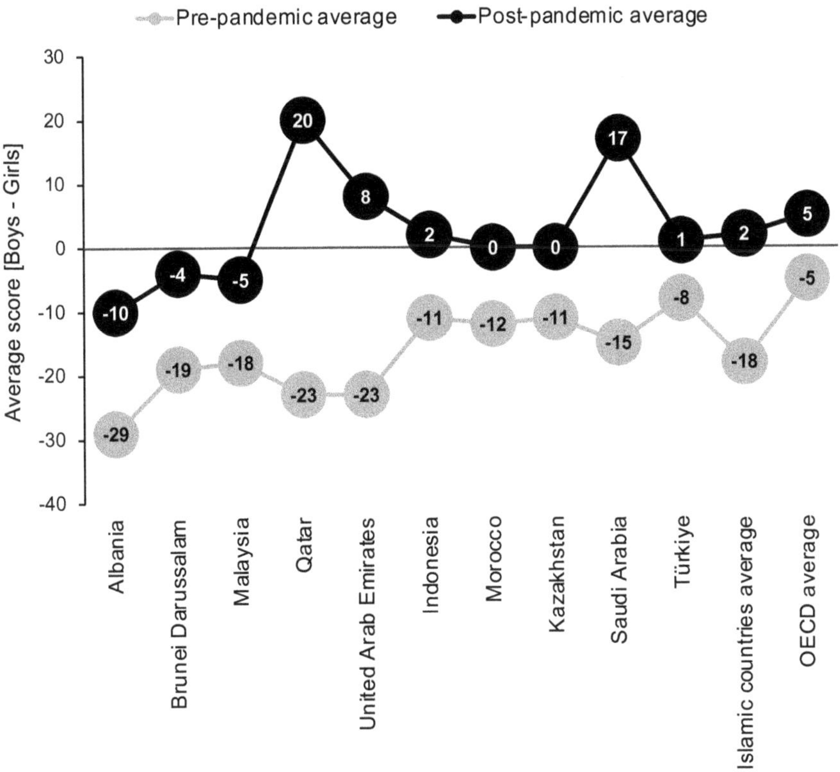

Figure 5. The difference between average scores (in mathematics, reading, and science) for boys and girls from PISA 2018 (pre-pandemic) and PISA 2022 (post-pandemic) for each of 11 Islamic countries. A positive score indicates that boys did better than girls; a negative score shows girls did better than boys. Palestinian Authority and Uzbekistan are excluded due to a lack of 2018 scores. For Jordan, only the mathematics scores were considered.

6. Learning Among Immigrant Students

The PISA survey also compared the mathematics scores of immigrant and non-immigrant students.[4] The latter group scored, on average, 29 points higher across the OECD countries. But once socioeconomic status and language barriers had been accounted for, immigrant students were only five points behind their non-immigrant counterparts. The average scores for OECD countries increased progressively from

[4]First-generation immigrant students are those born outside the country of assessment and whose parents were also born in another country. Second-generation immigrant students are those born in the country of assessment but whose parent(s) were born in another country.

first-generation immigrants (435) to second-generation immigrants (459) to non-immigrants (479), which is expected on account of getting used to a new culture, language, and education system. However, the average scores for Islamic countries went the other way: first-generation immigrants (414) fared better than second-generation immigrants (397), who in turn were better than non-immigrants (392).

Two groups of Islamic countries were apparent from the analysis. Six countries[5] with the highest share of immigrant students (7.4–59.1%) showed an average score of +40, indicating better performance by the immigrant students. But in the remaining seven countries[6] with a lower share of immigrants (0.4–2.2%), an average score of −45 indicated better results for non-immigrant students.

When the score differences for Islamic countries were plotted against the country's per capita GDP, they correlated positively with the performance of immigrant students (Fig. 6, top). In more affluent Islamic countries, immigrant students scored better than non-immigrant students, and the corresponding plot (Fig. 6, bottom) showed a slightly better correlation compared to all the Islamic countries combined. As a control, 24 OECD countries[7] with greater than 10% immigrant student populations were also analyzed; they showed no such correlation between score differences and the country's per capita GDP.

The dichotomy within Islamic countries can be explained by their population distribution and immigration policies. The population of Qatar (~2.7 million) includes only 11.6% natives, while the remaining are immigrants, with the majority hailing from South Asia, followed by the Middle East and North Africa (MENA) region [17]. In the UAE, the population (~10.2 million) includes 11.5% Emiratis, and the remaining are expats, which includes ~55% from South Asia [18]. The population of Saudi Arabia (~37.5 million) includes 38–40% immigrants, which includes about 40% from South Asia, 19% from MENA, and 12.6% from Southeast Asia [19]. Jordan's population (~11.4 million) includes about 33%

[5] Qatar (59.1%), the UAE (52.9%), Jordan (11.5%), Saudi Arabia (10.8%), Brunei (7.9%), and Kazakhstan (7.4%).

[6] The Palestinian Authority (2.2%), Türkiye (1.7%), Malaysia (1.5%), Albania (1.1%), Uzbekistan (1%), Morocco (0.7%), and Indonesia (0.4%).

[7] Australia, Austria, Belgium, Canada, Denmark, France, Germany, Greece, Ireland, Israel, Italy, Malta, the Netherlands, New Zealand, Norway, Portugal, Serbia, Singapore, Slovenia, Spain, Sweden, Switzerland, the UK, and the USA.

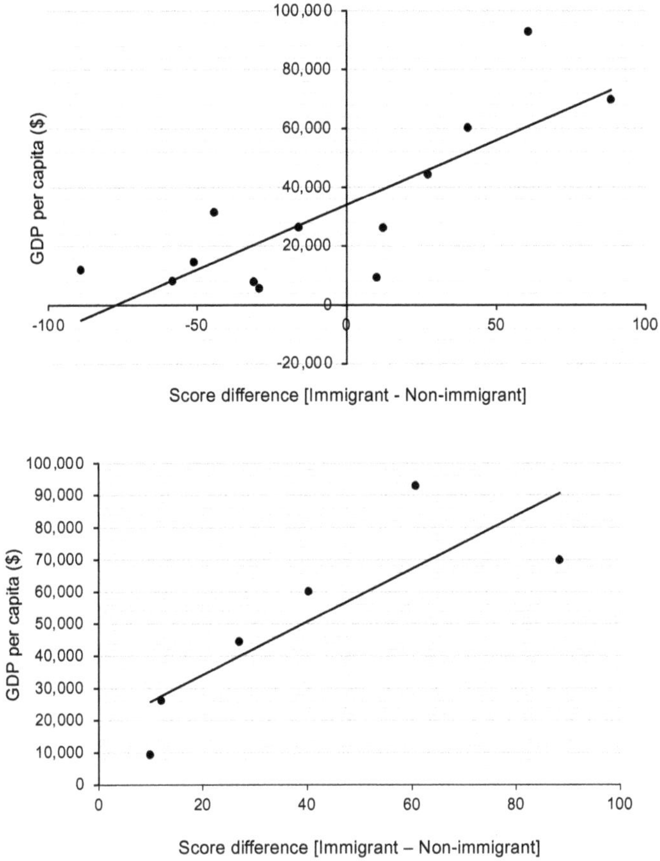

Figure 6. The differences in mathematics scores between immigrant (normalized for both first and second generations) and non-immigrant students as a function of the country's per capita GDP. The top graph includes data for all 13 Islamic countries; the trendline showed a positive correlation with $R^2 = 0.66$. The bottom graph shows data for only the 6 Islamic countries that showed positive score differences; the trendline showed a positive correlation with $R^2 = 0.68$.

immigrants, predominantly refugees displaced by wars in Iraq, Palestine, and Syria [20]. Brunei has a small population (~0.45 million), of whom about 24% are immigrants, mostly from Southeast Asia [21]. The population of Kazakhstan (~19.7 million) includes about 58% ethnic Kazakhs, with the remainder hailing from the Commonwealth of Independent States (CIS), Russia, and Germany, many of whom are skilled workers [22].

Islamic countries such as Qatar, Saudi Arabia, and the UAE have large expatriate populations that are granted long-term work permits; however, citizenship is very rarely available to them. Further, only those migrant workers with good jobs, which usually means professionals and white-collar workers, get family visas and thus have children attending school. The other three countries – Brunei, Jordan, and Kazakhstan – also have skilled migrant workers or refugees, both being groups that value education. In all these countries, a large fraction of immigrant students come from countries (e.g., in South Asia and Southeast Asia) that have strong traditions of learning. A combination of factors that include origin, immigration policies, and a desire to make a better future (e.g., refugees) appears to be responsible for the strong performance of immigrants in these Islamic countries.

This agrees with results from several industrialized countries such as Australia, Canada, New Zealand, Singapore, the UK, and the USA, all of which have significant immigrant populations. In all these countries, immigrant students performed better in mathematics by 15–28 points compared to non-immigrant students on PISA 2022. Skill-based immigration policies, supportive families, and strong work ethics are frequently cited as factors contributing to the success of immigrants in North America [23], Australia [24], and Singapore [25].

7. Discussion

COVID-19 was a huge disruption, unlike anything the world has witnessed in living memory. Besides the associated mortality and morbidity, it resulted in an estimated 3.4%, or US$2.9 trillion, loss in global GDP in just 2020 [26], with cumulative output losses predicted to be US$28 trillion for 2020–2025 [27]. It led to the 2020 stock market crash, the 2021–2023 global supply chain crisis, the 2021–2022 global energy crisis, and the 2022–2023 food crisis. Education was impacted as well due to school closures, with the maximum impacts felt by marginalized children and youth – this was predicted in a pandemic report we prepared for UNESCO and the Government of India [28].

As the world continued to reel under the pandemic's impact while trying to get back on track, about 700,000 students from 81 OECD and partner economies participated in PISA 2022. This was the first large-scale assessment of student performance, well-being, and equity during the pandemic, which used a standardized global format. The results showed a clear decline in the performance of 15-year-olds across the 81 countries and economies. They also showed some education systems to cope better than others. The resilient ones followed some common policies, which included: keeping schools open longer for more students; achieving high comfort levels and good access to digital technologies; and providing a more supportive school and online learning environment. Embedded within these learnings are lessons for the future and the identification of barriers that should be addressed through policy changes.

This chapter focuses on data from 13 Islamic countries in the PISA surveys. Though no Islamic country individually scored above the OECD average, all showed positive decennial trends. However, the pandemic reversed these gains, showing that, while investments in education help in normal times, they are not sufficient to build resilience during crises. This was seen particularly in Albania and Malaysia, which experienced average scores to drop 157 points (30%) and 80 points (16.5%), respectively. Albanian students reported to be curious and satisfied, with a positive experience of learning at home [29]. This helped in pre-pandemic times when the country registered an average score of 525 (OECD average: 505; Islamic countries average: 419). But the reported low numbers of computers per student and a significant disparity in the use of information and communication technologies (ICT) between private and public schools [29] could be reasons for low pandemic resilience. Students in Malaysia reported low confidence in self-learning and a lack of support from their families [30]. Together with the 61 weeks of school closures in Malaysia, these factors might be the possible reasons for the large drop in performance.

In every Islamic country surveyed, girls outperformed boys. But the pandemic led to a major reversal, with the average score dropping 20 points, which is double the OECD average. What might be the reason(s) for this? The largest drops were witnessed among the richest Islamic countries – Qatar, Saudi Arabia, and the UAE. Students from all these countries reported high levels of self-confidence, familiarity with digital devices, and schools that provided a supportive environment, preparation for remote learning, and good educational leadership [31–33]. With long school closures as the only confounding factor – Qatar: 56 weeks, Saudi Arabia: 63 weeks, and the UAE: 62 weeks – the environment at home and other cultural factors may be reasons for the significant decline in girls' performance. Three Southeast Asian countries also registered significant drops in the performance of girls: Brunei (15 points),

Indonesia, and Malaysia (13 points each). In addition to students in Indonesia and Malaysia reporting low confidence in self-learning and less supportive families, those in Brunei also reported low levels of assertiveness and stress resistance, as well as a system characterized by low levels of empathy [34]. All three countries also closed schools for longer-than-average periods – Brunei: 29 weeks, Indonesia: 77 weeks, and Malaysia: 61 weeks.

It is instructive to learn from resilient education systems. What did they do well? The PISA 2022 survey compared performance in mathematics, equity, and well-being as three key measures of resilience. Equity included both *socio-economic fairness*, i.e., performance unrelated to the students' socio-economic conditions, and *socio-economic parity*, i.e., the extent to which the performance of disadvantaged and advantaged students improved or remained stable between 2018 and 2022. Well-being measured the students' sense of belonging in the school and whether education systems improved or maintained it between 2018 and 2022. Only four countries – Japan, Korea, Lithuania, and Chinese Taipei – showed resilient education systems that performed well, were equitable, students reported a sense of belonging, and there was no change in these during the pandemic (Fig. 7). There were 21 others that showed one or two of these aspects of resilience, including Saudi Arabia, which was the only Islamic country that reported a good measure of students' sense of well-being.

Among the Islamic countries in the assessment, Türkiye had the highest scores in mathematics, reading, and science; it showed strong decennial indicators, and its average score decreased by only two points (from 464 to 462) between 2018 and 2022. It also recorded an average decline of 8 points for disadvantaged students, no decline for advantaged students (average of −15 points), and the smallest decline of 9 points in the performance of girls compared to boys (OECD average: 10 points; Islamic countries average: 20 points). Though schools in Türkiye remained closed for 49 weeks (Islamic country average: 27 weeks), students reported feeling safe in schools, there was effective enforcement of digital device policies to limit distractions in class, the mathematics performance of public and private school students was comparable, and the system showed high levels of empathy and assertiveness [35].

Based on its findings, the PISA 2022 report suggests a ten-point resilience plan for all countries and education systems [36]. The Islamic world would be well advised to heed and develop suitable policies toward

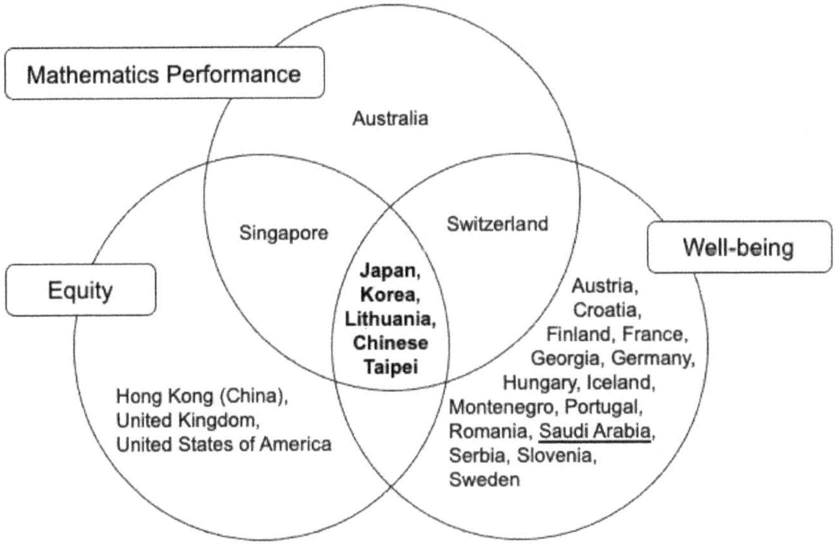

Figure 7. Resilient education systems based on a combination of performance in mathematics, equity, and well-being.

Note: The only Islamic country (Saudi Arabia) is underlined.

Source: Adapted from Ref. [36].

resilient education ecosystems. The lessons highlighted in this chapter should be disruptive, in a positive way, for Islamic countries as they improve student experience and learning toward developing knowledge-based economies. This would be especially true for Islamic countries that have invested heavily in education over the past decades. The effects of those investments are beginning to show; however, the pandemic, as a global disruption, also exposed the weak links that must be addressed.

Acknowledgments

I thank Adeel Malik, Muhammed Meki, Heiko Schuss, and Lavish Dudeja for reading drafts of the paper, on which this chapter is based, and for their suggestions. The Science, Technology, and Environment in Muslim Societies (STEMS) Project is supported by the Oxford Centre for Islamic Studies. Mr. Akber Moawalla is gratefully acknowledged for his early support of the project.

References

[1] Worldometers – Coronavirus. https://www.worldometers.info/coronavirus/. [Accessed 2024 Apr 4].

[2] Mark West. An ed-tech tragedy: Educational technologies and school closures in the time of Covid-19. UNESCO; Davison K, Yaghmour R, editors. 2023.

[3] Programme for International Student Assessment. https://www.oecd.org/pisa/. [Accessed 2024 Apr 4].

[4] Organisation for Economic Co-operation and Development. https://www.oecd.org/about/members-and-partners/. [Accessed 2024 Apr 4].

[5] Trends in International Mathematics and Science Study. https://nces.ed.gov/timss/. [Accessed 2024 Apr 4].

[6] Progress in International Reading Literacy Study. https://nces.ed.gov/surveys/pirls/. [Accessed 2024 Apr 4].

[7] Organisation of Islamic Cooperation. Member States. https://www.oic-oci.org. [Accessed 2024 Apr 4].

[8] Statistical, Economic and Social Research and Training Centre for Islamic Countries (SESRIC). https://www.sesric.org/sesric-about.php. [Accessed 2024 Apr 4].

[9] SESRIC. Socio-economic impacts of the COVID-19 pandemic in OIC countries: Pathways for sustainable and resilient recovery. The Statistical, Economic and Social Research and Training Centre for Islamic Countries. Ankara. 2022. https://sesricdiag.blob.core.windows.net/sesric-site-blob/files/article/802.pdf. [Accessed 2024 Apr 4].

[10] World Bank. Processed by Our World in Data. Average learning outcomes. [dataset]. World Bank, World bank education statistics (EdStats) 2023. [original data]. 2023. https://ourworldindata.org/grapher/learning-outcomes-vs-gdp-per-capita. [Accessed 2024 Apr 4].

[11] World Bank. With minor processing by Our World in Data. GDP per capita – World Bank. [dataset]. World Bank. World Bank world development indicators. [original data]. 2023. [Retrieved 2024 Apr 4] from https://ourworldindata.org/grapher/gdp-per-capita-worldbank.

[12] Roser M, Ortiz-Ospina, E. Education spending. Published online at OurWorldInData.org. 2016. Retrieved from: https://ourworldindata.org/financing-education. [Online Resource]. [Accessed 2024 Apr 4].

[13] Roser M, Ortiz-Ospina E. Literacy. Published online at OurWorldInData.org. 2018. Retrieved from: https://ourworldindata.org/literacy [Online Resource]. [Accessed 2024 Apr 4].

[14] UNESCO web archive. Education: From disruption to recovery. 2022. https://webarchive.unesco.org/web/20220629024039/https:/en.unesco.org/covid19/educationresponse/. [Accessed 2024 Apr 4].

[15] United Nations Children's Fund. Ensuring equal access to education in future crises: Findings of the new remote learning readiness index. New York: UNICEF; 2021. https://data.unicef.org/resources/remote-learning-readiness-index/. [Accessed 2024 Apr 4].

[16] UNICEF. Girls spend 160 million more hours than boys doing household chores everyday. 2016 Oct 7. https://www.unicef.org/press-releases/girls-spend-160-million-more-hours-boys-doing-household-chores-everyday. [Accessed 2024 Apr 4].

[17] World Population Review. Qatar. 2024. https://worldpopulationreview.com/countries/qatar-population. [Accessed 2024 Apr 4].

[18] Global Media Insight Blog. United Arab Emirates population statistics 2024. 2024. https://www.globalmediainsight.com/blog/uae-population-statistics/. [Accessed 2024 Apr 4].

[19] World Population Review. Saudi Arabia. 2024. https://worldpopulationreview.com/countries/saudi-arabia-population. [Accessed 2024 Apr 4].

[20] World Health Organization. Refugee and migrant health country profile – Jordan. 2023. https://www.emro.who.int/refugees-migrants-health/refugee_and_migrant_health_country_profile_Jordan.pdf. [Accessed 2024 Apr 4].

[21] Macrotrends. Brunei immigration statistics 1960-2024. 2024. https://www.macrotrends.net/countries/BRN/brunei/immigration-statistics. [Accessed 2024 Apr 4].

[22] World Population Review. Kazakhstan. 2024. https://worldpopulationreview.com/countries/kazakhstan-population. [Accessed 2024 Apr 4].

[23] Abramitzky R, Boustan L. Streets of gold: America's untold story of immigrant success. Public Affairs Publishers, New York, USA; 2022.

[24] Islam A, Sarkar D, Smyth R. How do children of immigrants perform? Evidence from Australian nationwide standardized tests. *Int Mig*. 2022;60(4): 93–136.

[25] Pan J, Theseira W. Immigration in Singapore. Background paper to the world development report 2023: Migrants, refugees, and societies. 2023. https://thedocs.worldbank.org/en/doc/080a4bc64cc8a9eb8a2a0e98d97a260a-0050062023/original/WDR-Immigration-in-Singapore-FORMATTED.pdf. [Accessed 2024 Apr 4].

[26] Dyvik EH. Impact of the coronavirus pandemic on the global economy - Statistics & facts. Statista. 2024. https://www.statista.com/topics/6139/covid-19-impact-on-the-global-economy/#topicOverview. [Accessed 2024 Apr 4].

[27] Gopinath G. IMF Blog. 2020. https://www.imf.org/en/Blogs/Articles/2020/10/13/blog-a-long-uneven-and-uncertain-ascent. [Accessed 2024 Apr 4].

[28] Duraiappah AK, Singh K, Mochizuki Y, editors. *Pandemics: Past, Present and Future Challenges and Opportunities*. New Delhi. UNESCO MGIEP; 2021.

[29] Organisation for Economic Co-operation and Development. Education GPS. Country Profile: Albania 2024. https://gpseducation.oecd.org/CountryProfile?primaryCountry=ALB. [Accessed 2024 Apr 4].
[30] Organisation for Economic Co-operation and Development. Education GPS. Country Profile: Malaysia 2024. https://gpseducation.oecd.org/CountryProfile?primaryCountry=MYS. [Accessed 2024 Apr 4].
[31] Organisation for Economic Co-operation and Development. Education GPS. Country Profile: Qatar 2024. https://gpseducation.oecd.org/CountryProfile?primaryCountry=QAT. [Accessed 2024 Apr 4].
[32] Organisation for Economic Co-operation and Development. Education GPS. Country Profile: Saudi Arabia 2024. 2024https://gpseducation.oecd.org/CountryProfile?primaryCountry=SAU. [Accessed 2024 Apr 4].
[33] Organisation for Economic Co-operation and Development. Education GPS. Country Profile: United Arab Emirates 2024. https://gpseducation.oecd.org/CountryProfile?primaryCountry=ARE. [Accessed 2024 Apr 4].
[34] Organisation for Economic Co-operation and Development. Education GPS. Country Profile: Brunei Darussalam: 2024. https://gpseducation.oecd.org/CountryProfile?primaryCountry=BRN. [Accessed 2024 Apr 4].
[35] Organisation for Economic Co-operation and Development. Education GPS. Country Profile: Türkiye 2024. https://gpseducation.oecd.org/CountryProfile?primaryCountry=TUR. [Accessed 2024 Apr 4].
[36] Organisation for Economic Co-operation and Development. PISA 2022 results (volume II): Learning During – and From – Disruption. Paris: PISA, OECD Publishing; 2023. https://doi.org/10.1787/a97db61c-en. [Accessed 2024 Apr 4].

https://doi.org/10.1142/9781800616295_0011

Chapter 11

Disruptive Innovation and Muslim Societies: The Need for Reforms in Higher Education

Ahmad Fauzi Ismail*, Muhammad Abd Hadi Bunyamin, Mahani Stapa, Rosli Md Illias, Jaffrey Samsul Bahrin, Rohaizan Khairul Anuar, and Nurul Amrie Abdullah

Universiti Teknologi Malaysia (UTM), Skudai, Johor, Malaysia

**afauzi@utm.my*

Abstract

The notion of disruptive innovation is not new, but it profoundly impacts the world and societies, including Muslim nations. Currently, Muslim nations are not essential inventors of such innovations. Steps toward empowering Muslim nations with disruptive innovation must be taken, particularly in higher education. This chapter discusses efforts made by the Malaysian government and an educational and research institution, Universiti Teknologi Malaysia (UTM), to promote and practice invention-based education. Universities should set clear plans and programs for making innovation a practice among students and academic staff and collaborating with industries. Such measures may enable disruptive innovation to transpire in the future.

1. Disruptive Innovation

Disruptive innovation refers to innovations that considerably change or transform established industries, often replacing conventional business leaders and profoundly changing how businesses operate or work. Christensen [1] introduced the concept of "disruptive innovation" in the mid-1990s. Some examples of disruptive innovation are the creation of personal computers replacing mainframes and minicomputers and cellular phones substituting fixed-line telephones [2]. Some other examples are digital photography, which replaced the traditional film photography industry, and smartphones, which significantly dominate the mobile phone industry worldwide, drastically reducing the influence of conventional mobile phones. Four key elements of disruptive innovation can be identified [3]:

1. Not all innovation is considered a disruption.
2. Disruption can be low-end or new-market.
3. Disruptive innovation is primarily a process rather than a product or a service.
4. Determining the right niche is crucial.

The first element of the above-mentioned disruptive innovation implies that an innovation need not be disruptive. This is understandable as a country may produce many innovations without successfully displacing the established products or services because they may not be good enough in quality or not fulfill the needs of the consumers. Displacing the established products or services will take time. Those who understand the importance of the "proper" process of making a new product or service will know that disruptions may occur if a new product or service can fulfill consumers' needs. This thinking reflects the need for proper research and development to produce a new product or service. In this vein, educational and research institutions must play a role.

The second element, "disruption can be low-end or new market," indicates that disruptive innovations can take place in a market that is never or rarely touched, and it may have a large number of consumers that may need a new product or service. For instance, many taxi drivers suffered following the development of digital applications such as Grab and Uber. These two companies managed to capture the market of consumers who prefer a service for which they can provide ratings and feedback for improvement. These measures were not available or applicable to traditional taxi drivers, whose consumers had no opportunity to directly influence the quality of service. Many e-hailing services now use consumers' feedback to improve their services, especially by identifying drivers who receive poor quality of service ratings from customers. Such drivers may be temporarily suspended from the company's fleet. This second element of disruptive innovation implies the importance of capturing the right market for innovations to thrive. Educational and research institutions will need to take part in educating and conducting research to determine under-targeted consumer markets.

The third element, "disruptive innovation is mostly a process rather than a product or a service," refers to the importance of patience in making the disruption a reality. In this vein, the innovators will need to ensure the process of producing a product or service is rigorous and systematic, and not take a "shortcut" or rush to create a new product or service. Replacing the established products or services will take time and not happen overnight. This notion makes clear the importance of emphasizing the proper innovation process among current and future innovators in a country. This particular emphasis is closely related to the first element, "not all innovation is considered disruption." To disrupt the established market, innovators must ensure they have the right "ingredients" to become quality innovators. This thinking in turn elucidates the importance of having an "innovators' mindset" among the current and future players in innovation. An entrepreneurial mindset can also be covered as part of an innovator's mindset. Educational and research institutions will need to play a role in cultivating this such mindsets among future innovators.

The fourth element, "determining the right niche," relates to the importance of having a distinct quality of products or services compared to the existing products or services. An innovator must think carefully about how to make a difference in the current market. This perspective emphasises the importance of creativity, critical thinking, and problem-solving skills among innovators. In order to make innovators genuinely creative and original, educational and research institutions will need to educate future innovators with these attributes. This is related to the third element mentioned earlier.

All four elements described reveal the essential measures needed to make disruptive innovations. Each of these measures implies the role of higher education institutions. In this current era, higher education institutions play dual roles as academic and research institutes [4–6]. Besides offering academic programs and providing certifications and degrees, higher education institutions, especially research universities, are also required to partake in research. These research universities become "the engine" of the economy of a nation [7] and a catalyst for innovation. This is especially true in Malaysia [8].

2. Higher Education, Disruptive Innovation, and Muslim Nations

Disruptions, including new technologies and innovations, also occur in higher education, especially in universities. These take place in various forms, such as online learning platforms, artificial intelligence (AI) in education, virtual labs, virtual reality and augmented reality, and open educational resources (OER) [9–12].

The effects of these disruptive innovations on higher education can be observed in multiple ways. A greater focus will be given in this chapter to AI because it has become a significant issue in education, specifically with the advent of ChatGPT in November 2022. Some studies discuss the effects of AI in education [13,14].

One particular issue is academic integrity. This is the key finding discovered by a study conducted in 2023 [13]. Participants of the study stated that university students outsourced essay writing and the completion of their academic assignments to AI tools. This is unsurprising because an AI tool, such as ChatGPT, can produce such an essay by simply giving a command to it, such as "Provide me an essay about innovation in business in 500 words." The AI tool can immediately produce such an essay with quite impressive quality. However, those who are experts in checking students' essays will be able to know that such an essay is not written by a student but rather by "someone." Luckily, other applications, such as Turnitin, can now provide the percentage of AI-generated sentences used. In this vein, students can check whether they produced original work or "asked" AI to do it for them.

Another study [14] provided a different point of view regarding the use of AI in education. It discovered the changing roles of academics or lecturers, from content providers to facilitators of students' learning, when AI is utilized. A lecturer will need to transform his or her roles to make students learn in a more personalized environment, assist students when they face obstacles in learning, and may also need to modify the academic assignments provided to their students. In this context, AI has been seen disrupting the roles of university educators. Students can now find learning content from various sources, including AI, and university educators can assist students when they need it.

Like it or not, AI will continue to disrupt higher education in the long run. With the awareness that this scenario cannot be avoided, universities must be able to adapt to this new reality. Changes should be made to ensure academics can cope with the future of higher education, where AI and humans (university lecturers and students) can "coexist" and professionally complement each other.

Additionally, during the COVID-19 pandemic, during 2020–2021, university teaching and learning immediately shifted to digital platforms, whereby university educators and students taught and learned using Zoom, WebEx, Google Meet, Teams, etc. The pandemic could prove to have been the catalyst for changes in higher education. As a result, any teaching and learning activities have been blended with a face-to-face and digital learning approach.

Nonetheless, the disruptive innovations around the globe, as discussed, are not led by Muslim nations. These innovations, especially AI research in education, are mainly led by the United States, China, and India [15]. The Muslim nations are not on the list of the top AI leaders. A question is addressed to tackle this central issue.

3. The Central Question

With disruptions taking place around the globe, the following question needs to be addressed: How do we equip the nation (at large) and universities (specifically) in Muslim countries with the necessary elements for them to lead the invention of disruptive technologies rather than just being consumers?

This question is crucial because it fosters discussions on strategies to empower Muslim nations, especially higher education institutions, with the elements needed to lead the inventions of disruptive technologies. Consequently, the execution of the strategy should be of the utmost priority.

4. The Theory and Concepts: Connectivism, Integrated STEM Education, and Invention-Based Education

4.1. *Theory*

The theory adopted for this writing is connectivism [16]. This theory of education is adopted as it provides a complete picture of the nature of education, especially teaching and learning, in the modern era. Connectivism sees learning as interconnected, whereby learners are always connected, learning together through tools or devices (especially digital tools). This learning theory emphasizes the following aspects of the nature of learning:

1. Learning may occur through non-human appliances (e.g., digital platforms).
2. Connection is critical; nurturing and maintaining it are needed to ensure continuous learning.
3. The ability to connect different fields, ideas, and concepts is a central skill.
4. Learning is a process of connecting information from different sources.

These four features of connectivism can be summarised as learning in the digital era [16]. The current generation of university students is Gen Z, who usually learn using digital tools, as they were born and grew up in an environment that uses digital media, such as social media (TikTok, Instagram, Facebook, etc.) [17].

Furthermore, this theory is particularly relevant because it emphasizes the importance of collaboration over individual efforts. In the current era of modern higher education in the 21st century [18], collaboration becomes crucial because it allows a learner to exchange views, thoughts, and even resources with other learners to produce a valuable product. Gen Z is a hyperconnected generation, and this provides them with opportunities to collaborate, either in digital or face-to-face settings.

4.2. *Concepts*

In terms of concept, integrated science, technology, engineering, and mathematics (STEM) education is adopted because it is closely related to the theory of connectivism [19]. Integrated STEM education emphasizes the interconnection between science, technology, engineering, mathematics, and other related domains, including economics and social sciences, to make learning connected with real-world scenarios and focus on solving real-world problems by applying science and mathematics via engineering design processes and relevant technological tools [20,21].

As the issue of disruptive innovations in education, particularly AI, is central, integrated STEM education provides a valuable framework for understanding the key features of education that are interdisciplinary, multidisciplinary, or transdisciplinary [22]. The creation of AI requires a focus mainly on STEM expertise, especially engineering and computer science [15]. Yet, knowledge of the social sciences is also needed [15].

A previous study [19] adopted the concept of integrated STEM education and used the theory of connectivism. A good fit between these two notions can be observed. They complement each other, especially when learners are required to work together (connect) to invent products. In many STEM projects in education, students are usually required to produce artifacts (prototypes, reports, etc.) [23].

Additionally, a nation should focus on empowering its citizens with invention-based education. High-quality education should enable citizens to achieve a higher order of thinking or cognition, which is "creative" [24]. Referring to the revised Bloom's taxonomy [24], one cannot create or generate if one cannot master all the lower-order thinking skills, which are remembering, understanding, applying, analyzing, and evaluating. It implies the supremacy of the cognitive level of creating, which may be thought to be the most desired stage of education, where all students can be creators. It is believed that a nation, particularly a Muslim nation, can thrive if its education system encourages, cultivates, and empowers its citizens to become inventors. An inventor will likely be born from an education system that practices and promotes curiosity, critical thinking, creativity, and collaboration. The concept of integrated STEM education, the theory of connectivism, and the significance of achieving the highest-order thinking, "creating," are all fit for and best offer a comprehensive view of the needs of a nation and higher education institutions to produce inventors or innovators, especially the ones who can lead disruptions rather than simply following them.

5. Equipping Muslim Nations with the Ingredients Needed for Leading Disruptive Innovation: The Cases of Malaysia and UTM

As the Muslim nations are not currently leaders in AI, strategies should be formulated to equip nations and educational institutions with invention-based education. The following strategies are proposed and discussed to illuminate how to empower nations, especially Muslim ones, with the concept and practice of invention-based education. These strategies are aligned with the theory and concepts described.

Malaysia and Universiti Teknologi Malaysia (UTM) are given as examples for these strategies. Malaysia is a Muslim-majority country that could be considered an exemplary Muslim nation [25]. It has five research universities in the top 200 in the QS World University Rankings 2024 [26]. This achievement shows a strong reputation gained by the nation through its research universities.

UTM is a STEM-based university that primarily focuses on science, technology, and engineering. It is also a university with a high reputation in education and research, especially in STEM and STEM-related areas, and robotics in particular. Currently, the government of Malaysia has selected UTM as the recipient of special funds for the establishment of a new faculty, the Faculty of Artificial Intelligence (FAI), starting in 2024 [27]. As a university that emphasizes science, technology, and engineering, UTM will likely provide examples for others to learn from, especially to produce graduates and ecosystems that can generate significant inventions or innovations.

5.1. *Strategy 1: Federal government policies on economic reforms, STEM education, and innovation ecosystem*

As a nation that practices centralization in many aspects of governance in education, the policies of the Malaysian federal government will always be the primary guide for many educational institutions, including higher education, to ensure they can fulfill the aspirations of the nation. The current Prime Minister of Malaysia, Anwar Ibrahim, established the notion of "Malaysia Madani" (translation: civilized Malaysia) in January 2023, two months after his appointment as the 10th Prime Minister. "Malaysia Madani" is a framework that emphasizes national holistic development, mentally, spiritually, physically, and socially, based on the local culture and wisdom [28].

This framework consists of six pillars: (1) sustainability, (2) well-being, (3) inventiveness, (4) respect, (5) confidence, and (6) manners [28]. One of the pillars, inventiveness, is especially relevant to the issue of disruptive innovation. The government has realized that Malaysians rarely consider themselves inventors, creators, or innovators [29]. Thus, the current government has included inventiveness as one of the key pillars in the "Malaysia Madani" framework.

The problem with the current education system in Malaysia is the lack of opportunities for students to achieve the highest order of thinking or cognition, which is *creating*. The current education system in Malaysia, especially at the school level, still revolves around the teacher-centered approach, where students learn science with minimal experience and teachers extensively give explanations while the students take notes [30]. However, efforts have been made to empower Malaysian students, especially university students, with the necessary knowledge, skills, and attitudes to become active learners and thus be creators, innovators, or inventors [31].

Integrated STEM has now become the focus of the Malaysian federal government, whereby the Ministry of Science, Technology, and Innovation (MOSTI) and other relevant ministries are working together to advance the nation's STEM agenda [32]. Integrated STEM education will nurture citizens to practice curiosity, critical thinking, creativity, inventiveness, and collaboration [33]. To date, integrated STEM education seems to be at a moderate level of development in Malaysia because, historically, the educational institutions in Malaysia do not strongly emphasize STEM in practice, even though the government has set a target of 60% total enrolment of science students for the nation [34]. The latest enrolment is at 45.73%, an increase from 2021, 40.95% [35]. The emphasis on integrated STEM education in Malaysia will benefit the country in the long run, whereby the nation will have a sufficient number of citizens who are able to become inventors, innovators, or creators.

If Malaysia continues to focus on integrated STEM education at various education levels, especially in schools and universities, the government can innovate and restructure the economy. The federal government has now focused on reforming the nation's economy through the "Ekonomi Madani" (translation: civilized economy) framework [36]. These economic reforms require adopting digital technology and innovation among industries [36].

The MOSTI released the 10-10 MySTIE (Malaysian Science, Technology, Innovation, and Economy) framework in 2020 [37]. This framework aims for a systematic approach to transform the nation into a knowledge-intensive economy. Ten science and technology drivers are determined: 5G/6G signal, sensor technology, 4D/5D-printing, advanced materials, advanced intelligent systems, cybersecurity and encryption, augmented analytics and data discovery, blockchain, neurotechnology, and bioscience technology.

Meanwhile, the ten socioeconomic drivers are energy, business and financial services, culture, arts and tourism, medical and healthcare, smart technology and systems, smart cities and transportation, water and food, agriculture and forestry, education, and environment and biodiversity. The 10–10 MySTIE framework will drive Malaysia to become a nation that creates global innovation [37].

Almost every year, the federal government allocates around MYR 500 million for research and development [38]. This allocation is shared mainly between the MOSTI and the Ministry of Higher Education (MOHE). Many researchers in Malaysia work at universities. Thus, research grants provided to Malaysian researchers can be obtained either from MOHE or MOSTI.

In sum, the federal government's policies for the economy and education are vital because they must be followed by educational and research institutions in Malaysia. With the right policies, they can help educational and research institutions carry out initiatives to deliver the policies at the grassroots level, such as at a university.

5.2. *Strategy 2: University policies and programs on education and research*

In UTM, the deputy vice-chancellor (academic and international) and the deputy vice-chancellor (research and innovation) are primarily responsible for delivering the academic and research missions of the university. The university's strategic plan of enVision UTM 2025 is the current document used to map the university's vision and mission with strategic thrusts and strategic priorities, as well as the university's core values. One of the strategic thrusts is for UTM to produce world-class holistic talents to extend the frontiers of education and research [39]. In achieving the strategic thrust, two strategic priorities are particularly important: producing holistic talents by developing high-quality graduates and strengthening UTM's research, development, commercialization, and innovation (RDCI) capability and resilience to champion emerging knowledge and research areas.

For its education mission, UTM has adopted the notion of UTMHyFlex to become a university that practices hybrid and flexible learning for students. Hybrid and flexible approaches require the curricula and the delivery of the curricula to be student-centered, have the features of dynamic curricula, and practice authentic learning and assessment. The university has provided many programs to equip lecturers with the necessary knowledge and skills to practice hybrid and flexible learning. One example is organizing the New Academia Learning Innovation (NALI) program, which is conducted annually. Lecturers at UTM are encouraged to showcase their practice of teaching and learning that incorporates online or hybrid learning approaches, project-based learning, problem-based learning, authentic assessment, or other innovative teaching and learning approaches. NALI also offers various teaching and learning trainings to assist lecturers in improving or strengthening their innovative teaching practice [40]. All of these initiatives ensure UTM lecturers can make students learn actively and nurture the students to become innovators, inventors, or creators of new knowledge and products.

As for research, UTM has produced the Research and Innovation Blueprint 2025 [41]. Furthermore, a unique research program named Fantastic4+ [42] has been set up. The research program initially covered four key research areas: integrated membrane wastewater treatment systems, next-generation battery technology and application, intelligent robots, and novel materials for biomedical devices. Then, four other research areas were added: affordable housing, spiritual technology, digitalization, and food security.

UTM emphasizes science, technology, and engineering in its research programs. As a STEM-based university, UTM comes out with research programs that can produce high-quality talents among lecturers and students so that they can become innovators, inventors, or creators.

One particular strength of UTM is robotics. The UTM robotic team has been the champion of the NI Autonomous Robotics Competition (NIARC), for three consecutive years, from 2021 to 2023 [43]. UTM has the Centre for Artificial Intelligence and Robotics (CAIRO) [44]. This research center plays a vital role in developing frontier intelligent systems for industries targeted at wealth creation, promoting and disseminating the knowledge of AI and robotics technologies, and providing state-of-the-art smart system solutions to society.

With outstanding reputations in robotics and AI-related areas, UTM is on the right track to lead the nation in developing more disruptive technologies and innovations, especially when the FAI is officially established in 2024. With this in mind, UTM can advise the government on advancing AI and other disruptive innovations to benefit the nation and society.

Overall, UTM's education and research missions are clear, with the direction to cultivate and produce talents that can become innovators, inventors, or creators, especially in AI and robotics education and research. UTM hopes that the policies and programs will assist all UTM staff and students to take up the challenge of producing innovations, which hopefully can create disruptions to the current technologies.

5.3. *Strategy 3: Collaboration across sectors*

Based on the university's strategic plan, enVision UTM 2025 [39], one of the priorities is nurturing a strategic nexus between the university, industry, government, and community. UTM has collaborated in various ways to achieve its education and research missions [45]. In a complex ecosystem, UTM connects with multiple stakeholders that can strengthen the impact of the university, particularly in education and research. For example, in 2022, a special research program, the Collaborative Research Grant (CRG), was set up [45]. The total allocation provided was MYR 4.0 million. CRG was introduced to encourage UTM's collaboration with other public and private universities, government agencies, and industries. A total of 54 CRG projects were awarded to UTM researchers, with 16 linkages with public universities, five with private universities, two with government agencies, and eight with industries.

UTM has also set up the Centre for Community and Industry Network (CCIN). It is responsible for "enhancing university-community-industry collaborations by engaging the university's academic resources in the enrichment of civic and community life in Malaysia" [46]. To date, a total of 2,137 linkages have been established between UTM and industries [47].

UTM believes that collaboration is the way to achieve a more significant outcome and impact on the university. In the context of innovation, a dynamic ecosystem is needed where many players, especially universities and industries, should work together to make innovations for the nation. UTM often collaborates with industries because the university believes that many benefits can be generated when multiple parties (especially universities and industries) work together for a common goal: building a knowledge-based economy for the nation [48,49].

5.4. *Strategy 4: Producing exemplary academics and researchers*

UTM has produced many exemplary academics and researchers throughout its history. In 2010, Hayati Abdullah, a UTM staff member from the Faculty of Mechanical Engineering, won the prestigious National Academies Award (Category: Teaching, Field: Engineering) [50]. This award is significant for UTM because Hayati is the first academic staff member to be recognized for excellence in teaching. She regularly practices active learning approaches with her students and often brings them to industry sites. This has enabled her students to understand the nature of industries while they are still learning at the university. In education, this may be called authentic learning, where the students learn at the actual site where they may be working in the future.

In 2012, another UTM staff member won the National Academies Award (Category: Innovation and Product Commercialisation), Ahmad Fauzi Ismail, a prominent researcher in membrane technology [51]. Fauzi believes in research-led teaching, where he regularly connects his students with membrane technology research in the laboratory. Fauzi founded a research center at UTM, the Advanced Membrane Technology Research Centre (AMTEC) [52]. Innovation (and commercialization) are essential for universities to create a more significant impact for themselves and their industries, whereby universities can share their expertise with industries. In contrast, industries can provide resources and devices to create innovation [48].

Many more academics and researchers at UTM have been recognized nationally and internationally. In 2019, the UTM team won the AKRI award for Immersive Learning Experience (Blended Learning Category) [53]. The award is significant because it is evidence that UTM staff have been recognized for excellence in blended learning approaches as part of the concept of hybrid and flexible learning described earlier. Even though UTMHyFlex approach was formally adopted in 2022, the foundations for this were already in place at the university. In other words, UTM already had the substance to make innovations in the context of teaching and learning before the initiation of UTMHyFlex. Such a base is significant because it provides students with an innovative learning environment, which may disrupt the long-standing practice of instructor-centered approaches in higher education [54].

Some other academics and researchers at UTM have also been recognized for their excellence. Two UTM academic staff members recently won the National Academies Award (Category: Teaching) in 2023. Adibah Abdul Latif [55] from the Faculty of Social Sciences and Humanities regularly practices authentic learning and assessment with her students. Adibah believes in students' well-being rather than merely good grades in a course or subject. Meanwhile, Norliza Mohd Isa [56] from the Faculty of Built Environment and Surveying often practices community project-based learning, where she connects her students with community members to apply their knowledge of architecture. These two teaching and learning practices, namely authentic learning and assessment and community project-based learning, are innovative, as many academics do not practice them and they are still uncommon at large. These academic staff may be able to "disrupt" the education market, whereby the recognition received from the federal government of Malaysia can prove their capabilities to transform and thus innovate the education landscape, especially in higher education.

6. The Way Forward

The four strategies described are based on the theory of connectivism and the concepts of integrated STEM education and invention-based education. The theory of connectivism is seen in all four strategies, highlighting the importance of connecting academics, researchers, and students to innovate. Strategy 1 focuses on the federal government policies in economic reforms, STEM education, and the innovation ecosystem, which can be thought of as the main drivers for innovation and, ultimately, disruptive innovation. As a nation that practices centralization of governance and management in many aspects, the Malaysian government's policies are the source of power for action for citizens and institutions to act and deliver the policies, particularly on innovation, in the context of education, especially higher education. The Malaysian government has set clear policies that can assist higher education institutions in taking action according to national policies. The federal government, through various ministries, especially the MOSTI and the MOHE, has worked together to achieve the national aspiration of "Malaysia Madani," especially in empowering and producing STEM talents that are highly needed for disruptive innovation.

Strategy 2 is about university policies and programs on education and research, which is vital for effecting national policies on economic reforms, STEM education, and innovation ecosystems. The universities must ensure their policies and programs can produce high-quality graduates, especially in the STEM fields, to create innovators, inventors, and creators. A particular focus is given to AI, where a university like UTM has strength in this crucial and promising field. By focusing on AI and AI-related fields, such as robotics, the aim of producing more talented students and academic staff for disruptive innovation can be achieved in the future.

Nonetheless, Strategy 2 may only be properly implemented if collaboration occurs across sectors. This is the crux of Strategy 3, which emphasizes the partnership of universities with industries, other stakeholders, government agencies, and communities. The aim of disruptive innovation may only be realized through regular collaboration, especially in universities and industries. Industries usually possess a better understanding of the market, while universities possess the expertise that industries can benefit from. This symbiotic relationship should be cultivated and nurtured. The essence of "connecting" is paramount because universities and industries have different interests and goals. Both parties need to reach a consensus to achieve a common goal.

The last strategy, Strategy 4, highlights the importance of having capable and well-recognized talents that may be able to produce disruptive innovation. Having a more significant number of prominent academics and researchers will inspire university students to follow their educators or research supervisors. In other words, showing a great example to students is crucial for generating greater motivation and inspiration. UTM is grateful for having many highly talented academics and researchers who have been recognized nationally or internationally.

The journey to produce many innovators, inventors, and creators will undoubtedly take time. Yet, plans must be set, and action must be taken to achieve this goal. Malaysia may be seen by Muslim nations as exemplary due to its research universities' reputation, both locally and globally. Nevertheless, Malaysia still needs to tackle economic and education issues that impede the nation's progress, especially economic uncertainties [57]. UTM received special funds from the federal government to establish the FAI starting in 2024; UTM will be committed to ensuring the best delivery of the new initiative while striving to produce talents that can produce disruptive innovations. The new tagline of the university, "Innovating Solutions" [58], is a manifestation of UTM as a university that emphasizes innovation, invention, and the creation of solutions for problems faced by humanity. With that, disruptive innovation may be fostered in Malaysia and around the globe.

7. Summary

Overall, reforms in higher education in the context of disruptive innovation in Muslim nations are imperative because many Muslim nations do not lead innovation in the current era. The West and the East still lead and dominate innovations across the globe, especially in AI. It appears that Muslim nations should work harder to equip their people with the attributes of becoming inventors, innovators, or creators. This effort can be realized through reforms in higher education that put into practice the theory of connectivism in education and research. As the West and the East still dominate many achievements in higher education, such as in the world university rankings [59], and also as both regions now lead in AI technologies [15], this implies that universities in Muslim nations should inculcate a culture of excellence in education, in line with Islamic values and teachings. World history shows the excellence of Muslim scholars such as Al-Khawarizmi, Al-Kindi, Ibn Sina, and many more who brought reforms to the world, and modern Muslim nations should strive to produce many more excellent scholars. By doing so, university students may be inspired to follow in the footsteps of exemplary scholars who serve as their lecturers or educators. Good teachers teach, while great teachers inspire. Hence, the "chain of excellent people" across generations in the Muslim nations can be realized, and the Muslim world can benefit from their expertise.

References

[1] Christensen C. *The Innovator's Dilemma: When New Technologies Cause Great Firms to Fail.* Boston: Harvard Business Review Press; 1997.

[2] Christensen Institute. Disruptive innovation theory. https://www.christenseninstitute.org/theory/disruptive-innovation/. [Accessed 2024 Dec 13].

[3] Larson C. Disruptive innovation theory: What it is & 4 key concepts. Harvard Business School Online; https://online.hbs.edu/blog/post/4-keys-to-understanding-clayton-christensens-theory-of-disruptive-innovation. [Accessed 2024 Dec 13].

[4] Hughes M. The mythology of research and teaching relationships in universities. In: Barnett R, editor. *Reshaping the University: New Relationships Between Research, Scholarship and Teaching.* New York: Open University Press; 2005. p. 14–26.

[5] Healey M. Linking research and teaching: exploring disciplinary spaces and the role of inquiry-based learning. In: Barnett R, editor. *Reshaping the University: New Relationships Between Research, Scholarship and Teaching.* New York: Open University Press; 2005.

[6] Robertson J, Bond, C. Being in the university. In Barnett R, editor. *Reshaping the University: New Relationships Between Research, Scholarship and Teaching.* New York: Open University Press; 2005. p. 79–91.

[7] Mohammad AW. Universiti penyelidikan enjin pertumbuhan ekonomi negara. *Berita Harian.* 2020 Jun 27. https://www.bharian.com.my/rencana/muka10/2020/06/704629/universiti-penyelidikan-enjin-pertumbuhan-ekonomi-negara?fbclid=IwAR3OMXrrLDmOR6_RUJmF3nlebKHWAXhHhNjTlQV3PUQYmjOJyyoKGeHD7U. [Accessed 2024 Dec 13].

[8] Mustafa Z. Research universities: Catalysts for innovation. *New Straits Times*; 30 Aug 2027. https://www.nst.com.my/education/2017/08/274535/research-universities-catalysts-innovation. [Accessed 2024 Dec 13].

[9] Vezne R, Yildiz Durak H, Atman Uslu N. Online learning in higher education: Examining the predictors of students' online engagement. *Educ Inform Technol.* 2023;28(2):1865–89. https://doi.org/10.1007/s10639-022-11171-9.

[10] Crompton H, Burke D. Artificial intelligence in higher education: The state of the field. *Int J Educ Technol High Educ.* 2023;20(1):1–22. https://educationaltechnologyjournal.springeropen.com/articles/10.1186/s41239-023-00392-8.

[11] Diwakar S, Kolil VK, Francis SP, Achuthan K. Intrinsic and extrinsic motivation among students for laboratory courses – assessing the impact of virtual laboratories. *Comput Educ.* 2023;198:104758. https://doi.org/10.1016/j.compedu.2023.104758.

[12] Tlili A, Nascimbeni F, Burgos D, Zhang X, Huang R, Chang TW. The evolution of sustainability models for open educational resources: Insights

from the literature and experts. *Interact Learn Environ.* 2023;31(3):1421–36. https://doi.org/10.1080/10494820.2020.1839507.

[13] Sullivan M, Kelly A, McLaughlan P. ChatGPT in higher education: Considerations for academic integrity and student learning. *J Appl Learn Teach.* 2023;6(1):1–10. https://journals.sfu.ca/jalt/index.php/jalt/article/view/731.

[14] Firat M. What ChatGPT means for universities: Perceptions of scholars and students. *J Appl Learn Teach.* 2023;6(1):57–63. https://journals.sfu.ca/jalt/index.php/jalt/article/view/769.

[15] Dogan ME, Goru Dogan T, Bozkurt A. The use of artificial intelligence (AI) in online learning and distance education processes: A systematic review of empirical studies. *Appl Sci.* 2023;13(5):3056. https://doi.org/10.3390/app13053056.

[16] Siemens G. Connectivism: A learning theory for the digital age. *Int J Instruct Technol Distance Learn.* 2005;2(1). http://www.itdl.org/Journal/Jan_05/article01.htm.

[17] Schwieger D, Ladwig C. Reaching and retaining the next generation: Adapting to the expectations of Gen Z in the classroom. *Inform Syst Educ J.* 2018;16(3):45. http://isedj.org/2018-16/n3/ISEDJv16n3p45.pdf.

[18] Thornhill-Miller B, Camarda A, Mercier M, Burkhardt JM, Morisseau T, Bourgeois-Bougrine S, Vinchon F, El Hayek S, Augereau-Landais M, Mourey F, Feybesse C. Creativity, critical thinking, communication, and collaboration: Assessment, certification, and promotion of 21st century skills for the future of work and education. *J Intell.* 2023;11(3):54. https://doi.org/10.3390/jintelligence11030054.

[19] Bunyamin MA, Rahman NF. Perspectives on reforming science teacher education programs toward integrated STEM in Malaysia. In: Al-Balushi SM, Martin-Hansen L, Song Y, editors. *Reforming Science Teacher Education Programs in The Stem Era: International and Comparative Perspectives.* Palgrave Macmillan: Cham; 2023. p. 143–159. https://doi.org/10.1007/978-3-031-27334-6_9.

[20] Roehrig GH, Dare EA, Ellis JA, Ring-Whalen E. Beyond the basics: A detailed conceptual framework of integrated STEM. *Discip Interdiscip Sci Educ Res.* 2021;3(1):1–8. https://doi.org/10.1186/s43031-021-00041-y.

[21] Bunyamin MA, Talib CA, Ahmad NJ, Ibrahim NH, Surif J. Current teaching practice of physics teachers and implications for integrated STEM education. *Univers J Educ Res.* 2020;8(5):18–28. https://www.hrpub.org/journals/article_info.php?aid=9218.

[22] Guan NH, Bunyamin MA, Khamis N. Perspectives of STEM education from physics teachers' points of view: A quantitative study. *Univers J Educ Res.* 2020;8(11C):72–82. https://www.hrpub.org/journals/article_info.php?aid=10082.

[23] Markula A, Aksela M. The key characteristics of project-based learning: How teachers implement projects in K-12 science education. *Discip Interdiscip Sci Educ Res.* 2022;4(1):1–7. https://doi.org/10.1186/s43031-021-00042-x.

[24] Krathwohl DR. A revision of Bloom's taxonomy: An overview. *Theory Pract.* 2002;41(4):212–218. https://doi.org/10.1207/s15430421tip4104_2.

[25] Bernama. Malaysia under Anwar a model Muslim country for Tunisia. *New Straits Times.* 2023 Nov 24. https://www.nst.com.my/news/nation/2023/11/982191/malaysia-under-anwar-model-muslim-country-tunisia. [Accessed 2024 Dec 13].

[26] QS Quacquarelli Symonds Limited. QS world university rankings 2025: Top global universities. https://www.topuniversities.com/world-university-rankings. [Accessed 2024 Dec 13].

[27] Povera A, Daim N, Mohamed Radhi NA, Azmi A. 2024 budget: Malaysia's first artificial intelligence faculty to be set up in UTM. *New Straits Times.* 2023 Oct 13. https://www.nst.com.my/news/nation/2023/10/966708/2024-budget-malaysias-first-artificial-intelligence-faculty-be-set-utm. [Accessed 2024 Dec 13].

[28] Pejabat Perdana Menteri. Malaysia Madani. https://malaysiamadani.gov.my/pengenalan/. [Accessed 2024 Dec 13].

[29] Ministry of Economy. Keynote address by the Honourable Rafizi Ramli, Minister of Economy: UK-Malaysia digital innovation programme demo day. https://www.ekonomi.gov.my/sites/default/files/2023-03/UK-Malaysia%20Digital%20Innovation%20Programme%20Demo%20Day.pdf. [Accessed 2024 Dec 13].

[30] Saleh S, Jing TA. Instructional practices in science education in German and Malaysian secondary schools: A comparative case study. *Int J Instruct.* 2020;13(4):267–82. https://doi.org/10.29333/iji.2020.13417a.

[31] Centre for Engineering Education. About us. https://research.utm.my/cee/our-objectives/. [Accessed 2024 Dec 13].

[32] *The Star.* STEM committee to be finalised this year, says Chang. Star Media Group Berhad. 2023 Sep 21. https://www.thestar.com.my/news/nation/2023/09/21/stem-committee-to-be-finalised-this-year-says-chang. [Accessed 2024 Dec 13].

[33] Saleh S, Muhammad A, Abdullah SM. STEM project-based approach in enhancing conceptual understanding and inventive thinking skills among secondary school students. *J Nusant Stud.* 2020;5(1):234–254. https://doi.org/10.24200/jonus.vol5iss1pp234-254.

[34] Emily C. Develop new ideas to promote STEM. *Star Media Group Berhad.* 2023 Jan 1. https://www.thestar.com.my/news/education/2023/01/01/develop-new-ideas-to-promote-stem. [Accessed 2024 Dec 13].

[35] Vethasalam R, Tan T, Yusof TA. STEM intake up at higher secondary level, Dewan Rakyat told. *Star Media Group Berhad.* 2023 Oct 19. https://www.thestar.com.my/news/nation/2023/10/19/stem-intake-up-at-higher-secondary-level-dewan-rakyat-told. [Accessed 2024 Dec 13].

[36] Pejabat Perdana Menteri. Ekonomi Madani: Memperkasa rakyat. https://www.pmo.gov.my/ms/membangun-malaysia-madani-2/ekonomi-madani-memperkasa-rakyat/. [Accessed 2024 Dec 13].

[37] Academy of Sciences Malaysia. 10-10 Malaysian Science, Technology, Innovation, and Economy (MySTIE) Framework. https://www.akademisains.gov.my/10-10-mystie/. [Accessed 2024 Dec 13].

[38] The Edge Malaysia. Cover story: Highlights of budget 2024. *The Edge Communications Sdn. Bhd.* 2023 Oct 26. https://theedgemalaysia.com/node/686441. [Accessed 2024 Dec 13].

[39] Strategy Management Office. envision UTM 2025. https://envision2025.utm.my/. [Accessed 2024 Dec 13].

[40] Centre for Advancement in Digital and Flexible Learning. New academia learning innovation model (NALI). https://utmcdex.utm.my/smu/about-nali/. [Accessed 2024 Dec 13].

[41] Mohd Nawi A, editor. UTM research and innovation blueprint 2025. Skudai: Penerbit UTM Press; 2021. https://research.utm.my/blueprint/. [Accessed 2024 Dec 13].

[42] UTM Library. Fantastic4. https://library.utm.my/fantastic-4/. [Accessed 2024 Dec 13].

[43] Universiti Teknologi Malaysia. UTM Airost team clinches 3rd consecutive NIARC championship for UTM. https://fke.utm.my/airost/2023/11/24/utm-airost-team-clinches-3rd-consecutive-niarc-championship-for-utm/. [Accessed 2024 Dec 13].

[44] Centre for Artificial Intelligence and Robotics. About us. https://research.utm.my/cairo/1about-us-2/. [Accessed 2024 Dec 13].

[45] Ismail AF. *Penyelesaian Radikal Memartabat Pendidikan Tinggi.* Skudai: Penerbit UTM Press; 2023.

[46] Centre for Community and Industry Network. Engaging towards a greater future. https://ccin.utm.my/directories/vision-mission/. [Accessed 2024 Dec 13].

[47] Centre for Community and Industry Network. Facts and figures. https://ccin.utm.my. [Accessed 2024 Dec 13].

[48] Ismail AF, Bunyamin MAH, Abd Razak S, Surif J, Khairul Anuar R. Transforming university-industry partnerships: Moving toward synergistic collaborations. In: Anuarudin AAS, Mohd Kasim AA, Manap MR, Mohd Ramli NF, Waheed M, Ismail O, editors. *Strengthening Malaysian Higher Education: A Contemporary Discourse.* Shah Alam: Penerbit Universiti Teknologi MARA Press. p. 85–102.

[49] Arshed N, Ahmad W, Hanif U. A spatial temporal exploration of factors motivating academia-industry collaboration. *J Knowl Econ.* 2022;13:521–540. https://doi.org/10.1007/s13132-021-00729-6.

[50] Kementerian Pendidikan Tinggi. Anugerah Akademik Negara: Anugerah Pengajaran (Kelompok Kejuruteraan). https://jpt.mohe.gov.my/aan/senarai-penerima/aan-2010/anugerah-pengajaran-kelompok-kejuruteraan. [Accessed 2024 Dec 13].

[51] Kementerian Pendidikan Tinggi. Anugerah Akademik Negara: Anugerah Inovasi dan Pengkomersialan Produk. https://jpt.mohe.gov.my/aan/senarai-penerima/aan-2012/anugerah-inovasi-dan-pengkomersialan-produk. [Accessed 2024 Dec 13].

[52] Advanced Membrane Technology Research Centre. Meet our experts. https://research.utm.my/amtec/prof-datuk-dr-ahmad-fauzi-ismail/. [Accessed 2024 Dec 13].

[53] AKRI. Senarai pemenang anugerah khas YB Menteri Pendidikan Malaysia: Rekabentuk kurikulum dan penyampaian inovatif. https://jpt.mohe.gov.my/akri/index.php/senarai-penerima/pemenang-akri-2019. [Accessed 2024 Dec 13].

[54] Stains M, Harshman J, Barker MK, Chasteen SV, Cole R, DeChenne-Peters SE, Eagan Jr MK, Esson JM, Knight JK, Laski FA, Levis-Fitzgerald M. Anatomy of STEM teaching in North American universities. *Science.* 2018;359(6383):1468–1470. https://www.science.org/doi/10.1126/science.aap8892.

[55] Kementerian Pendidikan Tinggi. Anugerah Akademik Negara: Anugerah Pengajaran (Kelompok Sastera Gunaan dan Sains Sosial Gunaan). https://jpt.mohe.gov.my/aan/senarai-penerima/aan-ke-15/pengajaran-kelompok-sastera-gunaan-dan-sains-sosial-gunaan. [Accessed 2024 Dec 13].

[56] Kementerian Pendidikan Tinggi. Anugerah Akademik Negara: Anugerah Pengajaran (Kelompok Sains Gunaan). https://jpt.mohe.gov.my/aan/senarai-penerima/aan-ke-15/anugerah-pengajaran-kelompok-sains-gunaan. [Accessed 2024 Dec 13].

[57] *New Straits Times.* Budget 2023: PM says Malaysia must embrace uncertainty in world economy this year. *New Straits Times Press.* 2023 Feb 24. https://www.nst.com.my/news/nation/2023/02/883136/budget-2023-pm-says-malaysia-must-embrace-uncertainty-world-economy-year. [Accessed 2024 Dec 13].

[58] Universiti Teknologi Malaysia. The UTM tagline. https://brand.utm.my/project/tagline/. [Accessed 2024 Dec 13].

[59] QS Quacquarelli Symonds Limited. QS world university rankings 2025: Top global universities. https://www.topuniversities.com/world-university-rankings. [Accessed 2024 Dec 13].

Part IV

Food Systems

https://doi.org/10.1142/9781800616295_0012

Chapter 12

Food System Innovations to Feed a Growing Global Muslim Population

Sophie Attwood[*,‡], Eman Alkhalawi[†], and Cother Hajat[*]

[*]*Real World Health, Oxford, UK*

[†]*Department of Community Medicine, Faculty of Medicine, King Abdulaziz University, Jeddah, Kingdom of Saudi Arabia*

[‡]*sattwood@realworldhealth.net*

Abstract

This chapter outlines major food systems challenges facing our growing global population, with a focus on high-growth Muslim majority countries where food security, human health, and the environment are all priority concerns. We outline key recommendations to ensure dietary demand in Muslim-majority countries can be met in future, including the adoption of plant-based diets, access to alternative protein sources, and greater use of technological and behavioral solutions to reduce household food waste. The viability of these solutions is considered in the context of Islamic religious beliefs and other practices unique to Muslim communities. We outline initial research insights and highlight key gaps in the current literature, including the need for more work exploring successful approaches to dietary behavior change in Muslim-majority countries, greater research coverage from a wider range of regions, especially in Asia and Africa, and the need for experts in Islamic faith and religious practices to contribute to research and innovation agendas to ensure that this work remains relevant, culturally sensitive, and acceptable to a rapidly expanding Muslim population.

1. Major Food Systems Challenges Facing the Global Population

1.1. *The environmental impact of our diets*

The global food system we rely on to feed the world's growing population is a significant contributor to climate change. Food production is a major source of greenhouse gases (GHG), such as carbon dioxide, methane, and nitrous oxide, which jointly account for around 30% of total emissions [1]. The agricultural sector is second only to the energy sector as the leading emitter of GHG emissions worldwide [2] and is also a major driver of deforestation: felling mature forests has a negative impact on biodiversity, as the habitats of many species are destroyed to make way for industrial-scale crop production, especially soybeans. This is primarily for animal feed and, to a lesser extent, for direct human consumption [3].

It is for these reasons that meat, particularly ruminant varieties such as beef and lamb, is a particularly concerning food from an environmental standpoint (see Fig. 1). Beef production emits around 60 kilograms (kg) of CO_2-equivalents (CO_2e) per kg of meat, which is more than double other types of ruminant meat including lamb (at 24 CO_2e/kg), around 10 times greater than chicken (at 6–7 CO_2e/kg), and over 12 times greater than fish (at 3–5 CO_2e/kg) [4]. Even more stark is the contrast between emissions from beef production and those from common plant-based sources of protein. Peas, for example emit 60 times less emissions than the equivalent weight of beef (at under 1 CO_2e/kg), whilst nuts produce just 0.3 CO_2e/kg and groundnuts (e.g., peanuts) just 2.5 CO_2e/kg [4].

The substantial GHG emissions footprint from beef is largely due to how it is produced rather than to later stages in the supply chain, such as its transportation, packaging, and preparation. As Fig. 1 demonstrates, most CO_2 emissions are the result of land use change (i.e., deforestation for cultivation and grazing cattle). This means less vegetation is ultimately available to absorb carbon dioxide back from the atmosphere. Livestock also emit considerable amounts of methane gas directly via their digestive processes through enteric fermentation [5], while manure from cattle is also responsible for about 65% of all nitrous oxide produced [6].

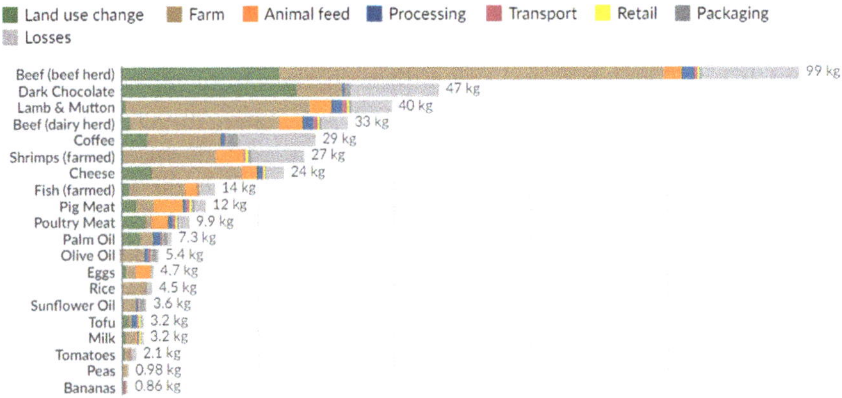

Figure 1. Food: Greenhouse gas emissions of different food types across the supply chain.

Note: Beef is one of the most GHG emission-intensive food to produce, with most emissions arising in production stages as a result of land use change and farming practices.

Source: Our World in Data CC BY 4.0 (https://creativecommons.org/licenses/by/4.0/).

1.2. *Population growth, food security, and health*

The global population continues to grow and is expected to reach almost 10 billion by mid-century [7]. These additional mouths to feed will place considerable strain on our food system, with important implications for food security, human health, and the environment. For example, if we compare current global food production capacity (in energy calories or kcals) to the amount of food energy that will be required to feed the world's population by 2050, we are estimated to be facing a 56% shortfall. Factoring in possible efficiency improvements over this time, such as reducing food waste by 25%, still leaves a possible 44% gap between the amount of food energy required and the amount actually available for human consumption by 2050 [8]. Exacerbating this problem is the fact that demand for resource-intensive animal-based foods is also rising rapidly as growing populations undergo economic development and, consequently, transition to more meat-heavy diets. Indeed, if current trends continue, demand for ruminant meat has been projected to rise by as much as 88% between 2010 and 2050 [9].

The possibility of insufficient food availability has serious implications for future populations, including increasing the risk of malnutrition.

This term encompasses access to too little food as well as access to the wrong types of food to ensure a healthy diet. In 2020, it was estimated that around 463 million adults and 155 million children were currently facing undernutrition, which is a major cause of health conditions such as stunting, wasting, underweight, and vitamin and mineral deficiencies [10]. At the same time, we are witnessing increases in overweight and obesity globally: 1.9 billion adults and 38.9 million children under 5 years are currently overweight or obese, and by 2050, this could be as high as 72% of the world's population [11]. Moreover, diet-related chronic diseases, such as cardiovascular disease, type 2 diabetes, and many cancers, are leading causes of mortality and morbidity in many countries, resulting from excess consumption of calories and sodium and insufficient intake of whole grains, fruits, and vegetables [12].

1.3. *Plant-based diets*

To better manage these outcomes, we require deep, swift, and effective changes to the global food system. This includes not only improving agricultural productivity to meet the rising demand for food but also maximizing available nutrition by changing what and how we consume and reducing the amount of edible food that goes to waste.

In terms of shifting dietary patterns, the current leading recommendation is to increase the quantity and diversity of plant-based foods in the average diet while simultaneously reducing the intake of animal-based products [13]. This recommendation is outlined in the Planetary Health Diet, first published by the EAT-Lancet Commission in 2019 [1], the exact constituents of which are detailed in Table 1 and Fig. 2.

The Planetary Health Diet advises limited ruminant meat consumption, at no more than 15 kcal/day per person, to be replaced with legumes as the primary source of protein in the diet, at 428 kcal/day. White meat and other animal-based protein sources, such as eggs and milk, may be consumed in smaller, recommended quantities [1]. As the name suggests, the Planetary Health Diet is intended to benefit human health as well as the environment. The diet is calorie controlled and encourages a diversity of highly nutritious plant-based foods, lower saturated fat intake, fewer refined grains, more fiber, and fewer added sugars. Modeled data indicate that around 11.1 million deaths could be avoided per year and premature mortality reduced by 19% by 2030 if populations in developed nations were to replace their current diets with the Planetary Health Diet [1].

Table 1. Planetary Health Dietary guidelines.

	Micronutrient Intake (Possible Range) g/day	Caloric Intake kcal/day
Whole grains		
Rice, wheat, corn & other	232 (grains 0–60% of energy)	811
Tubers or starchy vegetables		
Potatoes & casava	50 (0–100)	39
Vegetables		
All vegetables	300 (200–600)	
Dark green vegetables	100	23
Red and orange vegetables	100	30
Other vegetables	100	25
Fruits		
All fruits	200 (100–300)	126
Dairy foods		
Whole milk or derivative equivalents (e.g., cheese)	250 (0–500)	153
Protein sources		
Beef and lamb	7 (0–4)	15
Pork	7 (0–14)	15
Chicken and other poultry	29 (0–58)	62
Eggs	13 (0–75)	19
Fish	28 (0–100)	40
Legumes (dry beans, lentils & peas)	50 (0–100)	172
Soy foods	25 (0–50)	112
Peanuts	25 (0–75)	142
Tree nuts	25	149
Added fats		
Palm oil	6.8 (0–6.8)	60
Unsaturated oils	40 (20–80)	354
Dairy fats (included in milk)	0	0
Lard or tallow	5 (0–5)	36
Added sugars		
All sweeteners	31 (0–31)	120

Note: The Planetary Health Diet recommends limiting intake of animal-based foods and consuming legumes as the primary source of dietary protein.

The Planetary Health Diet is primarily to guide dietary intakes in developed and higher-income countries. For lower-income and developing countries, the issues of food affordability and accessibility must first be addressed as a priority. As a recent analysis shows, the current estimated cost of following the Planetary Health Diet is US$2.84 per person per day, which exceeds household per capita income for at least 1.58 billion people worldwide, rendering it unrealistic for around a third of the world's population [14].

Figure 2. Plate composition guidance for the Planetary Health Diet.

Note: The Planetary Health Diet recommends half of a typical meal is composed of fresh fruit and vegetables. This graphic was prepared by EAT and is included in an adapted summary of the Commission's *Food in the Anthropocene: The EAT-Lancet Commission on Healthy Diets from Sustainable Food Systems*. The entire Commission can be found online at eatforum.org/eat-lancet-commission.

Source: Used with permission of Elsevier Science & Technology Journals, from Inc., Willett *et al.*, 2019 [1]; permission conveyed through Copyright Clearance Center Inc.

1.4. *The environmental impact of food waste*

In addition to the types of food we consume, food that is never eaten is also a huge contributor to food insecurity and environmental damage. It is estimated that at least one-third of all food produced globally is wasted somewhere between the farm and fork [16]. This not only reflects a monumental mismanagement of valuable food and the energy and water used to produce it, but is also a substantial source of methane emissions as it decomposes in landfills [17]. Food waste is a particularly important problem in Muslim-majority countries in the Gulf Cooperation Council (GCC) region, including the Kingdom of Saudi Arabia (KSA) and Kuwait, which have some of the highest per capita levels of waste in the world and where over 50% of household waste streams are estimated to be comprised of organic matter [18].

As Fig. 3 shows, plant-based foods, including fruits and vegetables, are the most frequently wasted globally, followed by commonly consumed dietary staples, such as rice and wheat. When we consider the relative environmental impact of different types of wasted foods, however, a different picture emerges, and once again, ruminant meat is highlighted as a major problem. Because of the higher initial GHG footprint associated with ruminant meat production, wasting even relatively small quantities leads to the largest environmental impact of all food types [19]. As a result, shifting to sustainable plant-based diets will yield the added dividend of reducing the environmental impact of wasted food, as well as overall dietary intake.

The growing population is expected to worsen the already-sizeable problem of food waste. Accurate data on the exact amount of wasted food are relatively difficult to estimate at the global level, yet some recent attempts at modeling trajectories of change indicate that levels are expected to rise by around 2% per year between 2015 and 2030, reaching 2.1 billion tons of food waste per year by this date [20]. Given the pressing need to address the gap between future food production and projected increases in demand, effective solutions to tackle waste, especially household food waste, are urgently needed. In the following sections, we explore the two major issues of sustainable diets and food waste in the context of Muslim-majority countries worldwide, focusing on the intersection between population growth, religious beliefs, and food system issues, and identifying emergent solutions particularly relevant to a growing global Muslim population.

Figure 3. Major food groups that are wasted across the supply chain globally.

Note: Commonly, consumer vegetables are some of the most frequently wasted foods across the supply chain, while wasted bovine meat is associated with some of the largest GHG emissions footprints.

Source: Guo *et al*., 2020 [19] CC BY 4.0 (https://creativecommons.org/licenses/by/4.0/).

2. Food Systems Challenges Facing Muslim Populations

2.1. *Feeding a growing Muslim population*

When we consider where population growth is happening most rapidly, we observe that many high-growth countries are in fact home to large Muslim populations. Of the 10 billion people predicted to be living by 2050, around one-third, or 2.8 billion people, will likely follow the Islamic faith. This increase will almost close the gap on Christianity as the most followed religion worldwide (Fig. 4) and represents the fastest growth rate of any religion, at a projected 73% increase from 2010 [21].

India, despite being a Hindu-majority nation, is set to be home to the largest community of Muslims by 2050, at more than 310 million followers (18.4% of the population). As shown in Fig. 5, this will be followed by Pakistan, at over 273 million Muslims (96% of the population), Indonesia at 257 million Muslims (86.4% of the population), and Nigeria at almost 231 million Muslims (54.5% of the population) by mid-century.

The projected increase in the world's Muslim population will mostly be concentrated in Asia and Africa and will coincide with economic transitions in these regions. As incomes rise, dietary transitions are expected as more people access higher value foods, including those rich in animal protein. In Fig. 6, we chart the estimated changes in meat consumption (i.e., sheep, beef, veal, and poultry, combined) from 2023 to 2030 in the top 10 countries with the largest Muslim populations, excluding nations where meat intake data are not available (i.e., Bangladesh, Iraq, and Afghanistan) [23]. Projected increases in meat intake across high-growth countries with the largest Muslim communities range from 3% to 17%. These increases are highest in India, noting the lower 2023 baseline consumption in this country, and are lowest in Nigeria.

Considering these projected changes against Planetary Health Dietary guidelines (at a combined total of 77 kcal of ruminant meat and poultry per person per day), we find that consumption levels in Pakistan, Egypt, and Turkey will exceed recommendations by 2050, with consumption in Iran reaching over double the recommended amount by this date. If these predictions eventuate, the populations of these countries will need to find new ways to produce, or otherwise procure, the extra meat demanded by their populations. Currently, however, many do not have the capacity to produce

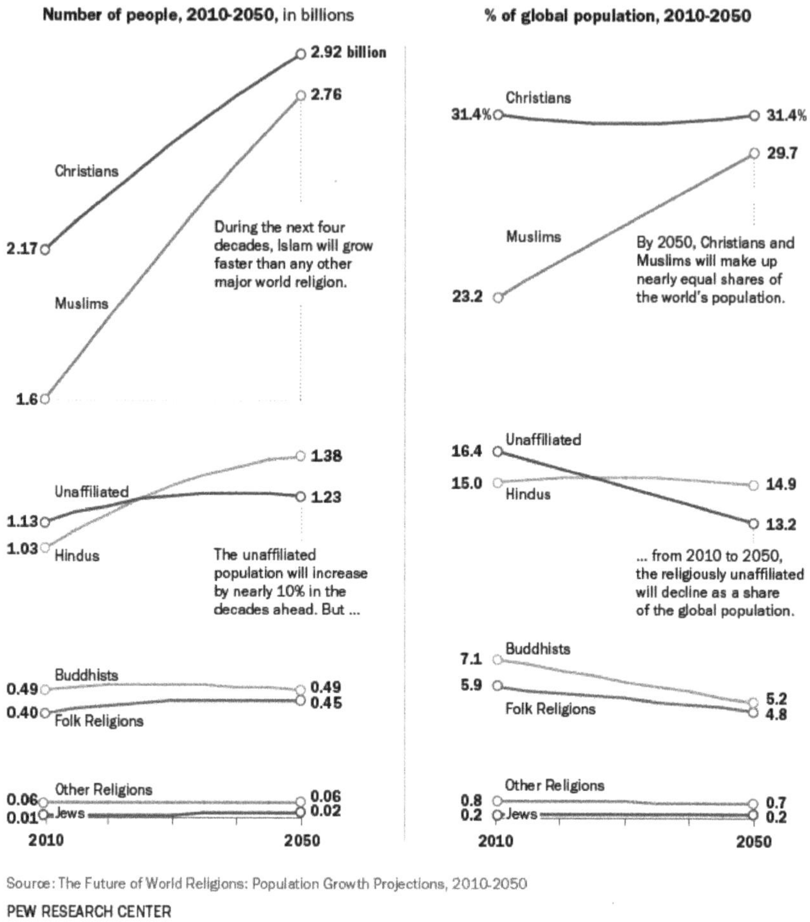

Figure 4. Projected changes in the global population following each major religion by 2050.

Note: Islam is projected to be the fasted growing religion between 2010 and 2050.
Source: With permission from Pew Research Center (2015) [21].

livestock in the quantities required and are thus reliant on imports from producer countries. This poses considerable risks for future food security. Indeed, most Muslim-majority nations do not produce or export significant quantities of ruminant meat. Of the top 10 most populous Muslim countries by 2050, India is currently the only major beef producer, ranking fifth in the world, at 5.8 million tonnes of beef produced per year [25].

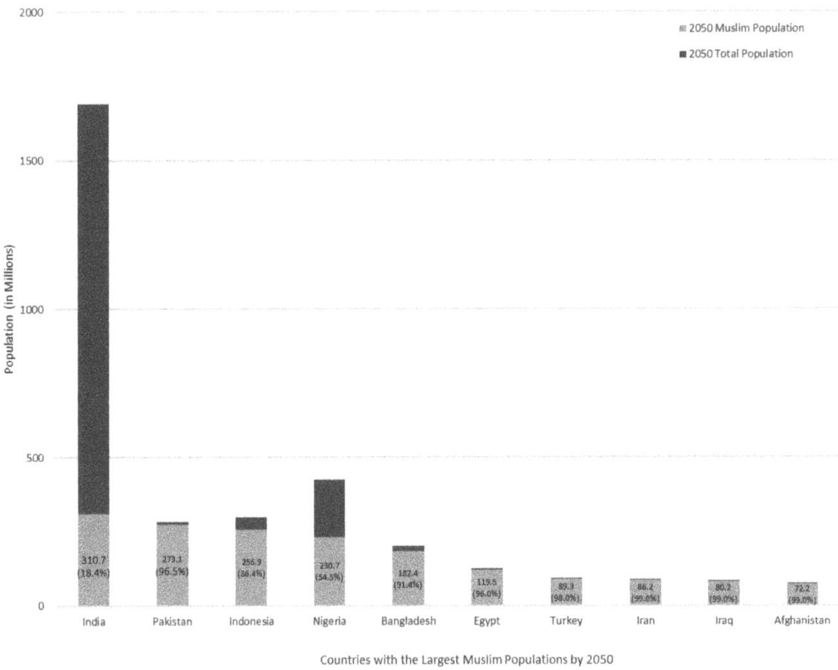

Figure 5. Top 10 nations projected to have the largest Muslim populations by 2050 (N and % of population).

Note: India, while remaining a Hindu-majority country, is expected to be home to the largest Muslim population of any country worldwide by 2050.
Source: Data from Pew Research Center, 2015 [22].

Predicted changes to the climate may also influence the availability of beef and other meats for import from producer countries. For example, increased temperatures may lead to heat stress in cattle, impacting live-weight gains, milk yield, fertility rates, and animal welfare. Changing temperatures may also increase the presence of ticks, flies, and worms, which carry pathogens and diseases that affect cattle and can degrade meat production efficiency. Drought may negatively impact the availability of sufficient pastureland, leading to poorer nutritional status and slower growth rates in cattle [26]. Altogether, despite rising demand, these factors may increasingly limit the supply of ruminant meat, resulting in price hikes and shortages.

Certain Muslim-majority countries, especially those in heat-stressed regions such as the GCC countries of Bahrain, Kuwait, Qatar, Oman, the

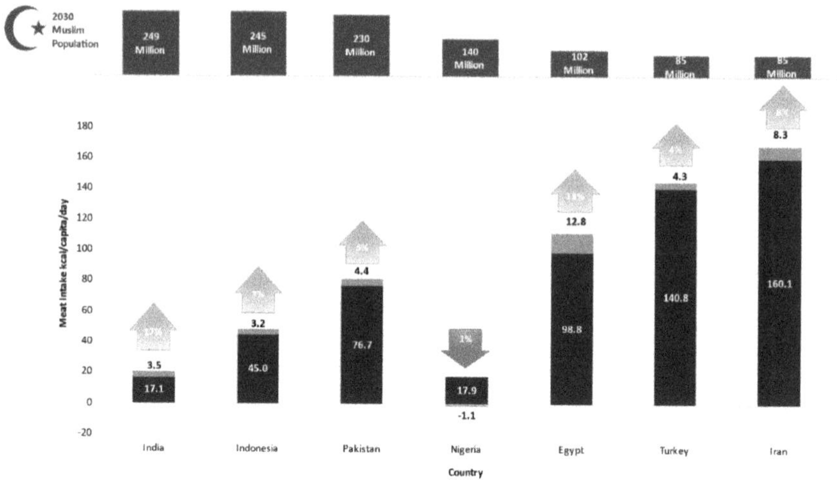

Figure 6. Projected change in meat intake in the most populous Muslim countries by 2030. Meat consumption is predicted to rise across all of the most populous Muslim countries except Nigeria by 2030.

Notes: Comparison with baseline year 2023; estimates are up to 2030 (not to 2050) due to the available projections for meat consumption. Darker bar color represents 2023 consumption levels and lighter bar color represents change in consumption to 2030. By courtesy of *Green Queen*.
Source: Hajat and Attwood (2023) [24] and reproduced by courtesy of *Green Queen*.

KSA, and the United Arab Emirates (UAE), are especially vulnerable to these risks. GCC countries already import over 85% of their total food and around 62% of their total meat [27]. Given the limited scope for increasing national production of beef due to the arid climate, topography, and limited space for large-scale livestock production, these countries have a particularly urgent need to find alternative ways to meet their growing demands for animal-based foods. This can include diversifying importer nations to reduce reliance on a sole partner country as well as encouraging changes to national diets, such as lower consumption of imported meats, greater intake of native plant species or underutilized crops, and changing farming practices to reduce requirements for imported fertilizers [28]. It is relevant to note that no Muslim-majority nation currently ranks within the top 10 on the Global Food Security Index (GFSI), with the highest listed currently being the UAE, at 23rd place [29]. Instead, Qatar, Oman, Bahrain, the KSA, Jordan, Turkey, and Kuwait all feature within the top

50, while the KSA has set a national target to fall within the top 10 most food-secure regions of the world by 2030 [29].

At the same time, many lower-income Muslim-majority countries are also facing challenges to securing access to food. These include nations facing prolonged food insecurity and acute catastrophic conditions, such as Yemen, Afghanistan, Somalia, Sudan, Syria, and Palestine. As ongoing geopolitical turbulence has already demonstrated in recent years, conflict within and between major food-producing nations can have severe downstream effects on importer nations due to export bans, logistical complications, and disrupted production [28]. Where these factors coexist with poverty, insufficient food reserves, political instability, a lack of infrastructure, problematic existing agriculture practices, and weak commodity prices, the risk of food insecurity increases substantially [30]. Of all the countries listed on the GFSI, for example, Syria currently ranks the lowest, at 113th on the index [29].

Adding to this, climate change has a strong potential to worsen food insecurity in many Muslim-majority countries. For example, one recent study focusing on the Middle East and North Africa (MENA) region (including the Maghreb, Near East, Middle East, and Turkey) estimated that climate change has the potential to increase food import dependence to 50% by 2050. The Maghreb region (Algeria, Libya, Mauritania, Morocco, Western Sahara, and Tunisia) may be particularly affected, potentially losing half its cultivable land and reaching 70% import dependency, while the Near East (Israel, Jordan, Lebanon, the West Bank and Gaza, and Syria) could lose a quarter of cultivable land, raising import dependency to 67% by 2050 [31].

2.2. *Food waste in Muslim-majority countries*

Compounding food security risks is the extremely high level of food waste in many Muslim-majority countries. For example, Fig. 7 displays levels of household food waste per capita across various Organization for Islamic Cooperation (OIC) member countries. This is compared against various non-OIC countries and against the global average. As is clear, food waste in OIC countries is considerably higher than in many other regions, reaching elevated levels in Nigeria, at more than double that found in the United Kingdom (UK), the US, and China [32].

Food waste is not just a by-product of a country's wealth and abundant access to food; it is a serious issue for regions with very different levels of development. For example, the highest levels of food waste, as previously noted, are in Nigeria, a lower middle-income country, followed by Bahrain, a high-income country, and then Iraq, which is upper middle-income. Considering differences in the causes of food waste between these regions, the exceedingly high waste levels found in Nigeria can be attributed more to factors at the pre-consumption stage, such as a lack of processing facilities and inefficient logistical infrastructure to transport food under optimal conditions. This means lower-quality products with shorter shelf lives eventually reach end-consumers, where they spoil more quickly [33]. Conversely, for higher-income OIC countries, such as the KSA, Bahrain, Qatar, and the UAE, more relevant drivers include over-purchasing of food and cultural norms that value abundance and demonstrating hospitality by serving food excess to guests [18].

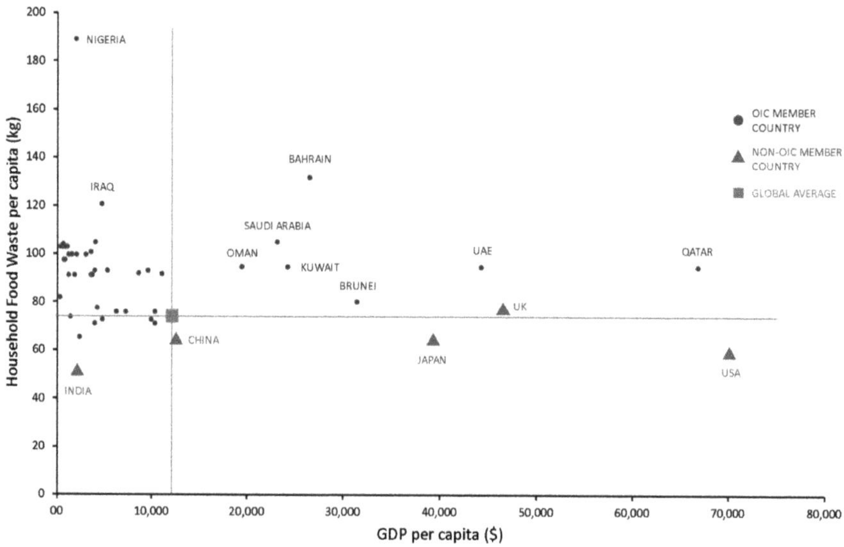

Figure 7. Household food waste per capita in Muslim countries compared to other regions.

Note: Food waste is high in OIC member countries compared to other regions globally, and is especially elevated in Nigeria.

Source: Used with permission of Elsevier Science & Technology Journals, from Jameel [32]; permission conveyed through Copyright Clearance Center, Inc.

3. Islamic Guidance on Diet and Food Waste

3.1. *Halal dietary guidelines*

Adherents of Islam are asked to follow a "halal" diet, which refers to food and drink consistent with Islamic dietary laws. Food restriction in Islam is centered around animal products in terms of the type consumed and the way in which the animal died (see Table 2 for further details). While some meat is explicitly forbidden in a halal diet (e.g., porcine-derived products), other types are not explicitly non-permissible but are broadly discouraged by Muslim scholars due to their "repulsive" or "suspicious" nature [34]. Most insects (besides locusts) and reptiles fall into this category, although recent Islamic schools of thought are shifting on the issue of consumption of other insect varieties, such as food worms [35].

Additional Islamic rulings are also related to concepts of necessity or a lack of an alternative. For example, some medicines that contain porcine derivates are acceptable for Muslims if they are the only options available or have been substantially physically or chemically transformed (e.g., heparin, heart valves, and gelatine in medication casing) [37]. Moreover, for safe consumption, all food should also be free of obvious harm, such as diseases or poisonous substances [34].

Within a halal diet, all animals that are consumed should be slaughtered, rather than killed by another method such as blunt force or electrocution, and should not have died naturally (e.g., from a disease or old age) or accidentally (e.g., fallen off a cliff or killed by another animal). Islam

Table 2. Animal-Based Foods Prohibited in a Halal Diet.

Prohibited Foods	**Further Details**
Pork (Quran 2:173)	Most scholars agree this includes pork derivatives such gelatine, collagen, and enzymes.
Predators (animals with fangs and claws) [36]	Including birds such as eagles and vultures.
Blood (Quran 5:3)	Including blood products. Liver, spleen, and bone marrow are permissible provided the animal has been slaughtered and bled.
Harmful [34]	There are various opinions on eating insects but a consensus that locusts are permissible while harmful, poisonous, or unclean insects such as flies and cockroaches are prohibited.

also states that meat should not have been sacrificed to another deity. The Islamic faith is clear that animal welfare should be observed throughout the slaughter process and measures taken to minimize suffering or stress to the animal: For example, a sharp knife or similar device is used for slaughter, the knife should not be sharpened in front of the animal, and the animal should not witness the slaughter of another animal or be exposed to its blood [36].

Muslim scholars generally agree that all seafood is permissible for Muslims to consume, regardless of the type or mode of death (Quran 5:96), while other issues have been disputed or are considered flexible: For example, stunning before slaughter, the slaughterer being non-Muslim (e.g., a Jew or a Christian), and the requirement to invoke the name of Allah (God) before slaughter.

Due to complexities in following halal guidelines and differences in how the rules are interpreted, several halal certification bodies emerged in the early 1990s to provide general oversight and regulation. The presence of halal certification is now required to clear products for import into Muslim-majority countries and provides assurance to Muslim consumers worldwide that production processes are compliant with Islamic principles. At present, there are over 400 halal-certifying bodies. The fact that no single universal halal certification exists is ascribed to differences in standards and practices between countries and the difficulties associated with unifying these, as well as competition between the certification bodies for brand awareness [38].

There remains considerable diversity among Islamic schools and scholars regarding other foods that may be considered permissible, especially regarding the purpose of the product. For example, the Malaysian Halal Product Research Institute has set an upper limit of 1% on the amount of alcohol permissible in food or beverages that is not intentionally produced as an alcoholic beverage [39]. This decision was based on confidence that very small volumes of alcohol would not impact the mental state of the consumer in regular culinary amounts, for example, as alcohol is used as a preservative in medicines or flavoring.

There are also different interpretations of the use of prohibited foods during production, which is important in the context of the increasing globalization of food markets and the complexity of international supply chains. For example, widespread production of processed food raises concerns among Muslims about the use of porcine derivatives in food manufacturing and processing (i.e., gelatine, enzymes, and fats), which renders products non-permissible even when present in small amounts. The acceptability of non-pork additives sourced from non-halal slaughtered animals is less clear, with important implications for some emerging food technologies, such as cell cultured meat (see subsequent sections).

3.2. *Islamic guidance on plant-based diets*

Plant-based diets are a simpler consideration within the Islamic faith, given that all fruits, vegetables, nuts, and legumes are halal by default. Within Islamic guidance, there is no explicit mention of restricting or eliminating animal products, except for prohibitions on hunting land animals by pilgrims and within the premise of the holy mosque in Mecca, while catching seafood is permitted (Quran 5:95). Traditionally, for many Muslim communities, meat has been viewed as a luxury, to be consumed only on special occasions (e.g., at Eid or at the birth of a child) or to be shared with a group. A saying ascribed to Ali ibn Abi Talib, the prophet's cousin, son-in-law, and fourth Khalifa, states, "*do not make your stomachs graveyards for animals.*"

Some Islamic scholars have actively encouraged vegetarian diets, acknowledging that the environmental benefits of a meat-free diet align with the Islamic teaching that humans are guardians of the earth and are therefore responsible for preserving it (Quran 10:14) and that Muslims must respond to emerging threats and adopt practices that benefit wider society and humanity. In addition, adopting a healthier and more sustainable plant-based diet may be considered a good way to uphold at least two of the five key objectives that must be preserved in Islamic law: the *preservation of life* and *lineage*. Opponents of vegetarianism do, however, view the exclusion of meat as "prohibiting that which is halal," or in contradiction to the Islamic tradition of the "Udhiya" (annual sacrifice at the end of the pilgrimage period), which is considered by some as a religious duty for those who have the means, but as Sunnah (the Prophet's tradition) by others.

Beyond plant-based foods, Islam also encourages various other practices around the diet, including exercising restraint and discouraging overindulgence. This is exemplified by the Hadeeth (the Prophet's saying) to moderate intake:

> *No child of Adam fills a container worse than his stomach. A few morsels that keep his back upright are sufficient for him. If he has to, then he should keep one-third for food, one-third for drink and one third for his breathing [40].*

In addition, regular fasting is also encouraged, as is taking care of one's body, as per the Prophet's saying in response to one of his companions fasting daily, "*your body has a right over you*" [41].

Fasting during Ramadan also has some potential to reduce the environmental impact of the diet by encouraging reduced consumption. However, recent research in Muslim communities in Iran, Ghana, and Lebanon indicates that changes to the diet during Ramadan are not always in the direction of reduced intake, with higher consumption of milk and meat witnessed in some cases and of sugar-sweetened foods, such as cakes and pastries, in others [42]. This shift in food choice may have negative downstream effects on the composition of leftover food, potentially increasing the GHG emissions of food waste during Ramadan. Conversely, other research exploring dietary changes during Ramadan in a sample of Nigerian Muslims found lower intake of pastries, salty snacks, and energy, carbonated, or sugar-sweetened beverages but increased consumption of home-made foods, dairy, and vegetables [43].

3.3. *Islamic guidance on food waste*

Islamic teachings also directly discourage food waste: "*Eat and drink and do not waste, for God does not love the wasteful*" (Quran 7:31). Moreover, feeding those in need is given a high priority in Islam and is emphasized on several occasions, such as donating a given amount of food on behalf of every household member at the end of Ramadan (Zakah), donating and gifting two-thirds of the Udhiya, and donating to repent for certain actions or in case of an inability to fast during Ramadan. The Quran also condemns the destruction of crops (Quran 2:204) and asks that Muslims eat of the fruit of gardens and give their dues (Zakah) on the day of their harvest and not waste (Quran 5:141).

As with research exploring the environmental implications of Ramadan fasting, studies of the relationship between the Islamic faith and food waste are also mixed. For example, one study of Muslim Arabs revealed that food waste increases during Ramadan, primarily due to larger quantities of food being prepared for Iftar meals to break daily fasts, which encourages diners to put more food on their plates [44]. At the same time, other research has found more beneficial associations between religiosity in Muslim communities and lower food waste [45–47], indicating multiple different pathways through which Islamic teachings can influence practices around food preparation, consumption, and waste.

Further research has also demonstrated strong links between local cultural practices and food waste across a range of Muslim communities. For example, in one qualitative study from Iraq, waste was associated with the habit of cooking fresh food daily and with an implicit cultural norm of demonstrating generosity. Conversely, Muslim Arabs in Israel have identified the collective experience of food scarcity as a driver of household food waste. That is, historical memories of times when group survival was dependent on the ability to stockpile food have led to present-day compensatory behaviors, such as overprovisioning of food at home in case of need [48].

4. Future Food System Solutions for Muslim Populations

4.1. *Actions to promote sustainable diets in Muslim-majority countries*

Recognizing the potential for future challenges to food systems, many Muslim-majority countries have already begun to develop and implement policies to shift their populations toward more sustainable plant-based diets. Leading this is the UAE, hosts of the 28th Conference of Parties (COP28) climate summit in December 2023, which led the Declaration on Sustainable Agriculture, Resilient Food Systems, and Climate Action. The declaration includes a clear call to shift from "higher greenhouse gas-emitting practices to more sustainable production and consumption approaches, including by reducing food loss and waste and promoting sustainable aquatic blue foods" but falls short of explicitly mentioning limiting the intake of ruminant meat, nor of the exact approaches to be implemented to reach these goals. The declaration has so far been signed by 159 countries, including the Muslim-majority countries Pakistan, Indonesia, Nigeria, Egypt, and Bangladesh. Further Muslim-majority signatories include leaders from all the high-income GCC countries, with the exception of the KSA, and a number of MENA countries, including Jordan, Lebanon, Morocco, Palestine, and Yemen.

At the country level, however, sustainability considerations have yet to be incorporated into national dietary guidelines or into nationally determined contributions submitted as part of the COP28 process. Indeed, of the GCC countries including the UAE, Qatar is currently the only one to explicitly recommend a plant-based diet, counseling its population to "*Emphasize a plant-based diet, including vegetables, fruit, whole grain cereals, legumes, nuts and seed*" [49]. Within the Qatari dietary guidelines, efforts have also been made to separate fruit and vegetables into two independent food categories to emphasize their importance in the diet [50]. Similarly, legumes and pulses are also now presented as independent categories in the updated Indian dietary guidelines for the same reason [51]. While not explicitly stating the recommendation to adopt a plant-based diet, the National Nutrition Strategy of Oman 2014–2050 places strong emphasis on promoting fruit, vegetables, and fish, recognizing the associated health benefits of these products as well as acknowledging that a greater consumption of these products would support national food security, given the high levels of self-sufficiency in their production, including 100% self-sufficiency for fish [52].

The Saudi Food Palm also emphasizes the consumption of a wide variety of different foods, recommending that most of the diet should be comprised of plant-based sources, such as cereals, fruit, and vegetables, while the consumption of meat and other foods high in saturated fat, cholesterol, salt, and sugar be limited.

In the future, sustainability considerations will need to be more explicitly incorporated into the dietary guidelines of many Muslim-majority countries, although care must be taken to ensure that these are tailored to local food contexts. For example, in India, the country expected to have the largest Muslim community by 2050, the typical diet currently contains 21% fewer calories from protein sources than is recommended in the Planetary Health Diet, with even the richest 5% of India's population consuming less than half of the 726 protein calories recommended per day, primarily in the form of milk and milk products [53]. Conversely, eggs are one of the most highly consumed foods in Muslim-majority Indonesia, with milk being a far less common source of dietary protein, [54] while the Iranian diet also contains low levels of milk and milk products, as well as plant-based foods, with an excess of bread, rice, pasta, red meat, eggs, fats, and sugar [55].

As is evident, the Planetary Health Diet recommendations must be tailored for each individual nation to ensure appropriateness, taking the current diet as a starting point for change and working to optimize this rather than applying a "top down" set of dietary recommendations that do not suit local food cultures (i.e., imposing the Mediterranean diet). In addition, how these guidelines are communicated to populations must be modified for each country, including through the use of relevant graphics, such as the Saudi Food Palm and the Qatari clam shell [49].

Dietary guidelines are, however, just one of the many tools available to Muslim-majority countries to encourage a shift toward healthier and sustainable diets. We know from existing efforts in other geographies that improvements in access to and availability of tasty and appealing plant-based options, supportive policies and fiscal measures, and extensive roll-out of behavioral change interventions are all required to meet the goals of the COP28 declaration. Following this, many Muslim-majority countries have started to implement a range of policies and actions to create change. For example, KSA has increased its national focus on food security and food sustainability by establishing a Food Security Authority which explicitly aims to measure and reduce food and water waste, increase crop efficiency, develop the national food security strategy, propose laws and regulations, and develop emergency response plans. Along with the UAE, the KSA has also started to position itself as a leader in food technology and innovation, launching a large regional food expo in 2023 and extensively promoting the nation's flagship "NEOM" project, which aims to build a healthy, sustainable smart city in the northwest Tabuk province. At the same time, the UAE has led the development and coordinated the signing of the aforementioned COP28 food declaration and demonstrated its willingness to take action on sustainable diets by ensuring that two-thirds of all food served during the conference was entirely plant-based.

Similarly, Iran is one of the more active Muslim-majority countries in terms of developing and implementing food-related policies, although to date, these have primarily been directed at improving population health. These include financial measures such as imposing a tax of 10% on unhealthy food, a 15% tax on soft drinks, reducing subsidies for sugar and vegetable oil, and eliminating milk subsidies [55]. These actions are not without criticism, however, given their potential to exacerbate food insecurity in vulnerable groups [56].

4.2. *Drivers of dietary change in Muslim-majority countries*

Currently limiting efforts to encourage dietary transitions in Muslim-majority countries is a lack of good-quality data on the reasons why people start and succeed in changing their diets. At present, there is little available research exploring plant-based food consumption patterns in many Muslim communities, which is a knowledge gap that must be rapidly filled if effective behavioral change approaches are to be successfully modified and adopted in high-growth Muslim regions.

For example, a recent review exploring consumer use of nutrition labels in Arab Muslim countries found research has so far been published from only 8 of 22 possible nations. In general, these studies showed that consumers were broadly aware that nutritional labels exist and, yet, do not necessarily have a clear understanding of their meaning, nor how to use them to inform food choices [57]. Moreover, an additional study has also shown that over half of Lebanese consumers stated that they did not look at labels at all when purchasing food, while only 42% of Bahraini shoppers reported reading these [58]. Another similar study examining the impact of calorie labeling in restaurants in the UAE also demonstrated that only a third of participants (34%) believed they had sufficient knowledge to make lower-calorie food choices when eating out [59].

In terms of plant-based diets, some recent research from the KSA has identified a range of prosocial and altruistic motivations for the adoption of vegetarian and vegan eating patterns, alongside the widely stated goal of wanting to lose weight. While these reasons are no different from those in many non-Muslim countries, the authors note comparatively lower perceived stigmatization associated with vegan and vegetarian eating patterns in the KSA because the diets themselves are not so explicitly linked to an ethical ideology [60].

At the same time, other studies exploring diet and lifestyle changes in the KSA have identified particularly poor dietary habits in the country, including low intake of fruit and vegetables, with only 6% of the population achieving the five-a-day goal and a very small percentage of the population following plant-based diets [61]. Yet, despite this and the fact that the Arab Gulf states, including the KSA, are currently home to around 93 million people, a recent review of behavioral change trials to promote positive lifestyle changes in the region found only three studies that had explicitly tested dietary change interventions. All of these studies were targeted at improving health endpoints rather than focusing on the environmental sustainability of food choices [62].

4.3. *Alternative proteins and food technologies*

To accelerate a transition toward lower meat consumption, many food companies are now developing alternative protein products. These are intended to provide consumers with a wider range of protein options, thus preventing them from solely consuming proteins from animal sources. They include inherently plant-based offerings as well as more novel products such as insect-based or lab-cultivated meat. These are displayed in more detail in Table 3.

If alt-protein companies are to succeed in attracting a substantial share of the global Muslim meat market, a fundamental issue to address is whether these products can be certified as halal or permissible. This is generally unproblematic in the case of 100% plant-based meat analogs but is more complex for cultivated or hybrid products that contain cells derived from animals or from insect-based sources of protein. Given the novelty of these foods, there is some evidence that Muslim consumers currently consider them as potentially risky or unsafe and strongly demand halal certification from known and trusted bodies in order to be willing to try or adopt them into their regular diet [64].

In 2022 the Assembly of Muslim Jurists of America deemed cultivated meat provisionally permissible by default for the first time, while in 2024, the Singaporean Islamic Council also announced that cultivated meat is potentially permissible for those following a halal diet if certain conditions can be met. However, an ultimate ruling on the issue will still depend on how these technologies develop in relation to the source of used stem cells, additives, and their health effects [65]. Key issues under debate include whether cultivated meat contravenes Islam's "Natural Law," as the production process can be seen as "playing God." Another issue is that cells are often harvested from live animals, which has been compared to the prohibited practice of eating parts cut off a live animal. Indeed, Nahdlatul Ulama, an Islamic organization in Indonesia, and scholars in Pakistan have both stated that cultivated meat cells must be taken from a halal slaughtered animal, while the head of the Association of Sharia Scholars in the GCC countries has said that cultured meats can be halal, even if taken from live animals [66].

Another potentially problematic issue for Muslims is the use of cell culture media (in which cultivated meat cells are propagated) that are inconsistent with halal laws. For many products, the medium in which extracted cells are developed currently contains fetal bovine serum, which is post-clotted blood fluid obtained from unborn cattle. Blood is

Table 3. Types of alternative proteins.

Name	Brief Description	Example
Plant-based	These products use plant-based ingredients, such as beans, peas, lentils, and soy, to create meat substitute products.	One market leader is Beyond Meat, which produces burgers and sausages from pea, mung and fava beans, and brown rice. Beetroot and apple extract are added to mimic the coloring of meat.
Cultivated meat	*In vitro* laboratory-grown meat from cultured cells. Also known as cell-cultivated, cell-based, or cell-cultured meat.	The first ever commercial sale of cultivated meat was by an American start-up, Eat Just, in 2013, served in a restaurant in Singapore. While still not widely available in many regions, there are rapid developments in this industry. Companies producing these products include Memphis Meat and Mosa Meats Inc.
Fermentation-derived processes	***Traditional fermentation*** uses microbial anaerobic digestion to improve the taste or functionality of plant-based ingredients. ***Biomass fermentation*** involves the rapid growth of microorganisms which form the basis of the product. ***Precision fermentation*** uses microorganisms as hosts to produce specific ingredients used in alt-meat.	Soybeans are fermented into tempeh. Mycoprotein Quorn is made from fermenting fungal spores. The heme protein (soy leghemoglobin) added to the Impossible Food burger to improve its distinctive meaty flavor.
Hybrid products	Produced by combining reduced portions of animal-based meat or cultivated ingredients (i.e., fat) with plant-based ingredients.	The Rebel Meat "semi-vegetarian" burger contains 50% beef and 50% plant-based ingredients.

Table 3. (*Continued*)

Name	Brief Description	Example
Insects	Processed edible insects, consumed either whole or ground, and used as ingredients to enhance the nutrient profile of existing products.	Fazer, a Finnish company that manufactures bread using cricket flour, and Eat Grub produce energy bars enriched with cricket powder.
Algae	Processed edible algae, mainly used as food ingredients or dietary supplements.	Examples include Spirulina or Chlorella.

Source: Reproduced from [63].

considered unclean according to Islamic scriptures (Quran 5:3), and this point has been specifically highlighted by the Malaysian Halal standard (MS 1500/2019) [67]. This problem may, however, soon prove obsolete given that wholly plant-based media have recently been developed, partly in response to demand from other consumer segments, such as ethical vegans and vegetarians, who are also unwilling to consume cultivated meat that contains animal-sourced ingredients [68]. Similarly, insect-based protein represents another area of debate, with locusts generally considered acceptable to consume by Muslims, but clear guidance on a wide range of other insect types is still pending [35].

Beyond halal considerations, far more research is still needed to understand the factors that influence the adoption of alt proteins in Muslim countries. Where sparse data already exist, there is some indication that Muslim consumers are willing to try these products but share many of the perceived barriers to habitual consumption as other consumer groups. For example, acceptance of novel proteins tends to be higher when Muslim consumers are more familiar with the products, if they taste good, are affordable, and when consumers are informed of their potential health and environmental benefits compared to traditional meat and dairy. Indeed, one recent study of Muslim consumers in the UK found that British Muslims participating in a willingness-to-pay experiment were willing to pay extra for cultivated meat (15%) compared to non-Muslim participants (6%), potentially reflecting greater latent demand for Muslim consumers who may have more stringent dietary requirements and thus fewer available choice [69]. In this study, cultivated meat characteristics (health, safety, and nutrition) were the leading drivers of greater willingness to pay more for these products among Muslim than non-Muslim consumers.

Additionally, there are a range of more specific drivers of alt-protein adoption unique to Muslim consumers. For example, given that plant-based, hybrid, and cultivated products can all be produced in highly controlled environments, this may limit the potential for contamination with non-halal animal ingredients, thereby overcoming fears around product impurity. This is particularly likely with the introduction of 3D printing technologies, which are currently being developed for the production of cultivated meat. These technologies will be able to assure Muslim consumers of the source of their halal products and so have strong potential to guard against food fraud in meat supply chains [70]. Similarly, in the future, halal products, including alternative proteins, can also be tagged and tracked using blockchain technologies, which will provide consumers with a transparent record of transactions for greater visibility on product and ingredient sources. Some have even suggested combining blockchain innovations with DNA-sequencing technologies to determine if halal products have become contaminated on their journey from production to consumer [71].

Alternative protein products may additionally help Muslim consumers navigate arguments around whether meat should be stunned prior to slaughter, which is generally considered more humane, but some believe it is inconsistent with halal rules [72]. Although Islam emphasizes the importance of animal welfare before and throughout the slaughter process, modern farming practices may fail to maintain these principles. As a result, consumers looking for halal products that ensure animal welfare are currently left with few choices.

Given the extent of population growth in Muslim-majority countries and the fact that demand for meat is also growing in many of these regions, alt protein is a highly promising solution with the potential to reduce the environmental impact of the diet in these regions. However, to ensure adoption, alt-protein manufacturers must develop products that are explicitly designed to meet the dietary expectations of different Muslim communities, including developing formats that align with local meat dishes (i.e., kebabs, stews, or curried/roasted meat dishes) rather than imposing formats developed for non-Muslim, Western markets (i.e., burgers, sausages, or nuggets). This gap in the market is beginning to be addressed by various start-up companies emerging from the Gulf region, including Switch Foods in Abu Dhabi and Myco Technology in Oman, plus those in India, including GoodDot, Imagine Meat, and Wakao Foods. Other examples of companies addressing food system issues in Muslim-majority nations include Sawani, a dairy company launched in the KSA in 2023, which produces locally sourced camel milk as an alternative to traditional dairy.

4.4. *Technologies to reduce food waste*

Many Muslim-majority countries have already made significant strides toward addressing the complex problem of food waste across food supply chains. One notable example is Turkey, which has worked with the United Nations Food and Agriculture Organization (FAO) to develop a national action plan on food waste reduction known as "SAVE FOOD" [73]. This outlines clear targets around technological innovation, including optimizing food packaging via modifications to sizing and novel materials, enabling better cold chain management by monitoring storage conditions, and developing innovative applications for food preservation and storage. One example is Farmhood, a Turkish start-up that produces a wide range of freeze-dried fruits and vegetables, thereby helping to preserve the nutritional value of food and extend product shelf life.

Another Muslim-majority country taking strong action on food waste is the KSA, one of the countries with the highest levels of food waste in the world, at between 165 and 511 kg per person per year, depending on the data source. Indeed, the problem of food waste is estimated to cost the KSA economy around US$13 billion annually [74]. Reasons for such high waste in the KSA have, in part, been attributed to unique cultural aspects, including the very high value placed on generous hospitality and serving abundant food to guests [75].

With the KSA also being an affluent country, food expenditure makes up a relatively small percentage of total household budgets, which is further supported by price caps and subsidies introduced by the KSA government to ensure that food prices remain relatively stable for the local population [74]. However, recent analysis has shown that levels of food waste are significantly higher in more food-insecure households in the KSA, suggesting a more complex relationship between food affordability, valuation, and waste [75]. Other research has also identified important conflicts between behavioral priorities in Arab states, which may inadvertently lead to higher levels of waste. For example, there are contrasts between food waste largely being viewed as "haram" (i.e., a behavior that is forbidden) and a desire to outwardly demonstrate one's affluence, including through food-related behaviors. These findings demonstrate the fact that food waste is rarely due to food being undervalued but is rather the result of competing aspirations about the role and purpose of food in daily life [48].

In response to this sizeable problem, the KSA government has launched a range of initiatives with a strong focus on utilizing technology and innovation, as well as making food waste a priority area in the KSA's Vision 2030. Examples of technological innovations include three deals signed by the Saudi Ministry of Environment, Water and Agriculture with organizations to employ artificial intelligence (AI) to tackle food waste, in addition to developing "smart farms" with calibrated lighting, big data analysis, remote sensors, and solutions to detect disease in food crops and potentially reduce waste on the farm.

The UAE government is another that has introduced various initiatives to cut food waste, which is also exceptionally high in this country. This has included activities to boost donations of viable excess food to the UAE Food Bank, which works to redistribute this to communities in need. In addition, the UAE has also launched programs to repurpose waste into animal feed and has encouraged hospitality companies, which make up a large part of the local tourist economy, to work toward concrete food waste targets [76]. Finally, the UAE is also currently exploring options to upscale their waste-to-energy capabilities, which involve using biochemical or thermochemical conversion techniques to turn wasted food into fuel sources, for example, using anaerobic bacteria to convert food waste into methane biogas, which can then be used as a source of fuel. These technologies are useful for small nations, such as the UAE, as they help avoid the accumulation of waste in scarce landfill sites. They can also help oil-producer nations such as the UAE adopt alternative fuel sources as they work toward their climate commitments of 44% of energy production from renewable sources by 2050 [77].

5. Conclusion

Rapid growth in the global Muslim population comes with the challenge of ensuring access to sufficient food for healthy and sustainable diets for all. Without substantial changes to the types of foods that are consumed and to the quantity of food that is wasted, we are likely to face difficulties in feeding the world's population – including 2.8 billion Muslim consumers – by the year 2050. Solutions are readily available, including widespread adoption of plant-based foods and alternative protein sources and greater implementation of technologies and policies to reduce household food waste. However, these solutions do not constitute a one-size-fits-all approach, and their success will depend on their acceptance and utilization among different populations worldwide. To ensure swift and timely uptake in Muslim communities spanning developed and developing regions of the world, far more research is required to understand how cultural practices and religious belief systems – including halal dietary requirements – will likely interact with food system policies, behavioral change interventions, and technological advances. Without addressing these critical gaps in our insights toward the soon-to-be 30% global Muslim population, we run the risk of missing current targets to tackle planetary health by transforming the food system.

References

[1] Willett W, Rockström J, Loken B, Springmann M, Lang T, Vermeulen S, Garnett T, Tilman D, DeClerck F, Wood A, Jonell M, Clark M, Gordon LJ, Fanzo J, Hawkes C, Zurayk R, Rivera JA, De Vries W, Majele Sibanda L, Afshin A, Chaudhary A, Herrero M, Agustina R, Branca F, Lartey A, Fan S, Crona B, Fox E, Bignet V, Troell M, Lindahl T, Singh S, Cornell SE, Srinath Reddy K, Narain S, Nishtar S, Murray CJL. Food in the Anthropocene: the EAT-Lancet Commission on healthy diets from sustainable food systems. *Lancet*. 2019;393(10170):447–492. DOI: 10.1016/S0140-6736(18)31788-4.

[2] World Economic Forum. 3 charts that show countries and sectors with the highest greenhouse gas emissions. https://www.weforum.org/agenda/2020/12/climate-change-greenhouse-gas-emissions-environment-paris-agreement/. [Accessed 2023 Dec 24].

[3] Pendrill F, Persson UM, Godar J, Kastner T, Moran D, Schmidt S, Wood, R. Agricultural and forestry trade drives large share of tropical deforestation emissions. *Global Environ Change*. 2019;56:1–10. https://doi.org/10.1016/j.gloenvcha.2019.03.002.

[4] Ritchie H. You want to reduce the carbon footprint of your food? Focus on what you eat, not whether your food is local. Our World in Data. https://ourworldindata.org/food-choice-vs-eating-local. [Accessed 2023 Dec 29].

[5] Chang J, Peng S, Ciais P, Saunois M, Dangal SRS, Herrero M, Havlík P, Tian H, Bousquet P. Revisiting enteric methane emissions from domestic ruminants and their δ13CCH4 source signature. *Nat Commun.* 2019;10:3420. https://doi.org/10.1038/s41467-019-11066-3.

[6] Rivera JE, Chará J. CH4 and N2O emissions from cattle excreta: A review of main drivers and mitigation strategies in grazing systems. *Front Sustain Food Syst.* 2021;5. DOI: 10.3389/fsufs.2021.657936.

[7] World Bank. World's population will reach nearly 10 billion by 2050. https://datatopics.worldbank.org/world-development-indicators/stories/world-population-will-continue-to-grow.html. [Accessed 2023 Dec 23].

[8] Searchinger T, Waite R, Hanson C, Ranganathan J, Dumas P, and Matthews E. World resources report: Creating a sustainable food future–A menu of solutions to feed nearly 10 billion people by 2050. World Resources Institute. Final report. 2019.

[9] Ranganathan J, Waite R, Searchinger T, Hanson C. How to sustainably feed 10 billion people by 2050, in 21 charts. World Resources Institute; 5 Dec 2018. https://www.wri.org/insights/how-sustainably-feed-10-billion-people-2050-21-charts. [Accessed 2024 Dec 29].

[10] World Health Organization. Malnutrition fact sheet. https://www.who.int/news-room/fact-sheets/detail/malnutrition. [Accessed 2023 Dec 24].

[11] Bodirsky BL, Dietrich JP, Martinelli E, Stenstad A, Pradhan P, Gabrysch S, Mishra A, Weindl I, Le Mouël C, Rolinski S, Baumstark L, Wang X, Waid JL, Lotze-Campen H, and Popp A. The ongoing nutrition transition thwarts long-term targets for food security, public health and environmental protection. *Sci Rep.* 2020;10:19778. https://doi.org/10.1038/s41598-020-75213-3.

[12] GBD 2017 Diet Collaborators. Health effects of dietary risks in 195 countries, 1990–2017: A systematic analysis for the Global Burden of Disease Study 2017. *Lancet.* 2019;393(10184):1958–1972. DOI: 10.1016/S0140-6736(19)30041-8.

[13] Poore J, Nemecek T. Reducing food's environmental impacts through producers and consumers. *Science.* 2018;1:360(6392):987–992. DOI: 10.1126/science.aaq0216.

[14] Hirvonen K, Bai Y, Headey D, Masters WA. Affordability of the EAT – Lancet reference diet: A global analysis. *Lancet Global Health.* 2019. https://doi.org/10.1016/S2214-109X(19)30447-4.

[15] EAT Forum. The planetary health diet. https://eatforum.org/learn-and-discover/the-planetary-health-diet/. [Accessed 2023 Dec 28].

[16] World Food Programme. 5 facts about food waste and hunger. https://www.wfp.org/stories/5-facts-about-food-waste-and-hunger. [Accessed 2023 Dec 24].

[17] Zhu J, Luo Z, Sun T, Li W, Zhou W, Wang X, Fei X, Tong H, Yin K. Cradle-to-grave emissions from food loss and waste represent half of total

greenhouse gas emissions from food systems. *Nat Food.* 2023;4:247–256. https://doi.org/10.1038/s43016-023-00710-3.

[18] El Bilali H, Ben Hassen T. Food waste in the countries of the Gulf Cooperation Council: A systematic review. *Foods*. 2020;9(4):463. DOI: 10.3390/foods9040463.

[19] Guo X, Broeze J, Groot JJ, Axmann H, Vollebregt M. A worldwide hotspot analysis on food loss and waste, associated greenhouse gas emissions, and protein losses. *Sustainability*. 2020;12(18):7488. https://doi.org/10.3390/su12187488.

[20] Hegnsholt E, Unnikrishnan S, Pollmann-Larsen M, Askelsdottir B, Gerard M. Tackling the 1.6-billion-ton food loss and waste crisis. Boston Consulting Group. https://www.bcg.com/publications/2018/tackling-1.6-billion-ton-food-loss-and-waste-crisis/. [Accessed 2023 Dec 24].

[21] Pew Research Centre. The future of world religions: Population growth projections, 2010-2050. https://www.pewresearch.org/religion/2015/04/02/religious-projections-2010-2050/. [Accessed 2023 Dec 29].

[22] Pew Research center. Religious composition by country, 2010-2050. https://www.pewresearch.org/religion/interactives/religious-composition-by-country-2010-2050/. [Accessed 2023 Dec 29].

[23] Attwood S, Jameel S, Fuseini A, AlKhalawi E, Hajat C Halal cultivated meat: An untapped opportunity. *Front Nutr*. 2023;10:1196475. DOI: 10.3389/fnut.2023.1196475.

[24] Hajat C, Attwood S. Unlocking Halal cultivated meat's potential: Exploring an untapped opportunity. Green Queen. https://www.greenqueen.com.hk/halal-cultivated-meat-opportunity-muslim-consumers/. [Accessed 2023 Dec 27].

[25] Ritchie H, Rosado P, Roser M. Meat and Dairy Production. Our World in Data. https://ourworldindata.org/meat-production#:~:text=Beef%20and%20buffalo%20(cattle)%20meat%20production&text=The%20United%20States%20is%20the,by%20Argentina%2C%20Australia%20and%20India. [Accessed 2023 Dec 27].

[26] Thornton P, Nelson G, Mayberry D, Herrero M. Impacts of heat stress on global cattle production during the 21st century: A modelling study. *Lancet Planet Health*. 2022;6(3):e192–e201.

[27] Oxford Business Group. GCC emphasis on food security is promising area for investment. https://oxfordbusinessgroup.com/reports/qatar/2022-report/economy/at-the-source-ensuring-food-supply-is-proving-a-promising-area-for-investment. [Accessed 2023 Dec 26].

[28] Neik TX, Siddique KHM, Mayes S, Edwards D, Batley J, Mabhaudhi T, Song BK, Massawe F. Diversifying agrifood systems to ensure global food security following the Russia–Ukraine crisis. *Front Sustain Food Syst*. 2023;7. https://www.frontiersin.org/articles/10.3389/fsufs.2023.1124640.

[29] *Economist*. Global food security index 2022. https://impact.economist.com/sustainability/project/food-security-index/. [Accessed 2023 Dec 29].

[30] Al-Saidi M. Caught off guard and beaten: The Ukraine war and food security in the Middle East. *Front Nutr*. 2023;10:983346. DOI: 10.3389/fnut.2023.983346.

[31] Le Mouël C, Forslund A, Marty P, Manceron S, Marajo-Petitzon E, Caillaud MA, Dumas P, Schmitt B. Can the Middle East-North Africa region mitigate the rise of its food import dependency under climate change? *Regional Environ Change*. 2023;23:52. https://doi.org/10.1007/s10113-023-02045-y.

[32] Jameel S. Climate change, food systems and the Islamic perspective on alternative proteins. *Trends Food Sci Technol*. 2023;138:480–490. https://doi.org/10.1016/j.tifs.2023.06.028.

[33] Haruna UA, Luther ML, Zubairu M, Abonyi EE, Dibal SM, Gegele TA, Gambo J, Garba SA, Musa SS, Manirambona E, Lucero-Prisno DE. Food loss and waste in Nigeria: Implications for food security and environmental sustainability. *Adv Food Secur Sustain*. 2023;8:217–233.

[34] Al-Sayyid Sābiq. Fiqh al-Sunnah, Volume 1 Fiqh al-Sunnah. Dār al-Hādī lil-Ṭibā'ah wa-al-Nashr. 2003.

[35] Tajudeen AL. Halal certification of insect-based food: A critique. *Int J Bus Ethics*. 2020;5(2):100. http://jurnal.unissula.ac.id/index.php/ijibe/article/view/10970.

[36] Sahih Muslim 1934a. *The Book of Hunting, Slaughter, and What May Be Eaten*. https://sunnah.com/muslim:1934a. [Accessed 2023 Dec 27].

[37] Mahamad Maifiah MH, Wan Ismail WNES. Porcine and bovine-derived ingredients: Islamic rules in Halal pharmaceutical products. *J Fatwa Manag Res*. 2023;28(3):41–57. https://doi.org/10.33102/jfatwa.vol28no3.549.

[38] Al-Mahmood OA, Fraser AM. Perceived challenges in implementing halal standards by halal certifying bodies in the United States. *PLOS One*. 2023;18(8):e0290774. https://doi.org/10.1371/journal.pone.0290774.

[39] Noor UMM. Irsyad Al-Fatwa Series 290: The ruling of food coloring containing 20% alcohol. https://muftiwp.gov.my/en/artikel/irsyad-fatwa/irsyad-fatwa-umum-cat/3097-irsyad-al-fatwa-series-290-the-ruling-of-food-coloring-containing-20-alcoho. [Accessed 2023 Dec 29].

[40] Jami` at-Tirmidhi (2380). Vol. 37, Hadith 77. https://sunnah.com/tirmidhi/36/77. [Accessed 2023 Dec 27].

[41] Sahih Al-Bukhari (1977). Vol. 30, Hadith 198. https://sunnah.com/bukhari:1977. [Accessed 2023 Dec 27].

[42] Trabelsi K, Ammar A, Boujelbane MA, Puce L, Garbarino S, Scoditti E, Boukhris O, Khanfir S, Clark CCT, Glenn JM, Alhaj OA, Jahrami H, Chtourou H, Bragazzi NL. Religious fasting and its impacts on individual, public, and planetary health: Fasting as a "religious health asset" for a

healthier, more equitable, and sustainable society. *Front Nutr*. 2022;9. DOI: 10.3389/fnut.2022.1036496.

[43] Sulaiman SK, Tsiga-Ahmed FI, Faris ME, Musa MS, Akpan UA, Umar AM, Abubakar SM, Allaham KK, Alyammahi T, Abdbuljalil MA, Syed FJ, Moien AK. Nigerian Muslim's perceptions of changes in diet, weight, and health status during Ramadan: A nationwide cross-sectional study. *Int J Environ Res Public Health*. 2022;19:14340. https://doi.org/10.3390/ijerph192114340.

[44] Aktas E, Sahin H, Topaloglu Z, Oledinma A, Huda AKS, Irani Z, Sharif AM, van't Wout T, Kamrava M. A consumer behavioural approach to food waste. *J Enterp Inf Manag*. 2018;31(5):658–673. https://doi.org/10.1108/JEIM-03-2018-0051.

[45] Elhoushy S, Jang S. Religiosity and food waste reduction intentions: A conceptual model. *Int J Consum Stud*. 2021;45:287–302. https://doi.org/10.1111/ijcs.12624.

[46] Chammas G, Yehya NA. Lebanese meal management practices and cultural constructions of food waste. *Appetite*. 2020;1(155):104803. DOI: 10.1016/j.appet.2020.104803.

[47] Hassan HF, Ghandour LA, Chalak A, Aoun P, Reynolds CJ, Abiad MG. The influence of religion and religiosity on food waste generation among restaurant clienteles. *Front Sustain Food Syst*. 2022;6:1010262. DOI: 10.3389/fsufs.2022.1010262.

[48] Elimelech E, Mintz KK, Katz-Gerro T, Segal-Klein H, Hussein L, Ayalon O. Between perceptions and practices: The religious and cultural aspects of food wastage in households. *Appetite*. 2023;180. https://doi.org/10.1016/j.appet.2022.106374.

[49] Coats L, Bernstein J, Dodge E, Bechard L, Aboul-Enein BH. Food-based dietary guidelines of Arabic-speaking countries: A culturally congruent profile. *Public Health Nutr*. 2019;22(6):1129–1137. DOI: 10.1017/S1368980018004093.

[50] Seed B. Sustainability in the Qatar national dietary guidelines, among the first to incorporate sustainability principles. *Public Health Nutr*. 2015;18(13):2303–10. DOI: 10.1017/S1368980014002110.

[51] Brown KA, Venkateshmurthy NS, Law C, Harris F, Kadiyala S, Shankar B, Mohan S, Prabhakaran D, Knai C. Moving towards sustainable food systems: A review of Indian food policy budgets. *Glob Food Secu*. 2021;28. https://doi.org/10.1016/j.gfs.2020.100462.

[52] Al-Jawaldeh A, Almamary S, Mahmoud L, Nasreddine L. Leveraging the food system in the Eastern Mediterranean region for better health and nutrition: A case study from Oman. *Int J Environ Res Public Health*. 2020;17:7250. https://doi.org/10.3390/ijerph17197250.

[53] Sharma M, Kishore A, Roy D, Joshi K. A comparison of the Indian diet with the EAT-Lancet reference diet. *BMC Public Health.* 2020;20:812. https://doi.org/10.1186/s12889-020-08951-8.

[54] Rahmi RN, Poolsawad N, Sranacharoenpong K. Environmental impacts related to food consumption of Indonesian adults. *J Nutr Sci Vitaminol.* 2020;66:S149–S154. DOI: 10.3177/jnsv.66.S149. PMID: 33612585.

[55] Sobhani SR, Omidvar N, Abdollahi Z and Al Jawaldeh A. Shifting to a sustainable dietary pattern in Iranian population: Current evidence and future directions. *Front Nutr.* 2021;8:789692. DOI: 10.3389/fnut.2021.789692.

[56] Saeediankia A, Majdzadeh R, Haghighian-Roudsari A, Pouraram H. The effects of subsidies on foods in Iran: A narrative review. *Front Sustain Food Syst.* 2023;6. DOI: 10.3389/fsufs.2022.1053851.

[57] Benajiba N, Mahrous L, Bernstein J, Aboul-Enein BH. Food labeling use by consumers in Arab countries: A scoping review. *J Community Health.* 2020;45:661–674. https://doi.org/10.1007/s10900-019-00750-6.

[58] Mohsen H, Sacre Y, Hanna-Wakim L, Hoteit M. Nutrition and food literacy in the MENA region: A review to inform nutrition research and policy makers. *Int J Environ Res Public Health.* 2022;19:10190. https://doi.org/10.3390/ijerph191610190.

[59] Cheikh Ismail L, Kassem H, Osaili TM, Hashim M, Obaid R, Radwan H, *et al.* Public's calorie literacy and perceived effectiveness of restaurant menu calorie labeling in the United Arab Emirates. *PLoS One.* 2023;18(10):e0293387. https://doi.org/10.1371/journal.pone.0293387.

[60] Alnasser A, Alomran N. The motivations and practices of vegetarian and vegan Saudis. *Sci Rep.* 2023;13:9742. https://doi.org/10.1038/s41598-023-36980-x.

[61] Salem V, AlHusseini N, Abdul Razack HI, Naoum A, Sims OT, Alqahtani SA. Prevalence, risk factors, and interventions for obesity in Saudi Arabia: A systematic review. *Obesity Rev.* 2022;23(7):e13448. DOI: 10.1111/obr.13448.

[62] Saquib N, Ibrahim AY, Saquib J. Behavioral trials in the Arab Gulf States: A scoping review. *SAGE Open Med.* 2019;24(7):2050312119846787. DOI: 10.1177/2050312119846787.

[63] Parkin B, Hajat C. Accelerating the market adoption of alternative proteins. A behavioural science approach. Real World Health; 2022. [Accessed 2024 Feb 18].

[64] Ho SS, Ou M, Vijayan AV. Halal or not? Exploring Muslim perceptions of cultured meat in Singapore. *Front Sustain Food Syst.* 2023;7:1127164. DOI: 10.3389/fsufs.2023.1127164.

[65] Assembly of Muslim Jurists of America (AMJA). 18th Annual Imams' conference, contemporary Fiqh issues related to technology, 2022 Sep 9–12,

Chicago IL. https://www.amjaonline.org/18th-annual-conference-contemporary-fiqh-issues-related-to-technology/. [Accessed 2023 Dec 29].

[66] Speed M. Islamic scholars rule on how to make lab-grown meat halal. *Financial Times*; 10 Sept 2023. https://www.ft.com/content/2f58f99e-5494-458a-9d71-8e6518012e56. [Accessed 2023 Dec 29].

[67] Halal Malaysia Official Portal. Malaysian standard on Halal food (MS 1500:2009). https://www.halal.gov.my/v4/index.php?data=bW9kdWxlcy9uZXdzOzs7Ow==&utama=panduan&ids=gp2. [Accessed 2023 Dec 29].

[68] Chelladurai KS, Christyraj JDS, Rajagopalan K, Yesudhason BV, Venkatachalam S, Mohan M, Vasantha NC, Johnson R, Christyraj SS. Alternative to FBS in animal cell culture-An overview and future perspective. *Heliyon*. 2021;17(8). DOI: 10.1016/j.heliyon.2021.e07686.

[69] Boereboom A, Sheikh M, Islam T, Achirimbi E, Vriesekoop F. Brits and British Muslims and their perceptions of cultured meat: How big is their willingness to purchase? *Food Front*. 2022;3:529–540. https://doi.org/10.1002/fft2.165.

[70] Baharuddin AS, Wan Ismail WAF, Mutalib LBA, Hashim H, Jusof N, Ghazali I, Alauddin MS, Harun MAH. Halal forensics issues involving three-dimensional (3D) printing technology of cultured meat. *Halal Rev*. 2021;1:3–15. 10.55265/halalreviews.v1i1.7.

[71] Alamsyah A, Hakim N, Hendayani R. Blockchain-based traceability system to support the Indonesian halal supply chain ecosystem. *Economies*. 2022;10:134. https://doi.org/10.3390/economies10060134.

[72] Fuseini A, Knowles T. The ethics of halal meat consumption: Preferences of consumers in England according to the method of slaughter. *Vet Record*. 2020;186:644. DOI: 10.1136/vr.105287.

[73] United Nations Food and Agricultural Organization. Food loss and waste reduction campaign of FAO and Turkey takes off. https://www.fao.org/save-food/news-and-multimedia/news/news-details/en/c/1276400/. [Accessed 2023 Dec 26].

[74] Baig MB, Gorski I, Neff RA. Understanding and addressing waste of food in the Kingdom of Saudi Arabia. *Saudi J Biol Sci*. 2019;26(7):1633. https://doi.org/10.1016/j.sjbs.2018.08.030.

[75] Althumiri NA, Basyouni MH, Duhaim AF, AlMousa N, Al Juwaysim MF, Bin Dhim NF. Understanding food waste, food insecurity, and the gap between the two: A nationwide cross-sectional study in Saudi Arabia. *Foods*. 2021;10:681. https://doi.org/10.3390/foods10030681.

[76] Essam S, Gill T, Alders RG. Dubai municipality initiative to reduce food loss. *Sustainability*. 2022;14:5374. https://doi.org/10.3390/su14095374.

[77] Abdallah M, Shanableh A, Shabib A, Adghim M. Financial feasibility of waste to energy strategies in the United Arab Emirates. *Waste Manag*. 2018;82:207–219. https://doi.org/10.1016/j.wasman.2018.10.029.

https://doi.org/10.1142/9781800616295_0013

Chapter 13

Food System Transformation: A Society-Based Approach

Saher Hasnain

Environmental Change Institute, University of Oxford, Oxford, UK

saher.hasnain@ouce.ox.ac.uk

Abstract

Food system transformation research has been limited to either the abstract or local levels with little practical engagement with societies. This chapter focuses on societies as mediators between transformations at a place level with changes at regional and global levels. This chapter identifies two categories for exploration in the transformation and food system space, explored through examples of Muslim societies. These are operationalizing aspirational transformational resilience strategies in the food system and managing trade-offs at a societal level. These provide a socially and spatially inclusive framework for exploring food system transformation for a resilient food secure future.

1. Introduction

Food systems are complex, deeply interlinked, and have significant inter-dependencies with other vulnerable systems. The relationships within food systems are dynamic and exist across multiple levels and scales of power and influence. Academic research on food system transformation has examined these power dynamics and inequalities and considers them critical to achieving systemic sustainability [1]. This chapter describes food system transformation, following Sonnino and Milbourne, as "a process of radical change in the structural, functional and relational aspects of the food system that leads to more just socio-ecological relationships, patterns of interactions and outcomes" [2: p. 915]. It further acknowledges Fazey and Colvin in terms of interpreting transformation as systemic and involving changes to the "core dynamics and goals of a system" [3: p. 4]. While transformation can take place at different spatial, jurisdictional, social, and temporal scales, internal transformation in terms of individual beliefs and mindsets is normally necessary for external transformations.

Debates and research on food system transformation have tended to be either on the global scale, leaning toward the abstract, or the hyper-local place-based scale for particular communities and groups of food system actors, such as producers [4,5]. This trend has the potential to be further enriched by national exercises on food system transformation, following the UN Food Systems Summit.

The underlying premise of the small-scale initiatives of transformation is that distinct action through personal and community alliance can take place at the local scale, which allows these food system actors to avoid and resist the global dynamics that are inherently "bad" [2]. While this "local trap" has been critiqued extensively [2,6,7], there is still an ongoing trend of drawing empirical research on transformation from the local level. Besides the potential practicalities of tracing transformational changes at a discrete local scale, there is a drive for deeper personal connections across the food system as an automatically "good" alternative to the impersonal and disconnected nature of the global food system.

There is a recognition that improving the food system will require the understanding and handling of features often considered emergent, such as resilience [8], while mediating with the complex web of stakeholders acting under their own worldviews and objectives. Comprehensively examining the impact of different and discrete food transformation initiatives remains a necessary and urgent task, currently being taken up by region-level research projects [9], and conceptualizations that facilitate deeper engagement with the system's complexity [10].

While the spatial nature of the system's actors and governance mechanisms as often explored through the jurisdictional nature is useful, more attention is needed on socially vertical dimensions [11]. Some of these are captured in research on household food security and behavior, food environments, and community-scale transformation efforts; however, engagement is needed on the scale of multiple communities or societies with distinct identities. This is necessary given the increasing dissonance between societal level perturbances and calls for localizing food systems to improve outcomes. Developing narratives in food system transformations may unintentionally leave out those who have been victimized by the food system in its current form [12] or drive views that are so context-dependent that they are out of tune with the complexities of global realities.

This chapter intends to contribute to debates on food system transformation by focusing on societies as mediators for transformation. The critical review and analysis challenge key thinking in this space by considering the role of scale in enacting resilience strategies, contributing to meanings and connections in the transformation space, and how interdependencies in systems are articulated at times of disruptive change at a societal level. This is exemplified through Muslim societies in the context of ongoing, projected, and aspirational food system transformations.

2. Food System Transformation: Place and Society

Food systems transformation is a high-priority agenda item for sustainability and green development.[1]

The consequences for the environment have become increasingly apparent, and the urgency of the matter has been noted in recent COP meetings. National strategies around net zero and just transitions are recognizing the vulnerability, complexity, and urgency of the situation. The food system is resulting in wicked problems of food and nutrition security, environmental sustainability, and livelihoods. Almost one in ten people in the world do not have enough food to eat [15], 26% of greenhouse gas emissions are attributed to food, 70% of global freshwater withdrawals are because of agriculture [16], and nearly 85% of the world's population lives on less than US$30 per day [17]. Global perturbations such as the COVID-19 pandemic, various conflicts across Africa and Europe, and the continuing influences of climate change further demonstrate that the food system is not functioning effectively.

---

[1] See Dengerink, Piters, Brouwer, *et al.* [13] on a comprehensive primer on food systems transformation and [14] on an analysis of the transformative potential of recommendations made in major food system reports.

The language of transformation has also been mostly abstract, with general calls for transforming outcomes without evaluating the adaptations needed by stakeholders and the drivers that will enable them [18]. There is a need to move beyond the abstract and into more empirically grounded engagements with transformation [3]. Feola [19] suggests a cautious approach toward a rigorous use of transformation because of the dangers of "attributing a transformative character to any instance of social change". There is, therefore, an encouragement of thinking of transformation broadly – even as a metaphor – with the hope of developing creative ways of fostering dialogue that does not reduce the term to a buzzword. Existing frameworks and guides to transformation have tended to emphasize the role of technological innovation and the chaotic dynamics inherent to change [20]. Major transitions across sectors always involve changes in technology, institutions, and the economy [21]. Changes in institutions have often been considered in response to transitions in technology and economic domains.

This chapter proposes an approach that bridges theory and practice for food system transformation. It keeps societies at the heart of the approach as conceptual and functional mediators. I argue that this approach has a substantial contribution to make in a field that prioritizes local spaces and places as locations of change. It has the potential to connect transformative efforts from the small scale to the global level while considering the drivers, activities, and outcomes of large, diverse, and spatially distributed communities.

Broadly, this society-based approach offers a lens to shift empirical attention away from isolated, place, and community-oriented analyses and challenges the dualisms in the food system (e.g., local vs. global, artisanal vs. corporate) [2,22]. This allows for a critical view of how resilience approaches consider scale and those who live at these scales, how meaning and connections work between communities and within societies, and how system interdependencies and trade-offs work at the levels between discretely conceptualized communities and "the food system" as an abstract object. These findings will also enable active engagement with societies as mediators and doers of change instead of passive recipients. There is an encouragement for geographers and food systems analysts to consider how questions of place function within questions of societies and in a future potentially characterized by significant migration: how can a just, healthy, sustainable, and resilient food future be reached in a global community with increased and often involuntary spatial mobility?

This then critiques Massey [23] and Gibson-Graham [24] on the imperative of anchoring transformative strategies to progressive senses of place and the relationships between places and scales. This is not to say that place and space should be reduced in priority in concerns of food system transformation, but to scrutinize the valorization of the physicality of place over the dynamic social relationships that exist between people across multiple spaces. I argue that while place-based approaches have the capacity of bringing together society and physical locations and natures, the societal element is often made subservient to places and spaces in a manner that disserves academia and the practices of transformation.

Elements of society-based change can be found in the Acknowl-EJ coalition's work on supporting radical transformation [25]. Questioning inequalities in the coalition process requires imagining and exploring how things could be done differently, with a drive toward challenging current conditions. The collective process of the coalition engages with various types of power: people and networks, structural power of institutions and political frameworks, and cultural power of narratives and values. With a range of strategies, the aim is to impact these current systems of power and engage closely with informal and often hidden structures of influence. While it offers a powerful tool for transformation through confronting injustice, the focus remains on supporting often local alternatives to dominant patterns. In effecting wider political transformations, the scrutiny of historical, social, and political issues is still performed with the dualism of alternatives in mind.

In the following sections, I introduce the concepts of resilience in the context of scale and space, investigating and fostering connections with the goal of enacting change and how interdependencies function when zooming out of a community and place scale.

2.1. *Food systems and resilience*

Resilience is understood in this study as a whole-system holistic concept that operates across many scales. This encompasses a range of different aims for building resilience that necessitate appropriate actions. [26] These aims include:

- Robustness: the ability of system stakeholders to resist disruptions to maintain the status quo.

- Recovery: the ability of system stakeholders to adapt activities to return to the status quo following a disruption.
- Reorientation: the ability of system stakeholders to adapt activities to accept alternative outcomes.

These three concepts require a comprehensive understanding of the system, its stakeholders, disruptions, and outcomes. All three concepts require the adaptation of system activities by the relevant stakeholders. While robustness and recovery are necessary to respond effectively to disruptions in the system, aiming for reorientation is an essential principle underlying most transformation and transition strategies. Bene, Frankenberger, Nelson *et al.* [8] propose that aspects of resilience are emergent properties of the food system at a system level, as opposed to the level of individuals. This proposal is based on the observation that connectivity, redundancy, diversity, inclusivity, and the rule of law play critical roles in building food system resilience.[2] These properties are functions of food system stakeholders, functioning at multiple levels and scales. In their adaptation of a social-ecological resilience framework for food systems, Hodbod and Eakin [28] point to the impacts of technological change on adjacent and distant systems and dynamics. Resilience in this context provides the structure needed for analyzing and anticipating complex interactions.

This chapter draws on the insights of these three papers and the broader food system resilience in the following ways: observing that resilience strategies across the literature tend to focus on robustness and recovery of food system activities and actors; operationalizing reorientation as a strategy is challenging in part because of the emergent nature of resilience; and connectivity within societies is a critical element of resilience capacity and aspirations toward radically different outcomes.

An important caveat is the recognition that a continuing and cumulative series of stressors strains the capacity of stakeholders and society to respond to loss and tolerate vulnerability in a system. Unavoidable trade-offs need to be made in managing the overall resilience of a system for the

[2]A systematic review of food system resilience is out of scope for this paper but Tendall, Joerin, Kopainsky *et al.* [27], Hodbod and Eakin [28], Zurek, Ingram, and Bellamy *et al.* [26], and Bene, Frankenberger, Nelson *et al.* [8] provide deep engagement and analysis of the literature.

future while providing morally just outcomes for reducing hunger, providing livelihoods, and avoiding environmental harm.

Evidence from practical engagements with the resilience concepts to develop strategies has demonstrated that it is challenging to enact a strategy for reorientation [14,29]. This challenge is related to the abstract nature of what food systems look like beyond the local scale outside the supply chain and a lack of clarity on what a transformative change would be.[3] Therefore, there is a danger that managing these trade-offs with a longer-term and aspirational view will leave many worse off and greatly strain societies' capacity for handling disruptions.

2.2. *Trade-offs for transformation*

A food systems approach invites the consideration of all the activities and actors involved in the supply chain, the systems they are embedded in, the supporting services and institutions that support them, the drivers that influence the actors in their functions, the outcomes the activities result in, and feedback loops [26,30]. In combination with the society-focused sense of place, this allows for an enhanced understanding of the power dynamics and interconnectedness in the system. Being cognizant of the local trap, this further allows for an extension of the system boundaries to include societies, as compared to spatially and jurisdictionally discrete communities.

Staying within the food system resilience framing, the recognition of interdependencies is essential in order to manage stressors and perturbations to the system and navigate trade-offs. This is a sensitive area, as fears of repercussions from change can hinder innovation and experimentation, which then further entrench existing food system dynamics [28]. Efforts to increase resilience in order to respond to vulnerabilities have tended to focus on the short term and a defined scale. An example is the widespread adoption of herbicide-resistant cotton, created to withstand cotton bollworm. An effective strategy in some regards by resisting disruption from pests and recovering to the status quo activity of monoculture production of cotton, but a poor reorientation strategy because of creating lock-ins for farmers for continuing production in a similar manner and being

[3]See Fazey and Colvin [3] for a comprehensive examination of transformation and food systems.

dependent on a small number of technology suppliers [31]. The system remains vulnerable to pests and diseases in service of the goals of food security and livelihoods. Trade-offs are made for ensuring environmental sustainability, biodiversity, and longer-term system stability.

This example's analysis of resilience is place-based and considers the impacts of technological innovation and the role of suppliers. A society-based approach can encourage thinking that challenges the core assumptions in the system, which may raise questions around why a particular commodity is being invested in, in that location, and how the impacts across a range of outcomes of that commodity travel through the entire society.

A society-based approach thus means thinking about high animal-welfare meat, for example, helps to approach it in terms of the supply chain, the supporting actors and systems, the embedded systems, and the values and worldviews held by all these stakeholders regardless of their spatial proximity to meat production. This allows for the trade-off discussion to take place earlier because the example is no longer tightly spatially bound. Questions of the livelihoods of small-scale producers and the affordability of healthy and sustainable food for lower socioeconomic populations can be addressed in service of the same lofty goals of resilience of food systems.

Considering food and nutrition security as an outcome that ideally should not be traded off reinforces the conservative trend in food systems [28]. This is also non-negotiable for populations today to respond to the urgent needs of regions and communities experiencing hunger and malnutrition. Strategies for transformation remain entrenched in securing food security in the now and the near future, following either the same mechanisms of mass production of a few commodities or driving for localized food systems that cater to the needs of the few in select geographies. How then can aspirational resilience be imagined and enacted to benefit present and future outcomes?

2.3. *Muslim societies, food, and transformation*

Historically, in academia and broader practice, discussions of the future and foresight are notably absent, except for responding to immediate or near-term threats to existing systems. While this has usually been assumed as a misunderstanding of Islam's relationship with the future, the religion encourages awareness of and planning for the future.

Sardar *et al.* [32] point to the difficulty of describing Muslim people and their society. The authors encourage paying attention to concerning trends across a range of spheres that are relevant to Muslim societies, such as income disparity and unemployment, social justice, the environment, and technological and cultural disruption. This paper is concerned with the self-identification of global Muslim society. It does not address the concept of community in the Islamic concept or engage with the colonial and racial history of categorization. The paper uses the term "Muslim societies" to refer to the diverse communities of Muslims living across the world, including but not limited to Muslim-majority countries. This choice is made partly to challenge place-based identities of communities and to decolonize the term to better examine Muslim societies *in their diversity and plurality* in the context of global food systems.

Locating Muslims in global food systems has currently been done in the following ways: explorations of halal food in terms of Muslim consumer acceptability, regulations, and standards, overlapping with issues of ethics, sustainability, and animal welfare [33]; current situation, operational elements, and business opportunities in the domain of halal food supply chains; and Muslim perspectives on emerging food trends, such as cultured meats and insects-as-food [34].

The conceptualization in this study invites a broadening of debate that allows for the inclusion of Muslim societies in the food system space beyond recipients of outcomes and mechanisms of carving out bespoke value chains. It encourages attention on Muslim societies beyond concerns of transnational migration and spatial displacement and to consider a range of systemic outcomes spanning environmental degradation and food injustice faced by diverse Muslim communities living in different contexts and experiencing different drivers of change.

This emerges from the recognition by Soja that "the scales of spatial justice are not separate and distinct; they interact and interweave in complex patterns" [35: p. 277]. Emerging from the food justice space, the sentiment can be equally applied to food system justice across variables in the environment and socioeconomy, and not just food and nutrition security. While this may take the form of de-centered assemblages of place-based social movements in the beginning [36], it is vital to keep scrutinizing the connections with broader society and transformation aims.

There is then a logical movement toward more distributed forms of knowledge and understanding for food system transformation that is located within societies and which allows for the diverse worldviews, narratives, and practices that drive everyday living and aspirations for the future. The invitation to consider the present and the future in this approach accomplishes the following:

(1) offering insights into the everyday practices of the food environment (e.g., enacting religious principles of production and consumption);
(2) clarifying engagements with the broader structural and institutional systems at a consumer and other food system actor level (e.g., compliance officer in the food industry);
(3) exploring social connections with other communities in society on shared interests and values (e.g., how Muslims in non-Muslim majority countries respond to concerns on sustainability and animal welfare); and
(4) actively exploring and co-creating futures within the global food system that step away from conventional dualisms and alternatives (e.g., reconfiguring microbiomes for complete nutrition retention).

3. The Framework and Approach

The relational and societal conceptualization of place has not been theorized or supported empirically to the same degree as the spatial imaginaries of localities [37]. The literature has tended to consider societal-level outcomes primarily in relation to translating policy and considering societies as "recipients" of change and needing capacity building from more powerful stakeholders "outside" of society [38]. The dualisms remain in the consideration of local/alternative versus global/conventional in a manner where communities have been studied in various contexts on the local and small scales, but societies and regional/global populations are not addressed beyond descriptors in data. The human population, on a broader scale, becomes dehumanized and addressable only by belonging to nations and metrics related to food system outcomes. Sonnino and Milbourne argue for a deeper engagement with a progressive sense of place by relating system-level properties with ideas of co-benefits, linkages, inclusions, and connectivities [2]. The framework is generative in its incorporation of social justice in concerns of food system transformation, strengthening linkages between places, orientating connections between everyday life and wider structures, and shifting toward action-based research.

The framework in this study takes inspiration – the ideas of connectivity and the call for socio-nature – from Sonnino and Milbourne to propose a society-based approach to food system transformation that connect the idea of reorientation as a resilience strategy with a societal-level consideration of interdependencies and trade-offs [2].

The framework challenges dominant thinking in transition literature by not focusing on the dynamics and outcomes of disruptions and disruptive innovation. It instead breaks down disruptive innovation (in technology, institutions, and the socioeconomic sphere) into system drivers, system activities, and system outcomes [39,40]. This accomplishes two main functions. The first is to emphasize the deeply embedded relationship between the innovation and the relevant stakeholders, and the second is to consider the disruption itself as a broader system that includes the product or service, the socio-technical frameworks around it, and the narratives that shape its influence in the system. Thus, the disruption is not simply a driver of a system influencing stakeholders to make a change, but it may also be an activity and an outcome. This theorization allows for the consideration of multiple scales (e.g., enterprise level for product-level innovation) and the macroscale (dominant narratives on employability).

This approach includes core concepts from the iceberg model of working with different levels of change [41] and leverage points [42]. This is done by retaining the social structures and relationships by considering societies at the heart of the approach and emphasizing the importance of mindsets, meanings, and paradigms on which systems are based on and from where transcendence can take place. Mechanistic traits of practice and resource flows are captured in the "everyday" aspects of the approach and refined by considering them in that broader structural and systemic context.

Figure 1 presents a framework for evaluating food system transformations in relation to resilience strategies and social levels. "Reactive" resilience here refers to resilience strategies that strive for the robustness and recovery of system activities and outcomes. I suggest that this mapping will be appropriate for most societies that exist in diverse regions and possess multiple demographic and economic descriptors. In essence, to have food system transformations that negotiate trade-offs effectively, action must be taken at the societal level while striving for aspirational resilience outcomes. I acknowledge that further research is required to explore other

Figure 1. A framework for evaluating food system transformations for a society-based approach.

resilience attributes, such as functional systemic diversity and response pathways to specific types of stressors.

The current food system situation in Muslim societies can be mapped onto the bottom left of Fig. 1 because of a primary focus on urgent responses to hunger and malnutrition. Challenges such as obesity and cardiovascular disease driven by poor diets are becoming increasingly apparent in Muslim-majority countries and in disadvantaged Muslim communities in other countries. Resilience strategies are focused on securing food production and ensuring that supplies are not interrupted. Responses to shocks and stressors are primarily aimed at returning to the status quo as rapidly as possible, with little investment in future-proofing systems. Aspirations and imaginative innovations are few and far between and tend to follow current dualisms. This has been observed in increased interest in "alternative" proteins for the Muslim world [34] in combination with a reactive response along the lines of "how will Muslim communities respond to this incoming change?" Societal agency can be denoted by the deployment of halal food chains, influencing national policies in non-Muslim countries for accepting halal certifications, and entrepreneurial efforts that seek to engender Muslim values in food products and processes.

Moving Muslim societies to the top right in Fig. 1 will be ideal because it will require the creation of imaginative infrastructures that drive transformational futures and interdisciplinary methods of engagement that consider how to enact and strengthen connectivity within societies. Such creative methods can be used to explore and change meanings and world-views, embody learnings across multiple spheres, change and inspire new connections, and empower societies to imagine and build truly transformational systems. While it is challenging to look for radically different futures through the lens of the present, evidence demonstrates that focusing on and supporting the preconditions of societal imaginations is productive and can engage with the deeper structural dimensions of systems that current practices do not necessarily allow for [13,43,44,45: p. 576].

Muslim societies occupying the top left in Fig. 1 also have the capacity to be a space of potential and possibility once there is a greater understanding of how transformations at a place and community level travel across to larger systems. Enacting aspirational resilience strategies has the potential to be a more approachable exercise in more localized systems of activity. However, even where Muslim communities are involved in local-scale endeavors, resilience strategies focus on the short term and small scale, with little consideration for how the systems can be changed at a fundamental level.

4. Conclusions

Calls for transformation are being moderated in recent times for greater clarity and detail in terms of objectives and expected outcomes. Responding to the recognition that despite the complexity and vulnerability of the deeply interconnected food system, empirical research remains at a local level and broadly divorced from global and abstract debates on food system transformations, this chapter has proposed an engagement with societies as mediators. Placing societies at the heart of the approach provides the space to hold multiple, potentially competing narratives and worldviews while exploring aspirations for transformation. A co-creative process that is not driven by an association with a place engenders elements of power and agency to step away from feelings of responding to change taking place elsewhere.

Practically, the approach presented here can guide the formulation of transformation pathways that can be tangible and directed, can respond to *societal* needs instead of just the context-specific needs of particular territories, and can include ways of addressing systemic trade-offs as a critical component of the transformation instead of a later consideration. It will also allow members of large regional and global communities to view themselves as agents of change and not simply receive the positive and negative consequences of transformative technologies and initiatives. It will invite systems experts, planners, and policymakers to develop aspirational strategies for food system resilience that are process- and outcome-focused instead of being purely responsive to stressors and challenge the underlying narratives of transformation strategies from the beginning. Actors across the food system will be able to see the societal impacts of their activities and better connect the metrics of measurement to consider trade-offs in the food security, environment, and livelihood spaces.

This has contributions to the research agenda on food system transformation and the studies on societies and geographies. Conceptually, it will encourage scrutiny of how space, place, and scale are conceptualized in an area where humans and non-humans are impacted across spaces, places, and scales in convoluted systems. Practically, it will drive interdisciplinary inquiry that can examine avenues of linking and measuring transformative impact from the local to the global and advise on methods of engagement that build on the plurality of diverse societies. Care will need to be taken in the inclusion of a diverse range of groups, experiences, and narratives, but there is opportunity in viewing from the lens of society instead of place. Questions are raised regarding boundary-marking in systems analysis in conceptual and practical terms of identifying the spatial boundaries of food system activities and the societal boundaries for actors in terms of drivers, activities, and outcomes of interest.

In conclusion, the approach will be applicable to societies with particular descriptors that participate in and experience food system outcomes. Muslim societies globally experience vulnerability in different forms and participate in global food systems in many ways. There are emergent concerns over the impact of disruptive technologies on issues of food security and environmental justice. There are opportunities and spaces of potential in developing innovative solutions to address these problems. A society-based approach to planning for such solutions for a radically transformed future food system is necessary if societal aspirations are to be addressed.

References

[1] Khan N, Ray RL, Kassem HS, Hussain S, Zhang S, Khayyam M, et al. Potential role of technology innovation in transformation of sustainable food systems: A review. *Agriculture*. 2021 Oct;11(10):984.

[2] Sonnino R, Milbourne P. Food system transformation: a progressive place-based approach. *Local Environ*. 2022;27(7):915–26.

[3] Fazey I, Colvin J. Transformation: An introductory guide to fundamental change for researchers and change makers in a world of crises – A report for the Transforming UK Food Systems SPF Programme. University of York, UK, 2023. p. 52.

[4] Sage C. Social embeddedness and relations of regard. *J Rural Stud*. 2003 Jan;19(1):47–60.

[5] Tregear A. Progressing knowledge in alternative and local food networks: Critical reflections and a research agenda. *J Rural Stud*. 2011 Oct 1;27(4):419–30.

[6] Born B, Purcell M. Avoiding the local trap: Scale and food systems in planning research. *J Plan Educ Res*. 2006 Dec;26(2):195–207.

[7] Libman K. Has New York City fallen into the local trap? *Public Health*. 2015 Apr;129(4):310–7.

[8] Béné C, Frankenberger TR, Nelson S, Constas MA, Collins G, Langworthy M, et al. Food system resilience measurement: Principles, framework and caveats. *Food Secur [Internet]*. 2023 Nov 8 [cited 2023 Dec 8]. Available from: https://doi.org/10.1007/s12571-023-01407-y.

[9] FOSTER. Fostering food system change. 2023 [cited 2023 Dec 1]. Available from: https://fosterfoodsystem.eu/.

[10] Lamine C, Garçon L, Brunori G. Territorial agrifood systems: A Franco-Italian contribution to the debates over alternative food networks in rural areas. *J Rural Stud*. 2019 May 1;68:159–70.

[11] Sarmiento ER. Synergies in alternative food network research: Embodiment, diverse economies, and more-than-human food geographies. *Agric Hum Values*. 2017 Jun 1;34(2):485–97.

[12] Dieterle JM. *Just Food: Philosophy, Justice and Food*. Rowman & Littlefield; 2015. 273 p.

[13] Advisory B, LEI International Policy, Advisory C, Dengerink JD, De Steenhuijsen Piters CB, Brouwer JH, *et al*. Food systems transformation: An introduction [Internet]. Wageningen: Wageningen Centre for Development Innovation; 2022 [cited 2023 Dec 8]. Available from: https://research.wur.nl/en/publications/ab4d6f4d-a1b8-487f-8295-5953d5a2acc1.

[14] Slater S, Baker P, Lawrence M. An analysis of the transformative potential of major food system report recommendations. *Glob Food Secur*. 2022 Mar;32:100610.

[15] Ritchie H, Rosado P, Roser M. Hunger and undernourishment. Published online at OurWorldinData.org; 2022. Retrieved from: https://ourworldindata.org/hunger-and-undernourishment.
[16] Ritchie H, Rosado P, Roser M. Environmental impacts of food production. Published online at OurWorldinData.org; 2022. Retrieved from: https://ourworldindata.org/environmental-impacts-of-food.
[17] Roser M, Arriagada P, Hasell J, Ritchie H, Ortiz-Ospina E. Economic Growth. Published online at OurWorldinData.org; 2023. Retrieved from: https://ourworldindata.org/economic-growth.
[18] Ingram J, Thornton P. What does transforming food systems actually mean? *Nat Food.* 2022 Nov 2;3(11):881–2.
[19] Feola G. Societal transformation in response to global environmental change: A review of emerging concepts. *Ambio.* 2015 Sep 1;44(5):376–90.
[20] Jesus A. Reimagining the food system through social innovations — European Environment Agency [Internet]. 2022 [cited 2023 Dec 8]. Available from: https://www.eea.europa.eu/publications/reimagining-the-food-system-the.
[21] Perez C. Technological revolutions and techno-economic paradigms. *Camb J Econ.* 2010;34(1):185–202.
[22] Wood A, Queiroz C, Deutsch L, González-Mon B, Jonell M, Pereira L, et al. Reframing the local–global food systems debate through a resilience lens. *Nat Food.* 2023 Jan;4(1):22–9.
[23] Massey D. A global sense of place. In: Timothy Oakes, editor. The cultural geography reader. Routledge, London, UK; 2008.
[24] Gibson-Graham JK. Diverse economies: Performative practices for 'other worlds'. *Prog Hum Geogr.* 2008 Oct;32(5):613–32.
[25] Temper L, Walter M, Rodriguez I, Kothari A, Turhan E. A perspective on radical transformations to sustainability: Resistances, movements and alternatives. *Sustain Sci.* 2018 May;13(3):747–64.
[26] Zurek M, Ingram J, Sanderson Bellamy A, Goold C, Lyon C, Alexander P, et al. Food system resilience: Concepts, issues, and challenges. *Annu Rev Environ Resour.* 2022 Oct 17;47(1):511–34.
[27] Tendall DM, Joerin J, Kopainsky B, Edwards P, Shreck A, Le QB, et al. Food system resilience: Defining the concept. *Glob Food Secur.* 2015 Oct 1;6:17–23.
[28] Hodbod J, Eakin H. Adapting a social-ecological resilience framework for food systems. *J Environ Stud Sci.* 2015 Sep 1;5(3):474–84.
[29] Food System Transformation Group. Enhancing the resilience of London's food systems. Food System Transformation Group; 2022.
[30] Stefanovic L, Freytag-Leyer B, Kahl J. Food system outcomes: An overview and the contribution to food systems transformation. *Front Sustain Food Syst [Internet].* 2020 [cited 2023 Dec 8];4. Available from: https://www.frontiersin.org/articles/10.3389/fsufs.2020.546167.

[31] Fernandez-Cornejo J, Wechsler S, Livingston M, Mitchell L. Genetically engineered crops in the United States, ERR-162 U.S. Department of Agriculture. USDA; 2014. Economic Research Service. Report No. 162.

[32] Sardar Z, Serra J, Jordan S. Muslim societies in postnormal times: Foresights for trends, emerging issues and scenarios [Internet]. International Institute of Islamic Thought; 2019 [cited 2023 Dec 8]. Available from: http://www.jstor.org/stable/10.2307/j.ctv10kmcpb.

[33] Tieman M, Hassan FH. Convergence of food systems: Kosher, Christian and Halal. *Br Food J.* 2015 Jan 1;117(9):2313–27.

[34] Jameel S. Climate change, food systems and the Islamic perspective on alternative proteins. *Trends Food Sci Technol.* 2023 Aug;138:480–90.

[35] Soja EW. *Seeking Spatial Justice.* University of Minnesota Press, Minnesota, USA; 2010.

[36] Sonnino R, Marsden T, Moragues-Faus A. Relationalities and convergences in food security narratives: Towards a place-based approach. *Trans Inst Br Geogr.* 2016 Oct;41(4):477–89.

[37] Woods M, Fois F, Heley J, Jones L, Onyeahialam A, Saville S, et al. Assemblage, place and globalisation. *Trans Inst Br Geogr.* 2021 Jun;46(2): 284–98.

[38] Singh BK, Fraser EDG, Arnold T, Biermayr-Jenzano P, Broerse JEW, Brunori G, et al. Ensuring societal considerations are met when translating science into policy for sustainable food system transformation. *Trends Food Sci Technol.* 2023 Jul 1;137:104–8.

[39] Geels FW. Disruption and low-carbon system transformation: Progress and new challenges in socio-technical transitions research and the multi-level perspective. *Energy Res Soc Sci.* 2018 Mar;37:224–31.

[40] Winskel M. Beyond the disruption narrative: Varieties and ambiguities of energy system change. *ENERGY Res Soc Sci.* 2018 Mar;37:232–7.

[41] Shi L, Moser S. Transformative climate adaptation in the United States: Trends and prospects. *Science.* 2021 Jun 25;372(6549).

[42] Abson DJ, Fischer J, Leventon J, Newig J, Schomerus T, Vilsmaier U, *et al.* Leverage points for sustainability transformation. *Ambio.* 2017 Feb 1;46(1):30–9.

[43] Hebinck A, Diercks G, von Wirth T, Beers PJ, Barsties L, Buchel S, *et al.* An actionable understanding of societal transitions: The X-curve framework. *Sustain Sci.* 2022 May 1;17(3):1009–21.

[44] Vervoort J. Transformative imagination: Linking resonant action, deeply creative practice, and imagination infrastructures. Anticiplay; 2023 [cited 2023 Nov 27]. Available from: https://anticiplay.medium.com/transformative-imagination-0cdec484f4c0.

[45] Hartmut R. *Resonance: A Sociology of Our Relationship to the World.* Wiley, Oxford, UK; 2019.

https://doi.org/10.1142/9781800616295_0014

Chapter 14

On the Consumption of Blood-Based Foods in Light of Two Old, Yet New, Legal Cases

Nour-Eddine Qaouar

Oxford Centre for Islamic Studies, Oxford, UK

nour-eddine.qaouar@oxcis.ac.uk

Abstract

This chapter addresses the consumption of blood-based foods, insects and sugar, in Islam through two legal cases scrutinized by premodern scholars. In terms of insects, the chapter discusses selected authoritative opinions in the four schools of law, including the Mālikī school known for its distinct flexible position on entomophagy, contrasting with the Ḥanafī, Ḥanbalī, and Shāfi'ī schools of law, which prohibited it on cultural grounds. Centuries later, the consumption of sugar, which some scholars in 19th-century Morocco prohibited due to the presence of blood, was prohibited following a similar line of reasoning used with entomophagy.

1. Introduction

There is no doubt that the Muslim food culture rests upon the teachings of the Quran and the *sunna*, or the traditions of the Prophet Muhammad peace be upon him; ﷺ. It also relies on culture itself when the aforementioned sources do not provide clear rulings for any given food. For instance, snails are not edible in many Muslim countries, but people in some other Muslim countries, such as those in North and West Africa, eat them. Also, entomophagy, or the consumption of insects, may serve as an excellent example here, as it has increasingly become a popular topic in response to recent developments in the food industry. In January 2023, the European Commission [1] authorized the consumption of *lesser worms*, which consist of frozen, paste, dried, and powder forms of house cricket. In the UK, Sainsbury's has been selling fried crickets since 2018 [2]. Entomophagy has entered the Western food culture as a more environmentally conscious alternative source of protein [3,4]. Yet, in certain cultures, the consumption of insects can bring about cultural anxiety, including some Muslim cultures where the issue is both cultural and religious. Indeed, no Muslim country has so far authorized the consumption of this *novel food*, in part because of past Islamic legal positions.[1] To my knowledge, no authoritative Islamic body has ever issued a fatwā validating or invalidating the consumption of insects.[2]

Although entomophagy has been receiving ever-growing attention, the scarcity of scholarly contributions to this particular topic is evident, especially from a historico-legal perspective. The studies carried out so far, particularly in the Muslim context, are mostly scientific, and hence their treatment of the case, at least from a legal standpoint, remains insufficient. They only provide brief accounts of the common opinion of the Jumhūr,[3] which consists of Ḥanafī, Ḥanbalī, and Shafi'ī authorities, as well as that of the Mālikī school with respect to locusts.[4] They mention nothing in regard to other insects, such as scarabs and mosquitoes, that medieval Mālikī scholars in particular scrutinized [3,9]. Yet, one may

[1]Novel food can be defined as "food that had not been consumed to a significant degree by humans in the EU before 15 May 1997" [5].

[2]Dār al-Iftā' al-Miṣriya [6] issued a confusing fatwā that responded to a petition about entomophagy with an answer regarding the use of insects for pharmaceutical purposes.

[3]The Jumhūr is a technical term that refers to mainstream scholars.

[4]The followers of these schools are Sunnī, the sect representing 89% of Muslims worldwide. These schools deal with legal cases in every area of Muslim life, including questions related to food. The Ḥanafī school is followed by roughly half of the world's Muslims and is especially prevalent in South Asia. The Mālikī school is followed by about 15% of Muslims, mainly in North and West Africa. The Shafi'ī school is followed by about 18% of Muslims mainly in South Asia and East Africa, and the Ḥanbalī school is followed by about 2% of Muslims, mainly in Saudi Arabia [7,8].

come across individual fatwās that provide useful information. Some of these fatwās invalidate insect-based food, while others permit it [10,11]. The fatwās that invalidate entomophagy build upon the Jumhūr's position, and those that permit it draw on the Mālikī's position. Even so, the proponents of this position do no justice to this case, as they largely ignore how it was treated within scholastic circles from medieval times up to the colonial era. Rather, these fatwās only cite one *ḥadīth* report and broad verses that even an opponent of their position could use as counter-evidence.[5]

Contributing to contemporary discussions on *novel food* in scholastic and academic circles from a historico-legal angle, this chapter seeks to shed light on Jumhūr's position prohibiting entomophagy as well as Mālikī's counter-position of allowing it. Irrespective of the broad proof-texts, particularly those of the Quran and *sunna*, this chapter will specifically demonstrate how both the Jumhūr and Mālikī scholars derived their rulings for this case, paying close attention to the common *ratio essendi* of each side,[6] with reference to the most authoritative texts of each school. For Mālikī scholars, blood is an essential factor that affected the permissibility of consuming not only insects but also plant-based food such as sugar, which was prohibited in Morocco in the 19th century. In addition to its discussion on entomophagy, this chapter analyzes two Mālikī fatwās about blood-based sugar: one in favor of the consumption of sugar, and the other against it. As we shall see, the fatwā that prohibited sugar entirely rested on the presence of blood, the same *ratio essendi* that Mālikī scholars relied upon to prohibit certain insects.

2. Ratiocinating Culture and Blood

In the absence of relevant scriptural texts, the consumption of insects other than locusts was subjected to *ijtihād*, or legal reasoning, and hence two trends have developed: the first trend draws on culture (the Jumhūr position), and the second on blood (the Mālikī position). On the basis of the well-known *ḥadīth* report on locusts, both the Jumhūr and Mālikīs agree on the permissibility of eating locusts, but Mālikī scholars slightly dissent from that common ruling by requiring the *dhakāt*, or killing

[5] ʻAbd Allāh b. "Umar reported that the Messenger of Allah said, 'Two kinds of dead meat have been permitted to us: fish and locusts'" [12].

[6] The *ratio essendi* is the legal motive.

locusts by any means such as boiling, roasting, or plucking off their heads. As for the Jumhūr, they see the *dhakāt* as unnecessary on the ground that the relevant *ḥadīth* does not require it.

2.1. *The Jumhūr position*

The Jumhūr's ruling for the consumption of insects is very common among the majority of schools, in which eating any type of insect other than locusts is not permitted. Their argument does not firmly stem from the Quran, nor from the *sunna* or any legal precedent. Rather, their ruling is grounded in culture, especially that of Arabs in the Ḥijāz, or western Saudi Arabia in modern times.[7] For instance, as a Shāfiʿī scholar, Yaḥyā b. Sharaf al-Dīn al-Nawawī (d. 676/1233) [13: pp. 23–24] expounds the Shāfiʿī position as follows:

> It is [illicit to eat] bees, wasps, flies, mosquitoes, and the like [...] Other than [these insects], all moving [or flying] creatures on earth are looked into [in the following way]. If Arabs regarded them as filthy, they are impermissible to eat; if not, then they are permissible for God says, "He makes lawful for them the good things, and forbids them from the evil things."[8] To ensure the permissibility of that, one should refer to [the food culture of] Arabs, including Bedouins and those who lived in the garrison towns [of Ḥijāz], and those who were rich unlike those who lived in the countryside and the poor. In case Arabs did not agree on the edibility of a [creature, either flying or moving on earth], then one may choose the opinion of the majority.

al-Nawawī builds his ruling entirely on cultural grounds, based on the food culture that was prevalent among Arabs. He specifically referred to those who were socially and economically privileged in the garrison towns of Ḥijāz, irrespective of the food culture that prevailed among the *Ajlāf min ahl al-bādiya wa-al-fuqarāʾ*, or the Bedouin and the poor who lived in rural areas. Additionally, the verse that al-Nawawī cited is vague and does not fit as an argument, provided that other scholars, namely Mālikīs, do not see it as relevant. Ḥanbalī scholars share the Shafiʿī

[7] Ḥijāz is modern-day Saudi Arabia.
[8] Sūrat al-Aʿrāf: 157.

position on the same ground. Ibn Qudāma (d. 620/1223) [14: pp. 105–106], for instance, argues as follows:

> Whatever Arabs regarded as repulsive must be impermissible because God says, "and forbids them from evil things." More specifically, those whose [attitudes towards food are referential] are the people of Ḥijāz because the Quran was revealed [to the Prophet Muḥammad (ﷺ)] among them, and his traditions were first formed and taught there. For this reason, scholars only refer to them when dealing with broad terms of the Quran and *sunna* and never take into account the [food culture of the] people living in rural regions as they used to eat whatever they came across out of necessity [...] Among the filthy foods are insects such as scarabs, cockroaches, beetles, mice, geckos, chameleons, *'dat*, rats, scorpions, and snakes.

Ibn 'Ābidīn (d. 1252/1836), who was a Ḥanafī scholar, had a similar position. In his illuminating commentary on *Sharḥ tanwīr al-abṣār wa-jāmi' al-biḥār* by Muhammad 'Alā' al-Dīn al-Haṣkafī (d. 1088/1677), Ibn 'Ābidīn [15: pp. 305–306] emphasizes the same argument as follows:

> [In his *Mi'rāj al-dirāya*, Burhān al-Dīn al-Marghinānī said], "There is a consensus among scholars on the impermissibility of filthy foods by virtue of the verse, "And [God] forbids them from evil things", on the contrary to what Arabs regarded as unfilthy." [This means that] whatever Arabs found filthy is illicit in strict accordance with the Quran, especially those who lived in the garrison towns of Ḥijāz on the ground that the Quran was revealed to them in their language [and culture] [...] Other than locusts, anything that has no blood is reprehensible such as wasps and flies, though there should be no concerns about eating wasp larvae as long as they do not mature into wasps for they are not considered as carrion.

Contrasting these rulings with each other, one notes that the Jumhūr built their ruling upon five arguments. The first argument is scriptural, using the verse, "He makes lawful for them the good things, and forbids them from the evil things,"[9] and yet, each scholar utilized this verse dif-

[9] *Ibid.*

ferently. Unlike al-Nawawī, who maintained the broad sense of the verse and did not attempt to tailor it to the specific implications of the case under consideration, Ibn ʻĀbidīn argues that the verse, notwithstanding its relatively broad sense, exclusively applies to what Arabs regarded as filthy or otherwise. He did not consider this verse with respect to the consumption of wasp larvae, which he allowed with no evidence. The same is true of Ibn Qudāma, who used the verse, stating that it only applies to the *ḥalāl* foods, as defined by the Quran and *sunna*; otherwise, whatever Arabs regarded as filthy would not be permissible. Additionally, provided that the *sunna*, especially *ḥadīth* reports, is of utmost importance within the Ḥanbalī legal system, Ibn Qudāma attempted to connect the verse with the *sunna* by arguing that, as the Quran was revealed in Arabic among Arabs, the *sunna* was taught in Arabic among the same Arab communities as well. He, however, did not include any *ḥadīth* report or tradition of the Prophet ﷺ related to the case under consideration. One observes that the employment of the *sunna* in this setting does not amount to an argument. Thus, al-Nawawī and Ibn ʻĀbidīn seem to be wary of incorporating the *sunna* as evidence to support their ruling.

The other argument pertains to *ijmāʻ*, or consensus – an argument introduced carefully by Ibn ʻĀbidīn. The formulation *ajmaʻa al-*ʻulamāʼ, or the consensus of scholars, is usually conceived as a consensus undertaken by all schools of law, and it hinges on *uṣūl al-fiqh*, or legal theory, rather than *fiqh*, or jurisprudence. Ibn ʻĀbidīn incorporated consensus without further clarification in his commentary, despite its paramount importance. *Ijmāʻ* is a very complex term, even in *uṣūl al-fiqh*, and scholars, especially in recent centuries, eschewed employing it in the cases that required reasoning, such as the consumption of insects. Nevertheless, it seems that Ibn ʻĀbidīn's wariness gave him leeway to engage in a somewhat similar case where he allowed the consumption of the wasp larvae on the ground that they are not regarded as *mayta*, or carrion.

The third argument relates to *ijtihād*, or legal reasoning. Unlike al-Nawawī, who did not develop this aspect, Ibn Qudāma and Ibn ʻĀbidīn wrestled with their ruling in more than one way. Ibn Qudāma asserts that the permissibility of eating any food (living creature) depends on whether Arabs consumed it; if they did so, then it is permissible, otherwise it is not. Ibn ʻĀbidīn espoused the same view as Ibn Qudāma on the same basis, but he added another feature to render his view more convincing: he made wasp larvae permissible to eat because they do not have *rūḥ*, or soul.[10]

[10] The soul in Arabic is often used as a synonym of maturity.

As I pointed out earlier, Ibn 'Ābidīn did not seem to share the view of *ijmā'* over eating insects, almost as if he was inclined to leave himself some room to defend his opinion about wasp larvae. It is also likely that he was aware of the Mālikī scholars who do not lend credence to consensus in this particular case.

The Jumhūr's position is thus entirely grounded in culture, not in strict legal premises such as *'urf*, or customary law. Food culture is restrained by many factors, including geographical exigencies. There were many species that did not exist in the Ḥijāz but did so in other parts of the world, and vice versa. If this cultural aspect was a legal precept, Mālikī scholars would have shared their position given their strict loyalty to the Medinese traditions, as Medina was a major garrison town of the Ḥijāz. From the Mālikī perspective, there is no such thing as *ma-istaṭābahū/istakhbathahū al-'Arab*, or what Arabs regarded as filthy or otherwise. As we shall see, Mālikī scholars did not use the Medinese traditions but rather wrestled with a different legal method that rests on the nature of insects themselves.

2.2. *The Mālikī position*

The *ummahāt*, or the early authoritative works of the Mālikī school compiled in the first few centuries after Hijra,[11] including the *Muwaṭṭa'* by Imām Mālik and the *Mudawwana* by 'Abd-al-Raḥmān b. al-Qāsim (d. 191/806) with the recension of Saḥnūn (d. 204/820), do not contain *ḥadīth* reports or opinions on the consumption of insects other than locusts. Thus, entomophagy has always been subjected to *ijtihād*, or legal reasoning, which often goes beyond legal precepts established by the Quran and *sunna* to include Arab cultural habits. Nevertheless, the area where one can find the relevant opinions of all Mālikī authorities, including the aforementioned ones, is the nawāzil compilations such as the *Mi'yār mu'rib* by Aḥmad b. Yaḥyā al-Wansharīsī (d. 914/1508) [16: p. 28], and the *Nawāzil jadīda* by al-Mahdī al-Wazzānī (d. 1342/1923), whose account on entomophagy is critical yet compliant with the *mashhūr*, or the commonly held view, of the *madhhab*. In his

[11]The Hijra, or migration, refers to the date when the Prophet Muhammad (ﷺ) and his Associates migrated from Mecca to Medina to escape persecution in 622 CE, which became the starting point of the Islamic calendar.

Nawāzil, al-Wazzānī [17: pp. 287–288] cites the most authoritative opinions and comments on them, as follows:

> Ibn ʻArafa -May God have mercy on him- was petitioned about the worms that feed on olives and honey and that cannot be removed from them when distilling [those foods] or can be difficult to remove. He responded: "To my knowledge and on the basis of the *madhhab* narratives, it is not permissible to produce what has been mentioned [olive oil and honey] until worms are completely removed. As for Ibn al-Ḥājib's statement: "It is not impermissible to eat food [mixed] with worms, it is an opinion that my Shaykh Ibn ʻAbd-al-Salām and Ibn Hārūn have espoused." I [Ibn ʻArafa] have never heard of a narrative that can be referred to [in this regard] except for the opinion of Abū ʻUmar who said: "some legists have allowed the consumption of food worms, fava beans insects, and bee larvae because they are not impure. Some scholars have made them reprehensible whilst other scholars have prohibited them." I [al-Wazzānī] reckon that such an opinion [prohibition] is not common in the *madhhab*. [For instance, al-Māzarī ...] is of the opinion that [food worms, grain weevils feeding on fava beans, and bees' larvae] are as permissible as all other earthly insects. al-Lakhmī was also asked about eating a dead worm on dates deliberately and said: "We have seen previously that it is not impermissible to eat worms feeding on dates and honey... As for the worms that feed on anything else [in dirt], then Ibn al-Ḥājib said in the end of his treatment of permissible food: "As for other filthy insects such as scarabs and the like, the [*mashhūr* of the] *madhhab* is that they are prohibited."

According to al-Wazzānī, the majority opinion of the Mālikī school is in favor of entomophagy, a majority opinion that crystallized with al-Māzarī in particular. Before delving into al-Wazzānī's position along with the other authorities that he cited, it is worth citing al-Māzarī's view in his *Sharḥ al-talqīn* [18], as follows:

> All living creatures on earth are divided into two types: The first type is the *bloody creatures* that we have treated previously such as birds and mice [...] The second type is *unbloody creatures* such as wasps, scorpions, beetles, crickets, cockroaches, and the like. The ruling for this type of insect is the same as the ruling for sea creatures because they do not become impure when they die [...] The reason why *unbloody creatures* are

> not considered impure because of death is what has been depicted before: that the *ratio essendi* of the impurity of an animal is twofold: death and bloodiness, two elements upon which there is an agreement [between scholars]. If either element lapses, then the ruling changes on the basis of the *ḥadīth* report of the Prophet -blessings be upon him- who said, "If a fly falls into the drink of anyone of you, s/he should dip it [in the drink], and then remove it." If this fly was impure by death, then the whole drink would be impure as well for the death occurred because of dipping; and if the fly died in food, then the food would become impure and eventually invalid [...] There are different opinions in the *madhhab* about [eating] fleas [...] Ibn al-Qaṣṣār's ruling is that they belong to *bloody insects* for their blood [...] It is, however, reported that Saḥnūn said that fleas should go *under unbloody creatures*. (pp. 237–241)

The first text above summarizes all the Mālikī authoritative positions on the consumption of insects, including the one that al-Wazzānī espoused *vis-à-vis* the position of other authorities, such as Ibn ʻArafa. The permissibility of consuming insects is a majority opinion, which is represented by Saḥnūn, Ibn Ḥabīb, al-Lakhmī, and al-Māzarī, while the prohibition of it is a minority opinion, which is represented by Ibn al-Qaṣṣār, Ibn al-Ḥājib, and Ibn ʻArafa. Unlike the Jumhūr, who expounded their ruling on cultural grounds, Mālikī scholars have used different approaches to derive their ruling. As an impure substance, blood seems to be the linchpin of their discussions over entomophagy by virtue of the verse, "He has only forbidden to you dead animals, blood, the flesh of swine, and that which has been dedicated to other than Allah."[12] From al-Māzarī's standpoint, insects containing blood ought to go under the general rule of the verse, unlike the ones that contain *hemolymph*.[13] However, the minority opinion is not as homogeneous as it may seem. Unlike Ibn ʻArafa, who holds a stricter viewpoint, Ibn al-Ḥājib allowed the consumption of worms contained in food but prohibited those that feed on dirt, such as earthworms and scarabs (insects of the beetle family).[14]

At the outset of his fatwā, Ibn ʻArafa mentioned the narratives of the *madhhab*, but his phraseology remains to some extent reluctant. His mention of the *ummahāt* is no more than an allusion to the fact that, due to the

---

[12] Sūrat al-Naḥl: 115.

[13] *Hemolymph* is a fluid equivalent to red blood in most invertebrates.

[14] al-Wazzani [17] also issued fatwā on scarabs and earthworms.

absence of any relevant authoritative text, eating food worms should be prohibited. In reaction to that, al-Wazzānī [17] commented that it was against the *madhhab* to hold such a view. Furthermore, unlike Ibn al-Ḥājib and Ibn ʻArafa, Ibn al-Qaṣṣār relied on the impermissibility of blood to support his view on fleas, which seems to be a stronger argument. This view may be regarded as a third type of argument in addition to the two types that al-Māzarī addressed in his *Sharḥ al-talqīn*.

As for Saḥnūn, he in turn built his opinion on fleas upon blood, which he allowed on the ground that fleas do not belong to *bloody creatures*, as the blood they contain is unnatural. The same is true of Ibn Ḥabīb, who allowed the consumption of mosquitoes in analogy with locusts. The rulings of both Saḥnūn and Ibn Ḥabīb for fleas and mosquitoes revolve around red blood cells and whether they are natural. Yet, neither authority distinguished between male and female mosquitoes, despite the fact that male mosquitoes only feed on plant nectar or alternative sugar sources [19]. Arguably, if male mosquitoes do not consume blood, then they ought to be edible, which is more likely what Ibn Ḥabīb was alluding to.

However, by dividing all *alive creature*s on earth, including insects, into two types: *bloody creatures*, such as birds, mice, and sheep, and *unbloody creatures*, such as scorpions, mosquitoes, and locusts, al-Māzarī's view is the opinion that gained wide acceptance among his fellow muftīs and subsequent scholars, including al-Wazzānī. Additionally, al-Māzarī restricts the impurity of blood to wetness and liquidity. Any creature, including insects, whose red blood cells are either dry or stagnant is no longer impure, and *vice versa*. Having said that, al-Māzarī does not distinguish between natural and unnatural blood. He suggests that insects with no red blood cells are edible, but seems to exclude the other types of insects that contain unnatural red blood cells. Mosquitoes, for instance, may contain it, but it is unnatural; the same is true of fleas that Ibn al-Qaṣṣār considered *bloody creatures*. Nevertheless, al-Māzarī seems to have been inclined to leave this third type open for discussion without providing any ruling or trying to compare the two opinions of Ibn al-Qaṣṣār and Ibn Ḥabīb.[15] Therefore, red blood cells should be thought of as a *ratio essendi* upon which Mālikī scholars allowed the consumption of not only insects but also any protein-free food, such as plant-based food. In what follows, I demonstrate how blood can affect the permissibility of

[15]al-Māzarī did not mention anything about the difference between male and female mosquitoes.

plant-based food through a case study: a debate between Mālikī authorities over the consumption of blood-based sugar in 19th-century Morocco.

3. Sugarcane Production: Rise, Fall, and Prohibition

Sugar consumption is a relevant and analogous case to entomophagy for two main reasons. First, the rationale behind the prohibition of certain insects from the Mālikī angle is identical to the *ratio essendi* (red blood cells) that certain Mālikī scholars relied upon to call for the prohibition of European sugarloaf in the 19th century. Second, the debate over the prohibition of consuming sugar is a case that helps us comprehend how delusion, especially if combined with what Christopher Melchert [20] calls *renunciant piety*, may dramatically affect the view of muftīs despite their authoritative stature. In what follows, I will demonstrate how sugar was prohibited in 19th-century Morocco by using the same reasoning that Mālikī scholars have used to invalidate the consumption of insects in the past.

Together with Egypt, Sicily, and Palestine, Morocco was a major hub for sugar production in the Mediterranean region for many centuries before and after the advent of Islam [21–23]. For instance, under the Sa‘dī dynasty in the 16th century, Morocco produced a considerable amount of sugar, especially during the reign of Sultan Aḥmad al-Manṣūr al-Dhahabī (r. 985/1578–1011/1603) after he boosted investments in sugarcane cultivation and established sugar factories in Marrakech, Agadir, and Essaouira [24]. After Sultan al-Dhahabī passed away, due to economic and political instabilities, sugarcane production declined, and subsequently the sugar market went bankrupt. The bankruptcy of Morocco's sugar industry continued for more than a century as it ceased to be a state-monopolized industry [24].

However, from the late 18th century onward, Moroccans began to find European sugarloaf in the markets. Rumors began to circulate that this type of refined sugar contained blood, which brought about a divisive debate among scholarly communities in Morocco.[16] Some muftīs prohibited the consumption of European sugarloaf completely, while others allowed it. The first fatwā was a response to a petition about the traders

[16] Sugarloaf is a conical loaf of concentrated refined sugar.

who crossed the Mediterranean Sea to trade goods with sugarloaf, while the second fatwā was a treatise against it.

3.1. *Blood as a ratio essendi*

The debate over the ruling for sugarloaf reached its peak under Sultan al-Mawlā Sulaymān (r. 1206/1792–1237/1822) in the 19th century [24]. A number of scholars issued fatwās prohibiting the consumption of European sugarloaf, including Ḥamdūn b. al-Ḥājj al-Sulamī (d. 1232/1817) [25: p. 356] who issued his fatwā as follows:

> Sugarloaf is no longer permissible to consume as a hard or liquid food. According to the *mashhūr* of the *madhhab*, anything impure that falls into a liquid food, this food becomes impure, too, irrespective of how small the amount of that impure substance is. The liquid food cannot be purified because the impurity is mixed with all the components of that food. It is cited in the *Mukhtaṣar* [of Khalīl] that "Any food [of that sort] is considered impure regardless of how small the impurity that touches it is." Based on what has been reported from some righteous and reliable [traders], Rum [Europeans] mix fresh blood with sugar and put them together on fire for distilling. They keep doing so until sugar takes the form of a loaf as it is exported to us now.

al-Sulamī's ruling builds upon three core elements. First, he expounds that his ruling complies with the *mashhūr* of the *maddhab* that invalidates the consumption of any liquid food mixed with an impure substance, such as blood, and therefore concludes that the ruling is completely compliant with that opinion. Second, al-Sulamī cites a statement from Khalīl's *Mukhtaṣar*, despite its vagueness, to support his ruling.[17] The other major element that contributed to the impermissibility of the sugarloaf is that the latter was originally liquid, while the position of the *madhhab*, the *mashhūr* to be specific, is very strict about mixing impure substances with liquid food, unlike hard food, where only the part that an impure

[17] Jocelyn Hendrickson [26] uses the term *manipulation* to describe how falsely many Mālikī jurists went against the dictates of juridical Islam, which apparently applies to al-Sulamī's ruling for this case.

substance touches must be removed while the rest can be edible.[18] Additionally, in response to the other fatwā that challenged him, al-Sulamī [27: p.175] employed another way to convince his fellow muftīs by saying that although blood might not be contained, it still ought to be void on the pretext of deteriorating one's *wara'*, or faithfulness,[19] as follows:

> Some people have heard about the sugarloaf production [in Europe], and some other people have witnessed it there. What [these people] have heard and witnessed is not a claim nor a lie. What they have [heard and witnessed] is accurate which no prudent person would deny. This is a fact that even people in Tunisia have witnessed everywhere is their region. Scholars there have prohibited it out of faithfulness, [and that is what] renowned scholars always do.

3.2. *Blood-based sugar as a delusion*

As expected, al-Sulamī's opinion brought about a massive reaction among the scholarly community of Morocco. Many muftīs issued counter-fatwās allowing the consumption of European sugarloaf, including Sulaymān b. Muḥammad al-Ḥawwāt al-Shafshāwnī (d. 1231/1816) [28: pp. 38–39], who produced a legal treatise on this particular case. In this treatise, not only does he draw on scriptural and Mālikī authoritative texts but also on *ḥikma*, or scientific evidence, as follows:

> The rumors about sugarloaf must be wrong because of a delusion that the red colour in sugar when being heated is caused by blood while it is not the case. Rather, the red colour that made the person who informed

[18] al-Sulamī used a binary argument that the petition was made by some petitioners who were both righteous and reliable. He used the expression, "*Akhbara ba'ḍ al-thiqāt*," which means that his ruling was responsive to a question raised by righteous individuals. Though, it is clear from the structure of the petition that the question was raised by one petitioner, not multiple petitioners, and the intriguing words here are *ba'ḍ* (some) and *thiqāt* (righteous). Even though the word *ba'ḍ* in Arabic is used with reference either to one person or multiple people, in this setting it seems to be linked to a single person as al-Sulamī used the relative pronoun *lahū* (him) instead of *lahum* (them).

[19] *Zuhd* and *wara'* have the same meaning in this setting.

> you believe it was blood is the nature of sugar itself just like *'andam*, or *Haematoxylum*. The original colour of sugar is [naturally] red and some of it comes back on [white] sugar when put on fire or it is in a cold and humid temperature. Specialists of *ḥikma*, or natural sciences, have thoroughly addressed this in their works and all agree that sugar becomes red at the first stages of making it. No natural scientist has ever said that [, when being heated,] sugar changes colour to red due to the presence of blood.

al-Shafshāwnī discussed al-Sulamī's fatwā on the basis of a threefold argument. First, al-Shafshāwnī considered the rumors *ghalaṭ*, or misleading, and pointed out that the red color has nothing to do with blood but instead with the nature of sugar itself. He expounds that when sugar is heated at a certain temperature, it naturally turns into a red liquid, as it does when exposed to a low temperature. al-Shafshāwnī also adds that natural scientists have described this effect of temperature on sugar when it is heated; therefore, sugarloaf must be permissible to consume either as hard food or as liquid food [29].

Although al-Shafshāwnī and al-Sulamī share their commitment to the *madhhab*, their misunderstanding of the case affected their rulings. al-Sulamī heard about the case but did not investigate further. Instead, he relied on the rumors and did not bother to scrutinize the case or at least ask the *ḥukamā'*, or natural scientists, like al-Shafshāwnī did. In addition to his *manipulation* of Khalīl's statement, al-Sulamī's renunciant piety contributed to the rigidity of his methodology to derive such a ruling. His advice for muftīs to avoid the consumption of sugarloaf is erroneous from the Mālikī perspective, as *wara'* is not a criterion in *ijtihād* upon which scholars of *uṣūl al-fiqh* agree.

4. Conclusions

The position of Islam on the consumption of insects is not homogeneous. The first position belongs to the majority of the schools of law, which are the Ḥanafī, Ḥanbalī, and Shāfi'ī schools. These schools prohibit the consumption of insects, except for Ibn 'Ābidīn, who made an exception for bee larvae before they mature into bees. The authorities of these schools have held such a view on the basis of whatever Arabs regarded as filthy in the early periods of Islam. A variety of arguments have been used to support this position, namely the Quran, the *sunna*, and consensus.

The second position belongs to the Mālikī school of law, which allows the consumption of all insects, depending on the presence of red blood cells. If red blood cells are present, then it is not permissible to eat those insects. Even so, certain Mālikī scholars, such as Ibn ʻArafa and al-Qaṣṣār, have not allowed the consumption of some specific insects, but their position remains a minority within the Mālikī school. The majority opinion is in favor of eating insects as long as they do not contain red blood cells, which al-Māzarī illuminatingly discussed in his *Sharḥ al-talqīn.* al-Māzarī depicted the Mālikī position by focusing on the *ratio essendi* of the impermissibility of insects with red blood cells. As an impure substance, blood is the rationale behind any prohibition.

It thus seems that the main issue with the consumption of insects revolves around red blood cells and yet goes beyond insects; it may even affect the permissibility of any other type of *ḥalāl* food, such as sugar, that al-Sulamī falsely disallowed on that basis. The red color produced by sugar while being heated was delusional. In addition, the *wara'*, or renunciant piety, played a role in establishing al-Sulamī's ruling as he urged his fellow muftīs who did not share his opinion to dismiss any *shubha,* or suspiciousness, surrounding sugarloaf as *taḥawwuṭ*, or act of wariness. What al-Sulamī did not pay attention to is that renunciant piety does not play a pivotal role in *fiqh* or *uṣūl al-fiqh* but instead in a different area, which is *ʻilm al-tazkiya*, or spirituality, which includes *taṣawwuf*, or Islamic mysticism. For this reason, al-Shafshāwnī disagreed with al-Sulamī on the basis of an array of proof-texts and evidence beyond the legal sphere, including the natural sciences. Interestingly, the Jumhūr did not employ piety as evidence, but instead they invoked Arab culture, even if it is an uncommon legal source.

The consumption of insects as addressed by premodern scholars of Islam is very similar to the discussion over the consumption of insect-based food nowadays. It is an old yet new case that requires further attention, especially the position of the Mālikī jurists who produced peculiar treatises on such a case. Although this chapter is no more than an attempt to depict the historico-legal implications regarding the consumption of insects and blood-based food in Islam and Muslim history, it is my hope that it will inspire reflections on incorporating the discussion of this case among Muslim scholars, from both the Mālikī and Jumhūr perspectives, into contemporary discussions over novel food technologies. Ideally, to have a more comprehensive understanding of the case in Islam, it is worth addressing the position of Shīʻī schools of law on this particular topic as well.

Acknowledgments

I am very grateful to the Oxford Centre for Islamic Studies for its support to conduct this research and for the beneficial discussions I have had with its scholars. I am also grateful to Christopher Melchert and Alice Catanzaro for their advice and helpful comments on the manuscript and the anonymous reviewers for their careful reading.

References

[1] European Commission. Approval of fourth insect as novel food. https://food.ec.europa.eu/food-safety/novel-food/authorisations/approval-insect-novel-food_en#:~:text=What%20was%20adopted%20by%20the,mealworm)%2C%20as%20a%20food. [Accessed 2024 Dec 13].

[2] *Independent*. Sainsbury's becomes first UK supermarket to sell edible bugs as crickets hit shelves. https://www.independent.co.uk/news/uk/home-news/sainsburys-first-uk-supermarket-sell-edible-bugs-insects-crickets-a8638581.html [Accessed 2024 Dec 13].

[3] Jameel S. Climate change, food systems, and the Islamic perspective on alternative proteins. *Trends Food Sci Technol*. Elsevier. 2023. https://doi.org/10.1016/j.tifs.2023.06.02.

[4] Attwood S, Jameel S, Huseini A, Alkhalawi E, Hajat C. Halal cultivated meat: An untapped opportunity. *Front Nutr*. 2023. DOI: 10.3389/fnut.2023.1196475.

[5] European Commission. What is novel food? Novel Food – European Commission. [Accessed 2024 Dec 16].

[6] Dār al-Iftā' al-Miṣriya. What is the ruling on eating insects? Egypt's Dar Al-Ifta. What is the ruling on eating insect... (dar-alifta.org). 2024 Feb 7.

[7] World Religion Database. Traditions of Muslims, global 2020. https://worldreligiondatabase.org/data/ [Accessed 2024 Feb 1].

[8] Melchert C. *The Formation of the Sunnī Schools of Law*. Leiden: Brill; 1997.

[9] Tajudeen AL. Halal certification of insect-based food: A critique. *Int J Islam Ethics*. 2020;5(2):100–112.

[10] Islamqa. Are insects Halal? Are Insects Halal? – Islam Question & Answer (islamqa.info). [Accessed 2024 Feb 7].

[11] Shaykh 'Ajīl al-Nashmī. Reaction to the recent authorisations of the European Commission. https://www.alanba.com.kw/1167454 [Accessed 2024 Dec 13].

[12] Ibn Māja. *Al-Sunan*. Muhammad Fu'ād 'Abd-al-Bāqī, editors. Vols. 2. Egypt: Dār Iḥyā' al-Kutub al-'Arabiya. Ḥadīth number 3218.

[13] Yaḥyā b. Sharaf-al-Dīn al- al-Nawawī. *Al-Majmū' sharḥ al-muhadhdhab*. A group of scholars, editors. 9 Vols. Cairo: Idārat al-Ṭibā'a al-Munīriya & Maṭba'at al-Taḍāmun al-Akhawī; 1928.
[14] Ibn Qudāma. *al-Mughnī*. Ṭāhā al-Zīnī, Muḥammad 'Abd-al-Wahhāb Fāyid, 'Abd-al-Qādir 'Aṭṭā, and Muḥammad Maḥmūd Ghānim Ghayth, editors. 10 Vols. Cairo: Maktabat al-Qāhira; 1968.
[15] Ibn 'Ābidīn, *Rad al-muḥtār 'alā sharḥ al-risāla: sharḥ tanwīr al-abṣār*. 6 Vols. 2nd edn. Egypt: Maktabat wa-Maṭba'at Muṣtafā al-Bābī al-Ḥalabī wa-Awlāduh; 1966.
[16] Aḥmad b. Yaḥyā al-Wansharīsī. *Al-Mi'yār al-mu'rib wa-al-jāmi' al-mughrib 'an fatāwā ahl Ifrīqiya wa-al-Andalus wa-al-Maghrib*. Muḥammad Ḥajjī and a group of the Qarawiyyīn University scholars, editors. 13 Vols. Lebanon: Dār al-Gharb al-Islāmī; 1981.
[17] Al-Mahdī al-Wazzānī. *Al-Nawāzil al-jadīda al-kubrā*. Muḥammad al-Sayid 'Uthmān, editor. 12 Vols. Lebanon: Dār al-Kutub al-'Ilmiya; 2014.
[18] Imām al-Māzarī. *Sharḥ al-talqīn*. Muḥammad al-Mukhtār al-Sulamī, editor. 5 Vols. Lebanon: Dār al-Gharb al-Islāmī; 2008.
[19] Barredo E, DeGennaro M. Not just from blood: Mosquito nutrient acquisition from nectar sources. Trends Parasitol. *CellPress Reviews*. 2020;36(5); 473–484.
[20] Melchert C. *Before Sufism: Early Islamic Renunciant Piety*. Berlin/Boston: De Gruyter; 2020.
[21] Galloway JH. The Mediterranean sugar industry. *Geogr Rev*. 1977;2(67): 177–194.
[22] Berthier P. *Les anciennes sucreries du Maroc et leurs réseaux hydrauliques*. Rabat: Imprimerie; 1966.
[23] Ouerfelli M. *Production, commercialisation et usages dans la Méditerranée médiévale*. Leiden: Brill; 2008.
[24] Aḥmad al-Nāṣirī. *Al-Istiqṣā li-akhbār al-Maghrib al-Aqṣā*. Ja'far al-Nāṣirī, Muhammad al-Nāṣirī, editors. 9 Vols. Casablanca: Dār al-Kitāb; 1954–1955–1956.
[25] al-Mahdī al-Wazzānī. *Al-Mi'yār al-jadīd al-jāmi' al-mu'rib 'an fatāwā al-muta'akhkhirīn min 'ulama' al-Maghrib*. 'Umār b. 'Abbād, editor. 8 Vols. Rabat: Ministry of Endowments and Islamic Affairs; 1996.
[26] Hendrickson J. Prohibiting the pilgrimage: Politics and fiction in Mālikī Fatwās. *Islam Law Soc*. 2016;3(23):161–238.
[27] 'Abd-al-Aḥad al-Sabtī, 'Abd-al-Raḥmān Lakhṣāṣī. *Min al-shāy ilā al-atāy: al-'āda wa-al-tārīkh*. Rabat: Kulliyat al-Ādāb wa-al-'Ulūm al-Insāniya; 1999.
[28] Sulaymān b. Muḥammad al-Ḥawwāt al-Shafshāwnī. *Taghyīr al-munkar fī man za'ama taḥrīm al-sukkar*. M'ḥammad Raḥmānī, editor. Fez: Markaz Fātima al-Fihriya li-al-Abḥāth wa-al-Dirāsāt; 2021.
[29] Deerr N. *Cane Sugar*. London: Norman Rodger; 1921.

Part V

Fintech

https://doi.org/10.1142/9781800616295_0015

Chapter 15

Fusion of Blockchain and Islamic Fintech: Unlocking New Possibilities in SME Financing, Financial Well-Being, and Trade Financing

Ahmet Faruk Aysan* and Muhammad Fazlurrahman Syarif†

Hamad Bin Khalifa University, Qatar Foundation, Doha, Qatar

*aaysan@hbku.edu.qa

†musy33188@hbku.edu.qa

Abstract

Islamic fintech refers to financial services that leverage modern technology to offer Sharia-compliant products, ensuring that transactions adhere to Islamic ethical standards. Using secondary data, we discuss Islamic fintech, focusing on small- and medium-sized enterprise (SME) financing, financial well-being, and trade financing in emerging markets, aiming to discover opportunities and challenges, the role of stakeholders, risk mitigation, and blockchain optimization. The results reveal that implementing various strategies is pivotal for mainstream Islamic fintech. This includes conducting risk assessments of business processes, introducing clear procedures for managing risk, ensuring an effective internal control system, building good relationships with regulators, implementing a robust cybersecurity system to accelerate these industries, increasing financial literacy, adopting blockchain technology, and adjusting business strategies. This research is likely to benefit industry or market players, regulators, and other stakeholders in developing better strategies to support the growth and development of SME financing, financial well-being, and trade financing.

1. Introduction

Islamic fintech applies advanced technology to offer financial services that comply with ethical standards by integrating digital innovations and Islamic financial principles. It is operated to provide accessible, transparent, and ethical financial solutions to meet the needs of both Muslim and non-Muslim populations globally. Since digital finance can benefit banks or financial institutions through financial inclusion, small- and medium-sized enterprise (SME) financing, financial well-being, and trade financing companies present significant growth globally [1]. Research shows that financial inclusion has a strong and positive relationship with financial well-being [2], with the latter considered a critical point of overall well-being worldwide. Financial well-being refers to the ability of a person or company to manage their finances effectively and to avoid financial problems that can harm business and individual well-being. Another fundamental aspect of the business context is trade financing, which involves financing imports and exports that can help businesses obtain the financial resources necessary to expand their operations. However, trade finance also comes with consequences and risks, and companies must consider these risks when choosing the right financing option.

Islamic fintech has emerged as a dynamic technology sector since 2010, playing a significant role in the global fintech ecosystem. It focuses on Sharia-compliant business and consumer finance, in which its growth and potential are evident, with close to 1,400 Islamic financial institutions operating across 80 countries [3]. This growth is attributed to the increasing adoption of advanced technology by Islamic banks, particularly in regions such as Malaysia, where technology support has been integrated to enhance financial services [4]. A study by [5] highlights how Islamic fintech effectively addresses the challenges of adhering to Sharia law in financial services by integrating modern technology with traditional Islamic finance principles. This has created innovative paths for implementing some of the most critical finance-related tasks applicable to the Muslim community. For example, Islamic fintech platforms have the potential to streamline processes related to Sharia-compliant transactions, such as Islamic philanthropy, by incorporating trust, religiosity, and image into technology acceptance models. Through the utilization of Islamic fintech, philanthropic institutions can improve their fundraising efforts in accordance with Islamic principles, thereby facilitating the flow of funds in a Sharia-compliant manner [6].

This study provides a more comprehensive view of the challenges and opportunities as well as the available solutions to promote the growth and prosperity of SME financing, financial well-being, and trade financing companies. It contributes to the ongoing discourse on this topic by providing a thorough analysis of the current landscape and offering suggestions for future improvements, which aim to generate insights and recommendations that can be implemented by policymakers, financial institutions, and other stakeholders to support growth and development. By creating an inclusive and supportive financial ecosystem, it is possible to empower these industries to overcome barriers that hinder their progress. Islamic fintech industries have significant growth potential despite facing challenges, including the necessity to adapt to regulatory changes and enhance risk control processes, alongside the critical need for collaboration between stakeholders to develop supportive policies and maintain Sharia compliance. Sustainable development can be promoted by providing innovative and affordable financial services tailored to customer needs and emphasizing the importance of risk control processes, regulatory change monitoring, and collaboration among governments, stakeholders, and industries. The study also highlights the benefits of leveraging artificial intelligence (AI) and blockchain technology to optimize credit risk analysis, improve business performance predictions, and provide transformative solutions for SME financing, financial well-being, and trade financing. Embracing infrastructure investment, education, and cultural change will help organizations leverage the benefits of blockchain technology, creating a more inclusive and efficient financial ecosystem.

This literature review outlines the methodology used to examine the importance of embedding SME financing, financial well-being, and trade financing and provides suggestions for future directions. A single approach is employed by reviewing the existing literature to generate insights into the topic. The study is conducted in three phases: understanding the current landscape, identifying gaps and challenges, and proposing recommendations. The first phase involves a comprehensive review of the academic literature, policy documents, and industry reports to understand the existing state of SME financing, financial well-being, and trade financing. It includes the challenges SMEs face in accessing finance, the role of financial literacy, and the impact of trade financing. Additionally, it examines existing financial products and services available to SMEs and the current government policies and initiatives to promote SME development.

In the second phase, secondary data sources are used identify gaps and challenges with regard to this topic. Secondary data sources, such as reports, are used to gain insights into the challenges faced by SMEs and their financial well-being and access, as well as the barriers that financial institutions face in providing services to these industries. Based on a literature review and data analysis, the third phase presents recommendations for improving SME financing, financial well-being, and trade financing. These recommendations were derived from the best practices identified in the literature and insights gained from secondary data sources. The recommendations focus on policy interventions, innovative financing solutions, and partnerships between stakeholders to create a more inclusive financial ecosystem for SMEs.

2. Setting the Stage and a Retrospective Analysis of the Literature

SMEs are considered Europe's core engine for future growth. However, to fulfill this potential, they need a continuous supply of long-term funding [7], which many find challenging and therefore fail to reach their potential. Interestingly, recent studies show that SMEs perform well and exhibit high resilience during crises [8]. Several financing options are available for SMEs, including traditional bank loans, government-sponsored loans, venture capital, crowdfunding, and alternative lending platforms. Government-sponsored loans usually have more lenient eligibility criteria, but the application process can take a long time. Studies have acknowledged that venture capital is another attractive financing option for SMEs with high growth potential. However, venture capitalists usually invest in businesses with a proven track record of success, despite their growth potential. Hence, they may not be the best choice for new or early-stage companies. Simultaneously, during a crisis period, there is a chance to create a market by tackling it with an innovative and proactive attitude [9]. Crowdfunding and alternative lending platforms have recently gained popularity as alternatives for SMEs to obtain financing without the use of traditional lenders. These platforms allow SMEs to raise funds from many investors or lenders, which is more favorable than traditional loans. According to [10], banking products are the most significant source of financing for SMEs. Other instruments offered in the market, such as stocks, debentures, and other financial instruments, are used on a residual basis.

Studies on financial well-being also show that it is a complex concept that extends beyond traditional financial literacy and the broader notion of financial capability [11]. Empirical investigations to measure the link between financial literacy and financial capability must be developed to achieve financial well-being goals [12]. Ongoing work on measuring financial well-being is considered relevant in today's highly challenging financial landscape, especially because this aspect is also expected to be the state balance in today's society [13]. Trade finance is essentially intercompany financing with established relationships between financial institutions [14] and refers to the range of financial products and services that facilitate international trade transactions between buyers and sellers. These financial tools are designed to mitigate the risks associated with cross-border trading, such as defaults, currency fluctuations, and political instability. Some of the most common trade finance products include letters of credit, export credit insurance, factoring, and supply chain financing. However, this trade finance service is well established for domestic and international trade financing [15]. Importers' risk shapes trade financing failure to pay the exporter and the possibility that the exporter does not deliver goods, as stipulated in the contract [16]. Furthermore, trade finance can reduce these risks to sellers and buyers (exporters and importers), which are fundamental to trading goods [17]. Trade finance is critical for businesses involved in international trade because it allows them to manage risk, improve cash flow, and facilitate the movement of goods across borders [16].

Islamic fintech has emerged as a key player in providing innovative financial solutions for SMEs to access funding and grow their businesses [18]. Research indicates that Islamic fintech can attract new customers and improve financial dealings, service offerings, and convenience, leading to higher customer loyalty [19,20]. It addresses financial inclusion and contributes to economic growth, especially in supporting SMEs [21,22] through solutions such as digital lending platforms, crowdfunding platforms, and invoice financing platforms, enabling SMEs to receive financing without needing collateral. By leveraging digital innovations, Islamic fintech can facilitate financial transactions, increase accessibility to financial services, and empower underserved communities [22–24]. On the other hand, it can promote financial inclusion by providing individuals with access to affordable and ethical financial products and services that can improve their financial well-being and eventually lead to critical drivers of economic development [25]. This includes personal finance management apps, zakat, and charity management platforms that enable users to manage their finances and charitable giving. It can also facilitate trade finance by providing solutions for cross-border payments and supply chain financing that comply with Islamic finance principles. Islamic factoring platforms, supply chain financing platforms, and cross-border payment platforms are a few examples that enable businesses to manage their working capital and cash flow. It also positively influences the development of Islamic finance [26].

3. Exploring the Landscape: Opportunities and Challenges in Islamic Fintech

In developing and developed countries, SMEs play an essential role in economic evolution, employment generation, output, technological innovation, and poverty reduction [27]. Previous studies have shown how well-functioning financing is necessary to maximize the potential of SMEs in Bangladesh [28]. Another study implies that SME financing has been extensively researched over a span of more than three decades (1986–2020) because of a notable increase in the number of publications exploring new and innovative sources of financing [29]. A novel bibliometric analysis of the academic literature on fintech as a financial disruptor reveals a growing number of publications on the topic, indicating an increased interest in and potential for future research [30]. Other findings also postulate that SME evolution has a positive effect on rural development [31]. It offers opportunities and challenges for the internationalization of SMEs, policy frameworks, finance, and market access, along with sociocultural norms, which have established a unique perspective [32]. The results of previous research show that this innovative model provides a new approach for the government to promote inclusive SME finance and alternative channels for SMEs for those who do not have sufficient collateral to gain access to finance [33]. Policymakers have raised concerns about the trade-off between increasing opportunities for SMEs and startups to raise funds and the challenge of protecting investors [34].

Financial literacy is crucial for financial well-being. However, other factors such as income, savings, and debt literacy also have an influence. According to [2], the critical elements of financial well-being are intervention, personal financial behavior, consequences, and contextual factors. Another opportunity is the increasing availability of digital financial services, which can provide individuals with greater access to financial products and services, particularly in underserved areas. Previous research has also affirmed that good self-control leads to better financial behavior and positively affects financial well-being [35]. On the other hand, trade finance plays a vital role in global trade, as it helps reduce the risks and uncertainties involved in cross-border transactions and allows businesses to access the capital they need to grow, including facilitating international trade, such as import and export financing, letters of credit, and trade insurance. Trade finance has evolved to address issues through financial intermediaries, such as banks that issue merchant credit letters [36]. It represents another vital form of financing that provides essential support for international and domestic trading activities, but it operates within a stricter regulatory and procedural framework compared to more informal, adaptable financing methods. It plays a crucial role in facilitating trade by providing the necessary funds and guarantees, yet it demands careful navigation due to its more rigid requirements and structures [37]. Other factors, such as the absence of strong trade facilitation and necessary trade-related economic infrastructure, are major barriers to building export capacities [38]. Today's trade finance is riddled with inefficiencies, and the industry is vulnerable to fraud. Therefore, paper-based trade financing processes must be improved or replaced by digital operations [39].

Even though fintech is empowering in terms of transparency and cost reduction, Islamic fintech faces several challenges. One of the main obstacles is that many SMEs hesitate to adopt new financial technologies, especially if they are unfamiliar with Islamic financial principles [4]. Additionally, the complexity of Sharia-compliant financial products and services could further deter SMEs from embracing Islamic fintech solutions [40]. Research shows that fintech adoption significantly affects sustainability, and thus its impact on economic, environmental, and social sustainability should be analyzed [41]. Regulatory challenges may also arise if Islamic fintech products and services are controversial and uncertain [42]. Another challenge is SMEs' lack of awareness and understanding of Islamic financial principles. This can hinder the adoption of

Islamic fintech products and services and limit their growth potential. There may be a lack of trust and confidence in new and innovative financial products and services, particularly if they are not tested or proven in the market.

With regard to financial well-being, the market for Islamic fintech products and services may be limited, making it challenging for startups to attract customers and generate revenue. Additionally, cross-border payments and trade finance can be complex and involve multiple parties, creating challenges for Islamic fintech platforms. Ensuring Sharia compliance in cross-border transactions and supply chain financing presents significant challenges for Islamic fintech startups, potentially restricting their capability to deliver these services. This difficulty stems from the complex nature of complying financial transactions with Islamic law, which can vary across different jurisdictions [43]. Some users are also skeptical of using fintech because of the risks linked with digital financial services [44]. Customer hesitation toward adopting new fintech solutions stems from concerns over the risks these technologies may carry, which are intensified by the unique requirements for Sharia compliance in financial transactions [45]. Thus, traditional financial institutions may have more experience and expertise in trade finance than Islamic fintech startups, making it challenging for the latter to compete in this market. Islamic fintech has the potential to grow and provide innovative solutions, particularly in SME financing, financial well-being, and trade finance, by enhancing access to financial products for the unbanked, supporting ethical investments, aiding poverty reduction, and triggering gender equality. This can play an important role in the socioeconomic development of emerging economies, with financial hubs in Malaysia, the United Kingdom, and the United Arab Emirates [46]. Islamic fintech also presents unique challenges that must be addressed, such as potential threats arising from rapid technological changes, regulatory uncertainties, the evolving landscape of digital finance, and the multidimensional aggregate demand and supply crisis triggered by the COVID-19 pandemic [47]. Therefore, Islamic fintech should promote economic growth and financial inclusion by overcoming these challenges and continuing to innovate.

A conducive government environment can contribute positively to the development of SMEs. As part of the Dodd-Frank Wall Street Reform and Consumer Protection Act, the US government created the Consumer Financial Protection Bureau, whose primary responsibility was to find more effective ways to increase consumers' financial literacy [48].

Similarly, previous research shows that, to promote environmentally friendly initiatives, SMEs can work with various stakeholder groups to gain legitimacy and social and moral capital to respond to environmental or sustainability demands [49]. Other stakeholders also play an essential role in supporting SME financing, financial well-being, and trade financing by integrating business transactions and collaborative processes [15]. Banks and financial institutions can help SMEs by providing various financial products and services that suit their requirements. Meanwhile, investors and venture capitalists can help strengthen working capital and grow the business by financing SME stakeholders (such as suppliers) that have recently increased their market share by using existing and new products [50]. It has also been documented that policymakers should be concerned with ensuring the availability of bank loans for SMEs during an economic downturn to reduce the harmful effects on investments [51].

Developing policies and regulations that encourage the expansion of Islamic fintech platforms is vital to the government's role in enhancing its growth. This can include providing financial and non-financial support to SMEs to increase their awareness and adoption of Islamic fintech solutions, as well as encouraging the development of Islamic fintech incubators and accelerators to support start-ups. By offering support, the government can help bridge the financial inclusion gap, especially for individuals, micro-enterprises, and small businesses, thereby contributing to the country's overall economic development [52]. Additionally, venture capital is essential for the growth of fintech start-ups, including Islamic ones. They can invest in start-ups to provide the capital necessary for growth and expansion [53]. Venture capital can collaborate with government agencies and industry players to support the growth of Islamic fintech platforms by providing mentoring, expertise, and networking opportunities for start-ups.

The Accounting and Auditing Organization for Islamic Financial Institutions (AAOFI) can also contribute to developing Islamic fintech sectors by developing Sharia-compliant guidelines and best practices, including crowdfunding, peer-to-peer lending, personal finance management, digital wallets, budgeting apps, factoring, supply chain finance, and other financial services. The Islamic Financial Service Board (IFSB), an international standard-setting body that provides regulatory and supervisory oversight to Islamic financing, can contribute by developing regulatory and supervisory standards for Sharia-compliant financing institutions, including risk management, governance, consumer protection, privacy, data security, and transparency measures. It can also provide technical assistance and capacity building for regulatory and supervisory authorities to better understand and regulate the financing, personal finance management, and trade financing sectors by promoting understanding of the Islamic financial model globally [47]. By doing so, the IFSB can nurture greater coordination and cooperation among regulatory bodies and other stakeholders to promote a level playing field, minimize regulatory arbitrage, and promote a more inclusive and competitive financial system.

Hence, improving Islamic fintech requires collaborative efforts from various stakeholders, including the government, venture capitalists, the AAOFI, and the IFSB. Each plays a role in promoting innovation and growth in this sector. Working together will accelerate the process of building trust and enhancing customer perception to overcome challenges and realize the potential benefits of this emerging field [54]. However, all these approaches have limitations and require careful consideration to ensure that they effectively promote innovation and economic growth in the Islamic fintech sector.

4. Unpacking Robust Risk Mitigation in Islamic Fintech

SME financing, financial well-being, and trade financing are expected to solve economic problems. However, these Islamic fintech categories have also experienced various risks, including operational risk, the macroenvironment, Sharia non-compliance, regulatory non-compliance, and cybersecurity. Operational risk mitigation can be achieved by conducting a strict risk assessment of business processes, providing proper employee training, and introducing clear procedures for managing operational risk. Operational risk mitigation requires close collaboration between Islamic fintech and Islamic banks, as well as regulators that focus on the harmonization of Sharia standards, pooling resources between Islamic banks, and training programs for human resource development [55]. Furthermore, macroeconomic risk affects a company's financing decisions [56]. This risk can be mitigated by diversifying portfolios, building long-term client relationships, and monitoring global and regional economic trends. Sharia non-compliance risk also occurs and may be assessed by internal and external bodies, such as the IFSB [57]. This risk can be mitigated by governance to ensure that products and services are Sharia-compliant. Cybersecurity risks should also be considered. This risk mitigation is related to cyberattacks and data theft, within a framework that integrates stakeholder values [58], and can be mitigated by implementing a robust cybersecurity system, protecting critical data, and developing emergency response plans to address cyberattacks.

Another risk emerged during the COVID-19 pandemic when small firms faced significant challenges in accessing formal finance and were more reliant on informal financing sources [59]. Therefore, SMEs require a good financing strategy to support business continuity, especially during times of natural disasters, which are predicted to increase with climate change. Financial well-being aims to support people in accessing the proper range of financial advice and services by providing knowledge, skills, and confidence to maximize their well-being and adopt social sustainability [60].

In trade finance, where interactions take place between the manufacturer and retailer [61], financial institutions and central banks can play an essential role in enhancing financial well-being through appropriate financing strategies. The banking industry is a prominent example of potential blockchain use cases that extend beyond digital payments, the settlement of securities trades, and trade finance [62]. Additionally, trade finance can be accomplished using blockchain-based solutions, which reduce the intermediaries required and are geographically agnostic because trade financing is a financing strategy that aims to finance international trade activities [63]. To mitigate this, financing institutions, investors, and trade partners can implement risk management strategies, such as diversification of portfolios, proper due diligence, effective monitoring and reporting systems, adherence to Sharia-compliant principles and ethical standards, and collaboration with regulatory bodies and other stakeholders. Implementing Islamic fintech solutions that prioritize transparency, accountability, and ethical behavior can help mitigate these risks and promote greater stakeholder trust and confidence [41].

Another critical risk in SME financing is credit risk, which can be addressed through AI-powered credit scoring and Sharia-compliant financing contracts that use risk-sharing. For financial well-being, operational risk can be managed through robust digital platforms that use advanced cybersecurity technologies, AI-powered chatbots, and Sharia-compliant financial products and services that comply with regulations and industry standards [64]. Trade financing enables real-time monitoring and transparency powered by AI.

Islamic fintech companies face significant operational risks that can be mitigated through several measures. These measures include using robust and secure digital platforms with advanced cybersecurity technologies, providing 24/7 customer support through AI-powered chatbots, and offering Sharia-compliant financial products and services that comply with regulations and industry standards. Digital financial platforms can also provide secure and efficient transactions. In contrast, AI-powered financial education and guidance tools can offer accurate and reliable information to help users make informed financial decisions. There are many charities that connect Muslims to the needy, and Islamic fintech can ensure system accountability, improving credibility and empowering more Muslims to contribute to society [45]. In trade financing, digital platforms can reduce reliance on paper-based transactions, minimize the risk of errors or fraud, and comply with regulations and industry standards through Sharia-compliant trade financing contracts. Islamic fintech companies can reduce operational risks by implementing these measures and ensuring platform and service safety, reliability, and compliance.

Liquidity risk is also a significant challenge in all three areas, but Islamic fintech can address this through digital financing platforms that enable faster and more efficient processing times and financial inclusion through collateral-free financing. Sharia-compliant financing contracts, which use risk-sharing and are backed by assets, could also be alternative solutions [65]. Market risk can be minimized through diversified portfolios, advanced financial modeling tools, and Sharia-compliant products and services that comply with industry standards. Interest rate risk is yet another critical risk that can be addressed using Sharia-compliant financing contracts that use risk-sharing and are not based on interest, collateral-free financing options that promote financial inclusion, and digital financing platforms that enable real-time processing and reduce interest rate fluctuations [47]. Compliance and regulatory risks can be managed through Sharia-compliant financing products and services that comply with regulations and industry standards, robust compliance management systems that ensure regulatory compliance, and transparent and auditable digital financing platforms that comply with regulations. Ensuring the security of digital financing platforms is essential for preventing cyber threats and fraudulent activities. One approach is to use advanced cybersecurity technologies to protect against such threats [66]. Robust data encryption and protection measures can ensure the privacy and security of customer data. AI-powered chatbots can also be implemented to detect and prevent fraudulent activities and enhance the security and reliability of the platform. By adopting these measures, fintech companies can safeguard sensitive customer information and ensure trust in their platforms.

Besides, the introduction of the Central Bank Digital Currency (CBDC) can also provide numerous benefits to Islamic fintech related to SME financing, financial well-being, and trade financing. It can improve efficiency, transparency, and security in financial transactions and promote financial inclusion and Sharia compliance. It may benefit Islamic fintech by providing a secure and efficient payment system for SME financing, efficient cross-border transactions, and a more inclusive payment system. CBDC may also contribute to developing financial well-being by providing a secure and efficient payment system for digital financial products and services [67]. CBDC may also help improve financial literacy and promote responsible financial behavior, as users can monitor and manage their finances in real time. For trade financing, CBDC may enhance the efficiency and transparency of cross-border transactions. This may reduce the cost and risk of trade financing, making it more accessible to SMEs. CBDC may also facilitate real-time tracking of goods and services, reducing the risk of fraud and error in trade financing transactions, and CBDC-powered remittance services for seamless and affordable international payments. Moreover, CBDC may promote Sharia compliance in Islamic fintech by providing a transparent and auditable payment system. Several banks are exploring CBDC to improve their financial inclusion [68]. Eventually, this may build trust and confidence in Islamic fintech products and services, as users can verify that they are Sharia-compliant.

5. Pioneering Efficiency in Islamic Fintech through the Advancement of Blockchain

Blockchain technology has been hailed as a game-changing tool for businesses, especially SMEs that frequently face difficulties in securing financing. By utilizing blockchain's potential, SMEs can gain access to new financing opportunities and streamline operations. According to

Aysan and Bergigui [69], blockchain has the potential to serve as an effective SDG accelerator, with Islamic finance facilitating a more circular economy by expanding the application of blockchain-enabled solutions. Aysan *et al.* [70,71] argue that blockchain's decentralized nature allows for the development of alternative financing models, such as peer-to-peer (P2P) lending and crowdfunding platforms, which can provide more accessible and affordable financial services to traditionally underserved populations. By directly connecting borrowers to lenders, bypassing traditional financial intermediaries, P2P lending platforms can offer SMEs a more efficient and cost-effective method of securing funding. Blockchain technology provides a secure, transparent, and immutable ledger for these transactions, thereby reducing the risk of fraud and boosting participants' confidence [72]. Aysan and Bergigui [73] find that blockchain's decentralized, transparent, and secure nature can contribute to various aspects of the SDGs, including financial inclusion and supply chain management.

Furthermore, the use of smart contracts, which are self-executing contracts with terms of agreement written directly in code, is crucial [74]. By automating contract execution, smart contracts can reduce transaction costs and the need for intermediaries, thereby increasing SME access to financing. Moreover, the transparency provided by blockchain technology enables all parties to track and verify the fulfillment of contractual obligations, thereby enhancing trust and reducing disputes [33]. Aysan *et al.* [75] assert that blockchain's inherent traits, such as transparency, immutability, and decentralization, complement Islamic finance principles such as risk-sharing, ethical investments, and interest prohibition. These enable Islamic finance institutions to streamline operations, cut costs, and boost transparency, thereby attracting investors. Tokenization can also optimize SME financing by enabling companies to issue digital tokens that represent real-world assets [76]. These tokens can be traded on blockchain-based platforms, providing SMEs with new ways to raise capital and boost investor liquidity. In addition, tokenization can enable fractional ownership by lowering barriers to entry for investors and creating a more inclusive financing ecosystem [77].

On the other hand, blockchain technology has also been recognized as a potent tool for improving financial well-being by expanding financial inclusion, empowering individuals to manage their financial resources, and promoting transparency and trust within the financial ecosystem. Aysan and Bergigui [69] showed that blockchain has the potential to support sustainable and inclusive financial systems, emphasizing its role in cross-border remittances, identity management, financial access for unbanked populations, and promoting transparency and traceability in supply chains for a more sustainable and circular economic model. Enhancing financial inclusion, particularly for unbanked and underbanked populations, is an essential aspect of optimizing blockchain for financial well-being. Digital identity solutions based on blockchain technology can provide individuals with a secure and verifiable means of establishing their identity, which is frequently a prerequisite for accessing financial services [78].

The development of decentralized finance (DeFi) platforms that use blockchain and smart contracts to create open, transparent, and accessible financial services is another area with optimization potential [79]. DeFi platforms can offer various financial products, such as loans, savings accounts, and investment opportunities, without the need for traditional intermediaries [80]. The democratization of access to financial services has the potential to enable individuals to manage their financial resources more effectively and attain financial security. However, Unal and Aysan [81] explored the challenges and opportunities of implementing blockchain technology in the public sector and warned against hype while stressing the importance of thorough assessment and due diligence before adopting the technology in public sector applications. Blockchain technology can be used to improve financial education and literacy through individualized and verifiable learning experiences, enabling individuals to acquire financial knowledge and skills at their own pace and thus becoming better equipped to make informed decisions regarding their financial lives. A study by Aysan *et al.* [71] examining the innovation performance of 5,273 Colombian companies across 64 sectors and 32 regions found that education and open economy variables significantly impact innovation at both firm and regional levels, with a focus on technology transfer and the role of education in the innovation process.

Improving trust and transparency is essential for optimizing blockchain for financial well-being. The decentralized and immutable nature of blockchain can promote trust in financial transactions because it enables the verification of transaction data without the need for a central authority [77]. Aysan and Bergigui [73] highlight the importance of collaboration among stakeholders in the blockchain ecosystem, such as governments, private sector organizations, and academia, emphasizing that improving partnerships and promoting knowledge sharing can drive innovation, tackle technical and regulatory obstacles, and unlock the technology's full potential for sustainable development. Increased transparency can lead to improved individual decision-making and promote a more equitable financial system. Blockchain technology can empower individuals to make better financial decisions and achieve greater financial well-being by promoting financial inclusion and enhancing the development of decentralized financial services, financial education and literacy, and trust. Aysan *et al.* [82] investigated China's and Venezuela's use of blockchain technology to build alternative financial systems, with China diversifying its network through investment and Venezuela circumventing the dollar-based system with a national cryptocurrency, both leveraging their respective technology's creative destruction potential within an international realist realm.

Additionally, the potential of blockchain technology to transform trade financing has gained significant attention. Unal and Aysan [81] contend that the fintech industry, which is focused on creating and implementing innovative financial technologies, can significantly benefit from incorporating blockchain technology to examine payment system efficiency, streamlining cross-border transactions, and bolstering security in digital identity management. One key area in which blockchain can optimize trade financing is in enhancing the efficiency and transparency of supply chain management. It can provide a secure, immutable, and easily accessible record of the movement of goods and services within a supply chain [42]. This not only increases trust among trading partners but also enables more accurate and timely risk assessments for financiers. Increased visibility in the supply chain can help identify and mitigate the risks associated with fraud, delays, and other disruptions [83]. Aysan *et al.* [70] find that blockchain's potential is an innovative solution to accelerate SDGs, emphasizing its role in post-COVID-19 recovery, building resilient economies, and addressing complex challenges while cautioning against the hype-cycle and emphasizing informed decision-making. Blockchain can optimize trade financing through smart contracts. These programmable contracts can automate the execution of contractual terms and conditions, thereby reducing the time and expenses associated with manual processes [84]. This automation can streamline the trade financing process, allowing for faster transaction settlement and reducing the need for financial intermediaries, such as banks and other financial institutions [85]. Moreover, blockchain technology can facilitate the digitization and standardization of trade documents, such as bills of lading, letters of credit, and invoices. By storing and managing these documents on a blockchain-based platform, businesses can ensure the authenticity and accuracy of the data and reduce the likelihood of errors and fraud. This can result in faster processing times and greater trust between trading partners and financiers, making trade financing more accessible and efficient [86].

The discussion in Dosso and Aysan [87], the authors underlines the importance of collaboration among fintech companies, financial institutions, and regulators to cultivate a conducive environment for blockchain adoption, enabling stakeholders to establish suitable regulatory frameworks, exchange best practices, and tackle technical and logistical hurdles in implementing blockchain technology within the fintech sector. Therefore, blockchain technology provides significant opportunities to optimize trade financing by increasing supply chain transparency, streamlining processes through smart contracts, and digitizing and standardizing trade documents. Aysan *et al.* [88] find that, while Islamic banks recognize the importance of digitalization and have begun implementing essential digital technologies such as mobile banking, they need to expand their digital transformation efforts to include more advanced technologies, such as AI and distributed ledger technology (DLT), and consider partnerships with fintech firms to remain competitive and future-ready in the rapidly evolving financial landscape. Aysan *et al.* [75] suggest that Islamic financial institutions can enhance their competitiveness by evaluating stablecoins for payments and remittances, creating an Islamic stablecoin based on gold and other stable assets, adopting CBDCs and DLT, addressing clients' data privacy concerns, and deploying AI and big data in their operations.

6. Conclusion: Toward a Paradigm of Inclusive Financial Futures of Islamic Fintech

Despite challenges in the business sector, Islamic fintech industries have many opportunities to grow by providing innovative and affordable financial services to society based on customer needs. However, this study reveals that it is necessary to strengthen risk control processes and pay attention to regulatory changes in the financial sector. Governments and stakeholders play pivotal roles in creating a conducive growth environment. With good cooperation and collaboration, SME financing, financial well-being, and trade financing can lead to better and more sustainable development in the future; however, several steps are also needed to mitigate the risks associated with them. These include carrying out a rigorous risk assessment of business processes, introducing clear procedures for risk management, ensuring an effective internal control system, building good relationships with regulators, implementing robust cybersecurity, and continuously monitoring Sharia compliance. Therefore, this study recommends policies and procedures that comply with applicable laws and keeping abreast of the latest developments in regulations and legislation. Appropriate risk-mitigation steps are expected to minimize losses in SME financing, financial well-being, and trade financing. Several strategies can be implemented to optimize Islamic fintech industries by utilizing AI technology to improve credit risk analysis, increase the accuracy of business performance predictions, and optimize blockchain toward transformative solutions.

The potential of blockchain technology to revolutionize various aspects of finance and trade is immense. It can enable SMEs to gain access to new financing opportunities, streamline operations, reduce transaction costs, and increase trust by utilizing P2P lending, smart contracts, and tokenization. Moreover, it can promote financial inclusion by providing secure and verifiable digital identities, democratizing access to financial services through DeFi platforms, and enhancing financial literacy toward a more equitable financial system. Blockchain technology can also optimize trade financing by enhancing the efficiency and transparency of supply chain management, reducing the time and expenses associated with manual processes, and facilitating the digitization and standardization of trade documents. By providing a secure, immutable, and easily accessible ledger for transactions, blockchain can increase trust among trading partners and financiers and enable more accurate and timely risk assessments. Despite the numerous benefits, blockchain technology also faces challenges such as scalability, interoperability, and regulatory frameworks that need to be addressed. The adoption of blockchain technology also requires significant investment in infrastructure, education, and cultural changes. However, with rapid advancements in technology and the growing demand for transparency and efficiency in finance and trade, the potential benefits of blockchain technology are difficult to ignore.

References

[1] Lu Z, Wu J, Li H, Nguyen D. Local banks, digital financial inclusion and SME financing constraints: Empirical evidence from China. *Emerg Mark Finance Trade*. 2022;58(6):1712–25. Available from: https://doi.org/10.1080/1540496X.2021.1923477.

[2] Brüggen E, Hogreve J, Holmlund M, Kabadayi S, Löfgren M. Financial well-being: A conceptualization and research agenda. *J Bus Research.* 2017;79:228–37. Available from: https://doi.org/10.1016/j.jbusres.2017.03.013.

[3] Ali M, Raza S, Khamis B, Puah C, Amin H. How perceived risk, benefit and trust determine user fintech adoption: A new dimension for Islamic finance. *Foresight.* 2021;23(4):403–420. Available from: https://doi.org/10.1108/fs-09-2020-0095.

[4] Shaikh I, Qureshi M, Noordin K, Shaikh J, Khan A, Shahbaz M. Acceptance of Islamic financial technology (fintech) banking services by Malaysian users: An extension of technology acceptance model. *Foresight.* 2020;22(3):367–383. Available from: https://doi.org/10.1108/fs-12-2019-0105.

[5] Syed M, Khan S, Rabbani M, Thalassinos Y. Artificial intelligence and NLP-based Islamic fintech model combining Zakat and Qardh-Al-Hasan for countering the adverse impact of COVID-19 on SMEs and individuals. *Int J Econ Bus Admin.* 2020;8(2):351–64. Available from: https://doi.org/10.35808/IJEBA/466.

[6] Usman H, Mulia D, Chairy C, Widowati N. Integrating trust, religiosity and image into technology acceptance model: The case of the Islamic philanthropy in Indonesia. *J Islam Mark.* 2020;13(2):381–409. Available from: https://doi.org/10.1108/jima-01-2020-0020.

[7] Dowling M, O'Gorman C, Puncheva P, Vanwalleghem D. Trust and SME attitudes towards equity financing across Europe. *J World Bus.* 2019;54(6):0–47. Available from: https://doi.org/10.1016/j.jwb.2019.101003.

[8] Godke Veiga M, McCahery J. The financing of small and medium-sized enterprises: An analysis of the financing gap in Brazil. *Eur Bus Organ Law Rev.* 2019;20. Available from: https://doi.org/10.1007/s40804-019-00167-7.

[9] Eggers F. The COVID-19 resource center is hosted on Elsevier Connect, the company's public news, and information. *J Bus Res.* 2020;116:199–208.

[10] Mueller A, Sensini L. Determinants of financing decisions of SMEs: Evidence from hotel industry. *Int J Bus Manag.* 2021;16(3):117. Available from: https://doi.org/10.5539/ijbm.v16n3p117.

[11] Drever A, Odders-White E, Kalish C, Else-Quest N, Hoagland E, Nelms E. Foundations of financial Well-being: Insights into the role of executive function, financial socialization, and experience-based learning in childhood and youth. *J Consum Aff.* 2015;49(1):13–38. Available from: https://doi.org/10.1111/joca.12068.

[12] Mahendru M. Financial Well-being for a sustainable society: A road less traveled. *Qual Res Organ Manag Int J.* 2021;16(3–4):572–93. Available from: https://doi.org/10.1108/QROM-03-2020-1910.

[13] Mahdzan N, Zainudin R, Abd Sukor M, Zainir F, Wan Ahmad W. An exploratory study of financial well-being among Malaysian households. *J Asian Bus Econ Stud.* 2020;27(3):285–302. Available from: https://doi.org/10.1108/JABES-12-2019-0120.

[14] Iacovone L, Zavacka V. Banking crises and exports: Lessons from the past. *J Dev Econ.* 2019;138:192–204. Available from: https://doi.org/10.1016/j.jdeveco.2018.12.005.

[15] Korpela K, Hallikas J, Dahlberg T. Digital supply chain transformation toward blockchain integration. *Kari. Filozofska Istrazivanja.* 2017;29(2): 325–33.

[16] Antrás P, Fritz Foley C. Poultry in motion: A study of international trade finance practices. *J Polit Econ.* 2015;123(4):853–901. Available from: https://doi.org/10.1086/681592.

[17] Tripoli M, Schmidhuber J. Emerging opportunities for the application of blockchain in the agri-food industry agriculture. Food and Agriculture Organization of the United Nations. 2018;21. Available from: http://www.fao.org/3/CA1335EN/ca1335en.pdf.

[18] Adelekan A. Islamic financing effects on small medium enterprises competitiveness. *J Islam Econ Bus Res.* 2021;1(1):100–113. Available from: https://doi.org/10.18196/jiebr.v1i1.11753.

[19] Ahmad A, Sohail A, Hussain A. Emergence of financial technology in Islamic banking industry and its influence on bank performance in covid-19 scenario: A case of developing economy. *Gomal Univ J Res.* 2021;37(1): 97–109. Available from: https://doi.org/10.51380/gujr-37-01-09.

[20] Rabbani M, Khan S, Thalassinos E. Fintech, blockchain and Islamic finance: An extensive literature review. *Int J Econ Bus Admin.* 2020; VIII(2):65–86. Available from: https://doi.org/10.35808/ijeba/444.

[21] Fadillah, A. Acceleration of financial technology growth towards inclusiveness of unbankable society in achieving the vision of the Islamic banking roadmap 2020-2025 (case study: generation z, jabodetabek). *Airlangga Int J Islam Econ Finance.* 2021;4(2):158. Available from: https://doi.org/10.20473/aijief.v4i2.31434.

[22] Winarsih W, Mutoharoh M, Tahar E, Aziz I. The role of fintech and financial literacy on SMEs sustainability. In: Proceedings of the 1st International Conference on Islamic Civilization, ICIC 2020, 27th August 2020, Semarang, Indonesia (168). European Alliance for Innovation. Available from: https://doi.org/10.4108/eai.27-8-2020.2303270.

[23] Oktavendi T. Islamic financial technology usage: An investing perspectives on Generation Z. *Riset Akuntansi Dan Keuangan Indonesia.* 2020;5(2): 151–158. Available from: https://doi.org/10.23917/reaksi.v5i2.10100.

[24] Yuneline M. Implications of shariah financial technology in increasing financial inclusion to micro, small, and medium enterprises. *Islamiyyat.*

2022;44(1):89–99. Available from: https://doi.org/10.17576/islamiyyat-2022-4401-8.

[25] Rahman M, Isa CR, Masud MM, et al. The role of financial behaviour, financial literacy, and financial stress in explaining the financial well-being of B40 group in Malaysia. *Futur Bus J.* 2021;7:52. Available from: https://doi.org/10.1186/s43093-021-00099-0.

[26] Kou G, Olgu Akdeniz Ö, Dinçer H, *et al.* Fintech investments in European banks: A hybrid IT2 fuzzy multidimensional decision-making approach. *Financ Innov.* 2021;7:39. Available from: https://doi.org/10.1186/s40854-021-00256-y.

[27] Eniola A, Entebang H. SME firm performance-financial innovation and challenges. *Procedia Soc Behav Sci.* 2015;195:334–42. Available from: https://doi.org/10.1016/j.sbspro.2015.06.361.

[28] Qamruzzaman M, Jianguo W. SME financing innovation and SME development in Bangladesh: An application of ARDL. *J Small Bus Entrep.* 2019;31(6):521–45. Available from: https://doi.org/10.1080/08276331.2018.1468975.

[29] Rao P, Kumar S, Chavan M, Lim W. A systematic literature review on SME financing: Trends and future directions. *J Small Bus Manag.* 2021; 1–31. Available from: https://doi.org/10.1080/00472778.2021.1955123.

[30] Aysan AF, Nanaeva Z. Fintech as a financial disruptor: A bibliometric analysis. *FinTech.* 2022;1(4):412–33. Available from: https://doi.org/10.3390/fintech1040031.

[31] Manzoor F, Wei L, Sahito N. The role of SMEs in rural development: Access of SMEs to finance as a mediator. *PLoS One.* 2021;16: 1–18. Available from: https://doi.org/10.1371/journal.pone.0247598.

[32] Anand B. Reverse globalization by internationalization of SMEs: Opportunities and challenges ahead. *Procedia — Soc Behav Sci.* 2015;195: 1003–11. Available from: https://doi.org/10.1016/j.sbspro.2015.06.359.

[33] Wang R, Lin Z, Luo H. Blockchain, bank credit, and SME financing. *Qual Quant.* 2019;53(3):1127–40. Available from: https://doi.org/10.1007/s11135-018-0806-6.

[34] Giudici G, Sannajust A, Van Auken H. Special issue on small business financing: New actors, opportunities, and challenges. *J Small Bus Manag.* 2021;59(2):219–22. Available from: https://doi.org/10.1080/00472778.2020.1865540.

[35] Strömbäck C, Lind T, Skagerlund K, Västfjäll D, Tinghög G. Does self-control predict financial behavior and financial well-being? *J Behav Exp Finance.* 2017;14:30–8. Available from: https://doi.org/10.1016/j.jbef.2017.04.002.

[36] Dewey J, Hill R, Plasencia R. Blockchain and 5G-enabled internet of things (IoT) will redefine supply chains and trade finance. Holland&Knight;

2018, p. 42–5. Available from: https://www.hklaw.com/files/Uploads/Documents/Articles/Blockchain5GEnabledInternetofThings.pdf.

[37] Dreher A, Fuchs A, Parks B, Strange A, Tierney M. Apples and dragon fruits: The determinants of aid and other state financings from China to Africa. *Int Stud Q*. 2018;62(1):182–94. Available from: https://doi.org/10.1093/isq/sqx052.

[38] Mclean S, Charles D. A preliminary review of policy responses to enhance SME access to trade financing in the Caribbean. United Nations Publications. 2020. Available from: www.cepal.org/apps.

[39] Wang S, Ouyang L, Yuan Y, Ni X, Han X, Wang F. Blockchain-enabled smart contracts: Architecture, applications, and future trends. *IEEE Trans Syst Man Cybern Syst*. 2019;49(11):2266–77. Available from: https://doi.org/10.1109/TSMC.2019.2895123.

[40] Darmansyah Fianto BA, Hendratmi A, Aziz PF. Factors determining behavioral intentions to use Islamic financial technology: Three competing models. *J Islam Mark*. 2020;12(4):794–812. Avalable from: https://doi.org/10.1108/JIMA-12-2019-0252.

[41] Abdul-Rahim R, Bohari SA, Aman A, Awang Z. Benefit-risk perceptions of FinTech adoption for sustainability from bank consumers' perspective: The moderating role of fear of COVID-19. *Sustainability*. 2022; 14(14):8357. Available from: https://doi.org/10.3390/su14148357.

[42] Saberi S, Kouhizadeh M, Sarkis J, Shen L. Blockchain technology and its relationships to sustainable supply chain management. *Int J Prod Res*. 2019;57(7):2117–35.

[43] Alam N, Zainuddin SSB, Rizvi SAR. Ramifications of varying banking regulations on performance of Islamic banks. *Borsa Istanbul Review*. 2019; 19(1):49–64. https://doi.org/10.1016/j.bir.2018.05.005.

[44] Ryu H-S. What makes users willing or hesitant to use Fintech?: The moderating effect of user type. *Ind Manag Data Syst*. 2018;118(3):541–69. Available from: https://doi.org/10.1108/IMDS-07-2017-0325.

[45] Rabbani M, Bashar A, Nawaz N, Karim S, Ali M, Rahiman H, *et al*. Exploring the role of Islamic fintech in combating the aftershocks of Covid-19: The open social innovation of the Islamic financial system. *J Open Innov Technol Mark Complex*. 2021;7(2):136. Available from: https://doi.org/10.3390/joitmc7020136.

[46] Türkan KG. The emergence of Islamic fintech and its applications. *Int J Islam Econ Finance Stud*. 2023;9(2):212–236. Available from: https://doi.org/10.54427/ijisef.1328087.

[47] Glavina, S, Aidrus I, Trusova A. Assessment of the competitiveness of Islamic fintech implementation: A composite indicator for cross-country analysis. *J Risk Financial Manag*. 2021;14:602. Available from: https://doi.org/10.3390/jrfm14120602.

[48] Mende M, van Doorn J. Co-production of transformative services as a pathway to improved consumer well-being: Findings from a longitudinal study on financial counseling. *J Serv Res*. 2015;18(3):351–68. Available from: https://doi.org/10.1177/1094670514559001.

[49] Baah C, Opoku-Agyeman D, Acquah I, Agyabeng-Mensah Y, Afum E, Faibil D, *et al*. Examining the correlations between stakeholder pressures, green production practices, firm reputation, environmental and financial performance: Evidence from manufacturing SMEs. *Sustain Prod Consum*. 2021;27:100–14. Available from: https://doi.org/10.1016/j.spc.2020.10.015.

[50] Park S. Corporate social responsibility, visibility, reputation, and financial performance: An empirical analysis on the moderating and mediating variables from Korea. *Soc Responsib J*. 2017;13. Available from: https://www.emerald.com/insight/content/doi/10.1108/SRJ-01-2017-0012/full/html.

[51] Zubair S, Kabir R, Huang X. Does the financial crisis change the effect of financing on investments? Evidence from Private SMEs. *J Bus Res*. 2020;110:456–63. Available from: https://doi.org/10.1016/j.jbusres.2020.01.063.

[52] Dewi I, Adinugraha H. The role of sharia fintech in improving halal financial inclusion in MSMEs in Indonesia. *Likuid Jurnal Ekonomi Industri Halal*. 2023;3(1):18–29. Available from: https://doi.org/10.15575/likuid.v3i1.18693.

[53] Ressin, M. Start-ups as drivers of economic growth. *Research in Economics*. 2022; 76(4), 345–354. https://doi.org/10.1016/j.rie.2022.08.003.

[54] Albertsen L, Wiedmann KP, Schmidt S. The impact of innovation-related perception on consumer acceptance of food innovations: Development of an integrated framework of the consumer acceptance process. *Food Quality and Preference*. (2020);84:103958. https://doi.org/10.1016/j.foodqual.2020.103958.

[55] Malim N. Islamic banking and risk management: Issues and challenges. *J Islam Bank Finance*. 2015;64–71.

[56] Kuehn LA, Bhamra HS, Strebulaev IA. The society for financial studies the aggregate dynamics of capital structure and macroeconomic risk. *Oxford J*. 2016;23(12):4187–241.

[57] Bhatti M. Managing Shariah non-compliance risk via Islamic dispute resolution. *J Risk Financial Manag*. 2019;13(1):2. Available from: https://doi.org/10.3390/jrfm13010002.

[58] Alvarenga A, Tanev G. A cybersecurity risk assessment framework that integrates value-sensitive design. *Technol Innov Manag Rev*. 2017;7(4):32–43. Available from: https://doi.org/10.22215/timreview1069.

[59] Aysan AF, Babacan M, Gür N, Süleyman S. Firm size and financing behavior during the COVID-19 pandemic: Evidence from SMEs in Istanbul. Munich Personal RePEc Arch. Forthcoming. 2023.

[60] Brookfield C. Financial well-being strategy. City of Wolverhampton Council; 2022. Available from: wolverhampton.gov.uk.

[61] Chen X. A model of trade credit in a capital-constrained distribution channel. *Int J Prod Econ.* 2015;159:347–57. Available from: https://doi.org/10.1016/j.ijpe.2014.05.001.

[62] Vukolić M. The quest for scalable blockchain fabric: Proof-of-work vs. BFT. The quest for scalable blockchain fabric. 2017.

[63] Carson B, Romanelli G, Walsh P, Zhumaev A. Digital McKinsey. 2018. p. 1–13. Blockchain beyond the hype: What is the strategic business value? McKinsey&Company. Available from: https://www.mckinsey.com/business-functions/digital-mckinsey/our-insights/blockchain-beyond-the-hype-what-is-the-strategic-business-value.

[64] Rahman M, Ming TH, Baigh TA, Sarker M. Adoption of artificial intelligence in banking services: An empirical analysis. *Int J Emerg Mark.* 2021;18(10):4270–4300. Available from: https://doi.org/10.1108/IJOEM-06-2020-0724.

[65] Abdul-Rahim R, Abd Wahab A, Hudaib M. The effects of foreign currency exposure and Sharī'ah-compliant status on financial hedging strategy. *Int J Islam Middle East Finance Manag.* 2023;16(2):323–42. Available from: https://doi.org/10.1108/IMEFM-08-2021-0352.

[66] Kim J, Park M, Kim H, Cho S, Kang P. Insider threat detection based on user behavior modeling and anomaly detection algorithms. *Appl Sci.* 2019; 9(19):4018. Available from: https://doi.org/10.3390/app9194018.

[67] Banerjee S, Sinha M. Promoting financial inclusion through central bank digital currency: An evaluation of payment system viability in India. *Australas Account Bus Finance J.* 2023;17(1):176–190. Available from: https://ro.uow.edu.au/cgi/viewcontent.cgi?article=2331&context=aabfj.

[68] Zams B, Indrastuti R, Pangersa A, Hasniawati N, Zahra F, Fauziah I. Designing central bank digital currency for Indonesia: The Delphi–analytic network process. *Buletin Ekonomi Moneter dan Perbankan,* 2020;23(3): 413–440. https://doi.org/10.21098/bemp.v23i3.1351.

[69] Aysan AF, Bergigui F. Sustainability, trust, and blockchain applications in Islamic finance and circular economy: Best practices and fintech prospects. *Gulf Stud.* 2021;141–67. Available from: https://doi.org/10.1007/978-981-16-6061-0_9.

[70] Aysan AF, Bergigui F, Disli M. Blockchain-based solutions in achieving SDGs after covid-19. *J Open Innov Technol Mark Complex.* 2021;7(2):151. Available from: https://doi.org/10.3390/joitmc7020151.

[71] Aysan AF, Bergigui F, Disli M. Using blockchain-enabled solutions as SDG accelerators in the international development space. *Sustainability.* 2021;13(7):4025. Available from: https://doi.org/10.3390/su13074025.

[72] Gomber P, Kauffman R, Parker C, Weber B. On the fintech revolution: Interpreting the forces of innovation, disruption, and transformation in

financial services'. *J Manag Inform Syst*. 2018;35(1):220–65. Available from: https://doi.org/10.1080/07421222.2018.1440766.

[73] Aysan AF, Bergigui F. Blockchain paths in rebooting the global response to the sustainable development goals after COVID-19. *Gulf Stud.* 2020. Available from: https://doi.org/10.20944/preprints202010.0074.v1.

[74] Buterin V. A next-generation smart contract and decentralized application platform. 2017. Available from: https://github.com/ethereum/wiki/wiki/White-Paper.

[75] Aysan AF, Al-Ansari, Ahmed K. Central bank digital currencies, internet of things, and Islamic finance: Blockchain prospects and challenges. 2022. Available from: https://ssrn.com/abstract=4128096.

[76] Swan M. *Blockchain: Blueprint for a New Economy*. O'Reilly Media. 2015.

[77] Tapscott D, Tapscott A. *Blockchain Revolution: How The Technology Behind Bitcoin is Changing Money, Business, and the World*. New York: Penguin;2016.Availablefrom:https://www.amazon.com/Blockchain-Revolution-Technology.

[78] Zwitter A, Boisse-Despiaux M. Blockchain for humanitarian action and development aid. *Int J Humanit Action 3*. 2018;16. Available from: https://doi.org/10.1186/s41018-018-0044-5.

[79] Morkunas VJ, Paschen J, Boon E. How blockchain technologies impact your business model. *Bus Horiz*. 2019;62(3):295–306.

[80] Chohan UW. Decentralized finance (DeFi): An emergent alternative financial architecture. *Econ Model Int Financial Mark – Foreign Exch eJ* 2021.

[81] Unal IM, Aysan AF. Fintech, digitalization, and blockchain in Islamic finance: Retrospective investigation. *FinTech*. 2022;1(4):388–98. Available from: https://doi.org/10.3390/fintech1040029.

[82] Aysan AF, Sadriu B, Topuz H. Blockchain futures in cryptocurrencies, trade and finance: A preliminary assessment. *Buletin Ekonomi Moneter dan Perbankan*. 2020;23(4):525–42. Available from: https://doi.org/10.21098/bemp.v23i4.1240.

[83] Kshetri N. 1 blockchain's roles in meeting key supply chain management objectives. *Int J Inf Manag*. 2018;39:80–9. Available from: https://doi.org/10.1016/j.ijinfomgt.2017.12.005.

[84] Clack CD, Bakshi VA, Braine L. Smart contract templates: Foundations, design landscape and research directions. 2017. Available from: https://arxiv.org/abs/1608.00771.

[85] Huang J, Li S, Thürer M. On the use of blockchain in industrial product service systems: A critical review and analysis. *Procedia CIRP*. 2019;83:552–6. Available from: https://doi.org/10.1016/j.procir.2019.03.117.

[86] Fan K, Ren Y, Wang Y, Li H, Yang Y. Blockchain-based efficient privacy preserving and data sharing scheme of content-centric network in 5G. *IET Commun*. 2017;12:527–32.

[87] Dosso M, Aysan AF. The technological impact in finance: A bibliometric study of fintech research. *Eurasian Stud Bus Econ.* 2022; 193–209. Available from: https://doi.org/10.1007/978-3-030-94672-2_12.

[88] Aysan AF, Belatik A, Unal IM, Ettaai R. Fintech strategies of Islamic banks: A global empirical analysis. *FinTech.* 2022;1:206–15. Available from: https://doi.org/10.3390/fintech1020016.

https://doi.org/10.1142/9781800616295_0016

Chapter 16

The Potential Applications of Artificial Intelligence in Managing Zakat Funds

Kinan Salim*, Wan Nuriqlima Wan Mohd Noor, and Shamsher Mohamad Ramadili Mohd

School of Graduate and Professional Studies, INCEIF University, Kuala Lumpur, Malaysia
**kinan@inceif.edu.my*

Abstract

This chapter explores the transformative role of artificial intelligence (AI) in enhancing the collection and distribution of Zakat funds. It delves into the utilization of AI for streamlining collection processes, accurate identification of eligible recipients, and ensuring effective fund allocation. Various AI applications are explored, such as predictive analytics, chatbots, and real-time monitoring, highlighting their impact on improving efficiency, transparency, and donor engagement. The challenges and ethical considerations inherent in integrating AI into religious and social welfare contracts are explored. The exploration concludes by emphasizing AI's potential to revolutionize Zakat management, aligning technological advancements with the core principles of Islamic social welfare.

1. Artificial Intelligence

Artificial intelligence (AI) has transformed our capabilities, enabling us to achieve feats previously thought impossible. From the development of autonomous vehicles to the sophistication of search engines, and now the emergence of generative AI, this field has continually opened new doors.

The concept of AI was first introduced in 1955, originally defined as "making a machine behave in ways that would be called intelligent if a human were so behaving" McCarthy, *et al.* [1]. Since then, AI has demonstrated a remarkable ability to learn and emulate human skills, including learning, reasoning, and perception, by employing a cross-disciplinary approach that integrates multiple fields, including mathematics, computer science, linguistics, and psychology. In today's context, AI can be redefined as "the frontier of computational advancements, reflecting human intelligence to tackle increasingly complex decision-making challenges" [2].

Before delving into the modern marvels of AI, it is imperative to acknowledge the legacy of Islamic traditions and scholars in laying the groundwork for today's computational sciences. The 9th-century polymath Muhammad ibn Musa al-Khwarizmi[1] is revered for his seminal contributions to the development of algebra – a term derived from his work, *Al-Kitab al-Mukhtasar fi Hisab al-Jabr wal-Muqabala*.[2] Al-Khwarizmi's innovations in mathematics, including the concept of the algorithm, enriched the vocabulary of science[3] and provided the foundational tools for addressing complex computational problems. These early developments in Islamic mathematics were often motivated as a problem-solving technique for the practical needs of Islamic rituals and social practices, such as the calculation of inheritance shares and determining the direction for prayer.[4]

---

[1] Al-Khwarizmi (780-847) was born in Khwarazm in present-day Uzbekistan-Turkmenistan. He accomplished most of his work in the period between 813 and 833 at the House of Wisdom (a kind of academy of scientists in Baghdad that owes its preeminence to Al Ma'mun, a great patron of learning and scientific investigation) [3].

[2] *The Compendious Book on Calculation by Completion and Balancing* (830). In this book, several algebraic problems are presented, most of which were derived from applications (e.g., subdivision of legacies), in particular, a series of algorithms for the solution of first- and second-degree equations with numerical coefficients, duly organized into six different classes according to their structure [4].

[3] Some words reflect the importance of Al-Khwarizmi's contributions to mathematics. "Algebra" is derived from *al-jabr*, one of the two operations he used to solve quadratic equations. Algorism and algorithm stem from Algoritmi, the Latin form of his name.

[4] The problem-solving approach is clearly articulated by Al-Khwarizmi as he describes the purpose of his book: to teach "what is easiest and most useful in arithmetic, such as people constantly require in cases of inheritance, legacies, partition, lawsuits, and trade, and in all their dealings with one another, or where the measuring of lands, the digging of canals, geometrical computations, and other objects of various sorts and kinds are concerned" [5].

The intellectual heritage of scholars like Al-Khwarizmi resonates in today's AI-driven world, where the fusion of algorithmic logic and mathematical precision continues to solve complex societal challenges. This historical context enriches our understanding of AI's potential, bridging the past and present in a continuum of intellectual pursuit.

AI has permeated various aspects of our daily lives, revolutionizing numerous industries with its diverse applications. In healthcare, AI assists in diagnosing diseases and predicting patient outcomes. In the automotive sector, it powers the advancements in self-driving technology. AI also plays an important role in enhancing customer experiences through recommendation systems in e-commerce and streaming services. Additionally, it has led to significant research breakthroughs by processing large and diverse datasets (big data) and using predictive modeling.

The finance sector has also witnessed an AI transformation. It increases operational efficiency and customer experience and enhances personalized banking services by analyzing customer data for tailored product offerings. AI-powered tools such as virtual assistants and chatbots are able to provide 24/7 customer support, perform transactions, and address customer inquiries. It also transforms risk management and fraud detection by identifying unusual patterns of fraudulent activities. Financial institutions are able to conduct electronic know-your-customer (e-KYC) procedures quickly and securely using AI. In addition, banks leverage AI and big data to improve credit assessment.

Charity organizations can enhance the collection and distribution of aid using AI. It helps optimize donation collection by predicting the most effective methods and times for fundraising, hence maximizing the efficiency of collection while also effectively distributing the aid to the intended target groups most in need. Charity organizations can use AI to identify the areas and individuals most in need of assistance. Additionally, AI can aid in monitoring and evaluating the impact of charitable initiatives. This will enhance transparency and accountability in managing charity funds.

This chapter focuses on the potential of AI applications in effectively managing the collection and distribution of Zakat funds.

2. The Concept of Zakat

Zakat is one of the five pillars of Islam. It is a vital obligation for Muslims, who are required to pay a specified portion of their accumulated wealth to designated categories of people. It can significantly assist in poverty eradication and mitigate the income inequality gap. Zakat is not just charitable giving, but the right of the needy for a share in the wealth of the Muslim community, or *Ummah*. It is one of the main mechanisms for social welfare and communal responsibility in Islam.

There are specific parameters set by Sharia law for both the Zakat payer (or *Muzaki*) and the receiver (or *Mustahik*). The parameters consider the payer's personal and financial status and the nature of their wealth. The Quran (verse 9:60), explicitly delineates the lawful recipients of Zakat, stating: "Zakat is for the poor and the needy, and those employed to administer the funds; for those whose hearts have been recently reconciled to truth; for those in bondage and in debt; in the cause of Allah; and for the wayfarer. This ordinance is from Allah, and Allah is Full of Knowledge and Wisdom." This shows the broad spectrum of beneficiaries, ranging from the poor and needy to those working toward societal reconciliation and spiritual upliftment.

Zakat plays an important economic and social role and can reduce, if not eliminate, the inequality gap between the rich and the poor. Abdul-Jabbar explained that this redistribution mechanism mandates that a certain portion (2.5%) of assets (that qualify to be subjected to Zakat) must be paid as Zakat [6]. This process helps in poverty alleviation and fosters a sense of community and shared responsibility among Muslims, thereby reinforcing social cohesion and economic stability.

2.1. *Zakat management process: Collection and distribution stages*

The management of Zakat encompasses two primary stages: collection and distribution. The process of collection and later the distribution of collected funds is not merely a transactional activity but also a religious commitment that needs to be carried out with a high sense of integrity, transparency, and administrative efficiency. In the first stage, the Zakat administrator or institution collects it from eligible Muslims, and they are responsible for accurately determining the Zakat liability of each payer. This requires an in-depth understanding of Islamic jurisprudence and the individual financial circumstances of the contributors. Moreover, this stage is greatly facilitated if there is also awareness of the importance of paying Zakat and its benefits and ensuring compliance with Sharia principles.

Following collection, the second stage involves the distribution of Zakat funds to the rightful recipients as ordained under Islamic law. This stage is as crucial as the collection, as it directly impacts the lives of the beneficiaries. Zakat administrators must identify and verify eligibility based on the categories of recipients (*Asnaf*) mentioned in the Quran. The distribution process must be fair and carefully planned to prioritize and effectively address the needs of the community. Zakat administrators may also collaborate with other social welfare programs to maximize the impact of aid and foster social solidarity and upliftment. Proper management in this phase ensures that Zakat achieves its objective of reducing economic disparity and enhancing social welfare in Muslim communities.

Historically, the collection and distribution of Zakat were managed centrally by the state. However, contemporary Zakat administration varies across countries, with three primary approaches commonly observed [7]. In the first approach, a centralized Zakat administrator within a country or state bears the responsibility for managing the Zakat fund. In the second method, multiple social entities are authorized to collect and distribute Zakat. The process is decentralized, where these entities independently handle the collection from payers and distribution to eligible recipients. In scenarios where no specific legal framework for Zakat exists or in countries where Zakat payers may not fully trust the entities handling Zakat funds, a different approach to Zakat administration emerges. In this third model, individuals need to personally manage their Zakat obligations. They need to calculate their own Zakat and then choose to distribute the due amount directly to the eligible recipients. Alternatively, they can channel their Zakat through charity organizations to fulfill their obligation.

2.2. *Issues in Zakat management*

The management of both the collection and distribution of Zakat faces several challenges. These challenges have attracted the attention of both researchers and the public and need innovative solutions.

On the collection side, the main challenge is how to incentivize Zakat payers and maximize collections. This includes encouraging adherence to Zakat obligations and implementing strategies to increase the overall efficiency and yield of the collection process. Additionally, since Zakat records are largely non-digital, real-time information on collection and distribution is not readily available. There is limited adoption of mobile applications and online management system and a lack of integration with AI technologies. This lack of advanced technology penetration is an issue because it affects the stakeholders' perception of transparency surrounding Zakat management.

On the distribution side, the first significant challenge is to accurately identify rightful Zakat recipients. This task has become increasingly complex and vital as the number of people in need of Zakat continues to grow. The second issue relates to the effectiveness of Zakat distribution, namely allocating the collected funds in the most impactful manner, and finally distribution efficiency. Timely delivery of funds to recipients is often hindered by various logistical and administrative obstacles. Each of these challenges presents an opportunity to apply AI to enhance Zakat management. AI-driven solutions could optimize the identification of *Asnaf* and improve distribution strategies to address current challenges.

A prerequisite for applying AI in Zakat management is having a management information system (MIS) that facilitates data documentation and analysis, performance monitoring, and strategic decision-making. It can also enhance credibility and accountability by transparently presenting activities to the public. The core functions of a Zakat management information system (Z-MIS) include recording the collection and disbursement of Zakat and generating reports based on submitted data. Additionally, it can create real-time online reports of Zakat activities [8].

The following sections delve into each problem, examining how AI can play an important role in resolving these challenges in Zakat management.

3. Addressing Suboptimal Zakat Collection through AI Solutions

A primary challenge in Zakat management is the suboptimal collection of funds, which is attributed to several factors such as limited outreach, a lack of donor trust, and the cumbersome nature of traditional collection methods. These methods often require the Zakat payer to search for a nearby *Amil* (Zakat collector) or a trustworthy individual to distribute it. Technology helps address these issues. For example, to facilitate collection, the Z-MIS can connect with banks, payment gateways, and other payment points.[5] In addition, the Zakat institution can connect its MIS to crowdfunding platforms (or build its own) to engage the payers by communicating the story of the program, for example, building a school for orphans or providing productive assets for the poor to generate income. Indonesia's National Board of Zakat (BAZNAS) in 2012 launched SIMBA, a web-based Z-MIS through which Zakat payments can be executed. The implementation of SIMBA has shown a positive and significant impact on Indonesia's national Zakat collection [8].

Traditional MISs collect structured data, but they struggle to aggregate and analyze data from diverse sources to identify potential Zakat payers and understand donor behaviors. Through machine learning and big data analytics, AI can integrate vast amounts of structured and unstructured data from various platforms, including social media, bank transactions, and mobile apps, to identify potential donors and understand patterns in donor behavior, addressing the issue of limited outreach. AI can also employ predictive analytics for targeted campaigns to forecast the most opportune times and methods for reaching out to potential donors, thereby enhancing donor engagement. Unlike traditional statistical models, AI can process complex and nonlinear relationships within the data to make accurate predictions.

Engaging meaningfully with Zakat payers is important to gain their trust and encourage more donations. One way to achieve this is by providing details about how funds are utilized and their impact. For example, the Z-MIS could be connected to a crowdfunding platform, allowing Zakat payers to contribute to specific causes/programs and follow their progress [9]. AI can be used to create detailed reports on Zakat fund utilization and its impact on beneficiaries. Presenting these data through AI-generated reports and infographics may enhance transparency, thereby boosting donor trust and inspiring more generous contributions. Engagement with Zakat payers can also be enhanced by using gamification strategies in Zakat apps or platforms, incorporating features such as tracking progress,

---

[5]A successful implementation of digital Zakat payments needs both high internet penetration and robust digital payment system and infrastructure. For example, Malaysia had 33.59 million internet users at the start of 2024, with an internet penetration rate of 97.4%. According to Johari and Yusoff [10], 9 out of 14 Zakat institutions in Malaysia utilize internet banking systems for Zakat collection.

earning badges, automated matching contributions,[6] and recognizing consistent donors.

AI can analyze individual donor patterns and preferences to offer personalized engagement strategies, including custom reminders, educational content about Zakat's impact, and tailored Zakat payment amounts based on donors' financial profiles. Zakat institutions can assist donors with better financial planning by integrating AI-powered financial planning tools within the Zakat platforms. This enables donors to fit their Zakat contributions within their broader financial landscape, allowing for more informed and confident decisions about their giving capabilities, going beyond the basic Zakat calculators offered by some institutions.

AI-powered chatbots and mobile applications can revolutionize engagement with Zakat payers by enhancing accessibility and catering to a broader audience, including tech-savvy donors and beneficiaries. The integration of AI with chatbots can improve user experiences by providing quick and efficient responses to payment issues and queries. This enhanced communication through AI-powered voice and text interactions makes engagement more efficient between Zakat payers and institutions. For instance, the Rania Chatbot, developed by Rumah Zakat Indonesia, and the Tanya Amil feature by Lembaga Zakat Selangor (Malaysia) are examples of Zakat chatbots in action, offering Zakat education and interactive sessions with payers, thereby enhancing customer interaction and service efficiency [11].[7]

A fundamental prerequisite for developing AI chatbots or rule-based engines capable of providing expert Zakat advice is access to the rich corpus of *Fiqh* rules and judgments from various Islamic schools of thought. These resources must be digitized to serve as training examples for the AI systems. Significant efforts have been made toward the digitization of *Fiqh* and *Sharia* literature, providing a robust foundation for AI applications in Islamic jurisprudence. One notable initiative is Al-Maktabah

[6]This feature matches individual donations with institutions or wealthier donors, doubling the impact of the original gift. This strategy can motivate wider participation, as donors are aware of the amplified effects of their contributions.

[7]Collaborations like that between Baznas and Artina Digitama Indonusa (Artdigi) have led to the development of AI-based chatbots, such as "Zaki," which uses natural language processing (NLP) for user interaction.

Al-Shamela,[8] a comprehensive digital library dedicated primarily to Islamic literature. This platform hosts an extensive collection, encompassing approximately 8,000 books and over 7 million pages of digitized content, ranging from handwritten manuscripts to printed works and illustrations. It allows users to search, browse, read, and download a wide array of texts, facilitating easy access to crucial Islamic jurisprudential resources. Other digital libraries, such as Jami Alkutub Al-Islamiyyah,[9] the Golden Shamela,[10] and Al-Maktabah Al-Waqfiyyah,[11] further contribute to the availability of Islamic jurisprudential texts in digital form. Most of these digital libraries are publicly accessible and are offered free of charge, ensuring broad availability for research, educational, and developmental purposes. Moreover, there are specialized websites and mobile apps[12] dedicated to curating Islamic economics,[13] Islamic finance,[14] and Zakat-related literature,[15] providing targeted resources for developing AI systems with a focus on Zakat management. These digital collections are invaluable for training AI chatbots and rule engines, as they offer a comprehensive overview of *Fiqh* rulings and judgments across different Islamic schools of thought.

Zakat institutions can leverage the above-mentioned AI-driven algorithms to optimize their collection processes. This will create a more engaging, transparent, and supportive ecosystem for Zakat payers and foster an impactful system. In addition, Zakat institutions can enhance public and stakeholder trust by providing AI applications for real-time monitoring of Zakat collection and distribution. This will provide a clear and accountable view of fund management. Such transparency will maintain confidence among donors and beneficiaries, ensuring high levels of integrity in the Zakat ecosystem.

---

[8] https://shamela.ws/.

[9] https://ketabonline.com/ar.

[10] https://goldenshamela.com/.

[11] https://www.waqfeya.com/.

[12] https://ifikr.my/.

[13] https://kantakji.com/.

[14] https://iefpedia.com/arab/.

[15] https://baitalzakat.com/.

4. Identifying the Potential Deserving Zakat Recipients: Challenges and AI Solutions

One of the primary difficulties in Zakat management is identifying those in need (*Asnaf*), particularly in rural areas or among individuals unaware of the process to apply for aid through Zakat institutions. For instance, the National Amil-Zakat Agency (Baznas) in Pekanbaru, Indonesia, traditionally conducts manual procedures such as interviews and field observations to determine eligible *Mustahik* (legal recipients). This method, however, can be influenced by emotions and sentiments, leading to potential misjudgments and bias in Zakat distribution [12].

In the Malaysian state of Selangor, the Zakat institution (Lembaga Zakat Selangor) uses two main methods for *Asnaf* identification. Individuals approach the Zakat institution, providing the required information and documents. The Zakat institution appoints assistants (*amil qariah*) in each district to help identify potential *Asnaf*. Registration can be done through paper-based methods or a web-based application, with the latter being a pilot project in select districts. This system aids in registering new *Asnaf* applications and conducting an annual census of the applicants. Recently, Lembaga Zakat Selangor has initiated a proof-of-concept phase for enhancing the *Asnaf* registration process. This phase includes the implementation of AI technology to read supporting documents, such as bank statements and identity cards, through the system. This pilot project aims to augment existing web-based applications used by the appointed assistants who facilitate the registration of *Asnaf* applications. The integration of AI in this process is expected to streamline and improve the accuracy of the registration procedure.

AI can provide innovative solutions for determining Zakat receivers (*Mustahik*). For example, Baznas Acheh (in Indonesia) has experimented with a prototype using a Bayesian network classification technique to determine the eligibility of a person who asks for Zakat assistance [13]. This incorporates parameters such as name, age, marital status, dependents, occupation, and income. This AI-driven approach can significantly enhance the reach and accuracy of identifying potential recipients and improve the on-ground operations of Zakat institutions. Furthermore, the categorization of recipients can be refined using AI methods, such as the *k*-nearest network (KNN). It includes factors such as residential status, job status, disability, and chronic diseases. This method allows for a more precise categorization of *Asnaf*. It can help distinguish between the poor and the indigent, facilitating targeted and effective distribution of Zakat funds.

5. Enhancing the Effectiveness of Zakat Distribution with AI

Another main challenge in Zakat management is the effectiveness and impact of aid distribution to *Asnaf*. This includes proactive intervention, speed, and empowering recipients to progress toward better life conditions, with the goal of enabling recipients to become self-sustaining and, eventually, becoming Zakat payers themselves. Institutions typically provide two types of aid: consumptive and productive. Consumptive aid addresses immediate necessities such as food, clothing, education, and housing. In contrast, productive aid focuses on the economic development of *Asnaf*. This includes initiatives such as providing capital, training, facilitating meetings with potential employers, and placement in industries. Determining the appropriate type of aid for each recipient presents its own challenges. A major issue is the lack of standardization in aid allocation, which mainly depends on individual evaluations by the appointed Zakat collectors (*Amil*).

The use of technology in general, and AI in particular, could play an important role in addressing these challenges. For example, the disbursement of Zakat funds through mobile applications, such as e-wallets, can enhance the effectiveness of Zakat distribution. By using e-wallets, the transaction activities can be tracked, allowing institutions to monitor how beneficiaries utilize the funds. Data analytics, together with the integration of AI, can allow institutions to gain a deeper understanding of the impact generated by the disbursement of funds. This approach streamlines the distribution process and provides valuable insights into the effectiveness of Zakat. AI can also support decision-making processes, potentially leading to more standardized and effective aid allocation. A support decision system, informed by AI, could offer recommendations for aid types. However, we cannot depend solely on AI, and there is still room for human judgment, thus ensuring a balance between algorithmic efficiency and human empathy. This enhances the accuracy and consistency of aid distribution and reduces the variability inherent in individual judgments.

6. Enhancing the Effectiveness of Zakat Operation with AI

In addition to the previously mentioned examples for the collection and distribution of Zakat funds, AI can also be used to enhance operational efficiency. It can provide predictive insights into Zakat collections using robotic process automation (RPA) and historical data on collections. The forecast can be enhanced by using third-party data, such as those from the tax authority. However, integrating such data needs a careful approach to protect the customer's privacy. Furthermore, Zakat institutions can use AI to determine the adequacy of collections to meet the needs of the rising number of applications. For this, Zakat institutions need to conduct sensitivity analysis for fund collection and distribution, especially in scenarios where collections fall short of targets. This ensures that Zakat collection and distribution are both effective and aligned with the overarching objectives of Islamic social welfare. Furthermore, AI can enhance the efficiency of Zakat institutions by automating various tasks. For example, integrating tools such as online surveys, Google Analytics, and Microsoft Dynamics related to tax and wealth reporting can help identify individuals obligated to pay Zakat [12]. Innovations such as auto-debit systems, informed by AI, can also improve the efficiency of Zakat collection. These systems facilitate the work of officers responsible for collecting Zakat and provide convenient alternatives for Zakat payers to fulfill their obligations.

7. Facilitating AI Applications in Zakat Institutions

The integration of AI in Zakat institutions presents a promising avenue for improving efficiency and outreach. For successful implementation, it would be important to address the following:

Staff training: Adequate training to cover the technical aspects of AI tools and practical applications of AI in Zakat management tasks is needed for staff members involved directly in the process. Employees need to understand how AI can simplify their workflows, enhance decision-making, and improve interactions with Zakat payers and recipients. The training may include workshops and training sessions coupled with hands-on experience to transform the mindset of staff to adapt to AI-driven processes.

Literacy programs for the poor: AI applications often rely on digital platforms; therefore, it's crucial to address the digital literacy gap among the poor, who are the main beneficiaries of Zakat. Literacy programs can be designed to teach them basic digital skills, including how to access and use mobile applications and websites to apply for Zakat. These programs could be conducted at community centers or through mobile units, ensuring widespread accessibility.

Raising awareness: Campaigns to raise awareness are essential to educate both staff and beneficiaries about the benefits and usage of AI in Zakat management. These campaigns can utilize social media, community workshops, and even AI-powered chatbots to disseminate information. Clear communication about how AI enhances the Zakat processes is crucial for promoting buy-in, especially from the perspective of maintaining privacy and the ultimate benefits for all stakeholders.

Overcoming resistance to change: Resistance to change is a natural response, both among staff and beneficiaries. Addressing this requires a strategic approach that involves clear communication, demonstrating the tangible benefits of AI, and involving all stakeholders in the transition process. Providing a platform for feedback and concerns and addressing these empathetically can help ease the transition. Change champions who lead change within the organization and community can play a vital role in advocating for the positive impacts of AI.

Building a supportive infrastructure: A supportive technological and organizational infrastructure is crucial for the effective application of AI. This involves not only having the necessary hardware and software but also ensuring that there is a robust support system in place for troubleshooting and maintenance. Continuous evaluation and upgrades of the AI systems based on feedback and evolving needs will also be essential.

Partnerships and collaborations: Forming partnerships with technology companies and educational institutions can facilitate the successful integration of AI in Zakat institutions. These collaborations include sharing expertise, resources, and support for training, development, and implementation of AI systems.

8. Challenges and Ethical Considerations in Implementing AI in Zakat Management

There are several challenges faced in the implementation of AI in Zakat management. A primary concern is data privacy and security, particularly as AI systems handle sensitive financial and personal data of donors and beneficiaries. It is paramount to ensure the protection of this data against breaches and unauthorized access. Another challenge is the technological infrastructure required for AI, especially in developing countries where such resources might be limited. This digital divide can pose a substantial challenge to the effective implementation of AI solutions. The cost and resource allocation for setting up and maintaining AI systems can be significant, which poses a challenge for Zakat institutions. Moreover, there is the risk of inherent bias in AI algorithms, which may lead to discriminatory decisions affecting Zakat distribution.

Another significant challenge is the potential overreliance on technology. This might lead to a diminishment in human judgment and skills essential in Zakat management. It is important to balance AI assistance with human oversight to ensure that the system remains ethical and grounded. In addition, cultural and social barriers can hinder the acceptance and effective utilization of AI. Resistance from both staff and beneficiaries due to varying perceptions of technology is expected. These challenges necessitate a balanced and thoughtful approach for AI implementation in Zakat institutions to ensure that Zakat management is effective, ethical, and responsive to the needs of all stakeholders involved.

Zakat institutions need to consider several ethical issues: the need to ensure equity and fairness in AI algorithms to prevent bias that could affect zakat distribution; transparency and accountability in AI operations, which are critical to maintaining trust and integrity, and hence systems need to be effective, understandable, and explainable to all stakeholders; ensuring informed consent from both beneficiaries and donors, who should be aware of how AI is used in managing their data and contributions; and ensuring a human-centric approach in Zakat management, even with AI integration, particularly in handling sensitive cases or exceptions. Additionally, the sustainability of AI implementation must be considered, focusing on long-term societal and environmental impacts, including the responsible use of resources. Collaborative governance involving religious scholars, technologists, and community representatives can also play an important role in addressing these ethical concerns, ensuring that AI use in Zakat management aligns with both Islamic principles and broader societal values.

9. Conclusion

The integration of AI into Zakat management represents a significant step forward in addressing the longstanding challenges of collection and distribution of these vital funds. Through AI, we can enhance the accuracy, efficiency, and reach of Zakat institutions, potentially transforming the landscape of Islamic social welfare. The implementation of AI-driven systems promises improved identification of eligible recipients, streamlined collection processes, and a more transparent and engaging approach to Zakat management.

However, this journey is not without its challenges. We must navigate concerns around data privacy, technological infrastructure, cost, and potential biases inherent in AI algorithms. Moreover, the shift toward AI demands a careful balance between technological reliance and the invaluable human judgment that has traditionally underpinned Zakat management. As we embrace these technological advancements, it is imperative to maintain a strong ethical framework, ensuring fairness, transparency, and inclusivity in all AI applications within Zakat institutions.

The successful implementation of AI in Zakat management will require a concerted effort across multiple fronts. This includes comprehensive training for staff, literacy programs for beneficiaries, overcoming cultural and resistance barriers, and fostering a sustainable and responsible approach to technology use. Collaborative governance and stakeholder engagement will be key to aligning AI initiatives with the core principles of Zakat and the broader objectives of Islamic social welfare. The potential of AI to revolutionize Zakat management is immense. However, realizing this potential will require a thoughtful, inclusive, and ethical approach, one that respects the traditions of Zakat while harnessing the benefits of modern technology. As we stand at this intersection of tradition and innovation, it is an opportune moment to reflect on how we can harmoniously blend these realms to enhance the lives of millions, staying true to the spirit of Zakat and the principles of social justice it embodies.[16]

---

[16]This chapter discusses the use of artificial intelligence (AI) technologies in Zakat management, including examples such as natural language processing (NLP) and various machine learning algorithms. It is important to note, however, that our discussion is based on publicly available information, and there may be additional AI solutions in use that are not disclosed by Zakat institutions. Some organizations may utilize proprietary or undisclosed AI technologies, limiting our ability to provide a comprehensive overview of all AI applications in this field. Therefore, while we aim to present a detailed account of known AI implementations, the actual range of AI technologies applied in Zakat management could be broader. We acknowledge this limitation and suggest that the scope of AI use in Zakat management is an area ripe for further research.

The exploration of AI solutions in Zakat management highlights the innovative approaches that are being adopted. However, this chapter also acknowledges a gap in the detailed evaluation of the effectiveness and penetration of these solutions among the stakeholders. Detailed empirical studies focusing on the number of subscribers, their satisfaction levels, and the overall impact of these AI-driven solutions on Zakat management practices are sparse but necessary. Future research is encouraged to delve into these dimensions, assessing user adoption rates, satisfaction, and the impact of technology on enhancing the efficiency and transparency of Zakat management. Such investigations will not only fill a crucial gap in the literature but also guide the development of more effective and user-centric AI solutions in Zakat management, ensuring they serve the community's needs more effectively.

Acknowledgment

We extend our sincere gratitude to the Oxford Centre for Islamic Studies and the Securities Commission Malaysia for their invaluable support during the course of this research. This work was completed during the tenure of KS as an SC-OCIS visiting fellow. We are immensely grateful for the resources, insights, and hospitable environment provided by the Centre, which were instrumental in the completion of this work.

References

[1] McCarthy J, Minsky ML, Rochester N, Shannon CE. A proposal for the Dartmouth summer research project on artificial intelligence [Internet]. 1955. Available from: http://www-formal.stanford.edu/jmc/history/dartmouth/dartmouth.html.

[2] Berente N, Gu B, Recker J, Santhanam R. Managing artificial intelligence. *MIS Q*. 2021;45(3).

[3] Baki A. Al Khwarizmi's contributions to the science of mathematics: Al Kitab Al Jabr Wa'l Muqabalah. *J Islam Acad Sci*. 1992;5(3):225–228.

[4] Ausiello G. Algorithms, an historical perspective. In: Ausiello G and Petreschi R, editors. *The Power of Algorithms: Inspiration and Examples in Everyday Life*. Berlin: Springer; 2013. p. 3–26.

[5] Oaks JA. Medieval Arabic algebra as an artificial language. *J Indian Philos*. 2007;35:543–575.

[6] Abdul-Jabbar H. Challenges of Zakah management in Muslim developing countries. *Int J of Zakat and Isl Philan.* 2020;2(1):22–31.
[7] Hassan MK, Muneeza A. The role of technology in effective distribution of Zakat to poor and needy. In: Zul Hakim Jumat, Saqib Hafiz Khateeb, and Syed Nazim Ali, editors. *Islamic Finance, Fintech, and The Road to Sustainability: Reframing the Approach in the Post-Pandemic Era.* Cham: Springer International Publishing; 2023. p. 309–331.
[8] Swandaru R. Zakat management information system: E-service quality and its impact on Zakat collection in Indonesia. *Int J Zakat.* 2019;4(2):41–72.
[9] Beik IS, Swandaru R, Rizkiningsih P. Utilization of digital technology for zakat development. In: Mohd Ma'Sum Billah, editor. *Islamic Fintech: Insights and Solutions*; 2021. p. 231–248.
[10] Johari MSN, Yusoff AS. FinTech: ke arah keberkesanan kutipan dan agihan zakat di Malaysia. *Int J Zakat Islam Philanthr.* 2019.
[11] Che Mohd Salleh M, Chowdhury MAM. Technological transformation in Malaysian Zakat institutions. *Int J Zakat.* 2020;5(3):44–56. Available from: https://doi.org/10.37706/ijaz.v5i3.263.
[12] Nugraha F, Permadia S, Gunawan AR, Saeful E. Artificial intelligence usage in Zakat optimization. *Int Conf Zakat.* 2019:14–24. Available from: https://doi.org/10.37706/iconz.2019.144.
[13] Akbarizan, Kurniawan R, Nazri MZ, Sheikh Abdullah SN, Murhayati S, Nurcahaya. Using bayesian network for determining the recipient of Zakat in BAZNAS Pekanbaru. In: *2nd International Conference on Electrical Engineering and Informatics* (ICon EEI). IEEE; 2018.

https://doi.org/10.1142/9781800616295_0017

Chapter 17

An Analysis of Disruptive Technologies in Muslim Societies: Economic, Financial, and Ethical Implications

Erdal Harunoğullari

Oxford Centre for Islamic Studies, Oxford, UK

erdalharunogullari@gmail.com

Abstract

Disruptive technologies are innovative advancements that create opportunities for new markets and alter the dynamics of value exchange, frequently causing significant upheaval in current sectors. This chapter analyzes the effects of these issues, focusing particularly on their economic, financial, and ethical aspects. The research examines the Islamic ethical principles that regulate the utilization of technology, as well as the influence of technology on economic inclusivity and social equity. It further examines rules and regulations, provides strategic advice, and showcases case studies of technology adoption in other nations. Ultimately, it examines forthcoming patterns and developing technologies that are influencing Islamic civilizations while also delineating the corresponding obstacles and prospects.

1. Introduction

Technology has a huge impact on our society, fundamentally changing cultures by introducing new ideas and disrupting established markets. Disruptive technologies are revolutionary breakthroughs that provide prospects for novel markets and networks, eventually leading to substantial disruption and transformation in existing ones [1]. Disruptive technologies exert a significant influence on several facets of society, including economics, social norms, politics, and culture. They challenge existing structures and open up exciting possibilities, but they also bring risks such as inequality, conflict, ethical issues, and environmental concerns. In the Islamic world, home to over 50 countries and 1.8 billion people, the effects of these technologies are equally felt, presenting both challenges and opportunities.

Islamic nations and Muslim cultures have a range of obstacles and possibilities when it comes to embracing and adjusting to modern technologies. They must strike a delicate balance between their religious principles, cultural customs, and developmental objectives. They also face the complicated and dynamic realities of a globalized and linked world where technology drives and enables change.

In this chapter, we discuss the implications of disruptive technologies, including cryptocurrencies, blockchain, and FinTech, for the Islamic world. It evaluates present patterns, difficulties, and forthcoming results. Moreover, it analyzes the Islamic ethical frameworks and principles that govern the advancement and implementation of these technologies, as well as the impact of technology on fostering economic inclusiveness and social fairness. Moreover, it assesses the current standards and rules and offers strategic suggestions for lawmakers, professionals, and scholars. Lastly, it examines the prospective developments and nascent technologies that are expected to influence Islamic civilizations in the near future, along with the associated difficulties and prospects they present.

2. Economic Implications of Disruptive Technologies

Technologies can significantly reshape the economic situation of Islamic nations, which make up around 8% of the global gross domestic product (GDP) and 24% of the total global population [2]. These technologies possess the capacity to provide fresh opportunities for economic growth, productivity, innovation, and competitiveness while also presenting appealing prospects for job generation, business growth, and global trade.

It emphasises that the Fourth Industrial Revolution, encompassing artificial intelligence (AI), biotechnology, robotics and the internet of things, offers MENA countries significant opportunities to increase productivity, improve customer experience and adopt creative business strategies. However, it warns that without adequate investment in skills, infrastructure and governance, these technological advances could lead to challenges such as unemployment, skills mismatch and cyber threats, potentially hampering economic growth [3].

Productivity, quality, customer experience, and creative company methods may add value. New technologies may also lower GDP by US$614 billion due to unemployment, skill gaps, cyber threats, and social instability, according to the report.

The Organisation of Islamic Cooperation (OIC) report highlights that disruptive technologies have the potential to address key challenges such as economic growth, human resource development, infrastructure improvement, innovation ecosystems and regional integration. However, OIC member states face significant barriers, such as poor digital readiness, limited research and development capacities, inadequate regulatory frameworks, and social and ethical challenges, which may hinder the adoption and effective use of these technologies [4].

Islamic economies may either benefit from or suffer from disruptive innovations. This depends on technological adoption, dissemination, breakthroughs, and control. In the following sections, we examine disruptive technologies in the Islamic world and their economic impacts [5–7].

3. Cryptocurrencies in Islamic Financial Landscapes

Cryptocurrencies use encryption to secure and authenticate transactions and govern unit production. Blockchain and other decentralized networks operate independently of banks and governments. Cryptocurrencies are appealing because they securely store and transmit money and assets and allow rapid, inexpensive, and transparent transactions. Nevertheless, cryptocurrencies pose significant obstacles, particularly from an Islamic perspective. The primary concerns that emerge are the patterns of usage, adherence to Sharia principles, and regulatory reactions to cryptocurrencies in Islamic financial environments.

3.1. *Utilization trends*

Understanding, infrastructure and platform accessibility, its pros and cons, and cultural and religious difficulties impact Islamic states and Muslim consumer cryptocurrency adoption. In Q2 2020, CoinMarketCap assessed the 10 countries with the most bitcoin website traffic. Indonesia, Nigeria,

Turkey, Pakistan, Malaysia, Iran, Saudi Arabia, Egypt, Bangladesh, and the UAE attract the most visitors. These countries mostly follow the Islamic religion or have substantial Muslim populations, suggesting a considerable level of interest and involvement in cryptocurrencies among Muslim users.

Nevertheless, the practical implementation and acceptance of cryptocurrencies in Islamic nations and among Muslim customers could not be as substantial as indicated by online activity, owing to several obstacles and difficulties. The contributing causes to this issue include a lack of comprehension, subpar education, insufficient self-assurance, inadequate regulation, deficient infrastructure, inadequate security, and non-adherence to Sharia principles. In 2019, Statista conducted a poll that revealed variations in the ownership or use of cryptocurrency among Islamic nations. Turkey had the highest proportion of participation, accounting for 9%, and Pakistan had the lowest, with only 1%. By contrast, the global average stands at 9%. According to a 2020 study conducted by Chainalysis, the Middle East and Africa regions collectively represented a mere 1.2% and 2.5% of global bitcoin transactions in June 2020, respectively. In contrast, East Asia and Western Europe made significant contributions, at 28.4% and 17.4%, respectively [8].

Hence, it is apparent that there exists a disparity between the inclination toward and the practical use of cryptocurrencies within Islamic nations and among Muslim consumers. This disparity signifies both obstacles and prospects for the advancement and expansion of this industry.

3.2. *Sharia compliance*

Sharia-compliant cryptocurrency has been a subject of debate among Islamic academics, practitioners, and authorities: whether cryptocurrencies are currencies, whether they can be utilized easily, and whether they meet Islamic financial rules are pressing problems.

Sharia interpretation and implementation provide these issues with diverse viewpoints. *Riba* (usury), *gharar* (uncertainty), *maysir* (gambling), and *zulm* (oppression) are banned. Many religious authorities and institutions have issued fatwas endorsing Bitcoin. Some fatwas ban cryptocurrency, but others are cautious and dependent. In 2019 Securities Commission Malaysia Sharia Advisory Council [9] authorized licensed cryptocurrency exchanges. Following rules and boundaries is essential. However, in 2018, Egypt's Grand Mufti had already banned cryptocurrency transactions due to the potential for deception and fraud.

Islamic scholars have different perspectives and interpretations in terms of how the natural price volatility of cryptocurrencies creates an uncertainty problem, which expresses the concept of *gharar* in Islamic finance. Debates continue regarding the compliance of cryptocurrency trading with Sharia law [10].

Therefore, it is clear that there is a notable absence of consensus or set standards regarding the conformity of cryptocurrencies with Sharia principles. Consequently, additional investigation and discussion are important to tackle the diverse Sharia concerns and obstacles within this industry.

3.3. *Regulatory responses*

Islamic nations and Muslim regulators regulate cryptocurrencies differently based on comprehension, transparency, risk assessment, and Sharia and other legal frameworks. Some governments and authorities are tolerant and accommodating, while others are tough and limited, and yet others are neutral and cautious.

Bahrain is one of the countries that has taken important steps regarding cryptocurrency and digital asset legislation. The Central Bank of Bahrain regulates issues such as licensing, governance, capital, risk management, cybersecurity, reporting, and Sharia compliance [11]. On the other hand, Algeria banned cryptocurrencies in 2018 due to the perceived threat to the currency and financial system [12]. In Indonesia, cryptocurrencies were allowed to be bought and sold as commodities rather than being accepted as cash or a means of payment [12].

Consequently, there is no consistent oversight of cryptocurrencies by Islamic governments and regulatory bodies. Hence, it is imperative to establish improved coordination and teamwork in order to effectively tackle the multitude of regulatory challenges and obstacles faced by this industry.

4. Blockchain Technology: Applications and Innovations

Blockchain verifies and records transactions without the intervention of banks or governments. Peer-to-peer transactions are safe, transparent, immutable, and efficient. Blockchain helps finance, trade, health, education, agriculture, and government.

4.1. *Finance*

Blockchain technology might increase financial industry efficacy, safety, and inclusion, especially in Islamic countries where many people lack access to traditional financial services. Blockchain technology permits the production and transfer of cryptocurrencies, tokens, and smart contracts for Islamic financial products, including *zakat* (charitable donations), *waqf* (endowments), *sukuk* (bonds), and *takaful* (insurance). The first blockchain-based *sukuk* was produced by Indonesian FinTech business Blossom Finance. This innovative *sukuk* simplifies bond issuance, management, and payment with smart contracts [13]. Malaysian FinTech business Finterra has created a blockchain platform for *waqf* project crowdfunding and administration, including school, hospital, and mosque construction [14].

4.2. *Trade*

Blockchain technology might increase trade transparency, traceability, and reliability, especially in Islamic nations where Sharia requirements apply to many products and services. Blockchain technology verifies halal certification, quality, and origin and tracks supply chains and logistics. Singapore-based B2B e-commerce platform OneAgrix has teamed with the Malaysian halal certification company to verify and certify its halal products using blockchain technology. This partnership offers consumers products and historical data [15].

4.3. *Health*

Blockchain technology might improve healthcare confidentiality, privacy, and compatibility, especially in Islamic countries where patients have problems accessing and controlling their medical information. Blockchain technology can produce and share medical records, prescriptions, and test results. Patients, healthcare providers, and insurers may safely communicate this information. Blockchain can check healthcare professionals' credentials and performance. The Swiss blockchain platform MedXchange and the IsDB are testing a project in Saudi Arabia. The project aims to improve Hajj and Umrah tourists' healthcare with blockchain by implementing digital health passports, telemedicine, and smart contracts [16].

4.4. *Education*

Blockchain technology might make education more reliable, accessible, and personalized, especially in Islamic nations where many students face difficulties. Blockchain can produce, transfer, and authenticate digital credentials such as degrees, certificates, and badges internationally. Blockchain enables custom courses, resources, and exams to be easier to design and distribute. The Swiss blockchain platform ODEM and the EU Blockchain Observatory and Forum have jointly established a program that creates and distributes digital certificates to online blockchain course graduates using blockchain technology. Participants may showcase their expertise safely and easily using this initiative [17]. The Lithuanian blockchain platform BitDegree offers online programming, design, and marketing courses. Students receive incentives, feedback, and recognition via tokens, gamification, and certificates [18].

4.5. *Agriculture*

In Islamic nations, blockchain technology may improve farming efficiency, sustainability, and profitability. This is important because farmers in these areas often struggle to produce and sell crops. Blockchain can securely produce and distribute land titles, contracts, and invoices. This mechanism helps farmers, purchasers, and middlemen make safe payments. Digital weather, soil, and agricultural data may be generated and sent using blockchain technology to enhance production and distribution. The World Bank and UK-based blockchain startup AgriLedger are experimenting with this in Haiti. This blockchain project aims to boost fruit farmers' profits. Transparent and fair prices, traceable and high-quality goods, and secure and timely payments are essential to achieving this goal [19]. The Australian blockchain platform AgUnity improves smallholder farmer trust and collaboration. Farmers access and share resources and information via digital identities, wallets, and records [20].

4.6. *Governance*

Blockchain technology may increase government transparency, inclusivity, and efficiency, especially in Islamic governments where citizens face obstacles to exercising their rights. National IDs, passports, and voting cards may be created and sent via blockchain. Digital IDs authenticate and identify individuals for public services and activities. Blockchain technology can construct and transmit digital votes, surveys, and petitions. Community input on public policy may be collected through elections and referendums using this technology. For example, the Dubai Blockchain Strategy intends to change public services and transactions with blockchain. Visas, bills, and license renewals are also included. Dubai aspires to be the first city to effectively implement blockchain technology by 2020 [21]. Tunisia confirms ease of online voting for Tunisians abroad using blockchain technology. In this way, it promotes national policy and social responsibility to citizens [22].

5. Intersection of Islamic Banking and FinTech

FinTech improves payments, loans, investments, and insurance. FinTech may improve the accessibility, affordability, and quality of financial services while opening new markets for the underbanked.

Sharia prohibits interest, ambiguity, gambling, and injustice in Islamic finance. Ethics, risk-sharing, and social responsibility are emphasized. It supports FinTech's objective of providing fair and impartial financial solutions to boost economic and social well-being.

Islamic banking and FinTech can collaborate to achieve their goals. Therefore, Islamic banking and FinTech partnerships are possible and required. Digital disruptions present Islamic banking with numerous challenges and opportunities. The important issues here are innovation, expansion, efficiency, and competitiveness. More than 60% of Muslims worldwide are young people, and meeting the needs and expectations of this digitally skilled Muslim population is extremely important [23].

It is believed that combining Islamic banking with FinTech, along with a comprehensive study of various Islamic FinTech projects and platforms that have developed recently, will increase the resilience of the Islamic banking sector.

5.1. *Islamic FinTech initiatives and platforms*

Islamic FinTech platforms integrate FinTech with Islamic finance. These types of firms provide Islamic financing services. Islamic banking, capital markets, microfinance, crowdfunding, robo-advisory, and social finance. Based on their aims and attributes, these initiatives and platforms become Islamic FinTech facilitators, suppliers, or integrators [24].

Enablers assist Islamic FinTech firms and integrators grow with infrastructure, technology, and legislation. The global Islamic Financial Services Board (IFSB) develops industry standards. Islamic banking laws and regulations handle FinTech's regulatory and supervisory issues. The IFSB lists Islamic finance administration principles, information disclosure guidelines, and technical documents on financial inclusion and Islamic finance [25]. The web portal IslamicMarkets delivers Islamic economic information, perspectives, and education at a global level. It connects Islamic financial investors, entrepreneurs, professionals, and institutions. A directory, a Sharia screening tool, and financial courses are available at IslamicMarkets.

Islamic FinTech businesses supply Islamic financial products directly. Germany-based Insha focuses on Islamic banking. They provide kosher current accounts, debit cards, interest-free overdrafts, *zakat* calculators, and donation options. As of 2020, Insha's mobile app is the main way its consumers access and manage their accounts and transactions. US-based digital investment platform Wahed Invest provides Islamic financial services. It provides halal robo-advisory, portfolio management, exchange-traded funds, and savings programs. Investment accounts and portfolios are created and managed via its website and mobile app [26].

Islamic FinTech integrators enable banks and FinTechs to collaborate. They help Islamic banks transact with FinTech firms. Islamic banking goods and services utilize FinTech advancements. Malaysian internet portal IAP Integrated promotes Islamic crowdfunding [27]. This scheme facilitates SME finance using Islamic banks. Islamic equity, loans, and hybrid crowdfunding are available. The website serves as the main platform for Islamic banks and SMEs to participate in crowdfunding campaigns and transactions. Ethis, a Singaporean digital platform, facilitates the connection between Islamic social finance institutions and social impact initiatives. The website facilitates donations and investments and offers a variety of services and products related to Islamic social finance, such as *zakat* crowdfunding, *waqf* crowdfunding, and halal real estate crowdfunding. Ethis principally employs its website as a platform for Islamic social finance organizations and social impact projects to exhibit and support crowdfunding campaigns and deals [28].

6. Ethical Implications in Technological Advancements

The progression of technology has the capacity to improve human civilization by augmenting our quality of life, amplifying production and ingenuity, and tackling several obstacles and issues. Nevertheless, technological progress also gives rise to ethical quandaries and hazards, as it possesses the potential to undermine human dignity, values, and rights, worsen disparities and injustices, and jeopardize the environment and security.

Hence, it is imperative to establish ethical frameworks and standards that provide guidance for the advancement and use of technology, ensuring a harmonious and ethical cohabitation between progress and moral values. Islamic ethics derive from the principles outlined in the Quran, Sunnah, consensus, and logic. They offer frameworks and principles to accomplish the goals of Sharia, which encompass safeguarding and advancing religion, life, intellect, offspring, and wealth [29].

In this section, we examine several Islamic ethical frameworks and notions related to technological progress. We also examine instances of ethical dilemmas and difficulties that arise from technology, which encompass concerns such as confidentiality, safeguards, responsibility, and durability.

6.1. *Privacy*

Privacy refers to the rights and independence of individuals and groups to protect and control their personal information and communications, keeping them secure from unwanted intrusion and exposure. Privacy holds significant ethical significance in Islam, as it is closely intertwined with an individual's dignity, honor, and trustworthiness. It is safeguarded by Sharia laws and principles, which prohibit actions like spying, eavesdropping, backbiting, and slander to protect individual privacy [30].

However, technological breakthroughs, such as big data, AI, and biometrics, pose risks to privacy. These technologies may gather, analyze, and exchange massive quantities of personal and sensitive data, sometimes without the knowledge or agreement of the affected individuals. In this case, problems such as data breaches, identity theft, and cyberattacks may arise. It is vital to develop ethical rules and standards that protect people's privacy rights and strike a balance between the benefits and harms of data use. For instance, the International Telecommunication

Union (ITU) and the IsDB have produced a joint paper that proposes a framework for the ethical use of big data and artificial intelligence (AI) in OIC nations. According to the IFSB, data ownership, permission, disclosure, and protection affect privacy. A technical document from the IFSB promotes merging Islamic finance and financial inclusion. Data security, confidentiality, and governance privacy are the report's main themes.

6.2. *Security*

Security refers to the state or situation of being shielded and defended from potential harm, uncertainty, or risk. Security is a significant ethical principle in Islam since it is closely linked to the tranquility, fairness, and stability of society. The Sharia standards and legislation, as stated by Al-Raysuni [31], strictly forbid violence, tyranny, and corruption.

Nevertheless, the progress in technology, including cryptocurrencies, blockchain, and FinTech, presents a significant vulnerability in terms of security. Technological improvements enable digital asset and transaction generation and transfer without government or bank supervision. The potential hazards encompass fraudulent activities, money laundering schemes, financing of terrorism, and cybercriminal acts. Thus, ethical norms that protect digital assets and transactions while balancing technological innovation and legal limits are needed [32].

6.3. *Accountability*

Accountability is the act of people and groups acknowledging and taking responsibility for their acts and decisions. This includes offering explanations and accepting the outcomes and repercussions that result from these activities. Accountability is a core ethical principle in Islam that pertains to the dependability, integrity, and impartiality of individuals. The Sharia rules and regulations uphold the execution of contracts, rights, and duties and also foresee a future judgment and evaluation [33].

Research in AI, robots, and biotechnology complicates assigning responsibility. These improvements allow intelligent and autonomous entities and systems to conduct numerous tasks and make decisions. Significantly, these agents and systems are capable of operating on their own without any human interaction or supervision, which might result in errors, prejudices, and harmful outcomes. Hence, it is imperative to establish ethical guidelines and standards that guarantee the responsibility and openness of intelligent and autonomous agents and systems while simultaneously striking a balance between the autonomy of the technology and ethical considerations.

The WEF and the IsDB have jointly produced a paper that presents a framework and recommendations for the governance and regulation of AI in the nations belonging to the OIC. The study especially aims to tackle accountability issues and difficulties pertaining to ethical principles, norms, and policies. The International Islamic University Malaysia (IIUM) has released a paper providing a Sharia analysis and evaluation of biotechnology and its various uses. The article also discusses the difficulties and intricacies related to accountability, including Sharia goals, criteria, and consequences.

6.4. *Sustainability*

Sustainability meets current and future requirements and aspirations. Islamic morality emphasizes sustainability. This involves deliberate management, balance, and self-control in human activities. Islamic Sharia benefits society. These laws also prohibit public damage to safeguard current and future well-being [34].

Technology, industry, urbanization, and globalization threaten sustainability. These technical developments allow the production and consumption of goods and services without considering their environmental and social impacts. Thus, contamination, depletion, and deterioration may ensue. Thus, ethical standards are needed to balance technical innovation and ethical issues while ensuring commodity and service production and users' sustainable profitability and responsibility.

7. Promoting Economic Inclusivity and Social Justice

Economic inclusion and social justice guarantee equitable and unbiased access to economic and social resources and advantages, irrespective of an individual's history, identity, or status, while simultaneously upholding their dignity and respect. The fundamental principles of Islam center on economic inclusion and social equality, derived from the teachings of the Quran and Sunnah. The teachings prioritize the oneness, compassion, and fairness of God while also highlighting the fraternity, equality, and variety of humanity. Khan [35] highlights the authority, obligations, and dedications of both people and society.

Sustainability refers to the ability to fulfill present needs and wants while also safeguarding the rights of future generations. Islam places great importance on the principles of sustainable ethics. Stewardship, balance, and moderation in human acts. Islamic Sharia rules emphasize public welfare, benefit preservation, and improvement. These rules also prohibit public injury or destruction, emphasizing the need to care for the present and future.

Hence, it is crucial to implement policies and solutions that foster and augment economic inclusion and social justice while effectively tackling the diverse realities and challenges that impede and undermine them. Technology, a powerful and effective instrument, may greatly contribute to fostering economic inclusion and social justice. The platform provides a diverse array of opportunities and benefits, such as accessibility and empowerment, innovation and business creation, and collaboration and partnership.

These strategies and solutions leverage technology to foster economic inclusivity and social justice. We explore various initiatives and platforms that have successfully implemented and demonstrated these strategies, including digital financial inclusion, digital social entrepreneurship, and digital peacebuilding.

7.1. *Digital financial inclusion*

Digital financial inclusion refers to the utilization of technology to enhance the accessibility of formal and economically effective financial services, such as payments, savings, credit, and insurance. The primary goal is to provide priority to marginalized populations, such as the disadvantaged, women, young people, and those in rural areas, who are often neglected by conventional financial institutions. Utilizing digital financial services has the potential to effectively promote economic inclusiveness and social justice. It enables people and communities to participate in and take advantage of economic activities and opportunities. Consequently, this assists individuals in improving and safeguarding their means of living and general welfare [36].

Bangladesh's bKash is an example. Mobile financial services, including mobile money, banking, and payments, are available on mobile phones. Over 36 million low-income, rural customers have used bKash thanks to this strategy. It has greatly boosted Bangladesh's financial inclusion and empowerment [37]. US based nonprofit Kiva is another inspiration. Kiva's digital crowdfunding platform facilitates the connection between private lenders and low-income companies. Lenders and borrowers may efficiently enroll in crowdfunding projects and loans using the company's website and mobile application. Kiva has disbursed more than US$1.5 billion to over 3.8 million borrowers, a significant portion of whom are women residing in poor countries. The Kiva campaign has significantly enhanced financial inclusion and empowered communities on a worldwide scale [38].

7.2. *Digital social entrepreneurship*

Technology is used to provide creative and sustainable social and environmental solutions in digital social entrepreneurship. The allocation of healthcare, education, energy resources, and sanitary facilities is aimed at aiding refugees, those with disabilities, and underprivileged populations. Digital social entrepreneurship may promote economic inclusion and social justice by efficiently addressing and resolving the unmet needs and ambitions of individuals and communities, thereby improving their quality of life and well-being [39].

One example is Souktel, a social enterprise operating in Palestine. Souktel provides a range of digital solutions and services, including mobile job matching, mobile aid delivery, and mobile data collection. These services are accessed and used primarily through mobile phones. Souktel has successfully served over 1.5 million customers and beneficiaries, with a focus on youth and those in conflict zones. Its efforts have contributed to social inclusion and empowerment in the Middle East and Africa [40]. Solar Sister is a Ugandan social company that offers solar energy goods and services, such as solar lights, chargers, and cookstoves. The company predominantly hires women as agents and distributors. Solar Sister has effectively catered to more than 1.7 million clients and benefits, predominantly in rural regions afflicted by energy shortages. Solar Sister's endeavors have made a substantial impact on fostering social inclusion and empowering individuals and communities in Sub-Saharan Africa [41].

7.3. *Digital peacebuilding*

Digital peacebuilding is the application of technology to avoid and resolve conflicts and violence while simultaneously fostering and maintaining peace and solidarity across many societal groups, including those based on ethnicity, religion, and politics. Utilizing digital tools and platforms in peacebuilding endeavors has the potential to bolster economic inclusivity and social equity by fostering transparent dialogues, promoting empathy and tolerance, and enabling reciprocal cooperation and collaboration among individuals and communities. Moreover, it can significantly bolster security and stability [42].

PeaceTech Lab is a US-based nonprofit organization that provides digital tools and platforms, including the Open Situation Room Exchange, PeaceTech Exchanges, and PeaceTech Accelerator. These tools employ data, media, and technology to aid peacebuilding and empowerment in more than 20 nations and regions affected by war and catastrophe. PeaceTech Lab has made substantial contributions to promoting peace and enhancing communities globally [43]. Another instance is Build Up, a non-governmental organization headquartered in Spain that offers a variety of digital tools and platforms, such as Participatory Video, Digital Storytelling, and Online Dialogue. These are used to serve and empower communities more than 10 conflict and crisis-ridden countries and regions. Build Up's efforts have significantly contributed to peacebuilding and the empowerment of individuals and communities worldwide [44].

8. The Role of Technology in Advancing Islamic Societies: Public Services, Cooperation, Education, and Ethics

The adoption of disruptive technologies in Islamic societies plays a critical role in improving various aspects of public services, co-operation, education and ethical governance. Technology sector policy governs its growth and functioning. Policy makers, practitioners, researchers and users are greatly affected by it. Technology policy is particularly vital in Islamic countries and Muslim societies. These policy environments are complex, constantly changing and concerns are paramount.

Therefore, it is imperative and advantageous to conduct a policy analysis and evaluate existing policies and provide strategic recommendations, as well as suggestions for their development and improvement. This analysis should also address and resolve various policy issues and challenges, including digital readiness, digital divide, digital literacy and digital governance.

This chapter analyses policy analysis and strategic recommendations for the technology sector. It will also examine examples and cases of policy initiatives and actions implemented by Islamic countries and Muslim policymakers. By synthesising the effects of digital transformation, collaboration, education and ethical concerns in a coherent analysis, it will be shown how technological advances contribute to societal betterment while adhering to Islamic values.

8.1. *Digital transformation and cooperation*

Digital transformation plays a pivotal role in modernizing public services, driving innovation, and improving accessibility in Islamic countries. Key areas such as e-government, e-commerce, and e-health benefit from digital technologies, enhancing efficiency and citizen engagement [45]. Digitalization improves the effectiveness, efficiency, and accessibility of services in Muslim economies, fostering public sector innovation, productivity, and competitiveness. By enhancing the quality and convenience of public services, it contributes to improved community life and overall citizen satisfaction [46].

Saudi Arabia's National Transformation Program is an example of how digital services can be integrated across sectors like health and education to promote public welfare while adhering to Sharia principles. Saudi Vision 2030 emphasizes using technology to create a more sustainable future, supported by initiatives like the National Transformation Programme, Digital Transformation Unit, and E-Government Programme [45]. Similarly, Malaysia's MyDigital project and the Malaysia Digital Economy Blueprint aim to drive societal and economic progress through technology, focusing on areas such as finance, health, education, and government [47]. These initiatives align with Sharia principles, promoting public well-being and mitigating potential harm [29].

A comprehensive strategy for digital transformation should clearly outline a vision, precise goals, and measurable priorities, ensuring the active engagement of key stakeholders like policymakers, practitioners, academics, and users. Adequate resource allocation (financial, physical, and human) must support the effective functioning and management of digital services. Uniform regulations are essential to ensure data protection, privacy, and tracking capabilities. It is also important to focus on making these services more affordable and accessible for underprivileged populations, such as women, young people, and rural communities. The impact of digital transformation must be evaluated through robust data-driven metrics to assess progress and societal benefits.

Digital collaboration, on the other hand, facilitates interactions between regional and global governments, organizations, and institutions. It encourages the sharing of data, expertise, and best practices, which enhances integration and addresses challenges related to innovation, regulation, and ethical concerns in Islamic countries [48]. For effective digital cooperation, a supportive policy environment is essential to address issues such as trust, coordination, and harmonization.

Such collaboration strengthens international ties and fosters the growth of technology-driven economies in Muslim-majority nations [4]. The Organization of Islamic Cooperation (OIC) 2025 Action Program emphasizes technology to promote cooperation and solidarity among member countries. Initiatives like OIC-CERT, the Science, Technology, and Innovation Agenda 2026, and the Digital Economy and Entrepreneurship Summit aim to advance areas such as science, cybersecurity, and entrepreneurship, while addressing individual and societal rights [4,35].

These programs, including the OIC's Science, Technology, and Innovation Agenda, promote cross-border collaboration to tackle regulatory and ethical challenges. Such initiatives are crucial for regional integration and progress in adopting new technologies [4]. The Islamic Development Bank (IsDB) Transform Fund supports innovation and entrepreneurship aligned with the Sustainable Development Goals (SDGs) in member countries. The Transform Fund's programs—Engage Platform, Call for Innovation, and Reverse Linkage—focus on sectors like health, education, energy, and agriculture. These efforts align with Quranic principles of unity, justice, and social responsibility [35].

Digital platforms further enhance collaboration in Muslim societies, fostering shared innovation in areas such as cybersecurity and the digital economy.35 Islamic organizations like the IsDB also provide funding to support innovation through digital technologies, promoting social justice and economic inclusion in line with Sharia goals [49,50].

By leveraging digital transformation and collaboration, Islamic countries can advance their economies and societies while adhering to ethical and Sharia principles. A comprehensive strategy for digital collaboration should define clear goals, actions, and indicators for cooperation with regional and global partners. Stakeholders including legislators, researchers, and practitioners must take an active role in order to guarantee success. Clear legislation guaranteeing the security, confidentiality, and traceability of shared data must be in place, and sufficient resources must be allotted for the development and management of collaboration platforms. Collaboration should enhance accessibility and affordability, particularly for disadvantaged groups. The impact of these efforts must be evaluated based on measurable progress in regional and global integration, using reliable data metrics.

8.2. *Digital education: Enhancing human capital*

Education is a key area where digital transformation has shown significant potential, especially in improving human capital in Islamic societies. E-learning platforms and digital literacy programs allow for the customization of educational content and greater flexibility for students and teachers alike [51].

E-learning, digital literacy, and online learning increase educational resources. This technique enhances student and teacher resource flexibility, customisation, and engagement. The use of digital education in Islamic nations and Muslim cultures has the potential to augment human capital and capacities. According to UNESCO (2020), it has the capability to significantly improve the abilities, understanding, and expertise of both students and teachers, thereby enhancing the total excellence and influence of educational services and products [51].

However, digital education requires a comprehensive and inclusive policy environment and structure. Ensuring and promoting the progress and operation of digital education services and products is of utmost importance. It also helps address and overcome many policy issues and challenges, such as accessibility, quality, and fairness.

In nations such as Pakistan and Indonesia, national policies have been established to integrate digital tools into education, enhancing access and quality, particularly in underserved areas [52,53]. Pakistan has implemented the National Education Policy Framework 2018, a strategic plan aimed at utilising technology to enhance and reorganize the education system. The objective is to augment the accessibility, equity, and superiority of education. This project includes the National Education Technology Policy, Curriculum Framework, and Assessment Framework. The Ministry of Federal Education and Professional Training of Pakistan (2018) manages education, evaluations, and teacher training [52]. Al-Ghazali said in 1993 that Sharia guards and nurtures intelligence [29].

Indonesia's Merdeka Belajar (Freedom to Learn) policy aspires to reinvent education with technology. System adaptability, relevance, and innovation are programme goals. Government initiatives like Merdeka Campus, Learning, and Network are included. Curriculum includes higher education, vocational education, and lifelong learning [53]. This policy protects and promotes intellectual pursuits, one of the five Sharia aims [29].

The Islamic world has long prioritized education as a means of intellectual and social development. In modern contexts, digital tools provide new ways to realize these goals, allowing students to access knowledge beyond geographic boundaries and fostering inclusive education for disadvantaged populations, such as women and rural communities [29]. Moreover, digital education aligns with the objectives of Sharia, which emphasizes the preservation and promotion of intellect and knowledge [29].

A comprehensive digital education policy must outline a clear vision with specific goals and measurable benchmarks. This strategy should actively involve policymakers, practitioners, scholars, and users and should include:

- Resource Allocation: Ensure sufficient financial, physical, and human resources for the effective delivery and management of digital education services, with a focus on efficient budget management.
- Regulations and Standards: Provide precise, global standards for data security, privacy, and auditability as well as quality assurance.
- Accessibility and Inclusion: Encourage the use of digital education services, making sure that underserved populations, like women, young people, and rural communities, can access them at a reasonable cost.
- Impact Assessment: Continuously evaluate the impact of digital education on human resource development and societal capacity using reliable data metrics to track performance and improvements.

8.3. *Ethical use of technology in Islamic societies*

Digital ethics include using technology to uphold privacy, security, responsibility, and sustainability. It tries to avoid and resolve ethical issues including damage, injustice, and conflict related to technology creation and usage. In Muslim communities, digital ethics improves moral and spiritual well-being. It promotes human dignity, rights, and obligations and integrates technology with Sharia goals [54].

Nevertheless, the field of digital ethics necessitates a well-defined and unwavering policy setting and structure to establish and uphold ethical norms and guidelines for the advancement and utilisation of technology. It also aims to tackle and resolve policy concerns and difficulties, including principles, criteria, and consequences.

The fast pace of technological advancement may well present a great deal of room for advancements in several fields, but they also continue to uphold immense ethical concerns that must be solved within the context of Islamic values. In the current digital era, pragmatic issues such as privacy, security accountability and sustainability are fundamental concerns. The basic tenets of Islamic ethics found in the Quran and Sunnah gives rise to a roadmap on how to address these challenges so that technology does not take away human dignity nor social justice [30].

Science, Technology, and Innovation Strategy 2019–2029 is in force at ISESCO. This concept streamlines ISESCO-Muslim state scientific, technological, and innovation partnership via technology. The ultimate goal is to accomplish the vision and mission of ISESCO. It encompasses a range of policy efforts. This policy initiative aligns with the fundamental objectives of Sharia, which include safeguarding and advancing religion, life, intelligence, children, and wealth [33].

Another example is the International Islamic University Malaysia Institute of Islamic Banking and Finance (IIiBF), a strategic institute and centre that uses technology to advance and excel Islamic banking and finance education and research and achieve the IIUM vision and mission [55]. It includes policy initiatives and actions like the Master of Science in Islamic Finance, PhD in Islamic Banking, and Finance. This policy endeavour supports the Sharia's five key goals of protecting and promoting religion, life, intellect, offspring, and wealth [33].

Data security and privacy are major concerns in the digital era. Big data and artificial intelligence (AI) are two instances of technologies that jeopardise individuals' privacy. To protect personal data, certain ethical guidelines must be adhered to [25]. Guidelines have been established by the International Telecommunication Union (ITU) and the Islamic Development Bank to ensure that AI and big data be used ethically in Islamic countries [25].

Accountability is another crucial element, especially in the context of AI and robotics, where intelligent systems operate independently of human oversight. Islamic principles of justice and fairness dictate that the creators and users of such technologies must remain accountable for their actions, ensuring that their innovations do not lead to harm or injustice [31]. Thus, policies and guidelines that align with Sharia objectives are necessary to navigate the ethical complexities of these technologies.

Some strategic recommendations for the digital ethics policy are as follows:

- Comprehensive Strategy: Create a digital ethics road map that outlines the objectives, actions, and vision for promoting moral technology use. Involve all interested parties in the planning and execution process, such as legislators, practitioners, academics, and users.
- Resource Allocation: Ensure sufficient investment in digital ethics platforms, including budget, infrastructure, and human capital. Focus on optimizing the management and efficient use of these resources.
- Clear Regulations: Establish uniform legislation, standards, and guidelines to ensure the safety, privacy, and auditability of data in ethical technology platforms.
- Accessibility and Inclusion: Promote digital ethics platforms to developers and users, with a focus on making these platforms accessible and affordable for marginalized communities, such as women, youth, and rural populations.
- Impact Evaluation: Regularly assess the impact of digital ethics platforms on societal moral and spiritual well-being, using reliable data and performance metrics to measure progress.

9. Future Trends in Technology and Islamic Societies

Technology constantly evolves, presenting new opportunities and threats to humanity. The technological advances also affect Islamic nations and communities, which are part of our globalized society. It's beneficial to predict and adapt to future technological changes and their effects on Islamic nations and cultures.

This section examines upcoming technological breakthroughs and their potential impact on Islamic nations and societies. We also analyze leading and emerging technologies in these fields, such as AI, blockchain, biotechnology, and nanotechnology.

9.1. *Artificial intelligence*

AI enables computers and systems to demonstrate abilities similar to those of humans, such as acquiring knowledge, reasoning logically, making judgments, and producing effective solutions to problems. AI possesses the capacity to bestow benefits on several areas, including healthcare, education, the economy, and security. AI poses ethical, social, legal, and religious hazards and problems. The topics addressed include the concepts of human dignity, rights, and duties, the dynamics between humans and computers, and the principles of human values and ethics.

AI has the capability to enhance the accessibility and quality of healthcare. Highlighting the significance of disease prevention, treatment, and diagnosis is essential in rural regions with restricted healthcare infrastructure and populations. AI can increase online learning, digital literacy, and personalized learning resources. It can tackle educational inequalities among marginalized populations, including those living in poverty, women, youth, and refugees.

Islamic nations and Muslim communities must also be cognizant and vigilant regarding the potential hazards and difficulties posed by AI, as it has the capacity to impact and shape Islamic tenets and principles, such as *tawhid* (the belief in the oneness of God), *khilafah* (the concept of people as stewards), and *adl* (the pursuit of justice). AI can give rise to ethical and religious concerns and predicaments. These include questions about the nature and standing of AI agents and systems, the responsibility and liability of AI developers and users, and the compatibility and coherence of AI objectives and results with Sharia objectives and intentions. Therefore, it is crucial for Islamic states and Muslim cultures to define and enforce a definitive and uniform structure and guidelines for the advancement and use of AI. It is necessary to build a solid framework built according to Islamic sources and references based on the Quran, Sunnah, *ijma* (consensus), and *ijtihad* (reasoning). Moreover, the recommendations in this regard should be based on *maqam al-Sharia* (purposes of Sharia), *maslahah* (public benefit), and *khalq* (creation).

9.2. *Blockchain*

Blockchain technology facilitates the establishment and upkeep of a reliable, open, and unchangeable distributed record of transactions and data. Transactions may be verified without the participation of middlemen or regulatory authorities. Blockchain might transform banking, commerce, government, and identity management. It also poses hazards and problems. Technical issues such as blockchain system scalability and interoperability, regulatory concerns about blockchain transaction legal and institutional acceptance, and social factors like user and stakeholder adoption and cultural adaptation of blockchain are all important [56: pp. 33–46].

Blockchain technology can enable Islamic nations to circumvent the issues of interest (*riba*) and uncertainty (*gharar*) and facilitate the practice of almsgiving (*zakat*). Blockchain has the potential to enhance the accessibility and quality of Islamic financial services and products. This involves providing halal and Sharia-compliant banking, insurance, and investment choices to the poor, women, youth, and rural communities. Blockchain can also enhance Islamic social services, including *zakat*, charity (*sadaqah*), and endowment (*waqf*) for the poor, orphans, widows, and refugees. Technology can make these vital services more efficient, transparent, and accessible to the needy [56].

Blockchain hazards and issues might affect Islamic principles such as trust (*amanah*), consultation (*shura*), and accountability (*hisbah*); therefore, Islamic governments and societies should be aware of them. Blockchain raises technological and regulatory issues involving security and dependability, legal and political recognition of blockchain transactions, and Sharia compliance. Thus, these communities must build a clear and consistent framework for blockchain's growth and usage based on Islamic teachings and sources, including the Quran, Sunnah, *ijma*, and *ijtihad*. To link technology with Islam, this framework should be guided by Islamic ethics and values, such as Sharia goals (*maqasid al-Sharia*), public interest (*maslahah*), and moral and ethical concerns (*khalq*).

10. Conclusion

This book chapter thoroughly explores the technology sector's impact and influence on Islamic nations and Muslim communities. It delves into the various difficulties, challenges, possibilities, advantages, policies, and strategies that are important and crucial in this context.

The main findings and insights from this book chapter are as follows:

- Technology has a significant impact on several aspects of human life, including the economy, society, culture, and religion. Technology possesses the capacity to offer benefits, hazards, opportunities, challenges, choices, and dilemmas for human civilization.

- Islamic countries and Muslim societies are not exempt from the effects and influence of technology, as they are integrated into the global and interconnected world with varied requirements, capabilities, limitations, potentials, and challenges. Islamic countries and societies have a distinct viewpoint and method toward technology, guided by different factors.
- Islamic nations and Muslim communities have the potential to utilize the technology industry to efficiently address urgent issues such as poverty, illiteracy, sickness, and violence. In addition, technology may be employed to enhance vital elements of life, including health, education, economics, and security.
- Islamic nations and Muslim communities should exercise caution and awareness about the possible hazards and challenges presented by the technology sector. These hazards have the capacity to influence and mold Islamic values and concepts, including human dignity, rights, and obligations, as well as the interaction and relationship between people and machines. Furthermore, they can give rise to ethical and religious quandaries, such as the nature and status of technology agents and products, the accountability and responsibility of technology developers and users, and the alignment and compatibility of technology objectives and outcomes with Sharia objectives and intentions.
- Islamic countries and Muslim societies should establish a well-defined and uniform policy framework for the technology sector. This initiative will enhance the development and operation of the sector, address policy issues such as digital preparedness, digital inequality, digital literacy, and digital management, and protect economic and social advancement.

This chapter aims to offer a thorough examination of the technology sector and its influence on Islamic nations and Muslim cultures. Moreover, it provides crucial viewpoints and recommendations for legislators, practitioners, researchers, and technology users. We expect that this chapter will stimulate and encourage more in-depth research and discussion on the technology industry and its implications for Islamic states and Muslim communities. Furthermore, we believe that it will add to the current and developing body of literature and understanding on the subject.

References

[1] Christensen CM. *Innovator's Dilemma*. Boston: Harvard Business School Press; 1997.

[2] DataBank world development indicators. 2023 [cited 2023 Dec 8]. Available from: https://databank.worldbank.org/source/world-development-indicators

[3] Schwab, K. The Global Competitiveness Report 2019. In World Economic Forum. World Economic Forum; 2019. Retrieved December 13, 2024, from https://www3.weforum.org/docs/WEF_TheGlobalCompetitivenessReport2019.pdf

[4] Organisation of Islamic Cooperation. (2016). OIC – 2025: Programme of Action. Retrieved December 13, 2024, from https://www.oic-oci.org/docdown/?docID=16&refID=5

[5] World Bank. World development report: Trading for development in the age of global value chains. Washington; 2020.

[6] Alawode AA. Islamic finance. World Bank; 2015. Available from: https://www.worldbank.org/en/topic/financialsector/brief/islamic-finance

[7] Zawya Islamic Finance. State of the Global Islamic Economy Report 2018/19. In ZAWYA. Dubai International Financial Centre, Thomson Reuters; 2018. Retrieved December 13, 2024, from https://static.zawya.com/pdf/Others/2018%20Global%20Islamic%20Economy%20Report%20.pdf

[8] Chainalysis. The 2020 geography of cryptocurrency report. 2020. Available from: https://go.chainalysis.com/rs/503-FAP-074/images/Chainalysis-2020-Geography-of-Crypto.pdf

[9] Resolutions of the Shariah Advisory Council of the SCM. 2019. Available from: https://www.sc.com.my/development/icm/shariah/resolutions-of-the-shariah-advisory-council-of-the-sc

[10] Mohd Noh MS. The Fiqhi thought of price volatility in crypto asset. *J Fiqh*. 2022;19(1):27–48.

[11] Central Bank of Bahrain rulebook. Volume 6: Capital markets. Bahrain; 2019. Available from: https://cbben.thomsonreuters.com/rulebook/central-bank-bahrain-volume-6-capital-markets

[12] Algeria cryptocurrency laws. Law no. 18-01 on the finance law for 2018. 2024. Available from: https://freemanlaw.com/cryptocurrency/algeria/

[13] Blossom Finance. World's first primary Sukuk issuance on blockchain closes. 2019. Available from: https://www.blossomfinance.com/posts/worlds-first-primary-sukuk-issuance-on-blockchain-closes#:~:text=Blossom's impact investing platform is, that runs in the blockchain

[14] Finterra: The future of blockchain. 2020. Available from: https://finterra.org/

[15] OneAgrix to use blockchain to verify Halal food. 2019. Available from: https://www.oneagrix.com/

[16] MedXchange: Blockchain for healthcare. 2019. Available from: https://medxchange.io/

[17] ODEM and EU blockchain observatory and forum collaborate on blockchain education. 2019. Available from: https://odem.io/odem-and-eu-blockchain-observatory-and-forum-collaborate-on-blockchain-education/

[18] BitDegree: Revolutionizing education with blockchain. 2020. Available from: https://www.bitdegree.org/

[19] AgriLedger: A blockchain solution for the agricultural sector. 2020. Available from: https://www.agriledger.com/

[20] AgUnity: Empowering the last mile. 2020. Available from: https://www.agunity.com/

[21] Smart Dubai: Making Dubai the happiest city on earth. 2020. Available from: https://www.digitaldubai.ae/

[22] Alam, M., Yusuf, M. O., & Sani, N. A. (2020). Blockchain technology for electoral process in Africa: a short review. *International Journal of Information Technology*, 12(3), 861–867. https://doi.org/10.1007/s41870-020-00440-w

[23] The Changing Global Religious Landscape. (2007). Pew Research Center. Retrieved December 13, 2024, from https://www.pewresearch.org/religion/2017/04/05/the-changing-global-religious-landscape/

[24] Kılıç G, Türkan Y. The emergence of Islamic fintech and its applications. *Int J Islam Econ Finance Stud.* 2023;9(2):212–236.

[25] Islamic Financial Services Board: Promoting the soundness and stability of the Islamic financial services industry. 2020. Available from: https://www.ifsb.org/

[26] Wahed: Halal Investing is Going Global. (n.d.). https://www.wahed.com/eu

[27] Investment Account Platform: The world's first Shariah-compliant crowd-funding platform. 2020. Available from: https://www.iaplatform.com/

[28] Ethis: Islamic crowdfunding for social good. 2020. Available from: https://ethis.co/

[29] Al-Ghazali AH. *Al Mustasfa Min ilm Al Usul*. Dar UL Thaqafah; 2023.

[30] Al-Qaradawi Y. *The Lawful and the Prohibited in Islam*. 2nd edn. Cairo: Al Falah Foundation; 2001.

[31] Al-Raysuni A. *Imam Al-Shatibi's Theory of the Higher Objectives and Intents of Islamic Law*. London: International Institute of Islamic Thought; 2013.

[32] Rabbani MR, Hassan MK, Hudaefi FA, Shaikh ZH. Islamic finance and cryptocurrency: A systematic review. In: *FinTech in Islamic Financial Institutions*. Palgrave Macmillan, Cham, Switzerland; 2022. p. 279–306.

[33] Al-Mawardi AA-H. *Al-Akham al-Sultanniyyah: The Laws of Islamic Governance*. London: Ta-Ha Publisher; 1996. 1–381.

[34] Ibn Ashur M al-T. *Ibn Ashur Treatise on the Maqasid al-Shariah*. London: The International Institute of Islamic Thought; 2013.

[35] Khan MA. *What is Wrong with Islamic Economics? Analysing the Present State and Future Agenda*. Edward Elgar Publishing; 2013. Studies in Islamic finance, accounting and governance series.
[36] Demirgüç-Kunt A, Klapper L, Singer D, Ansar S. The global findex database 2021. Washington: The World Bank; 2022.
[37] bKash: Simplifying life. 2020. Available from: https://www.bkash.com/
[38] Kiva: Loans that change lives. 2021. Available from: https://www.kiva.org/
[39] Nicholls A, editor. *Social Entrepreneurship*. Oxford University Press, New York, USA; 2019. 1–37.
[40] Souktel: Digital solutions for development. 2020. Available from: https://www.souktel.org/
[41] Solar Sister: Light, hope, opportunity. 2021. Available from: https://solarsister.org/
[42] Tellidis I, Kappler S. Information and communication technologies in peace-building: Implications, opportunities and challenges. *Coop Confl*. 2015;51(1):75–93. Available from: http://dx.doi.org/10.1177/0010836715603752
[43] PeaceTech Lab: Technology for peace. 2020. Available from: https://www.peacetechlab.org/
[44] Build Up: Technology for peacebuilding. 2020. Available from: https://howtobuildup.org/
[45] Digital government review of Argentina: Accelerating the digitalisation of the public sector. 2019. OECD Digital Government Studies. Available from: https://www.oecd-ilibrary.org/governance/digital-government-review-of-turkiye_3958d102-en
[46] Saudi Vision 2030: Transforming Saudi Arabia's economy and society. 2020. Available from: https://vision2030.gov.sa/en
[47] Malaysia's digital economy blueprint. 2021. Available from: https://www.intanbk.intan.my/iportal/en/
[48] The age of digital interdependence: Report of the UN Secretary-General's high level panel on digital cooperation. United Nations; 2019. Available from: https://www.un.org/en/pdfs/DigitalCooperation-report-for web.pdf
[49] Islamic Development Bank. Bridging the digital divide to accelerate development. [cited 2024 Jan 8]. Available from: https://www.isdb.org/news/bridging-the-digital-divide-to-accelerate-development
[50] Islamic Development Bank. The Islamic Development Bank invites applications for Transform Fund Program. FundsforNGOs; [cited 2024 Jan 8]. Available from: https://www2.fundsforngos.org/latest-funds-for-ngos/the-islamic-development-bank-invites-applications-for-transform-fund-program/
[51] Education in a post-COVID World: Nine ideas for public action. UNESCO; 2020. Available from: https://en.unesco.org/news/education-post-covid-world-nine-ideas-public-action

[52] Pakistan - National Education Policy Framework November 2018. (2018). In Ministry of Federal Education and Professional Training. Retrieved December 13, 2024, from https://aserpakistan.org/document/2018/National_Eductaion_Policy_Framework_2018_Final.pdf
[53] Merdeka Belajar: Freedom to learn. 2020. Available from: https://merdeka-belajar.kemdikbud.go.id/episode_3/web
[54] Rice G. Business ethics: Theory and practice in an Islamic context. *J Bus Ethics*. 1999;18:345–358.
[55] IIUM Institute of Islamic Banking and Finance. 2020.
[56] Oseni UA, Ali SN, editors. *Fintech in Islamic Finance*. New York: Routledge; 2019.

https://doi.org/10.1142/9781800616295_bmatter

Index

J

K

L

M

www.ingramcontent.com/pod-product-compliance
Ingram Content Group UK Ltd.
Pitfield, Milton Keynes, MK11 3LW, UK
UKHW021913130525
458379UK00002BB/14

9 781800 616288